CLOCKWORK OF THE GODS

Clockwork of the Gods

Published by The Conrad Press Ltd. in the United Kingdom 2023

Tel: +44(0)1227 472 874

www.theconradpress.com

info@theconradpress.com

ISBN 978-1-915494-49-8

Copyright © Robert Bąkowski, 2023

All rights reserved.

Typesetting and Cover Design by: Charlotte Mouncey, www.bookstyle.co.uk

The Conrad Press logo was designed by Maria Priestley.

Printed and bound in Great Britain by Clays Ltd, Elcograf S.p.A.

CLOCKWORK OF THE GODS

ROBERT BĄKOWSKI

for Daniel

Contents

PRELUDE
We are — 11

CHAPTER ONE
The child who sees dead people — 15

CHAPTER TWO
Silver Jubilee — 23

CHAPTER THREE
Naturally the supernatural — 30

CHAPTER FOUR
Rude awakening — 40

CHAPTER FIVE
My haunted life — 48

CHAPTER SIX
Life after life — 73

CHAPTER SEVEN
Miracles — 88

CHAPTER EIGHT
Poltergeist — 98

CHAPTER NINE
Life before death — 114

CHAPTER TEN

Poltergeist 2 the sequel — 125

CHAPTER ELEVEN
Poltergeist 3 finale — 150

CHAPTER TWELVE
The light and the dark — 169

CHAPTER THIRTEEN
2009 – 2015 A new home, a fresh start — 186

CHAPTER FOURTEEN
2009 – 2015 They walk among us — 211

CHAPTER FIFTEEN
Astrology — 221

CHAPTER SIXTEEN
2015-2016 Alone — 233

CHAPTER SEVENTEEN
Regency charm — 244

CHAPTER EIGHTEEN
Reincarnation Part One –
Several lives in two chapters — 259

CHAPTER NINETEEN
Vacant possession — 277

CHAPTER TWENTY
In the bleak midwinter — 300

CHAPTER TWENTY-ONE
Reincarnation Part Two   322

CHAPTER TWENTY-TWO
The haunted lamp   339

CHAPTER TWENTY-THREE
George   356

CHAPTER TWENTY-FOUR
Do you want change?   365

CHAPTER TWENTY-FIVE
The most haunted house in town   375

CHAPTER TWENTY-SIX
Dark forces   382

CHAPTER TWENTY-SEVEN
Judging others   396

CHAPTER TWENTY-EIGHT
The beguiling of Merlin   404

CHAPTER TWENTY-NINE
Manifestation   429

CHAPTER THIRTY
Compassion for the self   452

CHAPTER THIRTY-ONE
The rescue   455

CHAPTER THIRTY-TWO
Visitations   469

CHAPTER THIRTY-THREE
Universal adapter   485

CHAPTER THIRTY-FOUR
Saved by the bell   494

CHAPTER THIRTY-FIVE
Sooty and Sweep   520

CHAPTER THIRTY-SIX
A spiritual life   534

CHAPTER THIRTY-SEVEN
Bohemian Rhapsody   548

CHAPTER THIRTY-EIGHT
Twin flames   562

CHAPTER THIRTY-NINE
Physical, mental and spiritual wellbeing   575

CHAPTER FORTY
Epilogue   590

Prelude

We are

We are one. Our desire for individuality creates a sadness that comes from the isolation caused only by a veil of separation placed over us at birth. Each one of us is God enjoying his or her own unique human experience. How much more thrilling it would be for God, or the 'Source' as I refer to Him in these pages, if He experienced a deliberate temporary amnesia and didn't know that He was everything that ever was or ever will be!

The human drama that unfolds every day in every household around the globe is a stage play put on by the Source and we are the main characters. Joy, sorrow, tragedy, loss and love are the rich rewards. But the drama must be realistic, and it would be fruitless if those main characters were to know that they are of the Source and are eternal.

So, the veil of separation ensures that we feel isolated from the Source and from each other, and the loss of the love and the connectedness to all things is almost unbearable. Our soul learns and grows as it progresses through manifold lifetimes and our energetic vibration rises ever upwards until one day we no longer need to reincarnate. We have then graduated what the late acclaimed psychic researcher Dolores Cannon referred to as 'Earth School.'

I have – literally - had the spiritual journey of a lifetime and now at the age of fifty-three, I am excited to be able to sit back and soak in the warmth that comes from the gifted knowledge that everything in my life had a divine purpose and I am thrilled that I can share this knowing with you. I hope that in some way the divine truth about the true reality of existence will help to lighten the heavy load that we all carry with us everywhere and perhaps help remove some of the weeds that crowd your pathway to your own ever continuing spiritual ascension.

Perhaps you are browsing this book in a bookstore in some far-flung amazing place that I have never travelled to and that I will never see - not in this lifetime anyway. Perhaps you are curious as to the spirit realm and the purpose of human life on Earth, and you thought that you would take a peek at these pages. Your curiosity satiated, you may now decide to place this bound bundle of cellulose and gum back onto the shelf and move on.

You are still with me? I am grateful to you. For you are a seeker and this is my story and I give it to you as my gift of love and by your reading of my words you give your gift of love to me. You have chosen to read on and give your consideration to my experiences through my written word. You have my gratitude, for deep within, you are aware that there is so much more to this physical existence than our mortal bodies permit us to experience. You know that there is an unseen world, somewhere just beyond the periphery of our vision and our limited hearing.

I will try, in my own way, here amongst these pages, to help you begin to discover that which you seek. What you will find is my story; a 'ghost' story unfolding over several chapters. These chapters are interspersed with others of a philosophical and inspirational nature that are the result of my years of spiritual learning and in part channelled from spirit.

If you have heard about this book and my story then it means that as I type this first page, sat here as I am during the lockdown of 2020, it means that my task has, perhaps, achieved its purpose. The world needs to know so much about the unseen-world and the nature of existence. It has been my unknowing and unwitting duty to have experienced manifold bizarre, other-worldly and consciousness altering events in my lifetime.

It is only now, after I have reached half-a-century in Earth years, that I can look back on my life and see what occurred, good and bad, had to happen and the relevance and importance of those events. My ever-expanding understanding of spirituality also allows me to see the irrelevance and unimportance of those same events. The comfort that arises from the gratitude and the empowerment that comes with this understanding I wish to share with you so that you too may perhaps change your outlook on life forever.

So how do you know that this guy is the genuine article and not another one of the multitude of social media egos espousing spirituality as some kind of currency? You don't. Or rather your mind doesn't know, but your heart will guide you if you allow it. I give you here the spiritual autobiography of my life's experiences so that your heart can follow its own intuition. A hundred or more lifetimes of sorrow and joy now gives rise to the burden of my spiritual duty to put my knowledge into words in the hope that somewhere out there, at least one person reads these same words and their life journey improves irrecoverably.

Perhaps there are many hundreds, or many thousands of 'persons' who may become positively affected by the words in this book. A conscious collective of spiritually enlightened souls of brothers and sisters. Thank you for choosing to read this and welcome to the global spiritual awakening.

As someone once said to me and I now say to you, 'You are blessed and you are chosen.'

CHAPTER ONE

The child who sees dead people

The cot

'You saw it too, didn't you?' he said with a look of total comprehension and amusement on his face.

I was in my cot when it happened. A bright morning and the sun was flickering through the drawn curtains of my small box-room bedroom. I must have been, I suppose, one or two years old. Like everything in my parents' house, the immaculately white gloss painted wooden cot matched my white gloss painted chest of drawers with its little black Bakelite knobs and this in turn matched the white gloss painted bedroom door. Everyone has familiar childhood scents that they can fondly recall and one of mine is of the smell of freshly painted white gloss.

This was to be my first remembered encounter with spirit. Something woke me. Defenceless, the tiny me lay on my back, my eyes opened and dazzled by the sunlight I gazed up at the comfortingly familiar jolly blue rabbit transfer adhered to the back of my white plywood panelled cot. Then, turning my head I saw it. It is hard to adequately describe the full terror that the apparition evoked.

My starkest memory of the incident with the shade is of my silent scream that I tried without success to release. I am sure that the entire episode lasted mere seconds and although the door to my bedroom was closed the entity had entered my bedroom unhindered. Suspended and stationary, the spirit was slightly above floor height and in silhouette against the cheery bright white bedroom door. What seemed like an age passed and all the while I was repeatedly trying to scream for help but to my horror there was only a silenced terrified rasp.

In these days of extreme horror films with their unpleasant spiritually and psychologically corrosive special effects, it is difficult for me to emphasise how terrifying it is for a small child to have the black silhouette of an adult-size skeleton hover close to your safe-space sleeping place. But whatever earth-bound entity chose to manifest in that room, it was fully aware of the intentional terror it was inflicting upon an impressionable baby. I was defenceless, alone, without a voice and without assistance. In that moment, the white bars of my cot may just as well have been the bars of my own inescapable prison.

I do not recall what happened after that. I believe that I passed out from terror. Upon regaining consciousness, the apparition had gone. It was the one and only time that I saw the spectre. I recall the relief that washed over me as my smiling mother finally entered my bedroom in answer to my now audible cries. With the spectre gone, the deceptive comfort that is provided by the normality of the familiar resumed once more. Too young to speak, I must have been making a fuss as I remember trying to tell my mother about what had happened. What to me was a concise and urgent account of events was to my mother simply her baby crying with ever increasing vented frustration as she calmly sought to soothe me.

Why had this ghost chosen to frighten me? I was a mere

baby. The answer must be 'because it could.' Whatever the reason, I am very grateful to it as this was to herald the beginning of a lifelong spiritual journey. This small and seemingly unimportant incident remained with me for my whole life. So much so, that it becomes the opening chapter in this book, some fifty years later. It poses several unanswered questions. Why would a ghost choose to materialise specifically as a skeleton and not in the form it took in its own lifetime? Had the spectre once been human at all? How does a small child or baby even know what a skeleton is, in order to be frightened of it? Surely the entire memory is an imagined episode from childhood, a recollection of a bad dream perhaps? Finally, why only me and no-one else in the household?

I never told anyone about the incident. By the time I was old enough to talk it was already a memory and one too awkward to admit to. In a household where my strict parents ruled with the ever-present threat of being given a 'thick ear' for any minor misdemeanour, I kept my silence. My draconian upbringing ensured that truths and untruths alike remained unuttered for fear of punishment. So this strange and dark memory from my younger years stayed with me and me alone, only to be repeated over and over in my mind's eye. So many times in fact that, just like my happier early childhood memories, it burnt itself into my reality. Yet still I doubted it.

Fast forward to the year 1997, probably some twenty-seven years later and the incident was all but consigned to that part of our brain marked 'childhood imagination.' Now aged twenty-eight and after several years of having moved around the south of the UK, I had settled in the county of Dorset. One day, while visiting a friend's house in a nearby town, the incident with the skeletal ghost resurfaced. My friend's cat had given birth to kittens and she was keen to show both me and a mutual friend with a view to finding adoptive parents. Her father, with whom she lived, would not allow the kittens in the house and so the three of us happily made our way out into the warm summer sunshine and into the double garage where the kittens were being weaned by an attentive mother.

The double 'up and over' garage door went up and over and in stark contrast to the daylight without, our eyes adjusted to the darkness within. There, in a large cardboard box, were the kittens with the mother. People who know and love me well will tell you that I am a cat obsessive. They are the most perfect creatures. I cannot today live without at least one in my life and as I write this, I am joint custodian of thirteen rescue cats.

However, that sunny afternoon I did not have eyes for the kittens. I only had eyes for what had been discarded and stored many years before at the rear of the garage. Despite the years of disuse, it remained still shiny in its white gloss paint, and a powerful recognition fired through my very being and for a moment I was a little boy once more.

With an overwhelming sensation of nostalgia for days lost, I exclaimed, 'Oh, this is just like the one that I had as a child!'

The not unreasonable snorted retort of, 'How could you possibly remember that far back?' came from my co-kitten-conspirator.

I made my way through the stored junk and furniture to the rear of the garage and towards the thing that had caught my eye and had piqued my interest. It beckoned me into a world of happy childhood recollections and that energy of nostalgia that can flood through us like a warming brandy on a cold day.

Now standing over the cot, I was no longer a small infant inside looking out but a full-sized adult towering above it. Just like ….

'That was my cot when I was a baby,' laughed my kitten owning friend. She was only a year older than me, so it was perfectly reasonable that she could have had the same make of cot as I'd had. In my silent rapture I failed to reply. I was mesmerised. There, on the rear white gloss painted plywood panel was a transfer sticker. A transfer of an oh-so-familiar jolly blue rabbit and still skipping its delightful 1960s cutesy dance.

'This isn't similar to the cot that I had,' I said in a quiet serious voice, 'It is identical.'

I stood looking down into the pretty little white cot and the memories came flooding back. The memory of a distant sunny morning in 1970 when perhaps the weather had not been too dissimilar to today. So, it had not been a false memory. It *had* happened just as I recalled, hadn't it? I clearly couldn't tell the two friends who were now impatiently waiting for me by a box full of warm excited kittens. After all, it was obvious that they did not even believe me capable of remembering my cot, so why would they believe a story about a phantom seen by a one-year-old? I remained silent, but my mind buzzed.

And there the story would be lost, forgotten, concluded, had it not been for a second synchronicity. Many years passed, life occurred as it does and once more the incident of the spectre at my cot faded to a memory. That is until one evening came a chance conversation with my brother, who is some ten years my senior. We had been catching up via a Skype video call from my home in Dorset to his house in Cyprus, where he and his wife had retired. As is often the case with family members who have not seen each other in many years, we recounted old stories and got chatting excitedly about the past. All of our older relatives were now dead and we two are the only surviving family members who can remember the 'old days', our own past and our own shared history. This eventually happens to us all.

We began to talk about the various homes of our childhood, working chronologically backwards and I described my bedroom with the cot. Until this conversation I had mistakenly thought that this room was in my favourite childhood home.

'Oh no, the small bedroom with your cot was actually in an earlier house,' my older brother corrected. Explaining, he continued, 'We moved from there when you were aged about one or two years-old.'

That came as a revelation but then all our childhood homes smelt of white gloss paint and so they perhaps all seemed the same to me.

Then a thought took me. Following the death of our parents my brother and I had been getting along well and could chat about most things unhindered. Upon his bittersweet departure from the UK, we had already experienced a paranormal moment in a public house where a large white orb had slowly encircled our dining table. While that is another story for another time, it reminded me of the supernatural, and so after briefly chatting about the public house orb, I decided to mention the incident with the skeleton.

Expecting a quizzical look or a disbelieving guffaw, I nonetheless began to relay my childhood recollection of events over a flashing and noisy Skype internet connection. Just why was Skyping my brother always accompanied by this strange flashing and these loud but incoherent male voices in the background? I was to find out many months later. For now, I dismissed the interruptions as electrical problems and I pressed ahead.

'So do you remember my small bedroom with the cot?' I enquired.

He confirmed that indeed he did and described accurately the contents of that room which matched and validated my own memories. Picking up the courage, I began my story, 'Well, my one memory of that room was of a sunny morning when I was woken in my cot and on looking out of ....'

I trailed off as my brother interrupted me.

'You saw it too, didn't you?' he said with a look of total comprehension and amusement on his face. My jaw must have dropped. My brother then confirmed that before I was born, my bedroom had in fact been his, and that as a small boy, he too had been awoken one morning by the apparition of a silhouetted skeleton against the bedroom door. Independent of each other, we had both experienced the ghost. With my brother some ten years older than me, we had seen it some years apart. We had experienced the same thing and in the same room of the same house. Yet it was only now that we felt secure enough to discuss the details.

My brother explained that a small boy had tragically died in that house a few years prior. He believed that it was the earthbound spirit of this boy that had created the mischievous apparition. Perhaps his theory is correct, though a psychic medium friend has more recently dismissed this idea, understanding the apparition to have been something else. Whatever it was, it was meant for me to see and it set me on course for a lifetime of supernatural encounters and an amazing spiritual journey for which I am so very grateful.

In later years I was to become involved in a small part with what is called 'rescue work.' This is where earthbound spirits who require help to cross into the Light are aided by one or more psychic mediums. It seems I have a talent for 'sniffing them out' as it was once put to me, or perhaps they have a talent for sniffing *me* out? Whichever way around, some earthbound spirits want and need some additional help to cross to the Light, others choose to stay Earth side, and some spirits resent and fear all assistance. All of us have total free will. As it is in life, so it is in death.

• Earthbound spirit – the spirit of a deceased person or animal that has not crossed from this 3D physical reality to the next 5D reality, commonly referred to as 'Heaven' or as the 'Light' in spiritual circles. When I refer in this book to the 'Light' or to the 'Source' I am referring to God, and so I am treating these two key phrases as nouns, differentiated as such by capital letters.

Chapter Two

Silver Jubilee

The haunted water closet

Once more the round Bakelite doorknob span back and forth and rattled and rattled as I called out that I wouldn't be long.

1977 and I was eight years old. We didn't take holidays. Our parents were very much stay-at-homes, and so when my older brother and I were told that we were setting off from our house in rural Essex to my paternal uncle's home in Brighton, East Sussex for a holiday, it was an exciting adventure. My uncle Gordon lived alone. His adult children had left home and sadly he had lost his beloved wife Joan to cancer when she was still quite young. I thought of him then as an old man, but I suppose he was the same age as I am today writing this book. I guess that I am an old man too now.

Uncle lived in a rented spacious terraced Victorian furnished house in Hove, which for those who don't know is a genteel part of the larger area of Brighton. It was not far from the seafront and we spent the week going to the beach and doing touristy things like visit the Royal Pavilion, then finally the week's highlight was standing as a family on the beach and watching the RAF Red Arrows fly overhead in formation as a part of the Queen's Silver Jubilee celebrations of that year. Strange to think that it has now been another forty-five years since then.

Back at uncle's house, his bedroom and my parent's guest bedroom were upstairs and on a different floor to where I was billeted. My brother was accommodated on the same floor as me, he given the enormous principal bedroom, which was replete with an ancient sprung double bed, to the left of which was an even more ancient and massive walnut wardrobe, plus elsewhere in the spacious room a few other items of dark and heavy old-fashioned furnishings.

I was given the adjacent box room. All this room had to stir the heart was a single bed located in the sunny and jolly front bay window. I say 'all' because the only other item of furniture in the room was a less jolly full-size oil portrait of a middle-aged Victorian gentleman. An original Victorian tiled fireplace was the only frivolous ornamentation in the otherwise stark room. The bedroom clearly hadn't been used or loved for many years and presumably, like everything else in the house, had been furnished by the prior occupant owner.

The painting was hung so that it faced the end of the bed precisely. My keen and disturbing memory of my stay in this room is of being unable to sleep and lying awake in the small hours trying not to look at the portrait, wishing and hoping for the household to wake and begin its friendly familiar noises and routines. This bedroom was anything but friendly to a small boy and being well illuminated by the light summer nights, I continually tried to not catch the gaze of the gentleman portrait sitter staring down from the wall. Somehow, this stern man's eyes, and he *was* stern, seemed to bore disapprovingly into my very being.

I am not one to be alarmed by inanimate objects and even as a child I was not scared of the dark, but I still recall lying on my back in bed and being unable to look up at this painting and into *those eyes*. There was something about it which to me suggested that the sitter was still with the painting. Today I know this to be an 'attachment' where an earthbound spirit, so attached as they are to the physical world, remains with the material belongings that they held so dear in their lifetime. Most mornings I woke early as if I had been intentionally disturbed and I lay on the bed desperately listening for any signs of life stirring in the house so that I could get away from that painting's unerring and ceaseless cold gaze. I do not recall getting a lot of sleep that week.

One morning soon after arrival, desperate to leave that tiny bedroom, I left my creepy room and crossed the landing to my brother's adjacent double bedroom. My brother is ten years older than me, and he was busily making the double bed. From the landing I made to enter his bedroom. I had not been inside it before, but not for the first time in my life, I hesitated and was held back by my own internal warning system. We all have this instinctive intuitive alarm that protects all creatures in the animal kingdom from danger. It is only mankind that has trained itself over centuries of 'reason' to no longer heed its klaxon call.

I am unable to precisely tell you why I could not enter that room. I can only explain that I knew it to be the wrong thing to do, and that there was something in that room, aside from my older brother(!), that didn't want me in there. Therefore, my brother and I had our chat with me stood in his bedroom doorway nervously kicking my heels and him inside tidying his guest suite, I can still picture him now.

My brother told me that he didn't like the room at all and

that it gave him the creeps. He said that perhaps it was the old heavy dark furniture, but in particular, he had taken a dislike to the large double bed and the massive wardrobe which dominated the room. I think that week he got even less sleep than I did. I relayed to him how much I did not like the portrait in my apparently sunny pleasant small room, though looking back I remember that it had anything but a sunny welcoming feel to it, the air in the room being somewhat electric and stifling.

Later that day, we took a trip into town for a leisurely walk where I bought a souvenir snow globe of a Household Cavalry Officer standing guard at Buckingham Palace. My father was an obsessive military man and had a desire for me to be conscripted into the Army and would regularly do anything to encourage this, even at my tender age of eight years. I also bought a glitzy souvenir teaspoon of Brighton which I still have and use daily.

Afterwards we returned home to my uncle's house and gathered as a family unit in the kitchen for afternoon tea. Slightly bored by the adult chat going on, I excused myself and went off alone to the downstairs loo, which was a short walk from the kitchen door and across some beautiful Victorian encaustic floor tiles in the entrance hallway.

Like all of the rooms in the house, the WC had a very large Victorian panelled door. A tiny room, it housed one of those huge black high level flush cisterns with a pull chain that hanged down and replete with a ghastly black plastic toilet seat. Those like me of an age familiar with British plumbing of that period will know precisely to what I refer here.

I closed the solid wooden door carefully and being a cautious shy child – to this day I still am shy - I made sure to lock the door behind me as I settled down. A few moments passed and ever embarrassed by any social gaff, I was mortified when one of my family tried the door. Once more the round Bakelite doorknob span back and forth and rattled and rattled as I called out that I wouldn't be long.

Finishing my job at hand, literally, I pulled the unpleasant chain and waited for the huge Niagara-Falls-like flush to do its work, watching fascinated as seemingly gallons of water cascaded into the toilet bowl below. Then, unlocking the door, I made my way back to the sun-filled kitchen. My family were seated, still agreeably chatting away over tea and biscuits at the kitchen table with its oil cloth covering.

Seeing and feeling a part of this adult gang, I felt like a grown-up and thus emboldened when I was asked, 'Everything ok?' referring to my toilet break, I replied,

'Yes thank you and it's free now to whoever (sic) tried the door handle.'

Astonished stares came back at me.

'Nobody tried the door handle my love.'

Still emboldened I replied, 'Yes they did, it rattled several times.'

My statement was not met by my expected response of, 'Oh, that was me,' from one of those seated there. Instead there was a furtive exchange of looks and a knowing collection of awkward smirks across the table.

With a collective clearing of throats my father told me that, 'I must have been mistaken.'

Why everybody treats children like fools I do not know, for without ego they are often more perceptive and intuitive than many adults. I remember the feeling of injustice and the creeping sensation of awkwardness that my toilet break had been met with such close scrutiny. With all eyes on me in my indignation, I looked at my older brother who was not above playing regular practical jokes against his smaller sibling. I decided that this must have been one of his tricks but not to make a fuss, for in our household there was no room for freedom of expression, it usually being met with a sharp word or an even sharper slap.

The holiday over, it was only after we left my uncle's house and we were on the long drive home with my father at the wheel of his Ford Capri, that the matter of my uncle's house being haunted was revealed to me. My mother preferred to keep quiet on such things, only chipping in occasionally but my brother and father chatted freely. My mother never did believe in an afterlife, at least, not until many years later when her own time came and together we met an angel just a few weeks prior to her death. But that is a story for later in the book.

As the car motored out of Brighton and as we passed the famous windmill high up on the hill (my uncle had told me it was the same windmill as used in the film Chitty Chitty Bang Bang and I was disappointed to discover many years later that it wasn't), it was explained to me that I hadn't been told about the house being haunted because they thought that I would be frightened. Nobody, it seems, had wanted to share a house with a screaming, nightmare-ridden eight-year-old. This is quite understandable, yet despite my well-remembered experience in my cot, I have never been one taken to hysterics over the supernatural. I can remember sitting in the back of the car, the only member of the family to have actually experienced any phenomena the whole time that we were there, and rather than feel frightened, I was fascinated.

And so, the full story was there and then relayed to the impressionable eight-year-old me. It transpired that when my uncle took the tenancy of the fully furnished property, the previous owner occupiers, an elderly Jewish couple, had not long since died in the house. Not only had they died in the house, but they died on the same night and in the same bed. The same double bed that was in my brother's bedroom and that he had been obliged to sleep in. While my brother hadn't experienced any psychic phenomena during his stay, he told me that he hadn't got a lot of sleep in that big bedroom either and that the behemoth of a Victorian wardrobe in the room had absolutely terrified him. Remember that my brother was not an impressionable child, he was an eighteen-year-old man.

After my uncle had moved into the property, he discovered a Mezuzah – a protective parchment scroll with verses from the Torah – placed on the front door doorframe. He had, rather foolishly I feel, removed this and thereafter the disturbances, or haunting, began. For those who do not know, it is a religious commandment in Judaism for a Mezuzah to be placed on the doorframe of the home. Thus affixed, it protects the occupants from the spirits of the dead.

When my uncle removed this, he was undoubtedly upsetting the previous owners, who it seems were still present. I did not know then, but I do know now thanks to my research for this book, that the protective Mezuzot (plural of Mezuzah) are often placed on every doorway in the house, with the sole exception, Wikipedia tells me, of the WC water closet.

Chapter Three

Naturally the supernatural

Terms and conditions apply

Strip away in your mind those associations with renaissance artistic interpretations of God and angels, or images of Victorian ladies in hats gathering around for an hour of table-tipping under a conveniently dimmed light.

Death is a myth. This is something profoundly empowering when we come to understand it. Most of us have been bereaved and all of us certainly will be at some point in our life. The loss that we feel is acute and yet a necessary part of our three-dimensional (3D) existence on Earth. But there is no need for us to hold onto that energy of loss, for we do get to be with our loved ones again. The separation is only temporary. Everything is energy and we know that energy cannot be destroyed, only transmuted.

Upon death, our energy or 'consciousness' leaves the physical body behind and transmutes from one reality to another. The survival of the spirit after the death of the physical body was common knowledge to most old 'pagan' religions and in many 'eastern' religions. Every town or village would have a wise man or woman with a degree of psychic ability, from the healer to the shaman. The ability to speak with departed loved ones was a part of the natural process of life and death and not in any way considered dark or unnatural. Rightly, humanity was considered to be a part of the natural order of things on Earth and not separate to it.

Regrettably, over many centuries some faiths, largely those based on The Old Testament, fused with governance and created a disempowering patriarchal control structure which by design sought to exert moral and physical control over the people. Our natural birthright of an equal seat at the universe's table was subverted into a hierarchical structure of God at the top and you, the mere mortal, somewhere at the bottom. Yet you are immortal and this does not come with any exclusions or clauses in the contract.

Death as a finality and the myth of divine retribution with eternal Hell fires burning served to keep the populace in order, rather than enlighten them as to their life journey, which is surely the true purpose of any organised religion. If the heart-rending story in the New Testament of the Resurrection of Jesus Christ and of the Holy Ghost tells us anything, it is to guide us to the knowledge that there is such a thing as a 'Holy Spirit' and that life after the death of the physical body is a reality to be celebrated. Yet I will wager that you have encountered many Christians who do not believe in ghosts or life after death, let alone the Resurrection ....

Historically, much has been written and spoken of the death and the resurrection of Jesus Christ as the Holy Spirit and yet little is discussed of his existence *before his natural birth*.

Whether the Christian believer or the theologian understands Jesus to have been either a prophet or God in living form, what is clear from the texts is that the soul who inhabited the physical human body of Jesus Christ *came from somewhere*. That notion is spoken of very little by western theology; we are told that we go somewhere when we die yes, but by extension, *we must also come from the same place when we are born*. So, consider where that place is and ask yourself the question 'If that place is so great, then what would be the purpose of incarnating on the physical 3D Earth?'

Whatever your religious denomination, faith or secular viewpoint, it can be upsetting when our preconceived ideas or beliefs are challenged. Our core beliefs, whether political or spiritual, are hardwired into us and we associate them with our foundation as an individual. This is why when someone challenges our political or religious belief structure it feels as though they are making an attack upon us personally. But unless we regularly put our own beliefs and notions to the test, we are at as much danger of ignorance as we are of blind faith.

Perhaps if we were to more closely scrutinise those beliefs and notions we hold onto so dearly, they may not in fact be our own at all but instead conceived by others and passed down to us in childhood as fact. It is hard to shift those 'facts' taught to us in our early years, for they form the very foundation stones of our ego. Re-examine your hitherto unquestioned beliefs with an open inquiring mind and heart. Sometimes we resist change and gain false comfort from holding on too tightly to the belief structure that seems so familiar.

Pure and of the Light when born, throughout our lives we pick up other people's conditioning, prejudices, falsehoods and fears. Whether that be from our parents' attempts to protect us, our peers' influence, the schoolteachers' reinforcement of your government's version of your geopolitical history, or just the chaos of hatred and fear broadcast into your home via twenty-four-hour news coverage and of course via those people who are paid to represent all the people; those subrogated to the position of power by us to govern over us.

This anger and frustration of many years becomes like dirty snow gathering on a rolling snowball of toxic memories accumulating within our minds. These toxic thought patterns are negative energies that then become stored in the very cells of our bodies. In the same way that we are what we eat, we are also what we think and as a result we become cynical and ill, and we get old before our time.

Eventually something must give and many of us reach middle-age feeling an innate desire to return to the innocence of youth, when we perceived things were 'better.' Were things really better? Or do we subconsciously know that our own personal story - our own personal 'truth' - has been corrupted by other people's views, opinions and prejudices? Unwittingly we have diminished our present-day experience by 'buying-in' to other people's unhealed psychological wounding.

Perhaps you feel unable to acknowledge this truth as to do so would mean having to reassess your beliefs, many of those you held dear for your entire lifetime. Remember that you were once a happy carefree child and that your present-day opinions came from learned painful experience or from other people's perspectives.

This accruing disparate collection of other people's shame, anger issues and storylines that we adopt as our own, 'helps' to create our 'ego' or 'personality.' Our ego is said to have crystallised by the time that we are aged seven years. The ego is a conceit of the brain and not of the heart. The brain seeks to protect us from physical and mental hurt, but ultimately fails, because life is meant to be lived. But when the ego fails at protecting us fully from all life's pitfalls, as it surely must, then it responds with anger and resentment. After all, the ego reasons, it must be other people and external forces that have derailed its finely laid plans.

Even where the ego has succeeded in protecting us from all of life's pitfalls, providing us with a dull and fully insulated life, then it has failed in its duty because we have failed to live. We incarnate and set out to experience life in its fullest, but a closed mind and a closed heart is living a life half in shadow. Many aren't living at all. There is the added side effect of the ego keeping us from our own truth.

Throughout this book I shall use terms and terminology in my native language that I am obliged to use simply because there are no alternative options available to me, restricted by the tyranny of language as we all are. Some people will find comfort in the familiarity of the terms I use and others will, understandably I feel, become uncomfortable. This may be due to a learnt dislike of the religious connotations often associated with spiritual terminology and stemming from their own negative experiences with organised religion.

As a child, I was not a fan of organised school sport. Sport is fun and healthy, but it is a frequent truth that the fun element is often crushed or eliminated where sport, or playing, becomes organised with a hierarchy of leadership and followers. So it is with religion, which we may term 'spirituality.' Once spirituality is formulated and coordinated as 'organised religion' it has the tendency to crush and squeeze out the empathy, the healing, the compassion and the love; replacing it with intolerance, fear and ideology. In short it squeezes out God.

When coming across terminology in this book that the reader does not care for, I would ask that we refrain from getting hung-up on the specific words used, but instead they open their heart to the essence of those words. We can strip away the centuries of abuse of the magical and wholesome, and open our heart to what lies behind the noun. The innocent wonder of childhood for words like 'angels', 'spirits' and 'God' can return.

My own name 'Robert' I never particularly took to. An unhappy childhood saw to it that I did not appreciate hearing my name being called, as it invariably meant trouble. This is a psychological trigger. But on the rare occasion that a person new to me also called Robert enters my life, I don't come to this new acquaintance with preconceived notions, instead I look for the man behind the name. And so, it should be with names used in esoteric spiritual matters.

For example, the words 'medium', 'spirit', 'seance' and 'spirituality' often conjure up negative mental images of early twentieth century sepia photographs comprising the fakery of phosphorous coated spinning trumpets or tambourines suspended on hidden wires and cheesecloth appearing from indiscreet locations. Could it perhaps be that part of the human condition is to have instant recall for the negative and a reluctance to engage with the positive.

Words such as 'angels', 'spirit guides', 'prayer' and of course 'God' may inspire mental pictures of respite, salvation and love to some. To others a wounded mind winces at a learnt toxic relationship with organised religion or fake spiritualists.

Many times we can become unstuck when hoping to discuss openly and cleanly the metaphysical world around us, only to be halted mid-conversation by a casual mention of a trigger word like 'angel' or 'God.' The brakes are applied, the wounds of the past re-open. Verbal hurts resurface and the conversation is relegated to the mental waste-bin marked 'mumbo-jumbo.' So, whether you come to this book with a personal belief of a strong faith in a divine God, a knowledge of metaphysics or even a secular or agnostic background, please do not choose to be offended by the nouns used. They are just words.

Until new words for these entities and supernatural happenings are invented, we are stuck with the old quasi-religious terminology. Strip away in your mind those associations with renaissance artistic interpretations of God and angels, or images of Victorian ladies in hats gathering around for an hour of table-tipping under a conveniently dimmed light. Please clear your mind of all you have learnt, been told and 'understand' as these are distractions.

When we refer to the great universal intelligence that many call 'God', we may instead use the words 'universe', the 'Source' or the 'Light', these words being neutral, non-religious and interchangeable. If we accept that God created the universe, then He, or She, is the divine source of everything and the universe is therefore God. God is therefore the universe and, by extension, we are all children of the universe. So we really have no need to get hung-up on name tags, and we can temporarily suspend our human inclination of being offended for the duration of this book.

Is everything we see, hear, touch and feel on Earth in the 3D all that there is? I would categorically answer 'no.' Is Heaven akin to a renaissance painting, a place filled with people floating on clouds and playing harps? Again, I would categorically answer 'no.' Our senses deceive us. When we choose to incarnate on this planet, for we do *choose* to, a metaphorical veil is placed over us in order that we do not see and sense everything that is all around us all the time. This is by design. In order to be fully immersed and experience all of the emotions that we enjoy and endure in the physical world, we must not be aware of our connectedness with all that there is. When I was a child at school I was hopeless at mathematics. Fortunately our maths exercise books had the answers to the test questions written in the back. I learnt nothing as a result.

With the known 'everything' that comprises our physical reality originating from that great energy explosion, 'The Big Bang', all that we see and all that we experience in the physical dimension (physical 'plane') is nothing more than energy vibrating at a low frequency. Energy, so dense on planet Earth that vibrating energy called atoms join hands in friendship with other atoms to make solid objects. Contrary to what our eyes perceive, physics tells us that things are not solid, what you see to be permanent is not and all that you see is not all that there is. All energy vibrates and we are all made of energy, hence we may say, 'I don't like his vibe (vibration),' or, 'She's on my wavelength.' Science has shown that the entire universe is giving off a continuous vibration, or musical note.

Quantum physics and metaphysics are at a delicious meeting point and these two previously mutually exclusive worlds begin to collide. 'Supernatural' is a well-used term we all know, but the reality is that there is nothing supernatural about the supernatural at all. It is as commonplace and as everyday as the physical world surrounding us, but in this low vibrational 3D physical reality, most of us cannot see it, hear it or feel it, so when we do it appears unnatural to us. But everything is energy, and energy vibrates at different frequencies, and sometimes those frequencies are outside of our physical perception. Just because your radio appliance is built only for FM does not mean that MW doesn't exist, it merely means that the apparatus you have is unable to tune-in to all the frequencies that surround it.

The spirit world, aka 'Heaven', or the '5D fifth dimension' if you prefer, surrounds us all the time. Sometimes 'the veil' (another delightful evocative expression from the era of afternoon seances at Aunt Maud's) is thin, perhaps at certain times of year, or at certain locations. Everyone is familiar with Hallowe'en, or the tradition of ghost stories at Christmas and with haunted places. This is when or where the veil between the two 'worlds' is at its thinnest and contact may sometimes, just sometimes, be made.

Each and every one of us also has the 'veil' placed over us at birth and as previously described, this is to ensure that we all have a unique human experience of individuality while we are given our time here on Earth. The veil prevents us from seeing what all around us is there all of the time, other vibrational realities or dimensions yes, but also the interconnectedness of all things.

I perhaps do myself no favours here. I am aware that there is a great attraction in the romanticism of the supernatural and yet here I am trying to remove some of that mystique. When I was younger, I fell for the romantic imagery of wizards, goblins and spooks in books and illustrations. If my life experiences have shown me anything, it is that many of these things exist and are ever-present and are around us all of the time. These experiences also demonstrated to me that there is far more to our universe than our restricted human consciousness could ever allow us to realise and yet, all this is in the natural order of all things and contained within a scientifically explainable universe.

There may also be stalwarts of the established religions who will cry 'heresy' at any attempt to help people with their personal journey. They would advise that we are at the 'mercy of God' and that we are powerless, or even insignificant. They may reject outright the truth that we are made of the same stuff as the universe and that therefore we *are* God and so thereby we are empowered and in charge of our own destiny. So much unnecessary and damaging effort has gone into negative religious liturgies which seek to make mankind a world of irredeemable sinners and separate from God. This surely, is mankind projecting its own shadow on a global scale.

If religious texts tell us anything, it is that God is with us at all times, and this is because we cannot be separated from our divine creator as we are made of the same stuff. Mankind now needs to awaken and to ascend to a higher vibration of being. The first step of that journey is for the imaginary mental barriers between us to be broken down and for our minds to now be open to the reality of the 5D fifth dimension that is within us and all around us. Only then can we join as the conscious collective and humanity will ascend in awareness to a whole new level of global understanding, love and compassion.

Chapter Four

Rude awakening

The haunted tambourine

My deep sleep was sharply interrupted by a very loud 'rap, rap, rap' apparently coming from the tall chest of drawers which stood opposite the foot of the bed.

1980 and I was eleven years old. We had moved house a few times. We were always moving house. My parents, having both been in the Armed Forces during and after the War had a frustrated wanderlust. My father was a keen Do-It-Yourself-er and it became a hobby of his to buy a house that needed repair, do it up until it was immaculate and then move onto the next big project.

We were living in a part of Kent which is now Greater London. Back then it was considered a rural village, and the house we lived in was a spacious three-bedroom bungalow built during the 1930s. The property had a lengthy garden which at the bottom stretched down to a steep railway embankment where Kentish cobnut trees grew. I spent much of my spare time in this part of the garden, well away from the house and playing under the apple trees. It may sound idyllic, it wasn't. My life as a child and teenager during my time here was a lonely, unpleasant and often dark one, with the garden and borrowed library books my only sanctuary.

We had lived in the house for two or three years without incident when one early Saturday morning I received a rude awakening. At the age of nineteen, my brother had already left home and so with his bedroom spare, I now occupied his former room. This was larger than my old bedroom, allowing space for my bed, some built-in bookshelves that my father had made for my brother, and my high chest of drawers. The same old chest of drawers that had occupied my bedroom when, as a one-year-old child in my cot, I experienced that terrifying apparition of a skeleton.

When my brother had lived at home, he had told me that the bedroom that I now occupied unnerved him a little as he thought that someone had 'died in there.' However, apart from it being north facing and therefore a little gloomy, I had experienced no problems with the room. My small single bed was placed so that the headboard was in the road-facing front window. Opposite stood the tall chest of drawers, doubtless freshly painted in another coat of white gloss paint. My parents always saw to it that everything was immaculate and everything was in its place, including their children.

It is while we sleep that we are at our most vulnerable, both physically and also psychically. I did not know this then, I do now. I would always recommend to anyone that you ask your spirit guides and angels for protection at bedtime. It is, after all, why we traditionally say our prayers before sleep. Experience has taught me that we are particularly vulnerable around the hours of 3am and 4am. Our bodies have pretty much shut-down at this time, and we are undergoing our nightly period of deep-sleep.

Since a particularly traumatic haunting event (in both

definitions of that word 'haunting') a few short years ago, I now always have a protective crystal by my bedside and I would recommend you do the same. I would recommend to you Black Tourmaline, Laboradite, or Rose Quartz as these are crystals with powerful anti-negative energy capabilities. Black Tourmaline will absorb negative energies, Laboradite will deflect them, and Rose Quartz has the most powerful remedy against any darkness that might be passing, and that remedy is the vibrational energy of love.

On this particular Saturday morning, the milky British sun was casting a dull glow through the bedroom curtains and dimly illuminating my bedroom with a greyish light. I wasn't aware of this fact until my deep sleep was sharply interrupted by a very loud, '*rap, rap, rap,*' apparently coming from the tall chest of drawers which stood opposite the foot of the bed.

My sleep was shattered in that second. Sitting bolt upright in bed, I stared wide-eyed at the cabinet in front of me and straining my ears in the contrasting silence for any new sound. It was still early and the house was silent, but I didn't have long to wait. I was fully, utterly and completely awake now and my heart was beating fast. Again, one more time came the three sharp knocks, '*rap, rap, rap.*'

Still sitting upright in bed, I stared and listened hard. The noise had most definitely come from the chest of drawers. A fleeting hope that I had dreamt the noise was dashed by the same urgent message being rapped out once more. Atop the chest of drawers was my collection of what, at eleven years old, I naively considered artfully placed ornaments, and this included a tambourine which I had balanced standing upright. The rapping ceased after only those three outbursts.

Seemingly, whatever had made the noise was satisfied that it had now got my attention. It could see me, but I could not see it. Before I could move, do or say anything I heard the loud and familiar sound of my tambourine. With disbelief I watched and listened from my bed as the tambourine started to make its unmistakable sound, yet in the morning gloom as I narrowed my eyes in focus, I could quite clearly make out that the metal discs were *not* moving. The tambourine was completely stationary, yet nonetheless sound was issuing from the instrument.

While the loud rapping noise was unlike any knock I had heard before, it was unmistakably from the chest of drawers, yet rather than the random sound of human knuckles on wood, the sound I heard was sharp, clipped, staccato and seemed to emanate from *within* the wood itself. There was no reverberation. Those familiar with vinyl records and the 1960s craze for playing and recording sounds backwards (think The Beatles' 'Sergeant Pepper' album) and you will know what I mean by a clipped end to a sound.

However, while the rapping was sharp and quick, the tambourine's unmoving metal discs made a deliberate slow sliding sound as if *every single one* of the metal discs were sliding one way in *total unison*. It was as though the tambourine was being slowly tilted one way and then tilted back again, with all the metal discs sliding one way and then back again. Only it wasn't and they weren't.

As I watched and listened with increasing fear mingled with a strange fascination, the tambourine remained resolutely unmoved. My logical brain raced. Had there been an earthquake? What, in Kent, England? 'No, don't be silly!' I thought to myself. The creeping sensation of awareness that this was a visitor from another dimension making its presence known began to sink in. The slow sliding sound was doubtless intended to emphasise the unnerving quality to the experience that this particular phantom had chosen, presumably to frighten me.

Similar to the unearthly quality of the rapping sound, the metal discs were making a noise that was impossible to recreate in reality. The tambourine made its laboured fanfare for only a few seconds and then stopped. Silence. I listened intently for what seemed like an age but was probably only a few seconds but there was nothing further. I leapt out of bed and cautiously I stood by the side of the chest of drawers, first looking all about it and then trying unsuccessfully to replicate the rapping sound.

Picking up the tambourine from where it stood, I discovered that the moment it was touched it made its more familiar jangly sound as the multitude of little metal discs started to clatter randomly into each other. I tilted the tambourine first one way and then back the other. But try as I might, I could not get anywhere near to the clipped sound that I had heard emanate from the tambourine seconds earlier or from the cabinet. The noises were completely impossible to reproduce accurately. The whole thing was *physically impossible by human hand*.

My parents were disinterested by my seemingly wild claims. I was not surprised. This was to be an oft repeated experience for me in the years to follow. The life of anyone who is open and psychically attuned to any degree is full of instances of psychic happenings and phenomena which are met by others with an unbreakable wall of disbelief. At best, well-meaning people who have never experienced such events listen to your recollection and sympathise with a warm but weak smile and a suggestion that 'perhaps you were tired.' At worst, you are met with scorn or open derision and a suggestion that you 'must be delusional.'

I have encountered both types of reaction many times and have repeatedly been frustrated by an apparent indifference to such phenomena. The inference is always the same, either that I am somewhat overwrought or that I am an attention-seeking liar. 'What makes you so special?' seems to be the underlying thought process. Yet I did not then and I do not now suggest that I am in any way special. These spiritual occurrences are just part of my journey this time around. In any case, I soon learned to shut up if I wanted to keep friends. These days of course, I choose better friends.

The resistance by some to the belief in anything supernatural or other-worldly is understandable to a degree but it does demonstrate an unwillingness to explore the unseen lest it disturb their own preconceived ideas that make up the safe and protected cocoon that we all mentally create for ourselves. It's that over-protective ego at work, shutting down the avenues of curiosity that might lead to some revealing truth or personal growth. In short, some cannot see beyond the length of their own noses, and even if they could, they would still choose not to. Why? Because of fear. Fear of the thought that an afterlife might actually exist. Fear that all we see, feel and hear in our physical reality might not be all that there is. Terrified that the tales and stories that they read in books as children might be based on a truth. In short, fear of the bogeyman under the bed.

The reality of life on this planet is often a harsh one. To distract ourselves from the harshness we create an illusory comfortable world for ourselves, perhaps of Cotswold villages,

Miss Marple on a bicycle, warm toast and cocoa and curling up on the sofa to listen to BBC Radio 4's Gardeners' Question Time. The truth is that we have little to fear from what is termed the supernatural and perhaps a lot more to fear from the harsh realities of the physical 3D world. The cruelties that we try to protect ourselves and our loved ones from in a lifelong struggle are actually caused by the same blinkered approach to life that gives away our empowerment to those very people with darkness in their hearts that we fear so much.

Those who we should fear are not disembodied spirits but living people who seek power and status. We create and manifest our world every second of every day. Thoughts and words are energy and energy become reality. We are therefore advised to keep our hearts bright and our thoughts light by always holding a space within us for love, compassion and gratitude. Most of you reading this will be doing so because your mind and your hearts are already open to receive and in turn you give out the natural energy of love that is within all of us. The task at hand is to help those still in the shadows.

So, you ask, what do I think that I experienced in my childhood bedroom that morning? Given some of the supernatural claims that I will make later in this book, you would be forgiven for thinking that I am a gullible man open to any passing snake oil salesman or practitioner of woo-woo. Instead, I believe that all claims of the supernatural should be thoroughly open to analysis as it is healthy to be an open-minded sceptic. It is good housekeeping to be analytical about all that you hear and read, whether that be from the media, your peers, your parents, or indeed from people like me.

So even as the child that I was, I tried to rationalise what had occurred. I knew that I was wide awake. I knew what I had heard. I established that what I had heard could not be replicated by human hand. I concluded that the sound emanated from within the inanimate objects themselves. I knew a little of the history of seances where rapping would be heard on wooden tables and the use of tambourines was not uncommon in proving the existence of a spirit presence at a seance of the nineteenth & twentieth centuries. I also knew that our home had been built sometimes in the 1930s or 1940s. Seances conducted at home were surprisingly commonplace following both world wars, with the grieving so desperate to contact their departed loved ones.

Would it be too far to presume that a spirit had been summoned in this way, at some point in this house's past and was perhaps still present? Whatever or whoever it was, it wanted my attention and it wasn't disappointed.

Chapter Five

My haunted life

Background

Once back in bed, and before the lamp was even switched off, the noise began again, the distinct sound of thin crinkly paper being crumpled or folded by unseen hands.

At the time of the incident of the self-playing tambourine in my bedroom, I was aged around ten years old. Between then and my late thirties I experienced, *or noticed*, only a few scattered incidents of supernatural phenomena and I shall briefly talk about some of them here. These incidents were so subjective that I leave it to you to decide whether they were real, or just the result of the mind failing to find a logical solution to a seemingly insoluble occurrence.

My first job of employment came about because of problems I was having at home in my teenage years. My parents - always looking for something in the material world to solve their emotional difficulties - had once again moved house on a whim, this time during my 'O' and 'A' Level examinations while I was at senior school. This latest house move resulted in my having to start at a new college somewhat late into the term and in a different city in a different part of Britain. The new college didn't offer any of the courses that I was already halfway through at my old school, and so several months into term time I had to begin new courses in different subjects and play catch-up.

I was aware of my social awkwardness and painful shyness but unknown to the sixteen-year-old me was that I was already suffering from Hyper Anxiety, Obsessive Compulsive Disorder (OCD), mild physical Tourette's and most seriously Complex (Childhood) Post-Traumatic Stress Disorder (CPTSD). These afflictions were so demanding that they took up more of my valuable time to feed than if I had just countered them head-on. When suddenly thrown into a bustling and vibrant college of seemingly happy young people, I didn't last long and after just one year, and at the pressure of my father, I left full-time education and instead looked for work.

Perhaps this may sound like an everyday normal experience of any boy in the 1980s, but I am playing down the extreme emotional and mental impact that the daily external negative influences had on me at home and at school. There was an absence of any emotional support at home or elsewhere and it left me profoundly alone and vulnerable. It has only been in the last two years, while writing this book, that I was to rediscover this truth about my childhood. In 2021, my late mother came through to me at an annual consultation with my favourite, trusted and always accurate psychic medium. My mother advised that I had placed hurtful memories from childhood into a metaphorical 'box' and that it was now time for me to, 'Lift the lid on that box and study what was inside.'

This then, was to reveal to me a lot about my life journey and the lessons I had set out to learn. At the time of the consultation, I had little idea of what my mother meant, but immediately my spirit guides began to place information about narcissistic parental abuse issues in my path, primarily through online media. I knew nothing of psychology. I began to study online clinical psychology lectures and wondered if it was any coincidence that in my personal life I knew three clinical psychologists who I class as friends. Questioning my own psychological motives and behaviours there came a realisation that I had encountered people suffering with behaviour traits on the spectrum of clinically recognisable Narcissistic Personality Disorder throughout my life, a repeating cycle that I hadn't even noticed – until now.

The term 'narcissist' is sadly overused these days and it is often misunderstood. Only a trained mental health professional such as a clinical psychologist or psychotherapist may diagnose clinical narcissistic personality disorder. It is a profoundly disabling mental health issue that affects not only the individual themselves, but also all those whom they encounter. The individual closely in contact with someone afflicted with clinical narcissism will soon find themselves doubting their own behaviours, abilities and even their reality over time, leading to a loss of personal empowerment as they unwittingly hand this over to the narcissist who has become the architect of a false reality or narrative that everyone must 'buy-in to.'

Now reviewing my childhood and teenager memories, the scales, as they say, fell away from my eyes. I had created a comforting fantasy world of a loving, warm and safe childhood home. I dearly wanted my parents to love me as much as I loved them – all children are utterly dependent upon their parents, they have no choice – but where one or more parents are emotionally unavailable and abuse the trust and power, it can create a situation akin to 'Stockholm Syndrome' where the love is travelling in only one direction; the child often facing the impossible herculean task of making up for the imbalance as I did.

Every single memory from childhood that I had stored away through the filter of rose-tinted spectacles was now coming up in a series of flashbacks for my review. Stripped away of this warm tint, I was left with the stark hurtful reality that my father was a cold, emotionally unavailable bully who had little or perhaps no regard for me. The memories flooded back, yet this time I saw them in sharp contrast. The verbal abuse and indeed the physical abuse where no matter how hard I tried and successful I became, I could never quite please my father. Indeed, any success was met with indifference or coldness.

My mother meanwhile was the narcissist's enabler, where I was told to put up or shut up in order to maintain the power equilibrium in the household where my father reigned supreme. Those of you who have suffered at the hands of narcissistic parental abuse will be well familiar with the adultification of the scapegoat child, for that was me, where an intolerable burden of emotions are placed upon the child and where he or she is responsible for keeping the narcissist supplied with their ceaseless requirement for emotional need, or trying to fill an emotionless void with love.

The enabler meanwhile is kept safe and loved by proxy, though keeping the child under constant threat of being reported to the narcissist parent for any misdemeanour. This conditional love and betrayal of trust leaves the child feeling insecure, unsafe and untrusting of adults. In short, the roles have been reversed and the child becomes the care and love giver to the parents - only a child isn't to know this. The narcissistic parents are themselves emotionally underdeveloped, probably caused by things that occurred in their own childhoods and the child becomes emotionally mature at an early age but left with a wounded unhealed inner child.

With narcissistic parents, where the child is a success, in public it is deemed completely down to the amazing parental skills of the mother and father. When the child fails at something, no support or solace is provided, instead the child is declared a loser and a liability as I was, many times. The child is left to bring themselves up emotionally and while this makes for an amazingly independent adult, it also leaves that same adult open to repeated patterns of narcissistic abuse in later life, where healthy boundaries are non-existent and red flags in any relationship or work situation, that would stand out a mile to those brought up in an emotionally stable environment, go past unseen and unidentified.

I do not wish to distract from the positive life-affirming message that I hope to get across in these pages and I had not intended to put so much of myself and my personal history into this book when I began writing. That was perhaps naïve of me as my lifetime of experiences are so incredibly relevant to the extent that sharing this private knowledge is essential to understand the extremes of emotional turmoil that can be encountered and endured yet yield a positive outcome.

A close friend of mine, when reading through the draft of my book, felt strongly that I had to explain to readers why, after such a difficult childhood, I still have such a powerful love for my deceased parents. The answer is that I have only love in my heart and I am thankful to all who I have encountered on my journey. Besides, a child loves their parents unconditionally;

they must, as a defenceless child has no choice in the matter. In my case, I had buried away the truth of my early years deep within my subconscious, only to 'open that box' in 2021 and thus beginning a new journey into self-healing.

The unhealed pain from childhood and beyond I had unwittingly carried with me throughout my adult life. It is relevant to the path that led to my fall and subsequent recovery through my ever-increasing spiritual awareness and the self-improvement that has occurred for me in the last five years of my life. If I wrote this book without a hint of the background of my struggle then you may rightly think of me, 'What does he know?!' It is true that there are many people with profoundly difficult lives and all too often more tragic than I endured. But then we cannot compare or judge another's experiences or progress with our own. Indeed, we must not judge at all. 'Never judge another man until you have walked a mile in his moccasins,' goes the saying.

This time around in this incarnation I have enjoyed the life of white privilege in one of the wealthiest countries in the world. Like most people in Europe, I am possibly in the top five percent of wealthiest individuals globally. I do not treat that privilege lightly. However it is peace of mind and a settled heart that pave the way to a happy life and not the balance at the bank – though that helps too.

Those who work with spirit will know how our progress on the Earth plane is watched over all the time and guided for our highest good *when we accept the help of our guides*. Many will also have encountered situations on their life path which demonstrate how clever our spirit guides can be, and sometimes how humorous. I was editing this very section of the chapter when I decided, on a whim one evening, to visit a local spiritualist meeting occurring in a nearby town.

I had been in the UK for a few days and I miss being able to go to spirit circles and to public meetings. A stranger, I had never been to this spiritualist circle before but the moment that the spiritualist evening began in earnest, the 'guest' psychic medium on the platform immediately crossed over to where I was sitting in the audience and she brought forward my father.

My father, an Englishman, gave conclusive evidence that it was him speaking through the psychic medium with a memory from my childhood about how he used to greet me in the mornings in German, which I had completely forgotten about until that moment. He expressed his excitement to be able to see me again at such an 'important stage in my life' and delight that I had opened-up after my lifelong karmic journey. He went on to explain that I had just 'passed the test' that I had set myself before birth and he was delighted for me. Everything that happens in our life is just a lesson and a test, but because we don't know this, we can harbour hate, resentment and anger against others and the universe, when we should encourage love, acceptance and release.

Some additional psychic evidence about my present ongoing circumstances was given and finally my father finished by explaining that in life he didn't like being 'Earth-side' (in the '3D') very much, which was his way of apologising. It was very true that sadly, my father didn't like life much. The message from my father concluded by him telling me something that he could never say to me in life, 'I love you.' This was the single most validating spirit message that I have ever received, and I thank my father for it. I love you too dad.

I was sixteen when, as I described, we had moved house once again forcing me to abandon my school classes and my friends to start over. Change had been and continues to be a repeating experience in my life. I was a keen musician at the time, though my father probably rightly, wanted me to concentrate on my artistic skills which were far better than my musical ones. The move from London to the extremely rural county of Somerset, to what was then a quiet backwater, coincided to what was probably the first time that I found occasion to stand up to my bullying and emotionally distant father.

The result of this brief foray into self-empowerment was my father attempting to throttle me, my mother desperately trying to pull his hands from my throat in what was a highly emotionally charged moment of unpleasantness. My crime had been to enquire about when I was going to be able to begin my piano studies which I had been promised by my father as part of the relocation. The piano lessons never materialised and I was likewise unsurprised by the attack.

At the age of ten years old, when playing cards with my father, I jokingly accused him of cheating, something every card player has uttered at some time in their life. My father flew into a rage – a daily occurrence – and told me that a few years before when he was in the Army he would have, 'Stabbed me with a knife,' for such a comment. Yes, my childhood was not of the Christopher Robin variety and beatings were not uncommon.

I had passed my 'Eleven Plus' exam at the age of ten years old. For those who don't know, in the UK, if you were in the catchment area of a grammar school and you passed this test aged ten years, you were given the option of avoiding the local state-run school and instead enrolling at the grammar school.

Whether a grammar school is superior or not, I cannot say, but rightly or wrongly a child's ongoing prospects were thought to be vastly improved.

However, despite being a bright child and academically ahead by two years at that time, my father considered me a failure and had me written-off. This I now know was much more about his own internal demons and the narcissism he suffered than any reality concerning his son's capabilities. My parents told me that I would be going to the local state-run school on the basis that it was but a short walk from our house, whereas the grammar school was some three kilometres distant. Sound logic you might think until you know that my father had to pass the grammar school in his car on his way to work each morning.

In fact, only once did my father ever give me a car lift to school, and this was because he had just bought a brand-new Ford Sierra, newly released back then, and he wanted to show it off to the other parents (who he didn't know) in the school car park. As I say, my father suffered from clinical narcissist tendencies. I was the scapegoated child in the family and expected to appear the best in order to further advance my father's public admiration, or publicly humiliated when it suited him, so that he would look better by contrast as he saw it. These are the standard actions of the narcissistic parent, though from the inside looking out, it appeared normal behaviour as I didn't know any different.

The problem with the local state-run school was that it was a failing establishment. There were regular teacher and supply shortages, and it was populated by disinterested pupils. The teachers weren't exactly motivated either and kept changing more times than the guards at Buckingham Palace. The school became so bad that after two rebrand name changes, the bulldozers eventually moved-in and I understand that the much of the site is now a development of luxury homes. I am sure that cheering could be heard from so many ex-pupils on that glorious day of demolition.

I pleaded to my parents regularly about the brutality there and how I wanted to move to a different school but my cries for help fell upon deaf ears. I was told to 'toughen-up' and that it was 'character building' though what damaged character they were hoping to build I daren't say. I therefore became deeply resentful that when it was suddenly convenient for *them*, my parents felt it perfectly acceptable for me to be uprooted and placed into a new school during the middle of my exams.

Before the move the tumultuous years at my London school had seemed endless. I endured all-day-long bullying and harassment over everything from my appearance and personality to my sexuality. This bullying was not only from fellow pupils but also on occasion by the teachers. The matter of my sexuality, hidden from my parents, did not become overly relevant until news of a new virus spreading across the USA become national news overnight in the UK following an investigative news programme on television one night back in the early 1980s.

I can still recall the reaction at school the very next day. My best friend who for two years I had sat next to in class, approached me in the school quad that morning and laughingly told me that I was going to, 'Die of AIDs' because, 'My father says that's what happens to gays like you.'

He didn't speak to me or sit next to me in class again. Perhaps the result of poor parenting skills, encouraging prejudice and nurturing an absence of empathy within your own children has to be one of the biggest cruelties, for both the victim and also for the perpetrator. I must have cut a lonely figure at school and nobody wants to be seen with the outcast just in case the loneliness is catching.

The bullying was relentless and appalling. There was no respite. My parents weren't interested in my need for help, again telling me that I needed to 'man up.' I was twelve years old. My adult brother, when I pleaded with him for assistance told me that he had experienced his own bullying issues at school and therefore I had to too. 'Had I spoken with my teachers?' I was asked.

The teachers at my school were a part of the problem, some of them actually instigating the bullying using the tried-and-tested 'divide and rule' technique to assert control and creating an insidious atmosphere of homophobia in the classroom, the corridors and on the playing fields. By the time I was aged twelve I was being attacked repeatedly and openly in the classroom. Being stabbed with a pair of compasses or attacked with a metal rule were two of the favoured daily techniques as these left only small cuts or bleeding marks on the skin.

Children like me who are seen as an obvious undefended victim, soon become the target of other predators. I was sexually assaulted on several occasions by one female pupil, and I was sexually assaulted by one senior teacher in the classroom – something he did openly to any teenage boy he felt was appealing. I began to dread breaks in the school day, as they were seen as open opportunities by bullies for attacks on vulnerable or younger pupils and there was for me none worse than what I am about to describe.

My grand humiliation, from which I will never quite recover no matter the healing work, was when I was stripped naked except for my shirt, humiliated, sexually assaulted and an attempt made to choke me to death in a truly terrifying and severe incident on the school playing fields at break time.

In one of my daily attempts to protect myself from harm on a dreary, damp lunchtime, I had found a secluded spot in the corner of the school playing field, far enough away, or so I thought, from seeing eyes. To my horror, I realised too late that I had been seen crossing the playing fields and I found myself alone, cornered by the school bully - every school has one it seems - and his entourage of dubious male and female hangers-on.

I was restrained and held down by three boys and two girls, forced to lie on my back on the cold damp grass as my clothes were removed and scattered. My legs parted, I was humiliatingly sexually assaulted for entertainment and then the school bully, an older and larger boy, sat on my belly and stuffed mud, grass and autumn leaves into my open mouth as I gasped for air. I've always been terrified of suffocation, I had choked on a boiled sweet when I was eight years old with only presence of mind saving me, and when I was aged ten years old, I nearly drowned in the school swimming baths, only to be rescued by a girl classmate who had seen my plight.

The weight on my stomach and chest already meant that I couldn't breathe, and this was exacerbated by my arms being restrained above my head with my mouth and throat filling with debris. I was terrified. Whilst looking directly into my eyes, a girl who stood over us repeatedly screamed at the lead bully incitement, 'Kill him!'

This was it. I am going to die here. Suddenly, the other girl who had actively encouraged the assault by the boy perhaps now realised that I was suffocating and things had 'gotten out of hand.'

The school bully however had bloodlust, and humiliation was no longer his aim, instead he wanted to extinguish my life. Panicking, the girl persuaded the school bully, albeit with some difficulty, to release me. Realising that they had gone too far, they quickly got up and walked off together laughing, my clothes, my school bag and belongings wet and muddy and scattered across the field. I was going to be in a lot of trouble that night with my parents.

I felt that I had come close to dying that day. In the days that followed I often wish that I had. The experience was profoundly cruel and depressing to bear. I was little more than a child and I couldn't understand the cruelty and darkness that lay in their cold young hearts. Could the daily reality of their lives that had made them so angry possibly be worse than my own? I couldn't confide in anyone what had just happened to me or tell of the miseries that I was undergoing on a daily basis. I was chiefly worried sick of what to tell my angry mother about my mud and grass-soaked clothes. To tell my father about such matters always resulted in one of his rages and possibly additional punishment. 'How dare you bother me with your problems! Don't you know that I have enough of my own?'

So, I was the abused child who kept quiet. I wasn't to know it, but this wasn't to be the last time in my life that I was to brush up against death only to be saved. I now know that these 'brushes with death' are not uncommon for those like me destined for a spiritual awakening followed by a healing and teaching pathway. Perhaps they are tests of fortitude, perhaps they are karma, or perhaps they are just unfortunate miserable events that shouldn't happen to anyone.

With my parents having moved house once more, I found myself at the age of fifteen being interviewed at a new college in a new town in order to be accepted as a new late entrant student. The head of form was a delightful man, not at all like the dreadful teachers at my failing comprehensive had been, and the interview went well despite my intense shyness and hyper-anxiety.

Unknown to my parents, I had ceased going to lessons for the last year of my schooling, instead preferring the comfort and security of the music department. Here it had been largely bully-free, and the music teachers did not care about my presence, so I went by unnoticed. Besides, there were plenty of sound-proofed music practice rooms to escape into. It was a miracle that I passed any 'O' Level examinations at all as I had given up on my schooling after the school had given up on me.

Yet for all of the charm and warmth that this new head of form was exuding as I sat in his little office, I had an overwhelming sensation of dread. At the time I put this down to my anxiety and stress of what the past had shown me and what an unknown future may hold for me. But this wasn't the first time that I had experienced this unsettling sensation. My intuition was usually on point, but in those days I was closed-off to it.

My parents were, as they always were with anyone outside of our family unit, charming and delightful (childhood sufferers of narcissistic parental abuse reading this will readily recognise this familiar sugar-coated trait) and the tiny office of the headteacher glowed warm in the light of the desk lamp and with his own spirit. Yet despite this warmth, the dread tightened around me in a cold vice-like grip.

Back in those days and for many years afterwards I saw this intuitive dread as coming from my own thoughts and my own energy. More recently I have come to be aware that this can often be spirit desperately trying to make contact, their message going unheard or unheeded. At other times forthcoming events can be of such a magnitude that waves in the Akashic energy field ripple outwards and anyone with psychic abilities can intuitively feel the disturbance before it occurs in linear time. But I was too young and inexperienced. As a claircognizant psychic, I just 'know' things and if something hugely unfortunate is going to occur then that feeling can become an overwhelming sensation of dread which can last for hours and sometimes days.

Just a few weeks ago, I lost a good friend to the present global pandemic. He was not much older than me and was always full of life. He lived in a major city in the USA, and we kept in contact via social messaging, which although irregular was several times a year. At the end of 2019 I got that unwelcome but familiar sensation of dread whenever I saw his social media posts. I wanted to write to him and suggest he look after his health. A forthcoming heart attack perhaps? That was how it felt to me whenever I looked at his photos. I confided in my best friend back home about my concerns, but I didn't tell my American friend of those same fears.

The curse of the 'Cassandra' effect, a syndrome that takes its reference from Greek mythology, is that no-one wants to hear your bad news. And what good would it do? How could it make any difference? With my sense of dread increasing over a few weeks and then having written to him and received no reply, it was with some trepidation that eventually I searched the online news local to my friend's American city. Immediately I typed his name into a search engine, there was his face and there were the obituaries. It was with immense sadness that I discovered he had succumbed to Covid 19 in hospital, one of the early American casualties. I now understand him to be one of my spirit guides, which is rather lovely and such an honour.

The incident at my college interview was not dissimilar. I started at my new college only a week after the over-shadowed interview. With horror, I learned on my first day of the terrible news that the head tutor who had interviewed me had tragically died on his way home that same night in a motor vehicle accident. The memory of this tragedy has stuck with me. Many psychics will know full well the awful feeling of guilt that perhaps they should have said something or could have done something. It isn't possible to of course and this results in many spiritual people, me included, considering themselves 'The world's worst psychic.'

These supernatural incidents did not make me feel in anyway connected to the universe but instead made me feel fearful of the psychic world and even a social outcast. In those pre-internet and pre-social media days there were no chatrooms or friends to discuss these things with and I thought that I was just 'different.'

After much soul-searching, a long winter of solitude and pressure from my parents, I left college the following summer, thinking that I was not doing at all well with my education. Looking back, I now realise that I was at one of the many crossroads that life affords us. I had told no-one about my quitting and on my actual day of departure I stood at the registrar's countertop and handed-in my leaving documents. I was mortified to suddenly discover my art lecturer stood behind me in the queue. He was pleasant but saddened when I explained to him that I was departing. He only then chose to advise me that I had received an 'A' grade in the mock exam. If only he had once mentioned to me that he thought that I was doing well during all those previous weeks, then perhaps I might have been more enthusiastic about staying on.

This is a lesson for us all to give encouragement to anyone we feel deserves it. I never received encouragement from my parents, only criticism, this often occurring like a ritual humiliation when guests were in the house, much to the guests' embarrassment or shock surprise. So my college lecturer had, at that moment, presented me with an opportunity to change my mind and perhaps change the course of my destiny. I was at a crossroads, but I failed to grasp the positive lifeline being offered to me and as so often in my life I snatched defeat from the jaws of victory, or 'self-sabotage' as I now refer to it.

Having made my mind up to leave college there then began further rows with my father as I searched the classifieds for a job during those difficult days of high unemployment. My father wanted me out of his house. As a sixteen-year-old student in full-time education he was prepared to have me at home. Now that I was looking for work, he considered me an out-of-work adult who should find his own way in life.

I got my first job by accident or perhaps divine intervention. After a very positive job interview at the Ministry of Defence with a surprisingly delightful, retired military officer of the Colonel Blimp variety, I was told by him there and then that I was already unsuccessful as the perfect candidates had been selected before I had even sat down in the interview chair. As I left the interview it began to snow outside and I felt very positive and optimistic despite the apparent result of the interview and the wintry weather. After all, the interview had gone well and I received welcome praise for my abilities and conduct, praise that I had always been starved of by the very people who should have supported me the most. Or was my feeling of positivity coming from somewhere else? I just *knew* that things were going to be ok as I walked through the now heavily falling snow that chilly winter's day.

I got a call a few days later. It was the kindly retired officer who told me that the candidate who had been selected over me had called him and withdrawn his application. I received a job offer by default, but it felt like a victory, nonetheless. I cannot here disclose the nature of the job. It was and remains restricted information as the employment was with the military. It is, perhaps, not relevant to this story but it had a profound effect on me, the nature of the work on an impressionable seventeen-year-old involved encountering daily some of the very worst of human depravity. The old decrepit Edwardian building in which I found myself working amongst a small team of people was, I discovered, haunted by a seemingly benign spirit.

The disturbing nature of the work and the decaying nature of the old building made all of us there feel a little uneasy during our daily work routine. As a restricted unit, the front and back doors were locked with no visitors. Twice a day we collected together in the large staff room for our morning coffee and biscuits. The building was single storey and set out in two corridors in a 'T' shaped construction. We worked in several different rooms which fed off from the two corridors, and so twice a day, plus lunchtimes, we would depart from our little rooms and, leaving the doors wide open, gather in the staffroom for refreshment.

It was a surprisingly long while before we collectively began to notice that the doors to our rooms were always closed once we had finished and returned to our work posts after our staffroom breaks. I suppose that for a long time we presumed that one or other of us was going around closing all the doors in order to keep the heat inside the rooms that chilly winter. But eventually we, one by one, began to realise by a process of elimination, that it was no-one working in the building who had been closing the doors.

One tea-break, someone finally mentioned it, asking, 'Had we noticed that the doors were always shut fast when we finished our break?' We all chimed in that we had, and we thereafter sought to find out which mischievous person amongst us had been pulling a prank.

So, at the very next coffee break, we checked that we were all inside the staffroom and, like we always did, we shut the staffroom door to keep the heat, and the staff, inside. When we finished our break, we had been chatting happily and had forgotten about the doors completely. It was only when we opened the staffroom door, which was at the end of one of the long corridors, that we looked out and saw that, once again, all the doors were shut the length of the corridor.

Much nervous hilarity as we questioned each other about who it had been who had sneaked out of the staffroom and shut the doors. No-one admitted to it and so we agreed to repeat the experiment at the next break. We did so, ensuring that all the heavy old large Edwardian doors were left wide open. Once again, when we finished our break some minutes later and went back to work, all the doors to the rooms off the corridor were closed shut.

We repeated this experiment a couple of times, all the doors left open, all the staff secured inside the staffroom with only the one exit door, and each time all of the doors in the *whole* building were closed fast. The old wooden floorboards were covered in ancient linoleum which made a clatter whenever anyone walked along it. The doors were heavy and old with their original door mechanisms and they did not shut quietly. Yet each time, *all* the doors would be noiselessly shut with no sound of anyone accomplishing the task.

Given the military background of the building, my guess would be that the spirit who remained earthbound at this place was a former military man, who was still at his post watching over the place and rather than trying to haunt or aggravate, he, or she, was merely doing their duty in keeping the heat inside the rooms and most probably, following Regimental Orders in closing the doors.

Three years later, in a new job and a new location, I was renting an old Victorian house with a female friend. My parents had kicked me out of the parental home, or rather, wouldn't speak to me or let me back in, because they had presumed that I was having an affair with my female co-lodger. They also disapproved of the visitors I had to my new home, one of whom was a friend who, unlike me, happens to be black. They strongly disapproved of such things, stating, 'What would the neighbours think?' with shocked horror. Yes, my parents really were that backward. If they had known the truth that in fact, I was a gay man with a boyfriend, then I cannot think how far further downwards my relationship with them would have spiralled.

The house I rented was dark and creepy and had a pall of misery over it. I had a miserable time there for personal reasons that are not apropos to this story, suffice to say that they involved betrayal and injustice on a vicious scale and based around bullying and homophobia against me at my place of work. Hatred which stretched its dark tendrils right into my own home; somewhere where I should have felt safe and secure.

It was wintertime again and I put my feelings about the negative energy of the house down to imagination and to what I was going through personally at the time. Nothing much happened at that house to be perfectly frank. At least, not on a scale similar to what was to come in later years, which I write about elsewhere in this book. There was, however, a single weird incident, which to this day I cannot explain.

Alone in my small gloomy single bedroom around midnight and before I had gone to sleep, I was in my single-bed and had just settled down and had switched off the bedside lamp. There was nothing else in the bleak little room save for a fitted single wardrobe where I hanged my few meagre clothes. I was very poor in those days and the monthly rent was greater than my monthly income. My parents gave me no help of any kind and I was alone in the world. As I lay there in the total darkness beginning to drift off for my night's sleep, I heard the loud and unmistakable sound of rustling paper from the direction of the top of the wardrobe.

There was a cupboard over the wardrobe and, switching on the bedside lamp, I leapt out of bed and with trepidation opened the pivoting door upwards expecting to reveal a disturbed mouse in its nest. Instead, the sight that greeted me was an empty cupboard and no sound. I checked inside the wardrobe itself, opening the large double wooden doors but there was nothing that could have made the noise. Confused, I shut the doors again and retreated back to bed.

As soon as I was settled back into the darkness, the sound started again, very distinct and definitely coming from the corner of the room right at the top of the wardrobe. Crystal clear, it was the sound of someone, or something, slowly opening or folding thin paper such as you would get with parcel paper or newspaper. The noise stopped and in the dark I fumbled for the bedside lamp. Getting out of bed one more time, I did another reconnoitre of the wardrobe and cupboard interior, this time pulling everything that was in the wardrobe out onto the bedroom floor, so convinced was I that it was a mouse. Finding nothing I put everything back where it came from.

Once back in bed, and before the lamp was even switched off, the noise began again, the distinct sound of thin crinkly paper being crumpled or folded by unseen hands. Irritated now, I repeated the inspection, the noise stopping as I exited my bed, and pulling everything out of the wardrobe once more I inspected my few belongings in fine detail, still looking for that elusive mouse. I found nothing of course and the noise began again as soon as I had returned to my bed and even before the bedside lamp was extinguished.

This time I remained in bed. I had satisfactorily convinced myself that there were no mice in the cupboard or in the room. The sound was too loud and clear to have been a mouse in the walls or in the attic. The sound was very much in the room with me. Perhaps bored of its game when I refused to play anymore

- I instead chose to stay in bed - the noise stopped just as quickly as it had started and I heard no more strange sounds in that house for the reminder of my time there. I should perhaps also mention that we did not have mice. I cannot remember if my sleep was disturbed again that night but some weeks after eventually moving out of the house, I discovered that local talk was of the house being haunted.

Sissinghurst Castle Garden in Kent, the magnificent world-famous gardens created by Vita Sackville-West and her husband Harold Nicholson has been a lifelong favourite of mine. I have visited many times and even stayed as a guest there for one blissful week in 2013. It was here, as a young man and soon after the incident with the scrunching paper in the wardrobe, that I paid my third visit to the gardens as a paying tourist with my parents. My thoughts extended solely to enjoying the vision that Vita and Harold created here in this corner of rural Kent. They most certainly did not extend to thinking about spirits or hauntings, and yet Sissinghurst is known to be haunted, unsurprising perhaps for a site that dates back to the sixteenth century.

It was a beautiful hot sunny day and I had left my parents relaxing in the cool under the shade of a large oak tree. I was strolling around the main formal gardens for the second time that afternoon, disturbed only by some very noisy German schoolchildren who were also enjoying the grounds but in their own way. Gardens are perhaps best enjoyed at dusk, when the sun is setting, and the birds have yet to sleep. A serenity unfolds over mature gardens at this golden hour, and I consider there to be no finer pleasure than to be in an English country garden at this time of day.

This particular day was not to be one of those occasions however, the sun was high in the sky and the heat penetrating. Try as one might it was difficult to relax properly with all of the noise around me. Just which one of those children was making that silly clicking noise?!

I sped up to escape the children all about me who were noisily laughing and joking. But it wasn't the loud voices and shrieks of laughter that had irritated me, instead it was one of the silly fools making the clicking noise with, I assumed, his fingers. I diverted down the yew hedge walkway and found myself alone in the cool of the shade afforded by the yews. Yet still the clicking noise persisted. I looked about me and could see no-one. Clearly one of these pesky children had seen me divert off and was following me, not that I could see anyone about.

I walked along the yew path and retraced my steps back to the garden proper. Yet every so often there was that annoying sound again. A 'clickety, click, click' of what I guessed to be someone snapping their fingers. It was only because the sound was following me about that I paid any heed to it. Yet I was surprised that no other tourists seem to pay attention to this irritating noise. Eventually, somewhere near Harold Nicholson's cottage in the grounds, the child must have given up as the sound stopped and I rejoined my parents under the cool of the oak tree. Contented, we sat there for a while on a wooden bench, watching a robin redbreast on the ground dart in and out of our feet, hoping for some crumbs and eyeing us suspiciously.

It was some twenty-five years later that I was once again on one of my many holiday visits to Sissinghurst Castle Garden and I purchased a beautiful hard-backed illustrated book about the history of this ancient place. A week or so on from that and back at home I was reading the book from cover to cover. I liked to read a little before bedtime each night and I thoroughly enjoyed this written tour into Sissinghurst's past. A section of the book was dedicated to the rare ghostly happenings at the famous property.

It was therefore to my complete surprise to read that some young adult male visitors are said to report being followed about the gardens by a curious loud 'clicking noise,' just as I had been many years before when I was in my early twenties. The book suggested that this may in fact be the ghost of Harold Nicholson, who in life was openly attracted to young men and had the unusual habit of strolling about his gardens making a loud 'clicking noise' with his tongue. Sometimes ghosts are in plain 'sight' in broad daylight, and we aren't even aware that we have seen or heard them.

CHAPTER SIX

Life after life

Death is a myth

*Death is not the greatest tragedy to occur in our life.
The greatest tragedy is where we allow ourselves to
die inside while we still live*

When you read of my childhood experiences of the supernatural, you will perhaps understand that I was not very old when I concluded that ghosts exist. At a young age, and throughout my life, ghosts represented the very real and frightening prospect of a night-time visitation at the bedside and of strange mists, misplaced shadows, strange sensations and loud rapports. But earthbound spirit is only one aspect of the afterlife. In the same way that a wayward teenager avoiding their responsibilities by hanging out at the back of the school bike sheds and smoking weed is not representative of teens as a whole, a self-trapped ghost with a mischievous or malevolent intent is not representative of the spirit world.

There is an overwhelming body of anecdotal evidence from centuries of human existence that ghosts walk amongst us. My own personal experiences as a child left me in no doubt. Having concluded that ghosts exist, it then follows that the spirit must survive the death of the physical body. It really is that straightforward. Some earthbound spirits are fully conscious and interact with the living (whether we want them to or not!) and some are less so, trapped by their own angst and undergoing a ceaseless Groundhog Day cycle of the emotional anguish that they suffered as they breathed their final moments. Then there are ghost sightings, such as the infamous marching of Roman soldiers through an underground cellar in York, England which are either an indelible energetic imprint of a past event, or a human experience of a 'timeslip' in action.

Some of you, curious as to the supernatural and to the proof of an afterlife will be asking 'but where is the scientific evidence?' We have become used to reliance upon science, where the only acceptable evidence is that which can be reproduced in a laboratory environment. We cannot hope to reproduce the spiritual in a laboratory and yet without science proving beyond reasonable doubt the existence of spirit, many people will refuse to acknowledge it. Yet what about that enormous body of anecdotal evidence?

Those who dismiss the possibility of the survival of the spirit after the death of the physical body and who consider those who *do* believe in this possibility as little more than superstitious fools, are denying the overwhelming body of evidence from centuries of encounters with spirit. Such encounters occur every day, all around the world, continually adding to the vast catalogue of evidence. Few people would these days refute the association between smoking cigarettes and the resultant increased likelihood of contracting lung cancer. Yet this association between cigarette smoking and lung cancer cannot be replicated in the laboratory. Instead scientists researching lung cancer rely on the overwhelming body of evidence from many decades of study.

One could therefore be forgiven for questioning why some people still choose to refute the possibility of an afterlife despite not just decades but centuries of evidence. Perhaps it is now time for those who dismiss the probability of spirit to submit *their* evidence as to why they believe it does *not* exist, rather than is more often the case the other way around.

As to the science, everything in our physical universe is energy vibrating at different frequencies. I suggest that the frequency of the energy that we vibrate at and the frequency of the vibrational energy that surrounds us establishes our reality. Consciousness is our energy vibrating at a certain frequency. We are all unique and therefore we all have our own frequency energy pattern. When the death of the physical body occurs, our consciousness as energy persists and merely transmutes from one vibrational reality to another. Accordingly, there is no death.

Our bodies are the physical vessels given to us to house and support our spirit energy through its lifelong journey of discovery on Earth. At the moment of birth there begins the lifetime of struggle between what our brain experiences and learns through the way it senses our physical reality, contrasted to what our heart, spirit or 'inner knowing' is telling us. Our mind comes from the evolutionary process of the animal kingdom and is resolutely based in the physical, evolving over centuries to protect us from harm. To accomplish its task, our brain keeps us in a perpetual state of awareness, anxiety and fear. The 'fight or flight' mechanism is closely associated with an over-anxious mind and this heightened state of chemical anxiety in the physical body can cause health issues in the longer term.

While this survival technique is essential if our physical body is to survive in the physical world, it has the unfortunate side-effect that it distracts us from our true purpose while we are here on Earth. Fear of failure, fear of poverty, fear of derision, fear of isolation and fear of death, causes our brain, or rather our 'ego', to seek out reassurance and physical comfort in all its manifold forms. Yet what of the spirit contained within our physical body? It too needs nurturing as much as the physical body requires sustenance to survive.

Our spirit is here to experience the 3D physical world, but we often ignore the need for spiritual growth. I wonder how many of us out there have a healthy physical body but with a spirit that is malnourished? We would not disregard our physical health and hygiene and yet many of us ignore our spiritual health and wellbeing. Our intuition, our destiny and purpose come from spirit but out of fear we can ignore our heart in favour of what our brain logically suggests is best for us. How many times have you tuned-out what your intuition or spirit is telling you, and instead listened to your logical brain, only to regret this later?

When the moment of death arrives, our eternal spirit departs the impermanent physical body and returns home to the Light where it originated. It returns to the Source, to God. It returns to the greater collective energy where we are all one and not separated by the veil as we are on Earth. This is not death at all, this is a return home.

My Uncle Gordon sadly died of terminal cancer in the early hours one morning in 1997 in his apartment in Brighton. Nobody was with him. He had not shared the news that his cancer was terminal and that he did not have long to live, preferring as he saw it not to trouble others. My father could not have known that his brother was close to death and yet Uncle Gordon paid my father a visit that night.

Moment of death visitations to loved ones are not uncommon. Those interested in sound scientific knowledge in this area would be recommended to look at the work and studies of renowned neuropsychiatrist and neurophysiologist Peter Fenwick who has established a body of evidence of end-of-life phenomena of over three-hundred examples.

My father was not a man given to histrionics or flights-of-fancy. Before we received the telephone call to say that my Uncle Gordon had been found dead, my father had tremblingly told me and my mother that he knew his brother had died. The body of my Uncle Gordon was discovered in his bed at home by the daily visiting specialist cancer nurse, but my father couldn't have known this. He explained to me how he had been awoken in the night with a mental vision of a long forgotten Victorian large, framed print of 'The Good Shepherd.'

This picture had hung over his and his brother's shared childhood bed back in the 1930s. With the image of that picture firmly in his mind, my father found himself to be lying in bed feeling 'freezing cold.' Icy cold air wafted over him, and my father distinctly heard the loud sound of ice cracking which he said went on for some seconds. My father described the noise as best he could, and it was the sound that ice cubes make when first plunged into a warm glass of water.

A year or so before, my father's sister Olive had been in hospital, having suffered a severe stroke and she was not expected to survive. Olive had been lying in her hospital bed unconscious for some days when without warning one afternoon she awoke and, ignoring the people in the room, she began a bright and animated conversation with her older sister Kathleen. This would have been quite normal if it weren't for my Aunt Kathleen having died the previous year. So, Aunt Kathleen couldn't have been in the hospital room that day. Or could she? Having finished her conversation with her deceased sister, Aunt Olive lay back down onto her bed and fell into a deep sleep once more. She died peacefully later the same day.

I nursed both my late father and my late mother at home until their eventual deaths from cancer in 2008 and 2015 respectively. It is a very special privilege to be able to nurse our ailing parents until they are able to finally depart their failing physical body. Death from a wasting disease such as cancer is not often the peaceful departure that we are given to believe it is in film and TV. 'Died peacefully at home' we read in the obituaries.

Anyone who has been through this mental and physical torture will understand. For all their faults, I loved my parents more than anything else in the world. I still do. The frustration, the pain, the tears, the emotional drain and the immense love that I put into caring for them was such an honour for which I am grateful. To look after your own parents at the end in a similar way to how they nursed you as a small baby-in-arms was profoundly rewarding and filled me with a love that was difficult to contain.

My father had lost his voice some weeks prior to his passing. I had presumed that this was a stage of his terminal pancreatic cancer but instead I was told that it was a side-effect of the extreme depression that he had understandably sunk into. His depression and illness worsening, my father would lie in his bed for hours just staring without facial expression. It was therefore a surprise one morning, when I spoke to him like I always did when checking-in on him in his sickroom that he seemed to be asleep yet was smiling to himself.

I asked softly, 'What are you smiling about dad?'

He opened his eyes and replied, 'Beautiful music!'

Surprised, I asked, 'You can hear music?' adding, 'What kind of music?' 'Loud' was the single word reply, a smile still playing on his lips.

'Is it nice?' I asked.

My father's smile flickered and faded, then with a wince and a frown he replied 'No.'

My father's silence then resumed.

My father passed away later that week. Following weeks of torrential rain, it was the first day of March and the heavens cleared, heralding a beautiful spring day. As per our routine, I went to see my father in his bedroom that morning and opening the curtains welcomed-in the sunshine. My father was unconscious by this stage in his illness, but I was going through the motions of talking to him like I always did. I told him, as happily as I could muster, what a fantastic sunny day it was and how the birds were singing.

He had been chain-stoking for several hours, a condition of heavy breathing when close to death, and for all intents and purposes in a comatose state. Yet as I talked to him about the day and sat by his bedside, holding his hand, he smiled. Had I imagined his hand clasping mine? The visiting nurse said yes, it was impossible. My father died a short while later that day.

Years after when I nursed my much-loved mother at home to her death from terminal bowel cancer, a similar but perhaps even more profound event occurred. I occupied the bedroom next to hers and caring for her had become full time. Without any carers, I was obliged to be locked in the house on call twenty-four hours a day. It had been that way for three months or more when my mother finally passed away. Anyone who has ever experienced this duty of care will know what a truly emotionally and physically exhausting task it is but once again it is a true privilege to demonstrate love by caring for any human being, let alone your own parent.

One afternoon when I was lying on my bed in my bedroom, I heard men talking outside my room. They spoke quite loudly but curiously not clear enough to make out what was being said. Getting up off my bed I checked out of the windows, half expecting the window cleaner and his mate who were in the habit of arriving each month unannounced. Yet there was no-one. Presuming that mum had once again accidentally switched on her television, I left my room and crossed to her closed bedroom door where I had left her sleeping only minutes before. Standing in the hallway I clearly heard at least two male voices having an intense discussion but oddly still not clearly enough for me to be able to make out what was being said.

Quietly, I opened the bedroom door expecting to see mum asleep in bed and with the television switched on. The male conversation ceased the moment the door opened. I could see immediately that the television was switched off at the set, just as I had left it. In this switched-off state the remote control by my mother's bedside could not activate the television. My mother had been unable to walk for months, so I knew that she hadn't got out of bed to switch the set on and off. She was by now wisp-thin, the cancer depleting her body of life and she existed half in and half out of delirium.

Yet despite this she was conscious and from her bed she looked right at me.

'Who were you talking to? I heard voices,' she asked.

I explained that I hadn't been talking to anyone. I began to comprehend what had just happened.

'I heard loud voices,' she insisted.

To comfort her I said, 'It must be the window cleaner,' peering out of her window for effect and knowing this to be untrue.

Satisfied with my explanation but with an unsettled look flickering across her face, I quickly made my way outside. The gate to the driveway was locked and there was no-one in the garden. There had been no window cleaner. There were no callers of any kind. Or had there been?

Later that same week and I was on one of my many visits into mum's bedroom, this time with some water which she couldn't really drink by now but with which she went through the motions, perhaps to please me.

Mum was lying back on her pillow and with a look of happiness on her face.

'Can you hear that music? Is it yours,' she enquired.

I listened, the bedroom was silent.

'No, I can't hear any music mum,' I said truthfully as a recollection went through my mind of the similar event with my father.

'I can hear loud music,' she insisted with a smile of rapture, as if for all the world she was listening to heavenly choirs of angels.

'Is it nice?' I asked. I saw the same familiar frown that I had seen on my late father's face some years before.

'No,' she replied, 'I don't like it,' and pausing added, 'It's very loud. Make it stop!'

Mum died the next day. As with my father, she had been too ill to talk for several days. Just like with my father she had heard loud music which made her smile with pleasure until questioned about it. And like with my dad, she had passed away a few hours later. Only this time mum had received unseen visitors in her bedroom. A heavy conversation had been had in her room by men unseen, presumably as they stood at the foot of her bed discussing how long mum had left before she was ready to leave her physical body and pass into the Light. This moment of clarity hours before death is called 'terminal lucidity' and is a known medical event and even occurs in those people who have suffered from afflictions of the brain including dementia.

So, what is our conclusion? Mine is that the spirit departs the body at the moment of death. That we are constantly watched over every day, our progress through life is observed and protected as best it can be, right up to our last moments in our body on this Earth plane. In the days and moments before death, our 'team' come to visit us and monitor us as our physical life energy ebbs away. As our spirit becomes ready to depart its ailing physical body the 'veil' between this world and the next becomes thinner and during our final hours we get glimpses of those in the 5D via audible and visual awareness. Our deceased loved ones come to 'collect' us at the point of death of our physical body and they escort us to the next world and to our new life. For our spirit is energy, and as our body dies, our energy can finally be released.

I mentioned earlier that published neuropsychiatrist and

neurophysiologist Peter Fenwick has accomplished many years of research and work into 'near death experiences' (NDEs). There is the question of '*Is consciousness a direct result of brain activity?*' and it is one which Fenwick convinces he has answered. He asks us to consider whether there is a transcendent reality that is actually filtered out by our brain, giving us a reduced picture (of the real world?) If we were to give this neuro-filter a name, what would it be? A 'veil' perhaps? Prominent Canadian neurosurgeon Wilder Penfield's life's work demonstrated that neurons communicate with one another all of the time but in and of themselves, they do not cause consciousness.

Of course, we rely heavily on the senses that we have to help us navigate our way through the 3D physical reality. As a part of the Earth's animal kingdom this protects us from making errors of judgment that could result in injury or death. But why do we think that all that we can see and hear and feel is the sole reality of the 3D universe of energy that surrounds us? We cannot see magnetic waves for example, nor infrared light under most conditions, yet we do not doubt that they exist.

Certainly, other animals can see and hear things that are invisible or inaudible to us. For example, dogs can see infrared and it is thought migrating birds navigate by the Earth's magnetic waves emanating from the planet's poles. Yet still many only accept what their eyes and ears tell them. If you find your way around a room by night with just the light of a single candle and you cannot see into the dark corners of the room, does that mean that the corners of the room don't exist?

If we are collected and escorted safely back to the Light in the company of a loved one, or someone whom we trust, rather than find our own way, there then must be a need for this. Similarly, in our final moments, if our hold on life is being constantly observed so that we are met at the moment that our spirit leaves the physical body then we must ask, 'Why?' The answer must surely be to ensure that we make the journey back to 'the other side' arriving safely at our destination.

If we fail to cross over to the Light then our spirit remains in the 3D, experienced as 'ghosts' by those still 'living.' Reincarnation and the incarnating into our physical body is a topic well-covered in the ancient and sacred texts of the Kabbalah. Here, it is described as the physical body being like a drinking glass holding water. The water is our energy or life force that is poured into the glass. When the body dies, or the glass is smashed, the water or spirit doesn't just disappear, it still exists but has escaped the glass. What if that water was collected?

In Christian teachings we are told that when Jesus died, His spirit left His body, and His resurrection proved the existence of eternal life. Jesus' spirit was seen after His physical death and the intention in the holy texts is clear. We do not die. We have an eternal life force that survives death. The story of The Resurrection tells us that there is an afterlife, that a spirit can walk the Earth, and that there is a likelihood of reincarnation.

It is estimated that there were in excess of thirty gospels written after the death of Jesus. The Coptic Christians kept these safe but the effluxion of time, a tumultuous history and the birth of the Roman Catholic Church with its founding on only four of the Gospels; Matthew, Mark, Luke and John has led to the patriarchal system that we globally still endure today, both in religious and secular societies. The tragic loss of The Gospel of Judas Iscariot, one of Jesus' closest disciples and also the loss of The Gospel of Mary Magdalene amongst others has to be one of the greatest historic criminal acts perpetrated against humanity, because the survival of these gospels may well have resulted in a vastly different improved existence for millions.

The intentional suppression of The Gospel of Judas, and the subsequent deliberate demonization of Jews in western culture has possibly led to millions of inhumane and untimely deaths over centuries by state sanctioned brutality. In a similar vein, the failure to include The Gospel of Mary Magdalene, presumably because she was Jesus' closest disciple, companion and, crucially, omitted because she was a woman, has led to a patriarchal domination of western culture. Centuries of peaceful pagan matriarchal societies were replaced overnight with a male dominated church and primogeniture feeding into politics and the wider social agenda, strangling and stagnating women's natural birthright for centuries.

It is The Gospel of Mary Magdalene which is of most interest as to the subject of what occurs at the moment of death. The papyrus was discovered in 1896 and has been widely written about for anyone to discover. Mary Magdalene was almost certainly not the prostitute portrayed by (male) theologians. This was another attempt to discredit her and simultaneously create a misogynistic viewpoint that bolsters patriarchal control.

At the beginning of this book, I asked you to forget what you have been taught to believe over your lifetime. I understand that this can be very difficult for those of us brought up within the paradigms of strict religious doctrine. However, with a blank canvas, you can begin to positively reconstruct yourself in your own true image and not that of others.

Mary of Magdala was Jesus' closest companion and disciple.

You only have to study the remains of the text in the papyrus to understand why; she was smart and asked the right questions. Karen Leigh King, Hollis Professor of Divinity at Harvard University writes The Gospel of Mary Magdalene provides:

'a radical interpretation of Jesus' teachings as a path to inner spiritual knowledge; it rejects His suffering and death as the path to eternal life; it exposes the erroneous view that Mary of Magdala was a prostitute for what it is—a piece of theological fiction; it presents the most straightforward and convincing argument in any early Christian writing for the legitimacy of women's leadership; it offers a sharp critique of illegitimate power and a utopian vision of spiritual perfection; it challenges our rather romantic views about the harmony and unanimity of the first Christians; and it asks us to rethink the basis for church authority.'

King concludes that *'both the content and the text's structure lead the reader inward toward the identity, power and freedom of the true self, the soul set free from the Powers of Matter and the fear of death.'*

These are powerful words. Karen Leigh King is here inviting us to rethink everything we think that we know about the death of Jesus. In her gospel, Mary of Magdala is talking alone with Jesus. He laughs at the other disciples in their inability to understand the true concept of what life is about, and our journey and purpose of our time here on Earth. After 'what is the meaning of life?' you would think that 'what happens when we die?' would be the first question asked of Jesus by his disciples. Mary doesn't disappoint.

Mary asks of Jesus, 'What happens when we die?' and, 'Where do we go?' The answer that comes confirms what spiritualists and psychic mediums have been telling us for decades.

We are told by Jesus that we are both physical and spirit, and that when we die our spirit departs our physical body to pass through and traverse a no-man's land, patrolled by entities, before we safely arrive in Heaven.

A void that we must cross inhabited by 'entities' demonstrates the need for our dearest departed loved ones and spirit guides to return to this physical plane in order to 'collect' us and escort us safely back home to the Light from where we came. For the 5D reality is our true home, this 3D Earth is merely a low vibrational physical interpretation of the 5D universe. Earth is where we come under our own freewill to learn the joys of physical living with the necessary exposure to pain, loss, heartbreak and suffering.

It is through this suffering that we learn and grow as souls. But throughout our earthly journey we are always joined to the Source, and it is that inner Light that guides us throughout our lives. The Light is the small voice of intuition inside of you that speaks to us constantly, always telling us in which direction to travel. The much louder voice of your brain-based ego speaks to you from a place of fear. Listen instead to that softly spoken inner voice of intuition for it is guiding you from a place of love.

Chapter Seven

Miracles

Guardian angels

Pushing through the darkness, still another mile.
I believe in angels. When I know the time is right for me,
I'll cross the stream. I believe in angels. ABBA.

For some years I had been living with and looking after my elderly parents at their retirement home in a rural part of the UK when I encountered my miracle. This home had been a happy house for me in-spite of what had come to be an increasingly difficult time in my adult life. The house was idyllically set in the countryside in large grounds and was adjacent to protected woodland.

When my parents had first moved-in it was a peaceful haven of woods and birdsong, with nocturnal visits from badgers and deer, a breeze in the trees in summer and rolling sea-mists during winter. Summertime was only interrupted by the occasional sound of an acorn plop as it fell from one of the many mature oak trees that surrounded the plot. If a car went past the house in the tree-lined country lane beyond, it was such an irregular sight and sound that there was a tendency to rush to the window to see who it was who might be calling.

Over time more and more relocated city folk moved into the village that our home bordered the edge of. The airport some ten miles away grew busier and busier and the resultant overhead flight paths started to drown out some of the birdsong. Development became the greater curse with much annual noise and disruption, and nature sought a different home as the deer and badgers vanished along with the peace. Nonetheless, this house remained my happy place.

Few others agreed or saw and felt what I did, but we had a small rural oasis of beauty in this wooded glen and the serenity and energy of this land was profound. It wouldn't be a proud boast to suggest that my father, a keen gardener, had created the most beautiful garden in the village. I learnt my love of gardening from my father having watched him many times when growing up, gardening being his penultimate favourite hobby, second only perhaps to 'Do It Yourself' (DIY). I felt secure here. Whatever kind of day I had enjoyed or endured, I would always return with a sense of excitement and anticipation that this was my home and safe place.

This sanctuary was shattered when one day my parents announced that they were selling up and moving on. Until that moment I didn't realise how important this small house with its disproportionately large garden was to me. Nothing lasts forever of course. It was to be several more months before we would sell and move out, and that would prove to be when the supernatural 'fun' would really start. Until then, there was just the one solitary but major incident that even today I am unable to explain, excepting to say a miracle occurred that day. I struggled with it for years, but I now believe that I was being divinely protected by the Source, or by my guardian angels, whatever those words mean to you.

It was bright but cloudy when I set off early to work that

morning. Unusually, the country roads were clear, and being in full 'corporate clone' mode at that time in my life, I was smartly suited and booted and ready for the office. Everything I did at this stage in my life was as if time was of the essence. I was driving my new corporate car, a green Renault that I was proud of, and my corporate career gave my ego the incorrect impression that I was successful at life. I wasn't. Life isn't about possessions, dressing smartly, cars and careers. A successful life is about emotional intelligence, kindness, compassion and most importantly, giving love and being loved.

Keen not to be delayed that morning I immediately made to overtake a painfully slow solitary vehicle on this long empty stretch of link road, approaching it swiftly from behind. Once around a dangerous bend I could see for some kilometre ahead of me and with the way ahead clear I indicated my intention and made to overtake. Everything looked fine and the difference in speeds between my vehicle and that of the other meant the overtaking manoeuvre should have taken just three or four seconds.

Overtaking now, as my car became level with the other vehicle, the driver suddenly and without warning, started to pull over to my side of the roadway. It was all so sudden. Drivers will be familiar with that split-second decision-making and in order to avoid collision, I had no choice but to either do an emergency brake or accelerate out of trouble. I chose the latter, but the other driver had either a similar idea and accelerated, or he just hadn't seen me. In a panic and confused as to why this driver wanted to run me off the road, my car did just that, as it began to crash and bump at some speed along the ditch and scrub at the opposite kerbside of the carriageway.

Clouds of roadside dust billowed up as my tyres scrambled for traction. My heart was in my throat but fortunately there were no other cars around and I pulled away and out of trouble. The whole incident was over with within a couple of seconds and that should have been that. The other driver seemed to have been racing me or was trying to run me off the road. Reasoning, correctly as it transpired, that the other driver must be dangerous, I took an alternative route, turning off down a narrow country lane that I often chose back in those days as it was usually a pleasure to drive along.

I was dismayed to discover that today was to be different as the driver of the other vehicle had also turned off the main road and was following me. What did this guy want and why did he try and force me off the road? I knew that up ahead was a busy junction and that I would have to stop. The driver of the car behind me was catching up fast. It was clear that I was in the middle of an unfolding road-rage incident with such things oddly commonplace in the UK at that time and often reported on the news.

The busy junction arrived all too soon and I was obliged to stop or cause an accident. Unhappily, the main road which I needed to join was unbearably hectic with quite literally ceaseless fast-moving traffic in both directions. My horror was confirmed when the driver of the vehicle who had just tried to run me off the road, pulled-up behind me and getting out of his car, made his way quickly towards mine.

What happened next may sound trivial, but it left an indelible mental scar. Never have I seen anyone so angry. A man who had so totally 'lost-it' that the red mist had come down. His eyes had become small yet staring wildly and he was foaming at the mouth. We often hear of the expression 'foaming at the mouth' and assume it only refers to rabid wild dogs, but it transpires that humans too can foam at the mouth when so angry that all connection to reality or to the Source has been lost.

He was screaming at me to get out of the car as he frantically yanked several times at the driver's door handle, then at the other doors which were locked from the inside. My mouth opened and closed but I said little, the look of shock and horror on my face doing the talking. It would have been extremely unwise to open the door and exit to an uncertain – or perhaps certain – fate, so I declined his invitation in my mind but not before his fist began punching the driver's-side door window in order to smash it and gain access.

They say that perception of time slows down when life-threatening incidents occur, and I can confirm that this is absolutely true. Whether this slow time is a 'supernatural' occurrence or merely to do with an instinctive animal survival technique is impossible to say, but yes, I can attest that time appears to slow and every passing second seems a minute to elapse. This permits a hyper clarity of thought with each and every unsavoury moment sharply recorded in the memory.

The door glass would not withstand this punishment for long. It was a surprise that it had withheld this far. I pulled back from the window as he gave it a few more punches and then, standing back he started to repeatedly kick the car door with such ferocity he almost fell over backwards. The dismay of my car being wrecked flashed through my mind but strangely what actually washed over me was a sensation of overwhelming remorse.

The remorse however was not for me, even though I instinctively knew that I wasn't going to come out of this alive; it was for my elderly parents. I was their part-time carer, and I knew that they would be so utterly devastated by my loss and the nature of it, that they would not survive the emotional impact. They had already suffered the death of one of their three children and to lose another would surely kill them. As time slowed to almost standstill, I could clearly see in my mind's eye my mother inconsolable at the news and my father unsuccessfully trying to comfort her.

The traffic in front of me continued to thunder past in both directions. Nobody slowed or seemed to notice my plight that morning. I was going to die here. I felt sad, small and helpless and so incredibly alone as I pictured the two people who loved me most happily starting their morning activities and routines without any realisation of the news that they would receive later that day. It's amazing what goes through your mind when you face your own immediate mortality.

I was surprised that I was so ready to accept it, at least if it were not for the devastation that it would cause my parents. I realised in that moment how much I loved them as the sensation was overwhelming. The entire scene was utterly surreal and as my attacker leapt onto my car bonnet to begin smashing at the windscreen with his fist, it all seemed quite bizarre. How could a man go from 0-100mph in anger in such a short period of time? What kind of life could make a man get so angry that he could sustain that anger and want to kill?

He had the intent and the face of a murderer. Was it alcohol, drugs, or just an argument with his partner that morning? Was it a lifetime of abuse, bad luck, indifferent parents and cruel circumstance? Was it a brutal lifetime of unhappy occurrences that had brought him to breaking point that morning? And why me? Why was I now a part of his life story? That's always the question isn't it, 'Why me?'

'Why not me?' is, I suppose, the answer. One good reason why not is because I too had suffered an abusive and sometimes cruel childhood and life had often been harsh. That is not uncommon, many experience suffering. Yet somehow, I had forgiven those people who I perceived had transgressed against me and I had grown stronger, not weaker, from my experiences. I had become a survivor, not a victim. How very different we all are, and how important it is to learn and grow from our struggles and to not harbour resentment.

So it was that I finally started to come out of my surreal sense of other worldliness as my assailant, giving up on the toughened windscreen, began to kick in the front of my car. Making his way to the passenger side, he kicked and thumped his way as he destroyed the car. The traffic continued to roar in both directions, and it was only afterwards that I thought it odd that no-one had stopped their car or taken any action to assist. I guessed that they couldn't see what was occurring or didn't want to get involved. Neither did anyone call the police.

It was after he had dealt a few more blows and a couple more kicks to the passenger side of my car that I knew for sure that my time was over. I watched in the rear-view mirror as he suddenly retreated and made his way to the passenger side of his ancient Volvo estate car. Yanking open his car door and leaning-in, it was to my horror that I realised he was rifling through the glove compartment feverishly looking for something.

At best, this 'something' would be a small knife or hammer of some kind, but what kind of person keeps such a weapon in their glove compartment? With time still slowed down, it dawned on me that he was most likely looking for a weapon, perhaps a gun which he kept in his car. I could see now that he was feverishly fiddling with something on the passenger seat, perhaps loading a weapon. I realised that was it, my end had arrived and I was ready for it. Looking away from the rear-view mirror for a second, I glanced at the roadway. It had fallen silent. Not just quiet but totally and utterly silent in both directions. *Not one single car was to be seen or heard.* Silence had descended. I needed no encouragement. I floored the accelerator and my car took off along the main road in the direction of my workplace.

I looked back repeatedly. As my car sped along the main road, I was constantly checking the rear-view mirror, expecting at any moment to see my assailant's Volvo behind me. But there was nothing, not even another car. Even more strangely was that there were no vehicles in front of me either, not that I considered this at the time, I was too busy with my foot to the floor putting as much space between me and the Volvo as I could. In all the years that I drove that same journey, I have never been able to drive at that speed along that stretch of road at that time of day. It was as though the roadway had been cleared for me. Nonetheless, I realised that I was going to be stuck in queuing traffic when I got to the city limits and that my assailant was likely to catch up with me in no time at all, and it was very clear that he didn't much care about being seen or caught.

So, I sped off on a detour journey, still panicked and driving for a good twenty minutes or longer all over the countryside and town until I was sure that I wasn't being tailed. I considered going to the police, but what would I say? I didn't have the guy's number plate and what charges would they bring other than perhaps for the damage to my car. Oh, the damage! I realised that I was driving about town in a car with fist marks and boot dents and multiple scratches over the paintwork. Yet this didn't seem to draw any attention.

I turned up at my workplace that morning expecting a dressing-down for being late. I didn't take long to get into the office and my boss who was waiting for me must have seen the look on my face as he didn't complain about my late arrival. Instead, I shakily told my tale and we discussed briefly whether I should contact the police and report a road-rage incident. I reasoned however that my attacker would get off any charge if it were a first offence. Knowing that he had murder in mind that morning, any criminal proceedings would reveal my personal details and that I certainly wanted to avoid.

My escape and the strange way in which it occurred was only part of my miracle. The strangest part was my car. You see, it didn't have a single scratch, mark or dent anywhere on the bodywork. This was an inexpensive car where just a parking ding from another vehicle made a scratch or gouge. Yet there was nothing. I think that my boss, who inquisitive, had come outside to inspect the car with me was somewhat disappointed and he must have thought that I was exaggerating the entire incident. And yet the assailant had repeatedly punched and kicked the car panels so viciously that he almost fell over. The only mark on the whole car was on the driver's side of the vehicle, which was lightly dusted with dirt thrown up from the verge that I had driven along.

So, what to make of it? All these years later I remain convinced that it was a real event and that I was being divinely protected that morning. The traffic was somehow quelled, and my escape made good. And yet, as I sit here and write this now, I do wonder how such busy traffic could suddenly just fall silent. Not only that but how did I not catch up to that same busy traffic when I eventually pulled out of the junction at speed and drove so fast? The road ahead was empty. It was some ten kilometres into town on this straight road and yet I passed no-one. Then there was the total absence of damage to my car. *Not a single scratch or blemish and no marks on the window glass.* Only the dust demonstrated anything unusual at all had occurred that morning.

Was this some strange psychological event? Had I suffered an inexplicable hallucination on an otherwise uneventful morning? Or perhaps I somehow encountered a haunting and relived a tragic event from many years before that had occurred on that same patch of road? After all, I remembered that the other vehicle was decades old and the other driver may in fact have been an earthbound spirit. Or, had the event been entirely real but that as it simply wasn't my time to die, my guardian angels contrived to save me. I shall not discover the truth until it is my time to pass on. In the meantime, I will leave you to draw your own conclusion.

CHAPTER EIGHT

Poltergeist

Part One 2006 - 2007

'What could possibly go wrong?' we asked ourselves. Odd how this house hadn't been let when all the others had. Odd too that this house had been repeatedly sold during the preceding years that we had lived locally. Even the house name had been changed twice since we had moved to the area. The clues were all there and hindsight, as they say, is a wonderful thing.

The autumn of 2006 arrived, and my parents and I finally moved out of the house that I loved, the home that had given me sanctuary and a haven in a time of need. I cannot overemphasise the overwhelming feeling that I had that 'something was wrong.' I'd had this sense of foreboding for some weeks before the move, but I had put this down to having to leave the house that I loved and the inevitable fear of an unknown future. I did not then trust my intuition or claircognizance, I didn't even know that it had a name, but had I trusted my foresight in the way that I do now, I doubt that I would have thought differently.

I have explained that my parents spent a lifetime moving home from one 'do-er up-er' project to another. This had become the background wallpaper, literally, to my life. So, despite having finally achieved the perfect retirement house and garden that they had always desired, wanderlust overtook them once more and against my wishes and better judgment, we sold up and moved out of our peaceful home and into temporary rented accommodation.

This new rental home was a large, detached house with well-established and stocked grounds that had clearly once been a beautiful home and garden for someone. I write 'was once' intentionally, for the house was now tired, dirty and not a little grim, the garden overgrown.

The original blue Formica kitchen with serving hatch through to the spacious open-plan dining/sitting room reminded me of my well-beloved childhood home that too had been built in the 1960s. Then there was the original primrose yellow bathroom suite upstairs with matching downstairs WC. The ground floor front bedroom had a bright blue ensuite bathroom and due to his increasing infirmity, this easily accessed bedroom became my elderly father's room. The carpets and flooring throughout the house were old, the wall paint tired and even the relatively new but cheaply made plastic conservatory was falling apart. Outside the beautifully landscaped gardens had once been well-tended and loved, with some wonderful specimen trees and shrubs all sited under a wooded canopy. Now however it was overgrown and weary looking.

On the whole, the entire house gave a neglected melancholy air. Yes, 'melancholy' is precisely the word. Yet when we viewed it one sunny September afternoon the house had welcomed us in, with its fresh zingy 1960s family home appeal and architect designed features. This was not to be the last time that a house lured me in without betraying its supernatural secrets until it was too late. I now wonder if this is because the house wants to be healed of the darker energy that lurks within. Or perhaps I unwittingly allow spirit to guide me to these places so that they may be healed, and the earthbound spirits therein rescued.

'What could possibly go wrong?' we asked ourselves. After all, although it was ridiculously overpriced in rental terms for the condition that it was in, we were only going to be there for the minimum letting term of six months, and we didn't have much choice as at that late time of year there were no other candidates to rent locally. Odd how this house hadn't been let when all the others had, we thought. Odd too that this house had been repeatedly sold during the preceding years that we had lived locally. Even the house name had been changed twice since we had moved to the area. Yes, the clues were all there and hindsight, as they say, is a wonderful thing.

The day we moved in it was late October and the weather was all very different to the day that we had viewed the house a month or so before. Traditionally, in the Northern Hemisphere at least, it is thought that the darker days of late October onwards is a time when the veil between this world and the next is at its thinnest. In the UK it is definitely a time of dark stormy nights, endless gales and heavy rain. This particular day was no exception to that rule. Dark, cold and soaked, we finally bade farewell to the removal men and with the sunlight gone and illuminated by electric lighting only, we realised just how dirty and shabby this house was.

The house's welcoming gift was the discovery that the downstairs smelt of excrement which we assumed was the drains, a logical assumption because we found that none of the drains worked, necessitating an emergency call-out that same night to a drain unblocking firm before we could settle-in. With the rain lashing down outside and overflowing blocked sewers, it was already beginning to look like the end sequence to the movie 'Poltergeist.' Oh, the irony.

I can't remember exactly when the first incidence of poltergeist activity started. I think that it just began slowly and built its energy quickly over the effluxion of time. What is unusual perhaps, is that all three of us in that house experienced poltergeist phenomena on a regular basis and yet none of us confirmed our suspicions to one another, at least not directly until many weeks had passed. I think that we all intuitively knew what was going on and so we were too scared to voice those suspicions lest that give them more power or perhaps make it a reality.

Some of the things that happened can be put down to natural occurrences or coincidence but not most of them. My father's irrational anger and sudden fiery outbursts, for example, could be put down to his diabetes which oddly was becoming more and more difficult for him to medically control as the weeks passed. All the same, he seemed in a terribly dark mood for much of the time. The smell of drains and excrement, the endlessly blowing lightbulbs throughout the house and manifold electrical and plumbing problems could be put down to the age of the house perhaps.

Even the mystery of why the original front door doorbell would occasionally give its harsh trill when no caller was stood outside could perhaps be explained as an electrical glitch. This repeatedly occurred in the first three or four weeks of moving-in. We established via the fully glazed front door that no-one was playing a game. The door itself could only be reached by first walking the forty or so feet across the entrance driveway, so any caller would be clearly seen arriving or departing. But if this was just a mere electrical fault, then why did it cease as quickly as it had started?

Then there was the strange incident of the daytime intruder that wasn't. My father was not a man prone to flights of fancy and so shortly after we had moved in, when I received a telephone call from him while I was at work to tell me that he had seen a male prowler walking around the outside, I immediately went into a state of anxiety that we were to be burgled. We had been burgled at our previous home which was just yards up the road, and that had been shortly after we had moved in there too. It was a natural conclusion and yet there was something about my father's attitude on the 'phone that told me he wasn't telling me everything that he either knew or suspected.

Later that night at home he told me the full story. He had seen the man, who he described as a 'dark figure', 'middle-aged' and wearing head to toe 'dark clothes' walk swiftly past his ground floor bedroom side window. The figure was walking from the front of the house to the rear and 'seemed to be looking for something' he said. My father had, as quickly as possible, walked from the bedroom to the kitchen window, a distance of only some twenty feet. Seeing the man in the back garden, still apparently engrossed in looking for something, and fearing that he was a burglar, my father gave out a yell and moved quickly the ten feet to the back door of the house. But when outside, my father had discovered that no-one was there.

In the time it took my father to move the ten feet, the man had apparently covered a distance of fifty feet or more along the uphill driveway and vanished into our empty country lane where there was no vehicle waiting. The lane was straight and narrow, and the naked eye could clearly see for a quarter of a kilometre, yet there was no vehicle and no pedestrian in sight. With deep muddy ditches and thick low hedgerows either side of the lane, hiding was also out of the question. At the time I put it down to a lucky escape from a burglar scouting out our house where the 'new people' had just moved in. I could tell however that my father was more disturbed by this unwelcome daytime visitor then he let-on. In light of future events, it seems that my father may have had his first encounter with the earthbound spirit tied to the property.

Burglar or not, other things were less easy to explain. Our microwave oven would regularly blow its fuse, several times a month, something it didn't do previously and not again in the years since we moved out of the house. I paid to have broadband connected to the house and despite regular confirmation from the utility company that it was working and the phone line in good order, I was paying for nothing as we never once achieved an operating broadband connection. Repeated calls of complaint to the telephone company resulted in being advised that there was interference on the line, but that this was, '*Coming from within the property.*'

My father discovered that he could not walk into the sitting room. I mean by this that he was *able to walk* with the aid of a walking cane but having strolled into centre of the open-plan dining room/sitting room, the same thing always occurred; he reached the archway connecting the dining room to the sitting room but was unable to advance further. To watch him, it was as if he was being held back by an invisible force. You could see his reaction, as he halted and recoiled and then as he clutched his walking cane, his entire body started to shake as if trembling with fear. This was an old soldier we are talking of, and he was not a man given to unnecessary bouts of hysterics or fear. Yet this happened almost every time and he refused to speak about what had 'stopped him' but it was obvious that he was shaken and upset, just repeating, 'I can't go in there.'

I began to encounter a similar thing on the turned staircase in the house. At first it was just an uneasiness but gradually over time that sensation grew and always in the same two places on the stairs. I would get to near the top of the first flight and pause as if I felt it was unwise to continue. Imagine how odd that intuitive feeling is. After all, I reasoned to myself, it's just a staircase! Once I had paused and gathered my senses, I berated myself for being foolish and I pressed-on with the ascent to the first-floor landing. Only I couldn't. In the same place every time, just two steps into the second flight, a fear gripped me which was overwhelming.

I knew at that point exactly what my father was encountering in the sitting room. I can only explain it by saying that it felt as though someone unseen and unheard was in front of me on the stairs screaming and shouting in my face and fully prepared to push me back downstairs again if I advanced further. It became apparent that I was not welcome upstairs.

I hadn't heard of 'claircognizance' back in those days. I knew a little of the paranormal, but I didn't know of the other 'clairs' (differing psychic abilities) or any great detail about poltergeists other than they were the 'noisy ghosts.' I began however to realise that I somehow 'knew' that the presence in the house was male, aged in his forties or fifties when he passed and I could even picture his build and hair colour in my mind. I also knew that this man was very angry and that he did not want us in his house. And it was *his* house as he saw it, with us as mere intruders. The house was already grim and with a pall of gloom which permeated its very core, but our fear fed the darkness and it spread like an unseen creeping toxic fog over the very atmosphere until the energy was dense.

I had the upstairs small bedroom that overlooked the rear garden. It was unbearably hot and stifling, something I put down to the kitchen beneath and the badly maintained central heating boiler being sited under my room. I didn't particularly want the spacious principal bedroom opposite which faced the beautiful front garden as this bedroom was gloomy and a little damp. However, when my brother who was visiting one day pointed out to me how stifling it was in that bedroom and that it was in fact the dining room underneath and not the kitchen with the boiler, I made the decision to move across the hall into the principal bedroom. Besides, I never once got a proper night's sleep in that small stifling room, I always woke feeling anxious. It reminds me now of that little guest bedroom in Hove, all those many years ago when I was aged seven on holiday at my uncle's haunted house.

From where I chose to place my bed in the principal bedroom, I could clearly see the corridor from the landing through to my mother's bedroom which had a sunny, cheerful and pleasant disposition and with a panoramic view over the garden. My mother's room was in fact the only bedroom in the house in which I didn't mind being, at least, not until one particular event occurred, but more of that later. My new bedroom was directly over my father's bedroom downstairs and when he started to complain about the night-time noises

I was alleged to be making I put it down to his ill temper and the exaggeration that comes with age.

Meanwhile, I found the bright cheerful and sunny primrose coloured bathroom that was next to my bedroom creepy, as was the loft hatch and cupboard immediately outside the bathroom door. This was an inexplicable feeling of fear, which was strangely exacerbated when the bath drain repeatedly blocked without good reason and the shower broke on two occasions. It felt as though the house was fighting us.

The smell of excrement from nowhere in particular but apparently emanating around the downstairs WC and entrance hall came and went without logic. Visitors would sometimes comment that they could smell it when I could not and vice-versa. A similar thing occurred with the kitchen drain for the duration of the time that we lived there but that was by no means the oddest occurrence concerning the kitchen. That came about soon after we had moved in and before things had begun to intensify. The three of us had sat down in the dining room to eat dinner one evening. We had barely started before there was an almighty crash and the unmistakable sound of saucepans falling over and pitching onto the floor with even the rolling noise of saucepan lids as they settled.

Startled, the three of us paused and open-mouthed we stared from our distant viewpoint through the serving hatch and into the dreary blue kitchen beyond. Seeing nothing, I got up, crossed the room and entered the kitchen expecting to have to begin tidying up a mess. But there was nothing. The saucepans were neatly stacked on top of the counter where they had been left and there was nothing on the floor or anywhere else to explain what had caused the crashing noise. I opened all of the cupboard doors to see if any accident had occurred inside but there was nothing to see.

Satisfied, I returned to my still seated parents who disbelievingly received the news that nothing was visible that could have caused the noise. When a one-off occurrence such as this happens, one may perhaps dismiss it as a fluke. However, when dining the next evening, an identical occurrence once again left us bewildered and without logical explanation. We were to discover that with all of these poltergeist events, they would cease as quickly as they started, only for an entirely new set of events to occur. What was clear was that someone, or something, was trying to get our attention.

My knowledge about poltergeist activity was limited back then. Through experience and study, I'm now less ignorant and as a result less vulnerable. What I did know was that these 'noisy ghosts' were capable of the kinetic movement of material objects and as their German name suggests, make noise. I knew it was sometimes the other way around whereby no noise would be heard and yet material objects, almost miraculously, are moved; the doors I talked of in a previous chapter is relevant here.

The event with the crashing saucepans was a pivotal moment for me with this haunting and I think it was for my father too, because without discussing it, we both knew at that point that we had a ghost. None of us in the house were stressed beyond normal realms of everyday weariness (at least at that time), and there was no teenage angst in the home and none of the usual trigger points that many of those who study the particulars of poltergeist activity claim can cause these events. The angst however did come later.

Springtime arrived and daily I tried to keep all thoughts of weird happenings to the back of my head. I was working hard and studying for some important law exams and my parents were actively looking for a house to buy in the vicinity. They eventually found one that suited their needs, and we viewed it on a couple of occasions, an oddity in itself when we were greeted only by the elderly female owner of the house, her husband refusing to meet people. He would leave the house during our three viewings in order, we were openly told, to avoid us. The house was a little too small for our needs but with everything else suiting requirements, my parents made an offer to purchase, and it was accepted.

It was the Friday prior to a family gathering at my brother's home. He lived in a large rambling rented farmhouse with an even larger original walled Victorian garden that my brother claimed to be 'haunted.' That day my father had received a phone call from his solicitor. We were told that he had left the checking of the Land Registry documents to the house that we were buying until the very last minute and only after he had returned from holiday.

We were due to exchange contracts on the Monday, tying us in to the purchase, yet the solicitor told my father that the house we were proposing to buy had no legal entitlement to be built on the land, and with no planning consent for the large double garage. We were also advised that there was a restrictive covenant from the original landowners preventing any buildings ever being erected on the site. The solicitor suggested that the original owner of the land could object at any moment and require the house to be demolished should he or she so desire.

Earlier that same week I had discovered that tragically a

murder had recently occurred in a house neighbouring our proposed new home. The house my parents were hoping to buy was a cheerful little place, but I felt a sensation of dread in my stomach each time I went there. Had the recent murder in the same small road something to do with my increasing sense of foreboding? The sensation of dread had started earlier the previous summer but by this time I was feeling physically sick daily. Why did I feel this way? What was I being warned of?

Because we were due to exchange contracts on the Monday, a decision had to be made that weekend; to risk all and proceed with the purchase or pull out of the sale and stay at the rented accommodation for a little longer. At that time in my life, and for some time to come, I was still picking up on the energies of places and of future events without being able to pinpoint to what the warning was alluding. I had found myself making several journeys to the potential new home, sitting outside in my car, walking about the village and trying to understand and dispel why I felt so utterly fearful about such a pretty little place. Only it wasn't the house at all. It was something else yet to come.

The weekend arrived and despite the bad news about the house my parents were in a good mood as we visited my brother and his family for a get-together at his home in the countryside. It was to be the last family gathering. My father struggled with his dinner that day, unusual for him as he was a hearty eater. And he looked a little off-colour by the evening. Nonetheless, we all enjoyed a nice time and family photographs were taken which were intended to celebrate the gathering but instead, for me at least, became a reminder of the last days of how things were.

On the Monday, my father, who was still off-colour, rang the solicitor and called off the purchase with much regret. The vendors had no trouble selling the property some four weeks later at a much higher price and so they were doubtless happy, but things were about to take a turn for the worse for us. By the evening of the Monday my father became ill and started to vomit. The vomit was unusual in colour and his skin started to look waxen. We presumed his diabetes was out of control and a doctor's appointment was made for later that week. As usual I accompanied my father, his disabilities and increasing vulnerability meant that I always accompanied him to his various medical appointments.

It was a different doctor to his usual one and the man was young and jolly and very soothing in disposition. Nonetheless he couldn't quite hide his alarm and concern at the bright orange-yellow my father's skin had turned in just a couple of days. A temporary diagnosis of something being wrong with my father's liver was given and an appointment for tests at the local hospital arranged immediately. By the time that this appointment was kept, my father was very sick indeed.

No formal diagnosis was forthcoming at the hospital but the medical staff clearly knew what it was. It was only at work the following day when I Googled my father's diabetes and his symptoms that the true horror entered my consciousness for the first time. My father had pancreatic cancer, almost certainly late stage and almost always fatal within weeks. Sitting at my office desk, I felt sick with prickly heat and dizzy with worry. Worst of all I had to keep this news to myself. I couldn't tell my mother or father, certainly not until it was professionally diagnosed.

Sadly, despite our enquiries, the hospital never sat us down and formally spoke to any of us about it. The news that my father had terminal cancer was therefore broken to him casually by a passing nurse on the ward who presumed, wrongly, that he had been informed and she read the medical records out loud as he lay there alone. It was only when visiting my poor father in hospital later that same afternoon that my mother and I found him weeping, the news having come as a total shock to him and now also to my mother.

From that moment my father went into a rapid decline of mood, later becoming clinically depressed, something my mother and I were unaware of until an equally casual comment was made to us some weeks later by another member of medical staff. Once again, they mistakenly thought that someone else had informed us of the diagnosis of severe depression, whereas we thought that the reason he had become unable to speak was due to the cancer.

Some days later, following an operation to put a permanent drain tube in his side, my father was discharged from hospital in order that he may 'die at home.' It really was that sudden and brutal. Our 'home' had in any case been sold and we now found ourselves living in someone else's house under these strange and difficult circumstances. My father was returned to our temporary lodgings and given a special bed for his ground floor bedroom complete with tubes, pipes, pills, human waste bags, syringes, medicines, bells and whistles.

Everything was supplied except for moral and physical support. It was left to me and my elderly mother to cope with all that was to come, as my father slowly faded away over the next nine months. This would be a tremendous struggle for any family to deal with, but for us the serious haunting activity now started. It seems that earthbound spirits who are angry at their plight have little or no compassion for the living or dying. As we are in life, so we are in death. For those of us who choose to not pass into the Light to receive our truth, clarity and remembrance of who we truly are from many lifetimes, we instead find ourselves stuck in the anxiety consciousness of the ego that we created when alive.

The sad circumstances, as you'd expect in any normal home, created a pall of gloom but there was something more than that. The house became even darker and thicker in atmosphere, and it became readily apparent that there were more than just the three of us existing under that roof. This was no normal home and the consolation of the lucky escape in having not exchanged contracts on the other house, which would have inevitably necessitated an upheaval and house move while all this chaos was going on, proved of little comfort. For the foreseeable future we were stuck in a haunted house.

A few weeks prior to all this happening and while the supernatural events and atmosphere were ramping up, we had a surprise visit from our next-door neighbour. She and her husband were retired and had happily lived next door in the detached twin house to ours for many years. Unlike ours however, their house had been looked after over the years and they had a smart home and a flourishing garden of which they were rightly proud.

The woman was cheerful and upbeat, and it was her one and only visit, perhaps just to check-out the new neighbours or perhaps to drop a bit of gossip into our metaphorical 'in-tray.' We sat around chatting as she found out all about us and our plans and happily told us about her love of gardening and the revisions they were proposing to make to their home over the coming months. The visit seemed a pleasant one and then she dropped her 'bombshell.' Had this bombshell perhaps been the real reason for her visit? Certainly, she must have realised that she had hit her target full on by our icy white faces and she left almost immediately afterwards with us never receiving a second visit.

'Of course,' she cooed 'you did know about the man who built this house and my house?' she enquired, already fully expecting our answer. 'No' we replied and encouraged her to continue. Now with the full attention of her audience, she visibly expanded. 'Well, of course this was many years ago, but he was a local builder of repute, and he built this home to the highest specification for his family to live in. There was him, his wife and his children.'

We looked on with an unsettling feeling that we somehow knew what was to come. 'Well, it should have been the happy family home but very sadly, one day, his wife up and left him and she took the children with her.' She paused for maximum effect before hitting home with her final sentence. 'The man was so distraught and angry at this loss and betrayal that he took his own life in this very house.' With that she collected up her handbag and belongings and bid a cheery 'It's been lovely. Goodbye.'

Chapter Nine

Life before death

Peeling the onion – the ego unravelled

*Do not allow others to write your story for you.
Take control of your own life and your own narrative*

I spent most of my adult life empty inside. I had done what we all do, because almost without exception all of us are trained this way; I had stopped being me and instead I learnt who I was from others. This is the very first mistake we make in life. We learn it young. We learn from our parents whether we are considered to be good, bad, ugly, clever or even loveable. Then the cycle begins again with our peers and friends at school, at college then at work and it continues throughout our lives. This is an indoctrination hidden in plain sight that permeates through our ego into our very being. This projection from others onto our ego is topped up throughout each day with images and stories in all forms from people and the media about who we are and how we fit in to society.

Yet when we are born we know that we are good and whole. We join the human race, loveable, happy and filled with infinite possibility. Pure, like a blank sheet of paper, we unwittingly allow others to write our story because we are not taught to grasp the pen for ourselves. Over time we absorb the fear-based prejudices of our parents, peers and society. Prejudice is inherited, it is learnt. No baby is born judging another.

The ego is created to protect the individual from emotional hurt and it spins a carefully constructed perception of a safe reality. This is a false construct created over many years. As a child we are taught to reject anything different or unusual to the norm because there lays danger or ridicule. Ultimately when the stimulus of the outside world is to be judged for safety purely based on appearance, then the neurotic ego can become triggered by differing skin colour, culture, sexuality, religion or even something as ridiculous as hair colour.

When we are small children, we play together happily no matter skin colour or religion, so what has happened to us? Our mother and father decide on our name and narrate a story to us of who we are, where we came from and what we should believe. What our parents think they are doing is teaching their child out of love to fit safely into an unsafe world. What they are actually doing is creating that very same unsafe world by indoctrinating their child with their own fears and projections. If you want to find out who you really are, then, like the shaman, you must metaphorically first go into the woods to unlearn all that your ego has cobbled-together from other people's narratives about you.

I have spent the last four years of my life slowly untangling and unravelling the false construct that I had created for myself about who I was, what I am and how I wanted to be seen in the world. The ability to be given the time to be able to do this was handed to me by divine providence. In the preceding years I had watched my life unravel swiftly and horribly, with several life-altering events occurring within a few short months. At first, I felt myself the victim of circumstance and perhaps even picked on by the universe.

However, self-pity is an unedifying quality and not to be recommended. When faced with the storms that life sends our way as it inevitably must, we have a choice of pushing on ahead with our journey or giving up. I knew that giving up was not an option and if you are reading this and on the point of giving up on life, please don't. There is hope and you are far more empowered than you may realise.

Should you be going through a difficult time when you read this book, or perhaps that is why you chose to read this book, then I first urge you to stop being so hard on yourself. Even if you think 'I'm not being hard on myself' there is no harm in giving yourself a little of the same loving kindness that you would extend to a friend in need. Life is a difficult journey at times and yet life is not happening to you as we are told, instead it is happening for you.

If you have recently lost someone, whatever the circumstances, or your domestic and work life is presently unravelling in the same way that mine once did, chances are you are punishing yourself and perhaps others. We are often unkind to ourselves, and we don't even realise when we are doing it. Negative self-talk and the bad-tempered internal conversations of, 'If only I had said this,' or, 'If only I hadn't let that happen,' or, 'If only I hadn't done that,' you need to release and let go.

Author Agatha Christie wrote, 'As life goes on, it becomes tiring to keep up the character you invented for yourself, and so you relapse into individuality and become more like yourself every day.' When we are given the gratifying opportunity and luxury of free time, like now as I write this during the pandemic lockdown, we can rediscover who we truly are. We can peel back those layers as you would with an onion.

Somewhere, deep inside you is still that small child. The happy, innocent, free-spirited and joyful child. The person you were and were always destined to be before all of the indoctrination, rules, social norms, peer pressure and cynicism made its mark on you. *Before you became frightened.* Imagine if you will, that small child now stood in front of you. What would you say to them? Say to you? What would your heart say? Would it scold? Or would you instead want to hug that child closely to you and tell it that everything is going to be alright and that you must always be your true self. For only by being your true self are you able to fulfil the destiny that was set out for you before birth. For you are a child of the universe and as with the universe, infinitely powerful.

Depending upon where you are in your life and where in your journey, will depend on whether these words about ego mean something to you that stimulates the will for change, or whether you resist. There is no right or wrong, we are here to experience, to learn and to grow. If you have the urge to cast off old, preconceived ideas about who you are and where you fit in to society, then you are on the first step of your amazing journey of self-discovery. Or perhaps that should be 'rediscovery?' I applaud you and wish you well and I hope that this book gives a few helpful tips for you along the way.

If you find that you are resisting your heart's call for change then perhaps you are not quite yet ready. This is resistance that comes from our ego's self-taught preservation instinct. We do not need to learn how to love, we carry love in our hearts from the moment we are born. Love is our birthright. But we do learn how to hate from pain and distress, both physical and emotional. In responding to these hurtful and negative stimuli, our brain tries to ensure that the events that caused us so much grief never occur again. It does this through the fear instinct. Yet the heart that is protected by a wall is a heart that can never experience love. You must be prepared to let your heart be broken time and again in order to fully feel life and to find love in all its guises.

Nature's 'fight-or-flight' mechanism means that the brain is ever alert for triggers. This natural conditioning results in a perpetual negative experience within our own lives. Our collective human condition in the age of Twenty-Four-Hour News coverage is to live in a permanent state of fear. Our brain's response to triggers, both positive and negative, is to create a release of the hormone dopamine, known colloquially as a 'dopamine hit.' Dopamine is a powerful drug which calms the mind but also elates.

How many times a day do you pick up your smartphone to check the news, or emails? Do you get together with friends at work or socially and gravitate towards negative talk? Do you gossip? Do you talk about politics, religion and the state of the world? Do you indulge in regurgitating old conversations and toxic events from years gone past and wondered why you do so? Dopamine is the cause, and it is the same chemical that is released when narcotics are introduced to the bloodstream. So, you can see that the dopamine hit is also a hard habit to kick.

With an addiction to dopamine comes an addiction to negativity. Have you ever known someone who every time you meet them for coffee or lunch they go round and around in ever increasing negative spirals about all of the terrible things that have happened to them and why they feel such a victim? You suppress a helpful or kind comment and you stifle a yawn as once more you hear the same old story, one that you've heard a hundred times or more. Yes, the story is tragic and yes, they probably are depressed and requiring help, but they resist any assistance and get angry if it is suggested that they need to change their approach.

Their addiction to dopamine has allowed the negative thinking to begin to run their life and as a result, the negativity becomes their very reality. I used to be this person. I still can be if I accidentally allow myself to slip back into the comfort of the negative. So many bad things had happened to me from childhood going forwards that it changed me from a happy cheerful child to a bitter and angry adult. This happens to a lot of us. The daily woes of just existing can sometimes seem exhausting. Yet over the last few years I faced the uncomfortable truth that I no longer liked myself and my perceived reality. Yes, my reality is just my perception of it, and I can choose to perceive my life as a positive experience, or I can choose to perceive it as a negative one. The choice is mine.

So, is the ego that part of us that struts brightly like a peacock? The truth is somewhat different. I believe that the ego can be best described as our attachment to objects and property, to opinions, to beliefs, to pleasures and to other people. The ego relies upon these external material things for comfort and there is an expectation that they must therefore remain constant and unchanged. The problem with this emotional reliance on things outside of us is the impermanence of all things, living or otherwise. Nothing lasts forever, people leave us, friends change, pets die, houses get old, cars rust, and places alter. We are setting ourselves up for a fall and the suffering in our lives comes directly from the expectations of our internal ego – *not* from those external people, beliefs and objects that the ego may seek to blame.

Western consumerism and the seemingly almost compulsory requirement to buy things to make us happy leads many of us to question why then are we not happy when many of us have so much? The 'if only I had syndrome' is where your ego convinces you that if only you had that new house, new car, new job, different partner, then you would be happy. This is little more than the carrot on the end of the stick enticing the donkey ever onwards until the end of its journey. The donkey never quite achieves the nirvana of eating the carrot and it dies of exhaustion and probably disappointment. Our own earthly journey ends with death and you don't want to be the donkey who never paused by the roadside for a while to eat the daisies before you push them up.

Western culture tells us that we must work harder so that we can earn more in order to buy things to impress people who we don't even know. In the meantime, our life and those of our loved one's ebbs away. Your ego tells you that you 'must have' whereas what it is in fact also telling you is that you 'do not have.' This perpetual state of 'not having' results in us living with a permanent feeling of 'lack' and thereby, we are miserable. To desire something is to lack something. To desire therefore simply leads to disappointment for the ego. It is therefore better to not desire in the first place.

Many taste all the earthly physical pleasures because they say, 'life is to be enjoyed' and they become burnt up by their experiences, or bitter and angry. Others, often driven in their piety by their inherited patriarchal religious beliefs go to the other extreme and suffer in a masochistic fashion. In this way, pious people are just as unhappy as decadent people. Although I have a keen idea of which option most of you would prefer to choose if push came to shove.

While hedonism in all its forms, from consumer spending to sexual orgies may remind you that you are alive, the reminder is only a post-it note of brevity. The moment soon passes, and you must repeat, often with greater fervour to achieve the same result. This then becomes a Groundhog Day of sexual pleasures, spending orgies or drug and alcohol use and avoidance. If you manage to survive this hedonism into middle age you suddenly wake-up desensitized to all pleasure and discover everyday life is dull by comparison. Meanwhile, those living uncomfortably, the self-suffering hair shirt wearers avoid all life's little physical pleasures, and this dullness leads to a life not lived and a piety that is unedifying to be around. In this way, hedonism and suffering are two sides of the same coin.

In my forties I had reached a point in my life where I had everything that I had ever wanted; a detached house in the country with a big garden, a double garage and a classic car. Yet I was dissatisfied and angry, a situation which worsened when I lost the only people I had ever loved. I began to live in fear of losing everything. I had what to most people is the epitome of middle-class status and comfortability, but I had encountered a life filled with bullying, jealousy, anger, betrayal, homophobia and violence. These overt negative experiences had come from outside hostile sources and were, by and large, completely undeserved. I bitterly resented this external undeserved negative input and effect on my life. I also resented all of the love and effort that I had put into nurturing friendships and loves but with little or no return. The people who had hurt me had done so because they themselves were hurting on the inside.

So why was I resentful? Why was I angry? And why was I living in fear of losing everything? The answer lies in my ego's expectation of how it thought my life *should* be. I resented putting so much love and effort into relationships of all kinds which, however altruistic I thought I was being, I soon began to perceive an imbalance or injustice from not being appreciated or from where my love became expected by the other person but unreciprocated. I also resented the years of homophobia and abuse, both mental and physical that I had received at the hands of my parents, peers, friends and work colleagues. I was angry at all these hurts and the loss of the things that I held dear in a rapidly changing world that did not appear to respect my core values. Finally, I lived in fear because of what I had already lost.

We are an eternal spirit enjoying a unique fleeting human experience. Our body and our brain are the vessels in which we have our experience. It is the tool that we use while we are here. However, the brain (our ego) would have you think that it is in charge and knows best. In this way the ego represents all that separates us as a collective human race and holds us back in our progression as an eternal spirit on a human journey. Our fears lead to anger. And fear is so easy to manipulate by those people who have power and influence but have turned to self-serving interests and negativity because of their own inner fears.

We have allowed our brain and our ego to run the show rather than it be the servant of our heart and spirit. In the same way we have allowed ego centred politicians worldwide to give us the impression that we are their servants and that we should obey their edicts unquestioningly and a compassionate heart-based solution to problems is rarely offered.

Those politicians of dubious integrity have for decades used fear to frighten the populace into submission in order to carry out actions on our collective behalf which perhaps *we wouldn't have sanctioned* if we hadn't been scared. 'The War On Terror' - were 'hearts and minds' really won over? 'The Cold War' - did the 'threat' of Communism really merit taking the globe to the brink of thermonuclear war with the consequence of the destruction of the very planet we live on?

We see the world around us change so rapidly these days due to excessive commercialisation and mass globalisation, turning our home, this planet, into an endless supply for ever expanding global corporations. The few make excess money at the expense of the many. Yet the supply is not endless. We know that now. And the changes to our planet and to our lives is occurring rapidly and seemingly ever accelerating. This rapid change has alarmed many, with some feeling left behind and others scrambling to keep up. At best we may feel unsettled and at worst we feel fear.

So, who do the more dubious politicians seek to blame when the people become frightened by rapid change? They blame minority groups, ethnic minorities, immigrants, Muslims, Jews, LGTB, the very poor. 'They are responsible for what is wrong in your life' the cynical politician thunders, grabbing tomorrow's newspaper headline and giving you that guilty pleasure dopamine hit as you read and secretly indulge in the misery through the shared anger of indignation. You are being used. Much of the world's media is in the hands of only a few multimillionaires who have vested interests in maintaining the current status quo. Malcolm X is quoted as saying, 'If you're not careful the newspapers will have you hating the people who are being oppressed and loving the people who are doing the oppression.' Well, perhaps we haven't been careful.

Is the ego therefore potentially counterproductive and sometimes dangerous? In its attempt to keep us safe and protected from harm it keeps humankind under the smack of firm government, our liberties policed and ultimately it can lead to our own destruction as we saw in 1930s Europe. The destruction caused by a downward spiral of negative emotions fuelled by resentment and hatred towards others, or on a global scale an out of control consumer society, war and the threat of ruination of the very planet we live on.

Peel back the layers of that ego and see what you discover. Perhaps under the years of built-up defences you will discover the small unprotected and isolated child that you once were. Unprotected and alone is exactly how you came into the world. Would you berate your inner child for not having enough fear to protect itself, or would you show it love, compassion and warmth? Show yourself some love and compassion today and start the process of loving yourself by beginning the long journey of ego deconstruction. Collectively, in this way we will save the planet and humanity.

CHAPTER TEN

Poltergeist 2 the sequel

Part Two - 2007-2008

Step into the light

Summer arrived at the 'poltergeist house' as I have now come to think of the rented property that we had to call our temporary home. It was 2007 and it wasn't a very good summer for a number of reasons, some mundane and some profound. I had bought a convertible car the previous November and the day that I collected my new car from the garage it began to rain and then, as many British people reading this will understand, it didn't stop. By the time it was the summer of 2007 a friend of mine laughingly begged me to sell my convertible, half-jokingly suggesting that it was this purchase of a topless car that was causing the endless quantities of rainfall.

With the bleak summer had finally come the official diagnosis that my father had terminal cancer. There was an understandable lack of willingness by the Health Service to put a timescale on how long my father had left to live, this onerous task was thereby passed on to a privately owned charitable hospice. The hospice looked after my father for a couple of weeks at their wonderfully staffed and purpose-built hospital. This was in order to give me and my mother a short respite break from the arduous duties of care before dad was then returned home.

'Eight or nine months' they accurately predicted, having seen this type of cancer many times before. My father was in his last summer and sadly it was a dark and rainy one, we were not in our own home and the house in which all this was going on had an extreme haunting. 2007 would be a year to remember for all of the wrong reasons.

There were so many supernatural occurrences to relay to you that I am not entirely sure where to start. My father, as I have previously said, was now effectively a permanent in-patient at our rented home. For the duration of his illness he remained in his own bedroom which was on the ground floor, directly beneath mine. This bedroom was fitted out with a special bed and hoist and all of his medical supplies and needs. I gave him an electric bell to push so he could call for us should he need assistance when we weren't in the room. It may sound cruel to say now, but *oh, how I hated that bell*. My father rang the bell many many times a day. Although I had been in denial of it since my childhood, he was an emotionally cold and selfish man, and illness did not improve his weaker attributes.

The bell would ring out every few minutes day and night. Before I was halfway back up the stairs or had returned to the kitchen to prepare food - the kitchen entrance being sited only just opposite his bedroom door – that accursed bell would ring out again. Night-time was no different. My mother or I would take it in turns to be summoned several times in the small hours, and in addition to my domestic duties I usually had a full day's work at the office ahead of me. Over the months this took its toll with my physical health deteriorating rapidly, becoming so physically and emotionally drained that I struggled to function. Late one night I heard the bell ringing and

I got out of bed, dressed quickly, and trotted downstairs still half asleep. It was by now a familiar routine.

'What the bloody hell do you think you're playing at, stamping around at this time of night?' he demanded to know from his bed. When I replied sleepily, with some confusion and not a little injustice that I hadn't been 'stomping around' at all but had been 'asleep in bed' I was called a liar. My father grumbled that he had 'distinctly heard' my 'heavy feet' on the ceiling above him. 'It sounded like you were throwing your boots about.' he added. I reiterated that I had been asleep and that the only footwear that I had moved was when I had put on my slippers to come downstairs. My father refused to believe me, and he had by then been prescribed a small amount of morphine to provide some pain relief, so there was always a suggestion that he may have been hallucinating. Yet hallucinations don't explain the manifold events that unfolded and were shared by the three of us in that house. Or the 'four of us' if you include the poltergeist.

It is only as I write this now that I realise that the vast majority of the disturbances in the house were seemingly directed at me. As an unwitting sensitive I guess that I was easier to affect and in those days I was not at all spiritually aware and as a result, unprotected. For example, these bell ringing incidences began to occur more often when I was upstairs in my room trying to catch up with my sleep. On further occasions over a four-week period, my father would summon me from my sleep with his bell and complain about noise. I knew a little of poltergeist phenomena and so when my father regularly demanded why I was, 'Dragging bloody furniture around your room in the middle of the bloody night?' it was cemented into my mind that we were indeed dealing with the typical 'noisy ghost.' Furniture moving and associated noises are not uncommon in such powerful poltergeist hauntings.

The 'dragging furniture' incidents became more and more upsetting to my father and the suffering from these night-time intrusions only added to his terrible decline. I can attest that I was not dragging furniture about in the small hours, nor was I stomping about in 'hob nail boots' as I was once accused of doing. Then, almost as quickly as they had started, the noises stopped but only to be replaced by an escalation in activity, which now seemed linked to my father's deteriorating health.

My father was very frightened of dying and quite understandably did not like to be left alone for even a short time, hence the manic bell ringing. I believe that the malignant spirit was drawing its power to manifest from the negative energy in the house which had been brought about by my father's suffering and the fear created by his slow death. Fear is the most powerful of energies for negative entities of all kinds as I have written about elsewhere in this book.

Always with an eye to the pragmatic and logical, there were some strange events that occurred that caused me to wonder if my fraught nerves had made them up. Yet I had been under extreme pressure before and after this time of my life with no noticeable poltergeist activity occurring. A good example happened one Saturday afternoon when I was stood at the kitchen sink washing up the dishes. With my mind in neutral and looking out of the kitchen window my attention was somewhere outside, so I did not notice my mother sneaking up behind me and lovingly placing her arms around me, her pale white limbs and elegant hands comfortingly placing themselves over mine.

She had given me a start as I hadn't heard her come into the small kitchen, the door being directly behind where I stood. The consequence was that I jumped with surprise, the arms vanished, and I span around to an empty room, my heart pounding. I wasn't to know it, but my mother was in a different part of the house. So, whose arms had they been? They had belonged to a slender elderly woman, of that I was certain. Was this just imagination caused by over-anxiety? Only I wasn't anxious in that moment, my brain was in a calm meditative state while I cleaned the dishes. If a supernatural solution was the inevitable conclusion, then who was this comforting spirit? Perhaps a deceased relative or, I thought with a chill, were we sharing the house with a female entity as well as a male. Had this manifestation meant to comfort at all, or to scare?

Then there was the incidence of an apparition in the kitchen, not of the deceased builder who belligerently haunted the house but that of another spirit. I now believe this to have been the spirit of the woman who had placed her arms comfortingly around me. Occurring only a few days after the earlier incident at the kitchen sink, it was a similar afternoon and I was once more washing up and gazing out of the window when I felt that I was being watched from the doorway behind me. Sensing feminine energy and expecting to see my mother, I span around only to catch a split-second glimpse of a partial figure stood in the doorway and facing me. There was nothing manifested above the knee, the only thing to be seen was a pair of lady's legs in navy blue nylon slacks with a sharply ironed crease, pale stockinged ankles with feet shod in navy blue velour ladies' slippers which vanished the moment that I sighted them. The appearance and *energy* of the spirit was of an older or elderly woman.

Whenever there is a malevolent entity or spirit in a house where the occupants are being directly affected, there is often a guardian spirit who returns to protect the living residents. Sometimes this can also be to protect other deceased occupants in the house who are yet to cross to the Light and who remain stuck. This 'guardian' spirit can be a deceased relative of the living occupants or often a spirit tasked and sent to rescue the 'stuck' spirit who is actually causing the problems.

I never did find out who the woman was, and she never manifested again after I saw her that second time. But I concluded that there was no negative intent with her, and I believe her to be related to the malevolent spirit, perhaps his mother, and doubtless trying to help him to the Light, simultaneously protecting the house and its occupants from the worst that the male spirit could do.

Time passed but the unpleasant odour in the hallway cloakroom area recurred occasionally and without cause now that the drains were clean. The doorbell perhaps rang once or twice more but any pause in spectral activity was deceptive as the energies in the house continued to ramp up in power. You could feel the malevolence. Then things got weird, or should I say weirder. Even with my father ill and with all that was going on, I was still working and simultaneously studying for my law exams. Things could not have been more stressful, so when I got a phone call at work from my mother to tell me that something extraordinary had happened at home, it was in part expected.

When we had moved into this neglected rented house,

among the many faults that we inherited was to discover that the rooftop television aerial no longer worked. In response to the landlord's lack of action I had rigged-up an indoors set-top aerial and signal booster which just about worked if placed atop the television at the correct horizontal angle and direction.

What my mother told me over the telephone didn't surprise me. It was unusual for her to call the office and so I knew that whatever the purpose for her call, it was important. Yet she made light of it and told me that it hadn't troubled her but, 'Could you please come home?' I hadn't spoken to my mother about my suspicions of the house being haunted, nor to my father. This might seem incredible to read but it was true. I think that separately we all knew the truth but that it was so awful that we kept it to ourselves or tiptoed around the edges of the topic so as not to upset or hurt the other, after all, we had enough going on already. I knew as soon as I heard the brief story from my mother that what she had seen was true because something similar had already happened to me a few days previously. I had also experienced an additional dubious bonus manifestation.

The television was in the corner of the sitting room, a large old-fashioned cathode-ray tube set which stood within an ostentatious 'faux Georgian' wooden television cabinet, once so popular in the 1980s. Atop was a large ceramic electric table lamp together with the set-top TV aerial. Facing and sited just a few feet away was a sumptuously upholstered single armchair, one of a set my parents had especially made for them nearly two decades earlier. It was in this chair, some week or two before my mother's call to the office, that I began to experience a most strange but not necessarily unpleasant sensation on the now rare occasion that I sat down to watch television.

Rather the sensation *would* have been pleasant if it weren't for the hand that caused the effect being unseen. You see, every time, and I mean *every time* that I sat in this particular armchair an invisible hand would oh-so-gently place itself horizontally across the back of my head. This would probably be an unsettling experience for anyone taken by surprise by a friend or family member, but when something like this occurs by the hand of someone apparently not of the living it shakes you!

I couldn't understand then, why a spirit with malevolent intent would wish to gently place his hand on the back of my hair, so soft and gentle but very definitely there. This strange sensation only occurred in that armchair when placed in that exact spot. At the time I presumed that it was the poltergeist messing with my mind but writing this now it has made me reconsider the matter. As I have written, I now believe that there was more than just one spirit in that house, not only of the former builder but also a second spirit of the older woman in the navy-blue slacks.

The hostility meted out by the angry poltergeist seems contrary to the soft touch and caress of a hand placed gently on the back of my head. Was this the caress of the elderly female spirit in the house, perhaps attempting to salve my rattled nerves? Or was it of one of my own deceased loved ones or ancestors offering me protection and compassion?

We can all be mediums for spirit energy, willingly or unwittingly. I didn't know then, but I am an easy conduit or medium for spirit energy and when my protections are low, I can be susceptible to influence by any earthbound energies. During those hyper stressful times, both physically and spiritually, my usual psychic protections would have been weakened or even left defenceless.

My later experiences in the field of mediumship demonstrated to me that when 5D spirit comes in close to us to make contact, or to speak through or influence a psychic medium, it invariably approaches the body from the rear. Indeed, in some cultures it is considered unlucky to walk backwards for that very reason. Was this the angry ghost attempting to make physical contact? I doubt this now as the energy seemed feminine or gentle in nature. Perhaps I was sitting in a psychic energy 'hotspot' within the house enabling spirit to more easily make contact.

One Sunday afternoon I had sat down to watch BBC TVs 'Countryfile' on the television and I settled into the armchair. I cannot recall on this occasion whether I felt the hand on the back of my head or not. I expect that I did because eventually it happened without exception. When the incidences with the invisible hand occurred, I must have looked comical, as I always leapt up frantically clutching at the back of my head half-expecting to find something there. No-one else ever reported this sensation but I noticed that neither my father, when he had been well enough, nor my mother ever chose to sit in the chair. This was despite the armchair being the most convenient from which to view the television. But on this particular Sunday it wasn't the hand on the back of the head that got my attention, it was the set-top television aerial.

On three separate occasions over the previous two weeks, I had the distinct impression that the aerial had moved as I sat and watched television. It was only out of the corner of my eye that I had seen this movement and so I had put it down to my imagination the very first time it occurred, after all, these were stressful times. The second time it occurred the movement was greater and the picture on the screen became distorted, indicating that the aerial had indeed been interfered with. Perhaps gravity had affected it, I reasoned. The third occasion was alarming as the aerial moved swiftly and violently to the right, clattering to the floor, the picture on the screen now waves and static.

My logical mind tried unsuccessfully to put this down to the aerial perhaps having been teetering on the edge of the television cabinet. In reality I suspected the truth of the matter as I had distinctly seen the aerial fly off the top of the cabinet with some force, though I didn't mention these events to anyone, after all, what good would that do?

This particular Sunday, whilst hoping to get some reprieve from the tragedy of my seriously-ill father slowly dying at home and the 24-hour care that this entailed, I had been hoping to achieve a little bit of mind-numbing sanctuary by settling down to watch something normal and comforting on the television. Therefore, I had seated myself in the infamous armchair, switching on the TV programme 'Countryfile' and anticipating watching restful countryside scenes. The opening credits rolled but I was unable to watch television or be allowed to relax.

This time, perhaps by chance, I was looking directly at the set-top aerial when noiseless unseen hands suddenly jerked the antenna sharply and swiftly through ninety-degrees from the horizontal to the vertical position. The effect on the television picture was immediate, the image instantly wavy lines and static. Without thinking I leapt out of the chair, corrected the aerial, switched off the television and I did not watch it or sit in that armchair again for many weeks.

My mother's telephone call to me at work therefore came as no surprise, but a creeping horror possessed me as to the safety of my loved ones at home while I was away at the office. My mother clearly did not want to worry me, or perhaps she did not want my father to hear what she had to say, simply telling me that 'something strange has happened' and 'not to worry' but 'would I come home please?' Without hesitating I apologised to my boss, and it was less than an hour later that I was home, and my mother told me her story.

Earlier that day she had just finished attending to my father and had chosen to settle in that very armchair in order to watch some television. She said that no sooner than she had begun to watch a television programme, the set-top aerial had suddenly and swiftly 'flown across the room.' Perhaps knowing that I was lying just to assuage her fears, I told her that the event must have been a 'one-off.' However, only a couple of days later the flying aerial occurred once more with my mother the sole occupant of the sitting room. It was a clear message that the television was *not* to be watched. It was to her regret that my mother broke this unwritten rule some days later.

Hauntings induce a reasonable but terrible fear in the recipient of the disruption and he or she reconsiders their sanity. A common response from others to such events is that the witness must be 'mistaken,' 'overwrought' or even 'unhinged.' It was therefore with cold comfort to discover that the poltergeist events were being experienced by all three of us. Some believe that because the events in a poltergeist haunting axis around an individual in the household, often at a time of high stress or anxiety such as teenage angst or an illness, that it is these individuals who are unknowingly creating the disturbances through their own kinetic energy. I have always failed to see why some seek comfort from this theory, as the *events are still occurring* whether they are caused by the energy of the living or the deceased.

It is true that my seriously-ill father understandably wanted constant company and could have inadvertently been causing these disruptions. However, having experienced poltergeist phenomena first-hand I am of the opinion that the powerful negative energy from emotionally disrupted members of a household is *not* creating the disturbances but instead they are unwittingly *creating a power supply* to a *pre-existing* disruptive conscious earthbound spirit or entity *already present* in the house. The residents are not in my opinion creating an energy field with a separate malevolent consciousness, though doubtless this could happen in theory, instead the residents fear-based negative energy is I believe providing sustenance to the disincarnate entity. The more haunting events that the poltergeist creates, the greater the fear and misery within the house and the more empowered the entity becomes, with the result that events ramp up in nature over time.

Ramp up in nature they did. Days later we were to experience the most bizarre and, I admit, the least believable part of the entire poltergeist phenomena, though by no means the last. My parents directly experienced this most strange of psychic phenomena, with me as a secondary witness as I was away at work. With the three of us now experiencing poltergeist events I stand firm to my attestation that these were very real and not psychosomatic, with us as three witnesses adding weight to their validity.

Those familiar with poltergeist and ghost hauntings will know that spirit often frequents any place where water is located, the theory being that it offers a storage vessel or conduit for their energy. Wells, ponds and millpools are traditional vectors for spirit entities but also the less romantic bathrooms, toilets and places where any static water is located. Those familiar with the Harry Potter series of fictional books will know that the author J K Rowling included a haunted lavatory at Hogwarts School in her stories. I have a friend who regularly used to see the earthbound spirit of a small boy in period clothing in the ladies toilets of where she worked. I would theorise that hauntings around water could be due to the crystalline structure of water resulting, as with crystals, that energy can be held by the water. It is no coincidence that 'holy water' which has been imbued with the positive incantations and intention of the priest, is considered to retain the positive 'holy' energy.

It was while resident in the house that we were to discover it had been built over both stagnant and running water. A small brook was opposite in the country lane, and we were advised that the house had been built not only on low-lying land where the water table was high but that another brook had originally run where the house now stood. All this low-lying water around and just under the property gave it a permanent damp air, even in high summer.

And it was a surreal summer, the air was tinged with a tangible melancholy surrounding my father's illness and comprising an atmosphere in the house that was so thick it really did feel as though it could be cut with a knife into slices. With heavy hearts our daily life continued. Life that existed through an oppressive 'summer storm' that never broke, though in many ways it did break all too regularly. I received another distressed telephone call from my mother while I was at work. 'Could you come home please? Something has happened.' The 'something has happened' transpired to be another plumbing emergency, this time centred in the upstairs bathroom.

Along with my mother's request for my help was a predictable accusation from my father that what had occurred must have been my 'fault.' I say 'predictable' because since childhood my father had a tendency to blame me for most things in his life that ailed him. Those who know something of child psychology will be familiar with the concept of the child 'scapegoat' in the dysfunctional family. This day was no different, with my mother relaying the message from my father that I 'must have left the taps running' in the bathroom that morning, notwithstanding my mother went on to use the bathroom after I had finished and already left for work. My lifetime Obsessive Compulsive Disorder (OCD) always ensures that the water, gas and electricity is checked several times as having been switched off, with this morning being no exception. Besides, if I had left any water running, then who had turned it off? When my mother had rushed upstairs to turn off the taps it was to discover a dry bathroom and no taps running.

I have spoken of the sitting room and the television with its set-top aerial sited next to the sumptuous but 'haunted armchair.' On the first floor, directly above this apparently cosy corner of the sitting room was the bathroom. The story told to me by my parents was that my mother had sat down in the infamous armchair (that was probably her first mistake) in order to watch television, only to find seconds later water pouring through the ceiling and onto the carpeted floor directly in front of her. Immediately apparent was that there was a burst pipe, or a tap had been left running in the bathroom above and had overflowed the basin or bath.

To her horror, this 'overflowing' water was now coming through the ceiling at quite a speed, leaving a large dark wet patch on the paintwork above her and an increasingly wet carpet beneath her feet. The television was close-by and there was a real threat to safety from an electric shock. With only my mother and I using this first-floor bathroom and having concluded our ablutions some hours earlier, why was it only *now* overflowing?

I rushed home, a drive in my car of some thirteen miles in, unusually for that year, dry and sunny weather which I remember thinking would have made for a very pleasant journey under any other circumstances. When I entered the house, it was to discover two very confused and dumbfounded pensioners who were now feeling quite sheepish at having called me home for this latest 'emergency.' They told me that straight after the telephone call to my office (I had left for home immediately), the water had ceased to pour through, leaving a large damp patch on the sitting room ceiling and a damp carpet beneath. My mother had made a cursory inspection of the bathroom but found that there was no indication of what had caused the problem. The basin and bath were completely dry, and it was clear that none of the taps or the shower had been in use.

The small second hallway outside of the bathroom door was one of my least favourite places in the entire house. It led from my bedroom to my mother's with the bathroom situated in between. Directly outside the bathroom door was the loft hatch with access to the attic and below this, a large hallway cloaks cupboard. I had never been into the attic. It is not that I have any unnatural fear of attic spaces, but rather this entire area of the house filled me with such a total dread, with a constant sense of being watched by unseen eyes, that it took all my nerve one day just to change a blown lightbulb directly outside that bathroom door.

Bulbs were often popping in this house. This is another phenomenon associated with poltergeist activity. This is entirely subjective, but I always had the impression that this was the area of the house where the original owner may have taken his life, perhaps occurring in the bathroom, or perhaps in the attic or attic hatch area. I also felt strongly that he wanted us to know this.

I checked for leaks in the small cupboard outside the bathroom where was housed the power shower plumbing and found there were none. I thoroughly checked in the bathroom unable to determine where the leak had originated. No taps had been left running and there was no sign of any water or damp anywhere in the room. The problem, I decided, must be underneath the bath, perhaps a leaking drainpipe. Yes, that was it I reasoned; the drainpipe must have worked its way loose from the bathtub.

I grabbed a screwdriver and began the task of removing the multitude of 1960s screws that still held on the original brightly painted plywood bath panel affixed to the side of the primrose suite bathtub. Once underneath the bath, aside from the to-be-expected cobwebs and decades of dust, there was no sign of any loose pipe, nor was there any sign of any water leak or damage. Indeed, the dryness of the entire area meant that there had simply not been any leak at all in the bathroom and the water that had been cascading into the sitting room immediately beneath had to have come from another source.

Without mentioning anything supernatural, the explanation of my findings was not well received by my parents. I had 'obviously left water running' I was told and that I would 'have to pay the redecoration costs of having the ceiling repainted downstairs' lest we lose our tenants' deposit. Incredulous, I went into the sitting room with my mother. There indeed was a large water stain on the ceiling and the colour of it, in stark contrast to the surrounding white painted ceiling, made it clear that a dirty stain would soon manifest. With no further emergency and finding myself at home on a pleasant sunny day, there seemed little point in returning to work that afternoon.

Some three hours later my mother and I were back in the sitting room to discuss the water leak and what to do to remedy the damage to the ceiling and carpet. As we looked up at the ceiling it was immediately apparent that not only had the ceiling already dried out but that there was now no stain. Not a thing, no damage, no mark, not a spot. I felt the ceiling. It was tinder dry. I felt the carpet beneath, it too was totally dry. This was utterly impossible. It was as though there had been no leak. Had the three of us imagined it? That was perhaps answered much later when this cascading water episode was to enjoy an encore on our very last day in the house, but more of that later. It is only some years after these events that I now know that cascading water leaks that appear and disappear just as quickly are not uncommon in houses with a poltergeist presence. Indeed, they can be considered a classic trademark of a powerful poltergeist haunting.

The psychic attacks by the entity that still resided in our

home – 'his home' as he doubtless saw it – continued unabated but from this time onwards they were directed solely at me rather than the three of us. Perhaps this was because I was the one who sensed and reacted most of all to his activities. Or perhaps it was because I was the most fearful, knowing exactly what was occurring and by whom. It was my fear, together with my psychic energy that satiated and quenched his thirst for manifesting.

Daily his power grew, the atmosphere in the house increasingly darkening over time, the air thick with his angry brooding male presence. Those of you reading this who have experienced a severe case of haunting may recognise what I say in that this spirit would follow you around the house, observing you at all times somewhat like an over-zealous store detective. A perpetual feeling of being watched by unseen eyes, you could literally feel his presence all around you, or, particularly on the stairs, directly behind or in front of you.

His constant observation became visually apparent to me when I became aware of what is commonly known as a 'shade' or 'shadow' figure. I soon recognised that the angry spirit was making his presence known by manifesting as a shadow, or perhaps that should be termed an 'absence of light.' Shadow figures are common phenomena when dealing with negative entities or negative earthbound spirits. Subconsciously, the brain automatically identifies where the light source is in a room and thereby, where the shadows should be. I can only describe to you that in this house the shadows were all 'wrong' but it took me quite some time to recognise it.

Walking into a room, you would intuitively know that something was wrong with the way the light fell and accordingly an unnerving feeling would ensue, but you didn't know quite why. A shadow might follow you around the house and be there one moment and gone the next. The property had large 1960s picture windows and accordingly it should have been a sunlit and cheery house, but instead there was a perpetual pall of gloom and darkness in almost every room, on even the brightest day.

It was many weeks after moving into the house and when I was lying in my bed at night and staring up at the ceiling that it suddenly occurred to me the shadows above were not being cast by the electric bedside lamp. The shadow was in the wrong place. Moreover, as I watched, the shadow kept subtly changing and altering position, yet always suspended directly over my bed on the ceiling. We instinctively know when what the eyes are detecting isn't right and this long dark shadow was accompanied by a negative, hostile energy. These were no normal shadows, but the spirit of the man watching me, hovering above my bed. It's unnerving to realise that a spirit is floating right above you, staring down at you from the ceiling, watching silently, observing and waiting. But waiting for what?

Any number of strange things started to occur in my bedroom at night, always when I was in bed, either about to sleep, reading a book, or when just lying on the bed watching television on my portable set. The constant bell ringing from my seriously-ill father continued and those repetitive endless trips up and down the stairs to assist him began to take their toll. Sometimes my mother and I took it in turns to sleep in a chair in his room, but little sleep was to be had.

My father's bedroom was alive with noise from the medical equipment, and without saying why, he now insisted on the lights remaining switched on at night, and I never was any good at sleeping in a chair. More often than not I would spend the night hours wide awake in my father's room, sometimes studying for my exams, sometimes reading and sometimes just with my eyes closed but always desperately tired. So, to be lying in bed in my own room watching television or reading a book before turning off the light was a luxury during those unhappy days.

I have forgotten to mention that the television in the sitting room, the one with the set-top aerial that the poltergeist so aggressively disagreed with, would often switch itself on and off. My logical mind had put this down to perhaps a strong infrared light from outside triggering the remote-control sensor on the television. Yes, I really was clutching at straws to convince myself that the haunting was not happening, when all of the evidence was to the opposite.

Then, around the time of the shadow figure making a regular appearance on my bedroom ceiling, my own portable television in my bedroom began to do the same thing. This was a much newer device than the set downstairs and I only watched TV at night-time and during these hours there can be no question of stray infrared light from outside. Once or twice my set would switch itself off when I was watching but more often it would switch itself on.

Rather like a scene from a horror movie, I would wake with a start during the night, only to find that the television had switched itself on of its own accord, wavy lines or 'snow' on the screen which flashed ghostly light across the darkened bedroom and the eerie sound of static emanating from the speakers. Sceptics out there will rightly question whether the television 'was left on timer by accident.' I've heard all the excuses that people come up with to explain away these types of events, I know them well as I made them myself at the time. The portable television in question didn't have a timer, and not once before moving into this house had the set malfunctioned like this, nor since departing.

The poltergeist spirit was deliberately causing sleep deprivation in order to maintain the fear and dominance within the house. This was the most difficult time in our lives and while we watched my father slowly fade away in a most painful manner from pancreatic cancer this negative-minded spirit played its vile jokes.

Then began the scratching sounds. The first-floor bedrooms were built into the roof of the house and so each room, by dint of the roof shape, had a small vertical door that led into individual cramped attic storage spaces in the eaves. My own attic door was just to the right of my single bed. One night, I switched the bedside lamp off and settled down for a fitful night's sleep, knowing full well that I probably only had about thirty minutes before my father would ring the bell again. On this night, the moment my head hit the pillow the scratching began. The scratching was in the darkness to the right of the bedhead just some two feet from my face. Being deep in the countryside and with no streetlamps, the night was very dark and very quiet. My senses piqued in the dark as I strained to listen.

Mice! I thought, or perhaps bats? The scratching was within the wall itself and was moving away from the bedhead towards the attic door. Whatever it was it seemingly passed through the door and into the attic. I leapt out of bed, put the main light on and strode swiftly to the attic door where I began my inspection for intruding mice or bats. There was nothing and the noise had stopped. I shone a strong light inside the tiny empty attic space and checked everything thoroughly, but it was clean and clear with no signs of any rodent infestation.

Shutting the attic door I returned to bed, only to find the whole thing repeated as soon as I had switched off the bedside lamp. I considered that this was reminiscent of the incident with my bedroom wardrobe in another rented house many years before. A further thorough check of the attic space was made, and I was satisfied that there was nothing in there. The mouse, for it must be a mouse, was somehow within the wall space.

Once the bedside light was switched off again, the scratching restarted. This was no mouse. Mice don't immediately go about their business the moment that a lamp is extinguished. If the mouse was inside the wall space, how would it even know that the lamp was switched on? The 'mouse' now restarted its journey from my bedhead. In the darkness I listened intently and recognised that if a mouse was within the hollow walls of the bedroom, it would have to come to a 'roadblock' at the wooden attic door frame.

Instead, the scratching ceased at the doorframe and after a silence long enough for the 'mouse' to have traversed past the closed door, it miraculously began again at the opposite side of the doorframe. Slowly the scratching continued and made its way to what I recognised must be the corner of the bedroom. Still in darkness and listening hard I heard the 'mouse' turn the corner and it made its way to the large picture window. 'Ah!' I thought, 'It won't be able to get past the window!' but

I was wrong. There was a silence again, a long silence, while the 'mouse' traversed the distance of the two-metre picture window. Once it had reached the other side of the window, the scratching noise began again.

'It' then headed onwards towards the built-in 1960s wardrobe in the corner of the bedroom. Facing my bed, this was a floor to ceiling monolith of solid wood. But it failed to stop the progress of the 'mouse,' the scratching turning the corner of the bedroom once more, still at the same height within the wall and heading to mid-point in my bedroom, the wall directly opposite my bed.

Opposite and facing my bed I had, as I have stated, a portable television sat upon a DVD player, which in turn sat atop a metre high chest of drawers. The frame of this chest of drawers was in painted wood, but the drawers themselves were of natural wicker. As the scratching reached the chest of drawers, it didn't continue its way inside the wall as I was expecting. Instead, to my dismay, I heard the wicker baskets begin to make the unmistakable creak and squeak sound of natural wicker being moved. This was no mouse! I knew that something, probably the shadow figure that often resided on the ceiling above my bed, was toying with me rather like a cat might play with, well, with a mouse.

The wicker creaked and groaned for a few seconds, but it was when the noises from the wicker stopped and the scratching in the wall continued again on the other side of the drawers that I began to feel a growing sense of fear. This wasn't a living mouse within the wall, *this was the spirit of a man walking around my bedroom*, tapping and scratching on the walls, the noises occurring at hand height. 'It' turned the corner again and, with an ever-heightening dread, I knew 'it' was heading back towards me.

I suppose in many fictitious horror stories the chief protagonist would pull the sheets over his or her eyes and pass out. I did not. Instead I lay there fascinated in mortification as the scratching reached the door to the bedroom. There was no way that a mouse could get past this doorway, the height of which reached almost to the ceiling. Only this wasn't a mouse, I had to admit it to myself now. This was the spirit of the dead man. The angry dead man. Still furious at the manner of his death and furious that we were in his house.

The scratching did not stop. After a brief pause while it impossibly passed the closed bedroom door, the noise began once more, this time from the opposite side of the doorframe. On and on it advanced, reaching the corner of the bedroom nearest my bed and now, in its final phase, it had reached the wall against which my bedhead stood. I pictured the glowering spirit of the dead man stood some two metres from me, his fingernails scratching at the wall, for the sound was definitely at waist height.

I cannot explain to you the fear induced by the certain knowledge that an unseen spirit of a man who apparently despises you, is now walking slowly and deliberately towards your bedhead in the darkness. He was advancing upon me as I lay in the most vulnerable of places, my own bed. I cowered as the scratching stopped about a foot from my face. *The ghost was stood by the side of my bed.* I couldn't see him. I couldn't hear him. And because the entire house was filled with his negative energy, I couldn't even sense him, his presence next to my bed making little addition to the heavy atmosphere already in the room. And then ... and then there was nothing.

I would like to report that this was to be a one-off event. It wasn't. This scratching episode repeated itself in exactly the same manner, on and off, over the following few weeks. Always the same. Always ending at my bedhead until I was in terror at what was to come and eventually, I made the classic mistake that all haunted people do when pushed too far; I got angry. My mother and I were exhausted by the constant twenty-four-hour care that my father required, together with the emotional fatigue and sense of creeping bereavement that occurs when someone you love is slowly dying in front of you over the long disheartening months. Sleepless, exhausted and empty of all vitality and hope, it was on the fourth occasion of this new night-time visitation that I lost my temper and shouted obscenities at the spirit. I could feel his anger palpable in the room now. He had been enjoying his party games like bullies do, but now, I had challenged him.

Chapter Eleven

Poltergeist 3 finale

2007-2008 – Part Three

The door moved a little more, as if someone the other side was pushing it open cautiously to see what was going on inside the room. As I tried to tell myself that the now stationary door was merely responding to gravity, with a jerk the door opened some four inches.

Christmas arrived and with it, my father slowly began to lose his fight for life. His entire world was restricted to his bedroom, either sitting in the health-service supplied electric riser armchair or lying on the supplied inflatable bed.

The decorated Christmas tree was only a token affair that year. I wasn't intending to put up any Christmas decorations as the occasion neither seemed joyful, nor could they be seen from my father's bedroom. Besides, my father always loathed Christmas. However, it seemed wrong to not have any suggestion of Christmas in the house and perhaps it would bring a little hope.

Always treasuring our vintage Christmas ornaments which I remembered fondly from my childhood, I knew exactly what should be present and I kept everything meticulously in the original boxes. So, with nothing ever having been lost over the preceding forty years, it was a surprise when, upon packing the Christmas tree ornaments away the following January, I discovered that a small hand-painted wooden ornament of a Christmas tree had vanished completely from where it had hung on the full-sized version. There had been no celebration of Christmas and with it no visitors to the house. The only two people in that room that Christmas had been me and my mother and neither of us had taken the missing ornament. Perhaps poignantly, it seemed that our poltergeist had wanted his own tree that year. It is not uncommon in poltergeist incidences for physical items to move or disappear completely. Things can even manifest seemingly out of 'thin air' and these can often be items that do not belong to the householder at all.

Having challenged the spirit loudly in my bedroom, the scratching episodes and the shadows on the ceiling and elsewhere continued unabated. He had doubtless learnt of my horror of spiders in the time that he had 'spent together with us' and it was therefore with some repulsion that one night at bedtime I discovered a small black and red shiny bulbous spider on my headboard. Being on the colder north-facing side of the house meant that my room was always cool and not a little damp and I therefore kept the bedroom window closed all year 'round. So where had this garden spider come from?

It was an evil-looking creature and not like anything that I had come across before, but it did remind me of something that I had seen in a book somewhere. The spider was safely removed, and I went online to check if my suspicions were correct. Yes, the spider closely resembled the Black Widow and I was to discover that the UK has its own False Widow spider which has a similar appearance but without the deadly venomous bite. However, even today I wonder if I had a lucky escape from the small gift left for me that night. After all, if he could apport a False Widow spider, doubtless he could conjure up the real thing too. Perhaps it was.

With my father's increasing incapacity, I started to leave my bedroom door ajar at night, just a crack, maybe no more than one centimetre where it would happily stay without opening further. Occasionally a slim chink of light would shine through the crack from the lighting downstairs, or from when my mother was in her bedroom, the entrance to which was just out of sight from my doorway, around the corner of the landing. The spirit would always wait for me to be awake in my bed and looking at the crack in the doorway before carrying out his newest mischief. Perhaps he waited until I was watching, or perhaps my own intuition told me that there was a threat and woke me. It is a very uncomfortable feeling being watched by something unseen. Make no mistake, I was living in a perpetual state of anxiety and sometimes of fear.

My father's deterioration in health meant that both mine and my mother's attention was keenly focussed on his needs. The spirit episodes became more of a background noise that we both lived with and tried to ignore. Sensing this, the angry ghost would seemingly try and think up new ways of manifesting his displeasure at our presence in his house. One such night I was in bed (it seemed that things now always occurred when I was in bed), the lights were off and I was about to sleep. One half-closed eye caught the door move slightly, the chink of light expanding and contracting as the door almost imperceptibly moved back and forth a few millimetres. It was as though someone had just gently touched the ajar door to test it. The door moved a little more, as if someone the other side was cautiously pushing it open to see what was going on inside the room. As I tried to tell myself that the now stationary door was merely responding to gravity, with a jerk the door opened some four inches.

Cautiously I got out of bed and pushed the door back to its original position but by then I was already wary to the spirit's night-time tortuous teasing and I knew that my actions were futile. I guessed correctly that as soon as I was back in bed, this procedure would be repeated. The sequence of events repeated itself once more that first night and then this became a regular occurrence over the following weeks, always when I was looking at the door and always at night. At no other time did this door opening occur and nor could it be replicated by manual means. The door was not prone to swinging open, nor could I get it to behave in the same smooth manner by my own hand.

Eventually, in the final two weeks of this unpleasant and irritating phenomena, it seemed as if the energy the spirit possessed had grown in strength, or perhaps he had become ever more petulant and aggressive. The door would at first be pushed gently and opened a centimetre, then a couple of centimetres, then three or four, when suddenly with a silent jerk, the door would be thrust open lustily by a strong shove.

Nothing else followed on from this strange and scary door opening episodes but there was always the background noise of the meandering scratching sounds to keep me occupied as these had become a regular feature together with the occasional appearance of the shadow figure on the ceiling. It was the shadow figure that once or twice, when it was aware that I observed it, slid silently across the ceiling and down the opposite wall, dissipating into the floor.

When the door-shoving phenomena did occur, I understandably just wanted to get out of the bedroom for a while and have some human company. Given the late time of night when these strange, unsettling incidences happened, my mother was usually to be found in her bedroom, though like me she was not often asleep given everything that was going on in the house at that time. So, disturbed by the poltergeist, I would saunter across the landing to her room, ignoring the awful sensation of being watched or followed by something unseen, and I would knock and enter her room.

Like my own bedroom, her door would always be open or ajar so that she could listen out for my father and that infernal bell. While my bedroom faced the quiet country lane that we lived on, with only occasional passing motor vehicles or horses, my mother's bedroom overlooked the colourful tree and shrub filled garden with a distant view of a paddock and fields beyond, the paddock usually containing two handsome white horses. A sylvan setting and a lovely bedroom view. The outside was beautiful, but it was just a shame about the ugliness that lurked within the walls of the house itself.

One night, as I lay in my bed in the dark, my electric bedside lamp had already been extinguished and I was trying unsuccessfully to sleep. Something made me open my eyes and I saw the door to my room once more twitching slightly with only a faint chink of light showing around the crack, doubtless light escaping from my father's perpetually illuminated downstairs bedroom. Something was outside the door again. The door opened another centimetre and with a familiar creeping sense of dread, I knew that the poltergeist was on the landing and about to make his nightly entrance into my bedroom.

However, then I heard footsteps and raising my head off the pillow and looking directly through the crack I saw that an electric lamp had been switched on in my mother's bedroom, the light casting a long welcome golden glow across the landing carpet. I watched as mum walked around her bedroom, the long-stretched shadow of my mother's legs swiftly moving across the landing carpet in stark relief to the bright light within. Such a relief! Not my usual night-time visitor at all, instead it was the comforting presence of my mother. She must have come up the stairs without putting the overhead light on. She was a thoughtful woman and wouldn't have wanted to wake me, so had crept upstairs all but silently.

Happy, and emboldened by the welcoming warm glow of the light, and wanting to escape my spectral visitor, I leapt out of bed, quickly put on some bedclothes and padded across the now dark landing to her bedroom to say 'hi' and have a chat. Odd that it was dark again, my mum must have already extinguished her light and gone to bed. As I turned the corner of the landing and faced my mother's bedroom door, I saw to my surprise that it was wide open. My heart was already racing as I anticipated what was coming next.

The dim light from my own bedroom was insufficient to light the way and I cautiously entered my mother's room. Peering in and peeping around the corner, I saw that the curtains were not drawn and that the bed was empty. Not just the bed, but the bedroom too. I rushed downstairs as if I had the Devil himself behind me, which in a way I did, and I found my mother downstairs in the sitting room, lights blazing and happily watching television, the set-top aerial behaving itself for a change, though I noted that as usual, the sumptuous armchair remained vacant.

'Have you just been in your bedroom?' I enquired hopefully.

'No dear.' came her reply as she saw the colour in my face drain.

'You've not been upstairs at all?' a desperate look on my face.

'No, not at all, I've been sat here all night watching TV.' and then, 'Why dear?'

I collected myself and answered, 'Oh, no reason, I thought I'd just heard you up there that's all.'

My mother didn't enquire further. She could tell that I was holding something back and she probably knew what it was.

We had all quietly accepted that the house was haunted but as a topic of conversation, it remained the ghostly elephant in the room. Nobody wanted to scare the other, especially with my father seriously ill in the house, that fact being a much bigger nightmare for all of us. I wasn't going to frighten my poor mother to tell her that her bedroom was also haunted. I had previously decided that it was the only room in the house that felt 'right' but now I doubted myself.

I considered that it was likely that the disincarnate legs of the elderly lady who I glimpsed in the kitchen doorway were one-in-the-same legs of the figure that I had just seen in shadow across the floor of the landing. The glow of warm light from my mother's bedroom had been so welcoming, that I struggled to believe that it had anything to do with the angry poltergeist. Perhaps the spirit of the elderly woman was there to comfort and protect. I suppose I will never know on this side of the veil, but I will find out in due course when my time comes. That, I suspect, will be a most empowering and enjoyable 'day' not unlike an episode of the now defunct television programme 'This Is Your Life.'

Time marched on but the appalling weather remained stubbornly resilient. My father was now so ill that I had taken unpaid leave from work in order that I could devote myself full time to his care. The letter containing the results of my legal examinations arrived one morning and I discovered that I had passed all but one of the papers which therefore counted as a 'fail/referral.' This was no revelation to me, for months I had been unable to devote the time and attention needed to my studies due to all that was going on at home.

When I told my father he burst into tears. It was a rare thing indeed for my father to cry. He had not been emotionally there for me during my life and had shown little or no interest in my career, so to see him react like this was a shock. Nobody wishes to see their parent weep and when he went on to apologise to me for the selfish decisions he'd made and for the harsh things he'd said to me in my youth, I felt truly humbled. Perhaps it was a little late in the day for me to hear this confession, but at least he had said it and hopefully he received some relief from the guilt. The lesson there is to not leave things unsaid that need to be spoken. All too many people think that there will always be another day to make up or apologise, only for all of us, that day eventually doesn't come.

My father then declined over his last few weeks into a depressive stupor but not before he had predicted the timing of his own death by quoting Shakespeare with 'beware the ides of March.' I presumed that he was indulging, understandably, in a little melodrama but prophetically he was correct. After months of truly abysmal weather the first day of March came and with it sunshine. It was one of those delightful spring mornings that make you glad to be alive, at least under different circumstances it would have. But these were not normal times for us, and this was no normal house. Despite it all, or perhaps *because* of it all, I saw no reason to reinforce the misery of the situation on the two people in the house who I loved and shared my life with, so it was that I burst merrily into my father's bedroom that morning and yanked open the curtains, letting the bright fresh sunny day flood in.

Turning and declaring, 'It's a beautiful morning!' I smiled at my father lying in bed, but by this time he was unresponsive and nearing his end. Crossing the room to sit with him for a while I noticed a weak smile come to his lips and I knew he could hear me, so I sat and chatted a while. It was the one-sided conversation that anyone who has ever looked after an unconscious loved one is familiar with. Afterwards, I went outside into the sunshine to begin the clean up after the long winter. When the sun shines on the bleakest day you can almost forget your troubles.

But within the hour I was called in by mum, my father had started chain-stoking, which is where the breathing becomes noisy and irregular as the body starts to fail. The district nurse was called and while I waited for her to arrive, I sat by my father's bedside and chatted to him again, holding his hand. He had been in terrible pain for many weeks, not just from the pancreatic cancer which is, I was told at the time, 'the most painful of all cancers,' but also because unbeknownst to us, he had developed a 'flesh eating disease' while in hospital and this had spread and formed a large hole in his back so that his vertebrae was exposed. This, he had told me, was more painful than the cancer.

As I talked to my father about the spring sunshine and the

garden birds, I saw him trying to smile and he weakly pressed my hand, after that, nothing. The district nurse arrived a short while later and I stood up when she entered the room. My father was still chain-stoking, an alarming sound to anyone who has heard it, and she told me that he was 'near the end.' I accepted this and knew it would be a release for my father who was suffering greatly and also a release for me and my mother.

I said to the nurse that I had been chatting with my father and that he had 'Smiled a little and weakly pressed my hand.' The response I received was unexpected and stayed with me to this day.

'No, no.' she said with a patronising air, 'Your father can't hear you now and he can't respond either.'

I was a shocked, aren't we always encouraged to talk with our loved ones at their moment of departure?

'So, there's no point sitting and talking to him now, he can't hear you.' and then with a cheery, 'Goodbye, this will be my last visit.' she was gone.

With my mother and I left alone in our grief, my father died later that morning with us by his bedside, talking to him. I consider what the nurse said that morning to be at best thoughtless but at worst, crass and deliberately hurtful. There have been many times in my life when I was tempted to say something, because it was the truth, but I didn't in order to spare the recipient. When there is an urge to say something unpalatable but it is unnecessary or unhelpful, then say nothing at all. To offer up your 'truth' or knowledge says nothing about how you want to help the other person and says everything about your own ego and the need for it to prove itself over the emotional needs of the other person. The nurse gave me an uncomfortable but very valuable lesson in compassion and ego that day and I am thankful for it.

After my father's funeral and once the shock and grief had subsided a little, my mother and I began to live what was by comparison a more normal life. Those of you who have experienced the lingering illness of a loved one, followed by the release that death brings will recognise the elation that follows the crushing loss. The inevitable guilt that rushes in from the feeling of freedom that the death of your loved one brings can be too much to carry. My mother bravely coped with it all, and I wasn't to know until after my father's death that she had been keeping a secret of her own. In the days that followed she told me that she had been carrying the burden of believing that she too had cancer but had felt unable to seek medical attention while her husband lay dying.

Now that her husband had passed, she felt able to confide in me and seek help. My mother must have been beside herself with worry over her health for some time. Yet she had carried on bravely and uncomplainingly, perhaps largely for my benefit. The morning that my father died, the atmosphere in the house lifted and the poltergeist, restricted in empowerment, no longer had the capacity to haunt us quite like he once had. Indeed, despite everything, mum seemed much jollier, as was I, but the long-term encounter with the poltergeist and the spirit realm had left me with an unexpected lasting blessing; the gift of claircognizance.

One week after the death of my father I heard from him one more time. Free from the electric bell that summoned us throughout the day and night my mother and I greedily caught up on our sleep. My father's car had been on hire purchase but with the death of my father the contract was cancelled by the hire purchase company, and arrangements made for the loan company to collect the car from our house. I woke with a start that morning, not from any poltergeist disturbance this time but instead to the sound of my late father's voice. '*Robert!*' I stirred in my sleep. Again, '*Robert!*' the voice was unmistakably my father's and was loud and urgent.

I sat bolt upright in bed and looked at my alarm clock. It was 7.30am and at that precise moment I heard the approach of a lorry down the country lane outside the house. I dashed to the window and pulled back the curtain. It was the car collection man in his truck! My father was a stickler for good time keeping and would have hated me being still asleep when such an important event as the removal of his car had to be attended to. I acknowledged my father out loud as I hurriedly dressed and ran downstairs to meet the car collection guy.

One beautiful sunny September evening I visited my mother in her bedroom. Late summer sunlight streamed in through the picture window and I looked out across golden fields to the horses playing in the paddock beyond. What followed was a claircognizant psychic moment. I didn't even know what that word meant back then, but I was gripped by an impulse. I suddenly realized or 'knew' that we had to mobilise into action. Mum was lying on her bed, happily chatting with me and I was stood at the end of the bed. I can picture well the scene in my mind even now, so clear was the spirit revelation that came to me in that moment.

Abruptly, I changed the topic and said, 'Mum, I think that we need to get away from here.'

'A holiday dear?' she replied.

'Well, yes that would be nice and well deserved but what I mean is we need to move out of this house. Rent somewhere else.'

Renting longer than six months had never been on the agenda when we had moved in a year before, but we couldn't have foreseen what was to come. As I have explained previously, I had encountered my sensation of utter dread in the lead up to moving into this house but that wouldn't have changed anything.

Now standing in her bedroom, to my surprise my mother replied, 'Yes, I've been thinking the same thing.' and then suddenly we found ourselves discussing the house and the spirit activity we had all experienced. The bedroom was filled with golden sunlight and there was a peace over the house as we talked.

Although the house had become quieter since my father had died, as though the negative energy the spirit needed to manifest had dissipated, this place would forever hold bad memories. So it was decided, even though it would be a massive upheaval to move from one rented home to another, that we would do it. In very little time I made the arrangements, and my mother and I viewed a 1960s property some miles away in a popular estuary town, only a short walking distance from where I worked. The landlady had inherited the house from her mother and father who had both lived in the property; her mother having died in the house in the preceding months. We loved it and signed the lease.

Moving day came and the removal men were busy loading up our furniture into a large removal lorry when there was a commotion from the sitting room. The head removal man came out of the sitting room and into the front hall where I was still packing boxes.

He looked alarmed and agitated and he said, 'Hey boss, you need to come and look at this.' He turned and sensing the urgency I quickly followed him back to the sitting room as he excitedly continued, 'I've never seen anything like this' and then without pausing, 'I wanted to be sure that you saw this before we got the blame for the damage.'

I saw, as I walked into the sitting room, his two subordinate removal men in blue overalls, a strange mixture of sheepishness and shock on their faces.

In front of them was the comfortable armchair, the same armchair where once seated one experienced the sensation of the ghostly hand on the back of the head. The removal men had moved it from its usual position, but it still sat squarely on the carpeted floor. The head man continued, 'Your armchair is completely wet underneath. My men had gone to pick it up and load it onto the van, but when we lifted it, we saw that it was dripping wet. I mean *absolutely soaking*!'

I didn't say a word but doubtless my face was bemused as he indicated to his two men to lift up the armchair so that I could see the underside. They did so and I could indeed see white mould marks on the black canvas base but that was all. 'Go ahead!' indicated the head guy to me, 'Feel the base and see how wet it is!' I moved forward to do just as he suggested. I touched the arm, the side and finally the underneath of the upturned armchair.

'It's completely bone dry.' I reported, almost sorry for the men as I already knew what was occurring.

With a 'tut' the head man lurched forward to the chair.

'Of course it's wet it …' he paused as he felt the 'soaking wet' base of the armchair.

He looked as if he had seen a ghost. Seeing their boss's reaction, the two men also felt the base of the chair while it was tipped up on end. Dry. The armchair was examined by the men all over and found to be dry. I moved to feel the carpet where the armchair had been sitting. It too was dry. There had been no water ingress here that morning, of that I was certain. The incident with the '*bathroom leak that wasn't*' had occurred only the once months before.

As I say, I did feel very sorry for the men who now looked uncomfortable and not a little nervous. I couldn't tell them that the house was haunted in case they abandoned the job, perhaps fleeing in terror but by the look on their faces I think that they had guessed, and they quickly finished the job of loading the lorry in super-quick time. The poltergeist was glad to be rid of us and the house had given us its final gift.

The house move went very well. I had packed and meticulously labelled all of the boxes myself. Just forty-eight hours later, mum and I were completely unpacked and settled in to our new rented abode, happy and looking forward to some respite and a new environment. An environment that was welcoming and non-hostile, unlike our last house. However, it wasn't long before I realised that we weren't entirely alone in the new house. My mother had the delightful sunny first floor principal bedroom suite which overlooked a beautiful well-stocked garden, and I had the first floor second bedroom, which was just as large, if not larger but was stiflingly hot.

The third and final bedroom was downstairs immediately below my own, a similarly large double bedroom with the same view of the road as mine. This had clearly been the previous elderly occupant's principal bedroom as it was equipped with fitted wardrobes and dressing table, plus it still retained the scent of the previous occupant. The style was quite old fashioned but exactly the sort of thing an elderly couple would want and need, and all available on the ground floor for easy accessibility for anyone with limited mobility. The strange and immediately noticeable thing about this particular room was that it was icy cold, even with the heating on. It was also quite dark and gloomy.

I put this down to it being north facing until I realised that my own stifling bedroom was situated immediately above and was sunny and welcoming. After the last house, I didn't want to admit to myself that our new home may have a former resident in occupation. If it did, they didn't give me or my mother any trouble as there was no poltergeist or angry spirit activity. The former elderly owners had been a happily married couple, who, for whatever reason, didn't pass into the Light and had chosen to remain.

I say 'owners' in plural but I believed it to have been the landlord's deceased father who remained in residence. He had predeceased his wife, and, on her death, I think that she passed over to the Light and he had not. It isn't unusual, when a couple very much in love and connected, when separated by the death of one of the pair, the first to die remains earthbound, unable to bear parting with their loved one, they choose to watch over them until such a time as they too are ready to pass to the Light together.

This sounds very romantic, but I should make it clear, in order to avoid this happening to you, we can pass into the

Light yet can come back to visit our loved ones at any time we wish. We have complete freewill. Indeed, we are better suited and placed to offer our loved ones any help that they need from *the other side* of the 'veil' than we ever could, should we remain Earth side.

The small office space built between the kitchen and the garage had clearly been the deceased man's office. Originally when the house was built there was a gap between the back outer door of the kitchen and the garage. At a later time, this gap had been bridged by a small porch and leading off from this porch was a small office room with a view to the front. I say 'office room' because although it was devoid of furniture of any kind it had shelving plus, tellingly, a telephone point with a built-in desk.

It was in this room above any other that I felt the definite presence of an older male spirit energy. I used this surplus room to house all the unopened removal boxes, but I hated going in there. There was an occasion called for where I had to spend two evenings in there sorting through the boxes, opening and re-sealing. It was not a pleasant experience. It was a small room, and I was acutely aware of sharing it, once again, with an unseen entity that seemed less than happy that I was occupying his personal space.

It was while we were at this house, which was for some six-month period, that we received two pieces of important news. One was from the local press and the other from the hospital. My poor long-suffering mother had been ill the entire time we had lived at the poltergeist house and she had kept her troubles secret while father was dying. Afterwards, she went to her doctor and scans revealed that she needed a hysterectomy and that a 'dark mass the size of a grapefruit' had appeared in the same area. A second scan revealed the same thing. Finally, a third scan showed nothing at all. The doctors, perhaps too hastily, and wrongfully as it transpired, decided to go with the result of the third scan.

The day of the hysterectomy arrived. I nervously hung around all day in the hospital waiting area for any news about my mum. I prayed like I have never prayed before for the Source to spare my mother. People came and went until at about 5.30pm I was emotional and on the point of tears, sitting alone in a now deserted hospital corridor. No-one would tell me anything and I began to fear the worst. Finally the smiling anaesthetist arrived in the empty corridor to speak with me and confirmed that the operation had been a 'success' but laughing, he considered that they had 'nearly lost your mum on the operating table.' My mother had 'gone under too deeply and they had trouble bringing her back.'

The news of my mother's near-death experience was not greeted by me in the same curiously jolly manner that it was being delivered but I was so relieved to hear that she had survived that I didn't care, and I just couldn't wait to see her again. But, as I was to discover, my mother was never to be the same again and I believe that some brain damage may have occurred perhaps due to oxygen starvation caused by the excessive anaesthesia.

The second piece of important news that we received during this time came only three weeks after having vacated the poltergeist house. Only a few weeks before on that fine summer's evening in my mother's bedroom, I'd had the premonition that we had to vacate. We did not have long to wait to find out the reason why. Local news broke of an intense isolated storm. In a rare 'freak weather event' one day in October, the village where we had previously been living in the poltergeist house had suffered an overhead cloudburst of hail. The storm clouds had stationed overhead and did not move on for a period of several hours. The hail had become intense and heavy, pinpointed directly over the village.

So heavy in fact that mounds of frozen ice began to build up in drainage gullies, gardens, roadways and on rooftops. So much ice accumulated that in the case of the poltergeist house the entire kitchen roof and ceiling collapsed under the sheer weight of the frozen water, leaving the house uninhabitable for several months. Had we not have moved out, we would have been homeless and much of our furniture damaged. It was obvious that I should listen to my claircognizance more often, but I had yet to learn the vital lessons that I was being shown by spirit.

CHAPTER TWELVE

The light and the dark

Seeing beyond the 3D mirage

What if each one of us understood that we are an eternal soul on an eternal journey and that no harm can come to us? What if we didn't fear death and we began to do all those things that we always told ourselves we would do?

Science shows us that our physical universe that we see, hear, touch, taste and smell is made entirely of energy. This energy is thought to have emanated from the explosion that occurred many billions of Earth years ago when the physical universe first popped into existence. And everything that you do see, hear, touch, taste and smell is just your own energy reacting and inter-reacting to and with an external energy.

Our eyes, for example, detect the energy of light reflecting off something and this is sent as an electrical energy message to the brain which then uses energy to unscramble the message and the brain recreates a virtual version of what the eyes have detected. The image now in the brain is merely a virtual reconstruction of what the eyes are actually looking at, it is not the actual object and it is not necessarily reality. Everything that our brain experiences is an imagined existence.

Based on learnt experience, the brain interprets the object as either 'solid', 'liquid' or 'gaseous.' In this way our brain has created a rather filtered and humdrum two-dimensional virtual world out of the amazing natural phenomena of the huge chemistry experiment that is happening all around it which we call our 'universe.' Our universe and our world is vibrating energy displaying its amazingness at differing densities. Our brain deceives us when it labels things as 'solid' or 'liquid' as everything around us is just energy 'holding hands.'

Imagine what might be around you that your eyes cannot see within their natural limitations. It is worthwhile taking a moment to also think about what is around you that your eyes can see but your brain then refuses to unscramble the electrical message it has received because it either has no comparable reference point or because your brain says that it 'should not be there.' If you've ever wondered why witness statements vary so wildly between one witness and another it is because each individual's brain puts its own set of learnt parameters and prejudices on what it expected to see.

Quantum electrodynamics shows us that over 99% of an atom is made up of empty space and that space is filled by an electron field around the nucleus. We cannot physically remove that empty space, but if we were to you would, for example, be able to hold The Empire State Building in the palm of your hand, albeit it would still weigh the same and give you a terrible wrist ache. So, solid objects are not as solid as they seem and the world you see around you is also not as it seems. Your eyes are filters of deception, and your brain imagines your perception of the physical reality.

It is the tradition of most religions that God is the source of everything and created the known universe. It is therefore logical to consider that God is the known universe or the 'Source.' The universe is entirely made of energy, and we may therefore understand God as energy. If all energy in the known universe is from the Source, or 'God' if you prefer, then the energy that created the planets and all living things including mankind are of the Source. We are made of the same energy as the Source, so by definition *we are* the Source, and we *are* God. The Source (God) is not therefore a distant separate entity who sits on a cloud patiently watching over his children's shenanigans with a benign and loving disposition, instead we, collectively *are God incarnate*. All of us, good and bad, all races, all creeds are the same energy because we are of *the same essence as the Source*. We are of the universe. We begin to understand that we are created from the same energy as the Source, so begin to consider how *truly powerful you actually are*. If the Source can create an entire universe, then what can mankind create by his or her own thoughts? Mankind can manifest anything it desires, and *this is why our thoughts, our words and our deeds are so important*. We are creating 'magic' every day with our thoughts, words and deeds. Good or bad, we manifest our own reality. With this in mind we can begin to understand how important it is to ensure good mental and spiritual housekeeping.

Familiar as we are with the science of light waves, radio waves and sound waves oscillating or vibrating at differing frequencies, this is no different to our own physical energy. All living and inanimate things vibrate at their own frequency and emit their own energy field as a result. In metaphysics it is believed that the physical 3D universe (and thereby the Earth) is at the lowest vibration. So low and dense that energy appears as solid, and therefore the physical universe is the densest energy to navigate of all the dimensions. At this low vibration both positive and negative energy can co-exist. This is Yin and Yang. It is this unique characteristic of Earth as a planet that can support physical life and also both positive and negative energies that makes it the perfect background foil for humankind to seek out and learn through chosen vital lessons and experiences.

Reiterating what I asked at the beginning of this book, please forget many of the pre-conceived ideas and notions about who and what we are in the physical universe that you have been taught to believe or that you are given to understand. It can be liberating to discard our rule book of restrictive thinking practices that we have inherited or learnt from others and instead create our own new way of thinking, experiencing and understanding the world around us. In a seemingly static solid reality, it is difficult to even grasp that everything around us is flowing energy.

Seeing the world in a different way takes us a little time to absorb, due in large part to what our own eyes deceive us to believe and because of what we are taught to believe from an early age. Seeing the universe with a fresh understanding can also be a little unsettling, as many of those dawning realisations can overturn our long-held beliefs about who we are and where we fit in and it is those beliefs that give many of us a sense of security in a universe of chaos.

Let us consider positive and negative energy. We know that energy is indestructible and transmutable, that positive and negative energy exists in the physical 3D reality and that all things have a positive or negative charge. Positive and negative energies have a purpose in the nature of the physical universe just as the light and the dark does, but could there be even more purpose to those energies than just creating energetic chemical reactions?

Your consciousness comes from the divine energy force that is within you. There is a great body of evidence to show that it does not come from the vessel that we call your body which contains your brain. Nor does it come from the neural transmitters and receptors in your brain. Medical science has been unable to find any link between consciousness and the brain and they never will because consciousness does not start with the brain. All sentient beings have a consciousness, and this consciousness comes from the energy or spirit contained within that creature while it is physically alive. By extension, all living things on planet Earth perhaps including Earth itself have a living energy field and as such many things in the natural world may possess their own consciousness.

Once we have considered that the indestructible energy field contained within our bodies has a consciousness, we can then consider that this consciousness continues to exist after the death of the physical vessel that contains it. We can also consider that the ethereal energy fields that are sometimes around us but which we do not see may also be conscious. This can be an alarming thought when you first consider and expand it as an idea. This is the thought that we are surrounded by spirit energy or entities all of the time though we usually cannot see them, though our own energy field may interact with theirs and we may then feel the energy.

Upon the death of our physical body our energy consciousness detaches from the lifeless body and returns to the Source, often with assistance from deceased loved ones or spirit guides. Sometimes, for a number of reasons this does not happen and the spirit, now released from the deceased physical body, remains detached but loose in the physical 3D reality causing the existence of earthbound spirit, or 'ghosts.'

Because the energies that come with or attach to a location carries a vibration, or 'vibes' as it is often referred, a house, building or any location such as a forest is often said by people to have a 'good' or a 'bad' vibe or feel to it.

'Oh, I bought this house because it had such a lovely *vibe*.' is something often said.

'I wouldn't go there on my own, it doesn't *feel* right.' is something we all encounter from time to time.

Perhaps one dark winter evening you may be happily walking alone until you stumble across one stretch of path or street that doesn't *feel* right. You may experience an involuntary shiver, pull up your collar and hasten your step with your head down and you push through to the end of the road. Have you considered what you may actually be *pushing through*? Positive or negative energy can attach itself to anything, the very walls of a building, to the very stones or just to the location.

What if, just like our own embodied spirit energy, we consider that disembodied negative and positive energy may also have a consciousness. In the same way that all living things must have an energetic life-force of their own and a consciousness and a purpose, consider whether incorporeal negative or positive energies may also have a purpose just like any physical being. If so, what would that purpose be? Positive energy would presumably bring higher vibrational peace, contentment and unconditional love to all who encountered it and as a 'living' entity, it would seek to reach out and assist. It would perhaps accumulate in areas or around people with a similar positive 'vibe' of their own. Negative energy would be attracted to people and places where there is a negative 'vibe.' It would seek to mislead, betray and cause mischief or worse with its low vibrational energy field.

Born innocent and of the Light, many of us succumb to the often unbearable darkness that we all encounter in our lives. The many unfortunate life events that can and do often occur sometimes make the ego turn good people into what we would mistakenly term 'bad people.' Yet this is not irreversible, their energy field has become afflicted and affected by negative energy in the same way that a physical body can become afflicted by illness. We attract the energy that we emit, our creating the conditions of what we emit and what we attract towards us. A positive minded person will attract more of the same and conversely, a negative minded person will drift ever further away from the positivity and love that is the Light. How do we stay grounded and remain in a positive minded disposition in a world that can be so cruel and difficult to navigate? I believe that this is one of our most difficult tests.

I understand that this is an oversimplification, but those who embrace positive thought patterns and lifestyles attract positive energy into their lives. As a result, their lives improve, they remain positive and more positive energy is therefore drawn to them. This perpetual state of positive consciousness is impossible to achieve in the real world, but we can try. There are external influencing factors too such as karma, our life purpose and the astrological weather forecast. Those who, due to experiences in their life, create a negative thinking may attract additional negative energy into their lives. This can be a self-perpetuating spiral with those afflicted individuals sinking lower and lower as they attract more and more negative energy which increases their negative thinking. A whole life can be lived and wasted this way. I know because I've been there.

We either find ourselves able to pull ourselves out of this rabbit hole through deep inner work on our shadow side and the inner wounded child, or someone such as a therapist helps to dig our way out and back to the Light. It is our impressionable brain with its overthinking and easily wounded ego that is creating these negative emotions, it is not our own life force energy. The Light (positive energy) seeks harmony, peace and love and the darkness (negative energy) seeks to extinguish it. Everything in the universe was created by the Light including the darkness. The Light has a consciousness and so we may be forgiven for questioning whether the darkness does too. With a consciousness the darkness would seek to create chaos, misery and unhappiness on a global scale and also in your life at a personal level.

Consider whether as a divine being you are content with being manipulated in this way. What if the darkness was not a concept of an ethereal energy source but instead possessed a physical body, would you not seek to remove that person from your life? Why is it that we tolerate the darkness when it is in the abstract, yet we would never do so if it were a manipulative person in our life? It is sometimes easier to think of negative energy and negative thinking as an annoying toxic person. Who would want this type of enemy around them for even one second? Now consider your thoughts, your words and your deeds and what you may be unintentionally manifesting in your life.

Recognising negative energy and negative thinking as our true enemy is the first step in freeing our energy field of negative external influences and making our lives a happier reality.

The mistake is to make other people our enemy for we are all of the Source and a part of the collective whole. 'Hate the sin and not the sinner' is a Biblical expression meaning to *reject the negative energy but not the person* acting as its conduit. See beyond the fear and begin to recognise that your enemy is the conscious darkness itself.

Your friend on the other hand is the Light, which is the energy of unconditional Love. The second step is to live without fear, without anger and without hate. That step can be achieved by the slow and often painful process of healing your wounded inner child and realising how powerful you truly are as an eternal being of infinite love and light from the Source, from the very universe itself.

How would a conscious 'darkness' or negative energy go about bringing the lowering of vibrational energies globally amongst the people occupying our planet? The darkness is equally as clever as the collective consciousness of Light. As with the Light it is an eternal energy connected to the Source and it will know us all inside out. The darkness will use and influence negative minded people to bring about change for the worse. The more fear and hate there is in the world the more that energy of hatred can be utilised to feed the darkness and the more the darkness flourishes.

All of us have many opportunities in our lives to seek positivity and keep love in our hearts, but out of fear some of us end up looking to the darkness for our security. Security is something that we think that we get from home, possessions and people, but all these physical things are ephemeral and will not last. When material things and possessions break or leave us, as they inevitably must, our ego is left feeling insecure.

Yet the reality is that as an eternal divine soul, you are always secure. This security goes beyond the 3D physical world, and it comes as your birth-right because the universe 'has your back' as an eternal soul.

You are loved and when your physical body dies, you return to the Source. Security is something that the darkness can *never* provide but merely contrives to give the illusion of by way of material possessions and financial wealth in the 3D physical world. Like an addiction, you require more and more to keep you distracted from the pain that comes from our separation from the Light and in doing so, it leads you further and further away from the very Light that you crave.

The brain has created the ego and the ego lives in fear. Fear of loss, fear of poverty, fear of change, fear of someone different to us. This comes from learnt behaviours and our body's animal heritage where survival meant a heightened awareness and thereby existing in a permanent consciousness of fear. Far from being empowering, the ego disempowers us by keeping us on guard at all times against any perceived threats. The darkness will seek out exploitation of anyone's weaknesses – and we all have those.

Egocentric people are those individuals who have created an inflexible comfortable reality for themselves and who must dismiss anything that their ego perceives as a threat to its construct. The egocentric person can be someone who is only rigid in their opinions all the way on a spectrum through to the clinical narcissist. What they all have in common is that their ego's protection of the false narrative of safety that they live by results in them perhaps being most at risk from the darkness. These are those of us who when faced with the challenges of life, seek to exert control over the uncontrollable.

My own father was a man who exerted his ego-based control by the elimination of clutter and mess. Thus he created an immaculate home and garden – to the point of madness – but this resulted in unfulfilled children as our emotional needs were neglected. The very purpose of a family home is surely to provide a loving and safe place for the family and children, but my father thought it to be about appearance, status and cleanliness. He was haunted by the darkness and as a result I also lived in the shadow of his fear as a child.

My father's own internal 'demons' and the negative energy he created and attracted overflowed into my own life. This is what can occur when the ego seeks to exert control and power over others and the material world in order to protect itself from harm. Time and again humanity has seen what happens when those individuals who live in such ego-based fear and who then seek power to control are given authority. Humanity becomes overshadowed by the same darkness that afflicts the egocentric ruler who sought the power. The negative energy has spread like a virus amongst the people.

The ego will create an overactive mind and it seeks to emphasise and exaggerate the perception of the dangers facing the individual. We exist in a physical world of random and sometime chaotic events that for the most part cannot be predicted. Yet our ego believes that it is able to plan ahead and control the outcome of any situation, all this in a universe of chaos and chance. When things go wrong, as they inevitably may, the person becomes ever more fearful and unwilling to accept responsibility for their part in any failure of their ego's life plan. When the person is rewarded for their efforts with wealth and influence, the individual starts to believe in their own brilliant planning and superiority over others and in the reliability of their own ego.

This successful person listening to his or her ego seeks out of fear to protect what is theirs, although we really own nothing, we are just temporary custodians. They become ever more fearful that the people their ego has learnt to distrust, or dislike may try to take away what it already has, and so the urge to gain ever more wealth and material 'things' grows, as does the loathing of people who have less. After all, the person's ego justifies, 'Isn't it their own fault that they have less than I do?'

Through their own guilt, they begin to build a false construct of superiority and self-justification for all they own and consequentially for all of their actions. When they have acquired much, they then seek to acquire even more physical wealth, their ego now concerned that the wealth of others is a threat and that there won't be enough pie to go around. The underpaid employee, the cleaner, the care giver, the nurses, these are just some of the people who give to our world their efforts, compassion and love on a daily basis.

Those who live by the values of love and compassion are some of the wealthiest people on Earth, and as they travel on their journey through life, they are unknowingly spiritually ascending. Those who solely seek physical wealth and power over others are unknowingly some of the poorest. At the end of the physical life, the person who has collected the most toys does not win the prize. Shrouds do not have pockets.

Existing in the physical 3D over many incarnations, each lifetime is a short one and each short life should be filled with the only wealth worth having - love. To clutter our lives with the fake symbolism of the physical world, money and material possessions, is a personal tragedy to the person doing it. The individual so afflicted by his or her ego has created a cage of gold in which to live his or her faux-protected life. Only there is no protection to be had in that gilded cage. Gilded or not, a cage of their own making is still a prison.

We must seek to live in the 'light' but as beings of light temporarily trapped within a physical body this is difficult to achieve in such low-density vibrational Earth energy. Each one of us adds our energy to the collective whole, and if we do not live in the light, the collective ego feeds the darkness with our fear and anger. The darkness seeks to manoeuvre well-meaning people by manipulating their fear-based ego with perceived threats to their physical existence.

The poor exploited underpaid worker gets fearful and angry. A meagre income from their miserly billionaire employer never quite seems to keep up with the ever-increasing bills from their miserly billionaire energy companies and landlord. The unscrupulous billionaire lives in fear of others trying to get what he or she perceives as 'theirs.' They therefore seek power and control over the majority to remain 'on top,' ensuring everyone else is diminished in power. The underpaid and exploited worker lives in fear of losing what little he has. The unscrupulous billionaire is experiencing the same fears. Yet there are enough resources to go around for everyone, only fear and greed suggest that there isn't.

What if each one of us understands that they are a unique spiritual entity having a unique physical existence on Earth and that we chose to incarnate here to have a physical experience? What if each one of us understood that we are an eternal soul on an eternal journey and that no harm can come to us? What if we didn't fear death and we began to do all those things that we always told ourselves we would do? Without a fear of loss would the employer have love and compassion in his or her heart? We enter the realm of Charles Dickens' 'A Christmas Carol' and the '*Spirit of Christmas in their heart all year around.*'

Without the employer fearing financial failure would his employees be paid a fair wage for their own needs and plenty more besides? Imagine a world where employees would receive a decent living wage and where they could pay their rent and their energy bills and not have to worry about when the next pay cheque was coming. Much global fear would be extinguished and perhaps many hearts would be that little bit freer to express love, as is the natural order of things.

Money is nothing more than energy in promissory form and holding onto energy stops the flow. As the late esoteric philosopher Alan Watts wrote, 'You wouldn't get a carpenter coming to your house and stating that he cannot work today as he has, "Run out of inches."' Yet we readily accept when it is said that there is not enough money to go around. The Gold Standard is long since gone and money is nothing more than an abstract notion of energy. There is plenty of energy for everyone.

The truth and ultimate irony for the person who knowingly or unwittingly has allowed the darkness into their lives for personal gain at the suffering of others, is that after the death of their physical body they will seek to repeat their life's journey in order to 'get it right' the next time around. We are an eternal soul on a karmic journey through many lives, here on Earth and elsewhere. The sum total of our existence over many lifetimes is great and we are far more powerful and experienced than the small physical body which encapsulates our eternal spirit would suggest. The darkness has manipulated and duped the ego of the individual into believing that this material world is all that there is.

For each person incarnates here on Earth with a specific purpose. We all have a life purpose, and through the fear of the ego we can allow ourselves to be led off our path. After the death of our physical body and returning to the Light we are shown and understand that we must work through any karma we have inadvertently created. Any 'undeserved' gains made in this lifetime will be repaid in a future incarnation, this is not a punishment, this is simply the universal law of balance. So it continues until the spirit of the individual has learnt the lessons that it set itself and has cleared all karma or broken the karmic cycle.

I'm sure that most of us have wondered why or how seemingly unelectable people who are utterly devoid of empathy, love and humility are elevated to positions of great power. The darkness and the manipulation and affliction of the ego goes someway to explaining this strange phenomenon. We have all seen these imposters over many centuries. Stalin and Hitler from the twentieth century are the obvious candidates. Just how did these cold-hearted and psychopathic people become powerful leaders? It was not through charisma and a loving disposition. They used fear, hatred and rage to manipulate the very thoughts and hearts of normal people.

Despotic or unhealed people still exist in power today. They are in plain sight and wrap themselves in a cloak of honour; a national flag metaphorically waved at a press conference on sovereignty, or a holy book held aloft at a press photo shoot outside a sacred place of worship. Times change but sadly some people do not. Our fear-based servant brain was never meant to exert control over our love-based spirit. It is a case of the master allowing the servant to control it. If we were to let our spirit which emanates from the Source to control our brain, as should be the arrangement, then overnight the world will become a more loving, compassionate place.

When we think, say or do bad things, we often try to convince ourselves that we were in the 'right'. But we all know the inner truth. That little voice inside is our soul speaking to us. When our spirit incarnates on Earth in human form to learn what we set out to experience and with the people we always travel with (our karmic family), we are separated from the Source (God). This shocking and scary separation from the love and the light that we know as God (the Source), our true home, causes a spiritual wound within us that we carry our whole life.

If we begin to understand who and what we really are, where we came from, what we are made of and who has truly 'got our back', then we find inner peace as we begin to relax into our life's journey. It is shock for our spirit to be incarnate and walk a lonely path on our life journey. Is it no wonder newborn babies cry?

You are made of the energy of love and light. The low vibrational density of the physical 3D world does not provide an entirely hospitable home to our high vibrating energy that is contained within our physical vessel. The more incarnations and the more spiritual lessons learnt, the higher our vibration and the more problematic and difficult it is for our spirit to exist in the 3D physical world. Those of you reading this who are of a very high vibration may have experienced a whole lifetime of aches and pains and feeling unwell in your physical body. You may never have felt 'right' or comfortable in your physical body or in the material world. You may have felt alone and separate from others, unable to explain why you feel that way.

The feeling of separation from the Source stays with us for our entire life until we die and return home. This is why we seek solace in relationships with loved ones or even with strangers, alcohol, food or drugs. Because we are made of the energy of love, we therefore seek love from others to endorse our existence. Or we look to the avoidance of having to emotionally experience the absence of love in our physical life by thrill seeking or from the temporary distraction brought about by mind-altering chemicals. The Source is where we came from and what we are made of. The Source is the Light and it is the energy of love. Any absence of love in our physical life leaves us with a profound longing. In each short incarnation we are always seeking a return home.

Chapter Thirteen

2009 – 2015 A new home, a fresh start

The haunted cashbox

*An attachment to an object, a place, or to a person
can prevent the passing of a spirit from the
third dimension to the fifth dimension*

Alone now without dad, my mother and I had moved out of the storm damaged poltergeist house and into our new rented home. But we faced the less supernatural and more practical concerns of the economic crisis of 2007, which had by 2009 led to a major dip in our savings. My late father had made me promise that I would look after mum after his death, I thought it obvious that I would and not for the first time my father had failed to understand me and what motivated me. I believe that I had never once failed them as a son, but my father had little faith in my abilities or integrity. To look after mum was an honour and my duty, so I didn't need to be told to do so by my father. He would often repeat a threat of, 'I'll come back to haunt you if you don't look after your mother,' which said far more about his attitude towards his son and life in general than it ever did about me as a person.

With the rent becoming a burden, mum and I decided to pool our resources and purchase a new home together in the lovely old village where we used to live. This was the same village where my happy 'safe haven' house used to be and, less favourably, the poltergeist house. The shocking loss of capital that my mother and I suffered - like so many did who had saved a lifetime and who then found themselves caught up in the economic crash, was about to be recouped. April of 2009 was a particularly good time to be buying property in the UK, simply because it was not a good time for those poor folks who were desperate to sell.

Mum and I viewed a handful of properties in the location we wanted, and we stumbled upon a three-bedroom bungalow with its own private lane not too far from where we used to reside. Understandably, mum had announced that she wanted to live once more in the village where she had retired with dad. This made her feel close to him and surrounded by familiar things in her old age. I just wanted somewhere peaceful to crawl away to and lick my wounds from the experiences of the last few months. Somewhere quiet and with no bloody ghosts.

The memory of me and mum walking down the long gravel driveway approach to view what was to become our next house has stayed with me. I even took a photo of the occasion, as if I already knew that this was to be our new home. I can still see my late mother now, happy and well dressed as always, turning to me and smiling because we both knew that this was it. What we discovered at the end of the drive was a tired 1980s bungalow in a very ugly dark red brick, with gloomy dark painted windows, unfashionable blown vinyl grey and ginger wallpaper and carpeted with ginger nylon carpet floor tiles.

The overall decorative effect was that the interior had come from a bank waiting room so municipal in appearance was the décor. I was later to find that it probably did, as the late husband of the vendor widow who still lived in the house had worked his lifetime for a large bank, retiring as a senior manager. Anyone who has discovered the 'joy' of these decades old nylon carpet floor tiles – I still remember them being demonstrated in the 1970s as the 'carpet of the future' on BBC TVs 'Tomorrow's World' – will know that the backing glue begins to break down over time and releases an acrid smell not dissimilar to cheesy feet blended with a vinegar dressing.

It was sad to see a house presented in such an unpleasant and not a little depressing way, and the garden that had been lovingly installed by the widow's late husband had been unceremoniously ripped out by her jobbing gardener who had complained to the widow that it was 'too much hard work,' recommending that it all be laid to lawn. I always presumed that once it had become much easier to maintain that he then reduced his weekly rates accordingly, but somehow I doubt it. A keen lover of gardening I hatched my plans. Here I had a perfect blank canvas, and I was ready to throw myself into this house and its garden wholeheartedly.

The lovely old, widowed lady who sold us the house was downsizing and had been concerned about all her lifetime of stuff which filled the property, attic and garage. When she knew that she had to move out sometime in the forthcoming months, she had begun the mammoth task of clearing everything out that she couldn't take with her to her new smaller apartment. Being elderly and frail, this onerous but essential job was completed by her able-bodied adult daughters. The garage however remained untouched and was stuffed with her late husband's tools, equipment, homemade shelving, old paint cans and a million screws and nails from literally a lifetime of Do-It-Yourself jobs. My mother and I therefore agreed to purchase the house complete with any remaining items, including any rubbish that the widow couldn't deal with being left in situ.

Everything went smoothly and upon moving-in it was amazing to discover that not only did all of our furniture fit the house perfectly down to the square inch but many of the old tools and hardware in the separate double garage reminded me strongly of my childhood. My late father's own 1940s and 1950s hand tools and gardening tools, which were now vintage items and which I still had and used, strangely exactly mirrored what had been left in the property by the previous owner. My childhood weekends had been spent watching my father use his tools on various projects and I had become fond of them as a result. To see an almost identical set of Do-It-Yourself and gardening tools from a long bygone era made me feel nostalgic for lost innocent days.

The day soon came, when for the last time, the widow left the home that she and her late husband had built for their retirement, moving into a warden assisted apartment in a nearby town. It must have been a very sad day for her, some twenty years of memories. Mum and I moved in a few days after her departure and it was as if, I commented to my mother, 'Father has somehow found us this house.' It was quite perfect for mum and dad's needs, had he still been alive. Less so perhaps for me but ever mindful of my promise to my father to look after mum, I began the slow task of replicating my father's vision of how his and mum's ideal retirement home would look. I stripped wallpaper, ripped up floors, painted walls and windows. I dug beds for flowers, shrubs, trees and roses. But one of the first jobs that I had to do was to gut and clear out the detached double garage in order to create a workable workshop space and parking for our two cars.

This was perhaps the first time that I had any sense of uneasiness in this, our new home. Mum, who despite endless evidence of the ethereal still didn't quite believe in such things, often complained about the energy of the new house, in particular the sitting room where she didn't like to sit for long when I wasn't about, stating that, 'She must have spent a lot of time crying in here.' Of course, mum was referring to the prior owner, the grieving elderly widow mourning the loss of her husband to cancer some six years previously.

But it was the modern and well-equipped double garage that gave me the creeps. Once more I ignored my claircognizance that told me this place was still occupied by someone unseen. You might think that with all that I had experienced, I would have learnt to trust my intuition by this point in my life. The former owner's workbench, tools and equipment stood empty and unused, yet whenever I was present in the garage, touched anything or worked at his old bench, I had the very clear unnerving sense of being watched. Not only observed but overseen with annoyance that I was touching his things and invading his personal space.

We had moved into the house in the April of 2009 and although it was first on my to-do list, I had already done a fair bit of work about the property before I started the arduous, dirty and arguably worst task of clearing out the garage. I had 'disenjoyed' a phobia about spiders since a child and this garage had lain undisturbed for years, which suggested a whole colony of unpleasantness resided within. Yet spiders were not to be my biggest fear. Unexpectedly and even more unpleasantly, was the unseen silent watcher; the previous owner still in residence. I found myself clearing out what was endless old junk to me but was once someone else's life story and perhaps what they considered priceless heirlooms and I felt that I did all of this under his invisible watchful gaze.

Into the two skips that I had hired for the purpose it all went: old childhood games that gave away summers past, old tools that had given a hard service, old boxes, timber, paint tins and all the usual sort of rubbish that is to be found in most garages. Finally, into the waiting skip went the prior owner's wooden shelving created from old timber and old crates knocked together in a 'Heath Robinson' effect. Clearly a life-long hoarder, all of these things had to be stored somewhere and so the man had installed handmade shelving throughout one half of the garage. The wooden shelves and racks spread like a rash over the walls and worked their way across the garage floor, stretching to the ceiling and engulfing the entire middle section of the generously sized building.

I was grateful to get rid of the old worm-infested wood and dusty junk, and the delight of having the benefit of an electric remote control up-and-over door aided my big clean out. Once done, I gave a thorough sweep, a lick of paint to the garage floor and finally a close inspection of each of the small jars and vintage green & gold tobacco tins, just like the ones my late father used to buy for his pipe smoking habit in the 1970s. These were filled to brimming with all sorts of useful small objects, screws, bolts, nuts and washers of all sizes and types. I stood at the workbench for hours while I studied this glossary of someone's past life and it brought back heady childhood recollections of my own, the scents, sound and tactile feel of the contents stirring memories of my own past.

Whether it was bright and sunny outside or wet and miserable, whenever I toiled in the garage in those first months, I was always jumpy and on edge. It was as if I was expecting to be interrupted at any time by someone stood just over my shoulder. Rather than fading, this sensation grew as time passed as I disturbed the prior owner's tools and belongings. I was fully aware that if the prior owner was still around, earthbound or perhaps curious and visiting from the 5D, he would likely be looking at my trashing of his life's collection with disapproval at best.

Inside some of the small tins and tiny little faded green envelopes were items from the 1930s, souvenirs and medals of merit awarded to the former late owner's father when he must have belonged to one of the many popular cycling clubs at that time. Amongst other small items of interest, too valuable and maybe priceless in a nostalgic way to ever dispose of, were precious little mementos of a life long gone and probably now forgotten by all those living. In one small ancient decaying paper envelope I was surprised to discover two solid-gold wedding rings, one of which was inscribed on the inside of the band. These were the late man's deceased parent's wedding rings. I was deeply touched by this find, although puzzled as to why something so important would be stored out here in the lonely garage, separate from the house and metaphorically separate from the heart of the former owner. Perhaps they weren't separate at all. Perhaps the late former owner had spent much of his retirement stood at this workbench, so much so, that he kept his mementoes and treasures closest to him here.

This was his special private place.

Although I left these items in the garage, I put all these small tokens of memory, including the wedding bands, carefully to one side, hoping to reunite them one day with the widowed former owner of the house. In truth I didn't want these items to come inside the house with me. I knew that if I did so, whatever was watching me, observing me silently from the shadows of the garage, may instead begin to watch me indoors.

The weeks passed and tasks were accomplished around the house as I transformed it into a home my late father would have been proud of, or I like to think so. I still wanted my late father to be proud of me. I don't know that he ever was or ever would be, but I was determined to not disappoint myself, let alone him. Eventually mum and I ended up with a home that I knew was better than any house they had ever lived in. Yet I also knew that had my father been alive, he would have scrapped all the hard work that I had accomplished and would have started over again. Such was the strange relationship that I had with him – or rather, he with me.

Many happy days were spent during these times with my widowed mother and although my income and savings were small, I twice drove her from the UK to Bruges, Belgium for a week's vacation on her October birthday where on both occasions we had such a lovely time together. A time together that could not and would not have happened if my father had been alive. He would never have countenanced such a holiday let alone enjoyed it. When we had holidays as a family in the past, a rare occurrence, he would get bored or anxious by the third or fourth day and intentionally wreck the holiday with one of his rages or mood swings and insist that we, 'Might as well go home early as the holiday was ruined anyway,' and we could, 'Beat the traffic.'

There was to be none of that nonsense with just me and mum. After her husband had passed away, my mother was so much more relaxed and younger in attitude than she had ever been. I took us to destinations in the Cotswolds, Kent and Sussex and although I spent a lot of money that I simply didn't have, I don't regret one single moment. I truly bonded ever more deeply with my mother during this time, and we made up for many lost years spent under the negative influence of my late father. Mum blossomed for a while after dad died and we made the most of it. We both knew that it was the end of the summer of her life, indeed it was more of an Indian Summer, but nonetheless my mother, who was already ill but kept it hidden from me, lived life to the full in those last snatched moments of happiness.

The house was reaching completion and one of the final but most essential things to be done was the installation of the new kitchen. It was this, the usually humdrum fitting of a new kitchen, which caused one of the rare poltergeist occurrences at this house and I was later to discover why. You may recall the incident of the water pouring through the sitting room ceiling of the rental house that I wrote of in a previous chapter. The property mum and I had bought was blessed with an unusually large kitchen, and together we purchased the most expensive kitchen that the store had. Not because we wanted to show off but because this model was the only one we liked and which suited the house.

The kitchen installation went ahead normally as a team of fitters came and installed the kitchen and appliances over four days. A lot of the electrics had to be upgraded which cost more money than foreseen and finally the plumber came on the final day and installed the gas oven and water supply. It was this last thing that stuck out in my mind as being not only odd but downright weird. The attic space was completely empty save for a brand new still-boxed 1960s projector screen and solitary plastic bath panel left by the previous owner.

The plumber and his mate went into the loft space for a period of around half-an-hour, did their work and came down again ready to leave. I can still recall the chief plumber walking towards me down the bungalow corridor with his young plumber's mate following behind. As he approached, the plumber had a big smirk on his face and was looking straight into mine. He said something like, 'All done,' and then as he passed added cryptically, 'Any cash you want to stash up there will be quite safe.'

I hadn't a clue what he was hinting at, but they soon departed and I forgot all about it. The kitchen was installed, and the services connected. Anyone who has had to wait days while their new kitchen is installed will know only too well the feeling of relief when the tradesmen eventually depart and the water supply is restored to your smart new kitchen.

But only some ten minutes after all of the fitters and their boss had left for what I thought was the very last time, I had to call the head kitchen installation manager on his mobile phone. Rusty looking water had formed a large damp patch on the newly painted corridor ceiling and was dripping onto the newly fitted pale carpet – disaster! I was fortunate that I quickly got hold of the kitchen fitters on the telephone and they immediately sent out to the property a different young plumber who, when in the attic, assessed the problem quickly and told me that I needed a new water tank as, 'The old one has split.'

Quite how a heavy-duty plastic water tank can split suddenly after twenty years of constant service was anyone's guess, but I was shown the bottom corner where the split had occurred, arguably on the toughest part, and indeed it was apparent by the wooden base beneath that it had very recently been profusely leaking water. Though curiously, the flow had now completely ceased. Just enough water had escaped the tank to alert me to the leak, and then the leak had stopped as mysteriously as it had begun.

The plumber explained that the tank had been fitted into the loft before the house was completed and that there was no way to get a new tank the same size through the small attic hatch. My heart sank, this sounded expensive, would the roof have to come off? No problem he declared, we could have two smaller tanks fitted together in tandem, which bless him, he did that same day and he cut up the old tank and took it away. It was one of many unexpected expenses to occur in that house and it was also such a curious event that it led me to recall the details in sharp focus for later.

I painted over the stained corridor ceiling one more time and with the kitchen fitted and everything working, the house was now complete. Mum and I had a little perfect haven to live in and enjoy, for a while at least when times were still good.

It was some weeks later that I had cause to go into the attic to look for the bathroom ventilation grille, that I began poking about in the thick glass fibre insulation material that lined the attic floor. Very quickly, something caught my eye which I had not noticed before. I had been in the attic many times and yet I had not ever seen this white plastic carrier bag now poking out, very clearly, from under the old wooden base which supported the new water tank. I crossed over to it and retrieved it, only to find that the bag was very heavy indeed and contained something large, rectangular and metal.

Opening the bag, I discovered a large green/blue metalled painted cash box. From the style and robustness, it dated from some time in the 1960s and it was locked but with no key to be seen. The kitchen fitter's comments about 'stashing my cash' in the attic now made sense. They must have found the box when installing the kitchen plumbing and thought that I had hidden it up there. It was fortunate that they were honest, or the box could have been stolen.

I took the bag and its contents downstairs to the kitchen and showed mum. She wasn't that interested, though exclaimed that if there was anything valuable inside, we should sell it to recover some of the unexpected costs the house had thrown up at us. Since it had been constructed, the house had only ever been lived in by the previous owners, so I knew that the box belonged to them. Intrigued, I ignored the sensation of being watched and spent some time in the garage that evening turning over the multitude of tins and envelopes looking for a key that might fit the cashbox. I knew there to be many old keys stored here from a lifetime of the prior owner's collecting. None fitted. If I wanted to see what was inside the box, I would need to break it open.

This seemed a shame, as the box was well-made and attractive. I considered whether to contact the elderly widow and just give her the still-sealed box as it had clearly belonged to her late husband. The next day I telephoned the warden assisted apartments where the former owner had moved but I was told that as a result of financial cuts by the bank landlord, the tenants were being moved out and the place to be closed. The former owner had already been moved on and shockingly they had no forwarding address or contact details. The poor woman, she had seemed so nice but was very frail and in poor health, and to be uprooted from her new home so soon after moving in seemed wicked.

I spoke with a neighbour, a nice man who always had a good word to say about people. I knew that he had been a good friend to the elderly widow and he told me that he did not have her forwarding address but would see what he could find out. I heard nothing more and in the meantime I decided to force open the box to see if it was even worth contacting the former owner at all. For all I knew, there could just be a bunch of junk rattling about inside.

Getting a large screwdriver to prise open the lock I began to tackle the box on the kitchen countertop. This however proved a harder task than I had imagined, requiring a large amount of effort and not a little swearing. It swiftly became obvious that I would need a greater degree of brute force as the cash box had been well-made and was still fulfilling its design brief and purpose decades after the UK manufacturer had undoubtedly ceased trading. A large hammer and screwdriver were sought and the lock began to give and my conscience too as I was acutely aware that the former owner of the house and of this cash box was undoubtedly close by, perhaps furious at my intrusion into his personal effects. On the other hand, I did seem to have been led in a very curious way to the box's hidden location as though meant to find it.

The lock gave and with a sense of trepidation and excitement I emptied the contents over the counter worktop. Coins - many very large coins. Some in velvet sleeves and others in hard plastic sheaths. Commemorative coins! The deceased former owner of the house had for decades worked in senior management at the bank and had doubtless been given or perhaps purchased these coins as an 'investment.' Fascinated, I looked up the coins online to see the huge worth that must have by now accumulated that encouraged the former owner to hide them under the attic water tank. The most expensive one to buy online was valued at around £5 retail. The entire collection was worth around £30. Nice, but hardly worth the effort and subterfuge of secreting the box in the attic.

There were other minor items of nostalgic value only and together with the garage find of the cycling awards and the wedding bands, I put the cash box away in the bottom of a cupboard in the dining room and promptly forgot about it. Forgot about it until the August of the following year, when 'someone' who had not forgotten, decided to remind me.

It had been a hot and sunny August day which had now turned into a hot and still August night when in the early hours of the morning something woke me from my slumber. I stirred in the small single bed that took up most of the space in my tiny bedroom of the bungalow I'd shared with mum for just over a year. Waking in the inky darkness, I was lying on my side facing the window. Monty my old ever-faithful cat was curled up asleep by my side. Perhaps aware that something was amiss, my eyes flickered open and in that second, I caught a double flash or 'pop' of luminous green light from behind the drawn curtain. It was not quite as bright as torchlight but rather more like someone had lit a match outside. But it was the strange *greyish-green* colour to the two flashes of light that didn't make sense. Panicked that we had intruders, I went from sleeping to wide-awake in a moment and leaping out of bed, I scrambled in the dark for my eyeglasses and for my mobile phone.

Illuminating the phone's powerful torch and dashing to the ground floor window I pulled back the curtains and checked the lawns outside. The gardens surrounded the house, and any intruder would not only be heard making their exit but also would be quickly and easily revealed by torchlight. There was nothing. Quickly, I threw my clothes on and made a thorough search outside. No intruder and no suggestion of what had caused the luminous green flare. No suggestion perhaps, yet intuitively I suspected what had caused it and it was not of the physical world. For those readers familiar with illuminated night-flying insects, where I lived at the time in the United Kingdom we do not get them, and self-combusting swamp gasses do not occur in suburban gardens …. Yes, I really did consider all pragmatic natural options before settling on the only one remaining: the supernatural.

Nonetheless this incident was almost forgotten when a year later and once again in the small hours of the night, I stirred in my sleep. Once again, the room was inky dark and stifling with the August heat. Once again Monty was asleep, my right hand feeling out for him from under the bedclothes. And once again I had awoken for no good reason except that I knew that in addition to my mother and me there was some other presence in the house. It is hard to define or prove '*knew*'.

There is something about the physical presence of a human or animal within the vicinity of our aura, particularly when you are 'safe' at home and familiar with all of the noises that your own home produces, which leaves you able to easily isolate and identify any changes to the norm. I could hear nothing, but something had awoken me to danger. We lived in the countryside and night-time came with a hushed silence. No road noise or other urban background sounds here, only the occasional hoot of an owl or screech of a fox disturbed the night.

I lay in the darkness and listened. We've all done this from time to time. Disturbed by something in the night, we lay still and listen intensely, straining our ears. Tuning in to the remotest sound, our senses amplify. As I listened, I told myself that I was imagining the ever-so-soft sound of the front door opening and closing. So quietly was this done, that it was as though the volume had been turned down low on an audio recording of the front door. I knew that the main door to the house was both locked and bolted with a security chain across. How could any intruder possibly have entered the house via this door as it would have to be forced? With my heart pounding in my ears, I strained to listen further. Was this an intruder inside the house?

With some relief I inwardly welcomed the brief silence that followed. Then, I tuned in to the ever-so-soft sound of footfall in the entrance hall. Had I imagined this too? The fear rose in me again as I now definitely heard the intruder turn and softly begin the approach along the long corridor which led to the bedrooms. Which led to my bedroom. The footsteps on the soft carpeting were almost imperceptible but nonetheless, they were definitely there, and they approached as cautiously as a cat burglar might. But this night-time intruder was not ransacking the house, looking for the family silver or cash, instead it was clear that whoever or *whatever* it was knew exactly where it was headed. *It was headed towards my bedroom.*

Silence again. The intruder was outside my closed bedroom door now. Did I have a weapon to hand to protect myself? No, there was nothing. I started to visualize what I could grab that was easy to hand to defend myself should the intruder suddenly burst his or her way in. The silence was palpable. Was the intruder waiting outside my door, their ear pressed against the wood, listening intently for any sign of breathing or stirring within? I waited for the sound of the door handle to turn in the darkness.

It was then that I sensed that whatever had been outside the door was now *inside the room*. It is difficult to explain a sensation and I can only suggest that we know when there is a human presence in a room with us. Even if that room is in total darkness, it makes no difference. At night and in the silence you can tell how many people are in a room by those tiny almost imperceptible sounds that *living* creatures make. In my bedroom that night there were two of us. I fumbled for the bedside lamp light cord and flicked on the switch. The room, now illuminated harshly in stark contrast to the preceding darkness told me that I was alone.

I checked the house thoroughly, switching on all the lights as I went, more out of fear than out of the need for good vision. There was nothing to be found of course. The house was deserted and quiet except for me and for my sleeping mother in her bedroom, undisturbed by the night-time visitor. I would like to say it ended there but a similar thing happened the following night. It wasn't so pronounced and I think that I was so tired from the previous night's disturbance that I fell asleep again almost instantly. Nothing more happened that year – almost nothing, I shall tell of that later - but I knew that I had experienced a spectral visitation that night and I wondered when it would next repeat itself. The question of *why* it happened did not occur to me.

I had to wait an entire year for the answer. Once again it was August and I wondered if events would conspire to repeat themselves. I didn't have to wait for long that month to find out. It was night and I woke, blearily coming into consciousness in the darkness of my single bedroom. Faithful Monty my cat was as ever, asleep at my side. Then I distinctly heard the front door making a noise as if being opened and closed, not softly or stealthily but normally, only with the volume of the sound turned right down low so as to be almost inaudible. This was pure spirit theatre surely?

Once again, I had been woken *prior* to the noises beginning as though I was meant to experience this haunting to its fullest. I turned up all of my senses to the maximum to listen and feel in the darkness for any sound or motion from the other end of the bungalow. I was not disappointed. I heard a shuffling noise in the entrance hallway and then slowly and steadily, I heard whoever or whatever it was approach my bedroom door along the long slender bungalow corridor.

The sounds were so imperceptible, it was to the point where you doubted whether you were hearing anything at all, but your inner senses were screaming that you did. I knew by now that this was a ghostly visitation. I knew too that it could be my late father – but why would he go to the trouble of scaring me? More likely it was the late husband of the widowed former owner of the house. After all, this house had been newly built for the previous owners on virgin land and no other residence had ever occupied this site.

If this were the ghost of the late husband of the prior owner why the hell was he haunting me? What did he want of me? Why only August? Was this the month of his birthday, or perhaps it was the anniversary of his death? Did it really matter? All that mattered to me in that terrifying moment was that once again he was now stood outside my bedroom door.

Just like the last time this had happened it went quiet. Then, just as before I sensed that silently and stealthily, the spectre had made its entrance into my bedroom without the need to open the bedroom door. He was in my room now. I listened and I stared into the darkness trying to see something, to see *anything*, but the room was inky black. The longest silence followed and then, just as I had told myself that it was over, or perhaps that I had imagined everything, came the unmistakable sound of the wicker chair in the corner of my bedroom. It was the sound of a wicker chair slowly taking the weight of an adult male, creaking and groaning as the occupant settled themselves in.

The chair, which faced me, was in touching distance of the foot of my bed. The spirit was sitting in the chair and watching me in the darkness. Hoping and praying that the show was now over I carried on listening with my eyes now tightly shut and my bedsheet up to my nose. But it was not over. Instead, I clearly heard the sound of a man brushing lint from his trouser leg as he sat there in the chair. My ghost was quite relaxed and intending to give me a bedside vigil.

If I didn't already have my eyes tightly shut I would have shut them anyway, hoping that it would make this nightmare stop. Instead, it continued. In the new silence that followed, I once again began to tell myself that this was imagined and that the chair was creaking due perhaps to damp air, even though it was another warm August evening. It was harder to explain away the sound of trouser brushing and then came an unmistakable noise.

Unmistakable because I made this same sound each day when getting dressed and undressed. To the left of my bed and between me and the chair in which the unseen spirit of the man was now comfortably seated, was my small low chest of drawers. On top sat a dressing mirror and a few personal items including a small blue ceramic bowl in which each day I placed my loose change and cufflinks. On this particular night I had placed my silver necklace which had a small silver cross attached. In the darkness came the unexpected but chilling sound of the chain being moved across the furniture and then a 'chink' noise as the cross was picked up, studied and then dropped back into the bowl again by unseen hands.

I grabbed for the bedside lamp switch. I could stand it no more and I wanted to see the invisible assailant. Of course, there was no-one there. There was nothing or no-one that I could *see*. And there lies the rub with ghosts, the electric light may provide some comfort and relief from the darkness but in reality, as I lay there in bed, I knew that the spirit of the former owner of the property was, likely as not, still sat in the bedside chair, studying me from his position of invisibility.

Nothing further happened that night, or that year, but it was an unnerving and unpleasant realisation that this spirit was not constrained to the detached double garage but had complete free run of the house and garden.

I have mentioned that the previous year something else supernatural had occurred. It was wintertime and I had captured an 'orb' of light on my smartphone camera when filming inside the garage. Invisible to the naked eye, the orb travelled high up around the roof of the garage, chiefly by the electric motor for the up-and-over door. It lasted long enough for me to study the area with the naked eye to ensure that this anomaly was not caused by any flying insects. It was bitterly cold and few flying insects were about anyway.

All the while that I checked with the naked eye and saw nothing, the orb continued to allow itself to be filmed. Or so I thought as it later transpired that either I never pressed the video 'record' button, or that the video had failed to save to memory. I did however manage to take one single photo before it chose to disappear. Over the next few days I puzzled over the orb photograph. In the photo, the orb was hovering right by the motor mechanism of the electric door. Then two weeks later, the usually trusty mechanism failed without warning, the lengthy drive belt breaking in *the very same spot* that the orb had allowed itself to be photographed. A helpful warning?

Some two or three months before that final spectral bedside visitation in the dead of night, I had received a much more pleasant visit from spirit. I'd planted three large rose beds either side of the pathway that led from the rear door of the bungalow to the rear entrance door of the garage. It was a beautiful sunny day in May and early warm weather had resulted in an early bloom of roses. The underplanting of lavender together with the mixed colourful blooms of the Old English Roses gave off a heady scent and the bees were in abundance and birds were singing their springtime songs while my dear old cat Monty revelled in the warm weather by rolling on his back, frolicking in a shaft of sunshine on the pathway.

It was one of those life-affirming days where you just smiled for the pleasure and on an errand I swiftly made my way from the back door of the house to the garage. I was assailed by the scent and the sounds of England in early summer, truly delightful but as ever I was half closed-off to it, doubtless stuck in my thoughts. Suddenly, halfway along the path, energy passed straight through me in the opposite direction. I span on my heels as though someone had literally walked quickly past me on the narrow path. The sensation to be felt was one of total love. Without even thinking I cried out in joy and laughed out loud the single word, 'Joan!'

Joan had been the wife of my late Uncle Gordon, my father's brother. It was at Uncle Gordon's house in Hove, all those years ago in 1977, that I had experienced the haunted toilet door.

Aunt Joan had died in the late 1960s and Uncle Gordon had passed some thirteen years prior to this warm sunny day. I had never met my Aunt Joan, at least in this incarnation, so it was extremely odd that I called out her name. I knew that she had been a lovely, warm, wonderful woman and mother who had returned to the Light too soon, but in that moment I felt as if both Joan and Gordon had passed through me on the path and had just wanted to say, 'Hello.' I am unable to explain it to you more than that.

Whatever or whoever the spirit(s) was that passed me on the pathway that lovely summer morning, they meant me well and no harm at all. I also knew that they had passed into the Light and were *of* the Light. The overwhelming sense of love, peace and comfort that travelled right through me I shall remember for the remainder of my days.

The following year I discovered that the widow who had sold the bungalow to me and mum had sadly passed away. Through the internet I managed to track down and find the email address of one of her three daughters. Recognising that the cash box was at the centre of the haunting of the bungalow, I determined to return it to the deceased's family where it rightfully belonged. The daughter, when told of the box, was delighted and I was so relieved to hear that she was keen to see and collect the contents.

By then I had thrown away the heavily damaged old turquoise box. Anyway, I would have been embarrassed for her to have seen it as a broken-open cash box never looks good! Arriving in her car one afternoon, I welcomed her into the house as she remarked how much had changed. She reminded me very much of her mother and seemed a lovely person. We briefly chatted in the kitchen about her memories of the house and then I showed her the cash box contents now spread across the kitchen countertop.

She was fascinated as we inspected the precious cargo that the cash box had once contained. I felt a bit of an intruder while we both studied the contents, yet it seemed that she had not seen these things before and they were therefore of a surprise to her. Clearly pleased to now be in possession of these precious few mementoes of her family she enquired as to whether I had also 'come across a green box?' She explained that her late father had often told her and her siblings that when he was 'gone' to look for his 'green box' which he'd said contained vast wealth. Without considering this question properly I stupidly said,

'No, I hadn't.' Perhaps I even felt a little accused, as though I had indeed come across a green box and was secreting it for my own avaricious ends. It was only after she had left, taking the contents of the cash box with her, that I realised what to me had been a *blue* cash box, was probably *turquoise* and therefore to most people would be called '*green.*' I could have kicked myself.

The woman's father had considered the contents of this blue/green cash box to be highly valuable and had instructed his daughters to look out for it upon his death. So valuable did he consider the contents to be, that he hid it out of sight under the water tank in the attic. Yet so out of sight was the cash box, that after his death, when the attic was cleared out of all rubbish, it remained hidden, only for my plumber to discover it years later. The spirit of the man had become earthbound, the cash box becoming central to his earthly entrapment.

Unfinished business on the Earth plane is what keeps spirit from moving on to the Light. So determined was he to get me to deal with the cash box on his behalf, that he even split the attic water tank in the very corner where the cash box had been secreted, hoping to get my attention drawn to the box hidden underneath. I figured, correctly as it turned out, that once the cash box contents had been delivered to his daughters as he wanted, the annual haunting would cease. With the deed completed, I hoped that he was able to cross into the Light.

Intriguingly, the daughter I met was a Reiki practitioner. I didn't know anything about Reiki then, but I do now. Had I then known that she believed in universal energy and doubtless also in the 5D spiritual realm, I would have felt able to openly discuss her late father and his spirit which was still present at the house. However, not knowing this, it hardly seemed appropriate and so she went away without ever knowing of the circumstances in which I found the cash box nor of the annual visitations meant to nudge me into dealing with this outstanding issue which kept him earthbound.

Certainly, this was not at all like the haunting at the rented poltergeist house where that spirit was angry and had set out to scare. Even the curious incident of the splitting of the corner of the water tank only allowed enough water to escape to raise attention and did not seem intended to cause damage to the house. I hope that if his daughter is reading this, she does not mind that I failed to discuss her father with her. I would add that there were no more visitations and no more hauntings, the heavy atmosphere in the garage lifting completely. I feel that the act of handing over the precious contents of the 'green' box allowed her late father to feel he could safely return to the Light.

Chapter Fourteen

2009 – 2015 They walk among us

Angels

An angel walks with you every step of every day

Mum was never actually diagnosed with cancer. We just sort of drifted into the realisation of what it was. That's not to say she didn't see her GP (general medical practitioner) about it. Indeed, she saw five different GPs at the same surgery and none of them took mum seriously by undertaking tests or referring her to a specialist. Mum's insistence that she go into the GPs office alone meant that I began to suspect that she wasn't discussing her fears with her doctor. Because of this I wrote a note to her GP, placed it in a personally addressed sealed envelope and asked mum to hand it to the doctor at her next appointment. She agreed.

The doctor not only read my letter but returned it with a handwritten note on the back suggesting that mum should take Vitamin C plus an echinacea supplement. This seemed bizarre but there was also included a prescription for medicine, so all hope was not lost. However, when the prescription had been processed by the pharmacy and I went to collect it I was surprised and not a little disappointed to be given a small bottle of nasal drops for a blocked nose.

Mum and I therefore found ourselves spending her last few

months together in the new home that I had created for us after dad had passed away. It felt like autumn was with us all year 'round and with a hard winter yet to come. I slowly released my grasp on my career, needing to spend more and more time with mum as she grew weaker and weaker and more and more confused and irrational. We lived close to the UK coastline and when not at the seaside one of our favourite places to go together was a Tudor manor house and gardens not far from our home in Dorset. Before the Dissolution, this was originally a monastery although all that remains of that time are the monks' fishponds. The amazing historic house dated to the 1500s but it was to the relaxing gardens – and the English tearoom – that drew our closest attention.

The gardens were lovingly maintained by volunteers and were replete with high stone walls, sweeping lawns, colourful flower borders and ancient Yew trees. They were also often to be found relatively empty of visitors if you chose the right time of day. One particular sunny late spring afternoon we found ourselves slowly walking about the mostly empty grounds having already enjoyed tea and cake in the relaxed tea rooms. I had also enjoyed looking at the plant stall located outside the barn that housed the tea rooms, this being where they sold home-grown plants which fed my burgeoning gardening habit.

We moved on to the garden proper and it was as relaxing as it sounds when I recount to you that we strolled down the long flower border with the other garden visitors and then we slowly made our way over to the small walled alcove garden which was sited under the shade of a large weeping tree and where there was a square formal pond and fountain. Here mum and I found ourselves alone and we enjoyed the cottage garden flowers in full bloom, the sound of splashing water providing the backdrop.

For what happened next, it is important to first understand the layout of this part of the gardens. From the entrance gateway, a narrow gravel path of some twenty metres led to the gardens. On one side of this path the ground sloped sharply down into the main large fishpond. On the other side of the path was a long flower border seated in front of an ancient and very pretty brick wall of around one-and-a-half metres in height.

The wall was covered with exquisite, scented flowering climbing roses and it ran for the length of the pathway until you turned left into the gardens where my mother and I were now stood under the shade of the enormous tree. From our slightly elevated position, anyone of average height could be seen over the top of the wall. Once you are on the path, you hoped not to meet anyone coming in the opposite direction such was the narrowness and the ever-present threat of being perilously close to the edge of the pond.

The whole feel and appearance of the grounds and gardens was one of serene natural beauty and peace. Mum and I particularly liked this little walled formal garden simply because it was a secluded and somehow even more peaceful and calm than the main gardens as a result. It was a sunny and warm day without being too hot, typical of early summer in the UK, the slight threat of rain had passed and the gardens were still cool and lush.

We were both dressed in our usual summer attire, with my ever elegant yet still gently glamourous mother wearing a taupe two-piece linen suit and matching Italian leather shoes.

I noticed that her encroaching illness was now beginning to reflect on her once youthful face. Etched lines of worry or pain were evident on her soft skin. But in this special moment mum's illness was not discussed, instead we were both feeling peaceful and happy, and we smiled as we chatted. Undisturbed by any passing garden visitors, we had spent an enjoyable short time together in this same spot and were just slowly making our way to leave and move on to another part of the grounds. Suddenly, we were stopped by a stranger.

I cannot now explain how we didn't see the man approach as the stranger in question was pretty much on top of us before we noticed him. He must have approached swiftly and silently. There was no-one else around with all other garden visitors having suddenly disappeared and he was seemingly a lone traveller. Looking back now and also at the time, the whole scenario was other-worldly, surreal even. Yet when I explain the events to you here it will sound perfectly normal and every day.

Still standing on the lush lawn in the small walled formal garden, we were now joined by the man who had intentionally approached us. He was only some one metre from me but he did not look at me at all, instead gazing unswervingly at mum. All of his comments were aimed at my mother and not to me. In fact, I think he hardly looked at or spoke to me at all except to tell us where he came from and then when he said his departing words.

The conversation was most unusual, with the only question that he asked the entire time he was with us, some three or four minutes, was whether my mother liked delphiniums. He spoke the whole time, chatting about flowers but it wasn't a conversation in the *true* sense of it. It was as though the words were unimportant but the time that he was spending with us was. And that is why it is so difficult to recall what was actually said. The content of the conversation did not seem as important as the energy and the feeling that something magical was happening here.

Time slowed, it was as though he was with us for some ten minutes, yet in reality it cannot have been longer than three or four. Gentle in appearance and mannerisms, he spoke with a masculine voice but softly, a man, if that is what he was, in command of his emotions. Then there were some words of explanation as to where he had travelled from and then he was gone. As I say, all very unremarkable, except you were not there to experience the *feeling* of the interaction.

Facing my mother, he stood close enough to allow me to study him in detail. However, even immediately afterwards I was unable to describe his facial appearance accurately, except to say that he was about 1.75 metres in height, white skinned with a healthy neat shock of thick white hair and he had a perfect complexion. I say 'perfect' intentionally, because his skin was just that. He was clean shaven and yet there was no stubble or sign of this man having ever shaved. His eyes and skin were clean and bright with no indication of any perspiration, sweat or *ageing*. There were no liver spots, no wrinkles, no fat and no creases in his clothes.

The man had an upright demeanour and was slim but not muscular, and then there were his clothes. His clothes were straight out of a 1980s Marks and Spencer sales catalogue, resplendent in perfect linen and cotton. On top of his head was an as-new panama hat with a coloured band. He wore a white shirt which was buttoned all the way up and a medium to slender striped pastel silk tie neatly tied at the neck, the kind that I hadn't seen since the 1980s. He wore white cotton or linen trousers which were brand new, and this was teamed with a pastel shade lapelled jacket and white shoes, again the likes of which have not really been available since the 1980s. I choose the phrase 'brand new' cautiously because his clothes were just that – brand new. They were utterly perfect, no marks, stains, creases, crumples or any indication of how he got there in such pristine fashion. Even walking in these fabrics would produce evidence of wear, particularly on this warm day, but he demonstrated none.

This was enough to puzzle me, because even the cleanest most scrupulous traveller from only a mile or so distant would have arrived that sunny summer's day a little crumpled or sweaty. Mum looked suitably bemused as the man chatted amiably and softly to her. It felt as if he was introducing himself to her for a purpose. The thought that perhaps he may have been attracted to my mother passed briefly in my mind but no, there was no suggestion of flirting. My mother was nearly eighty and yet this man who stood before us was aged around fifty. Or perhaps he was sixty. Or maybe seventy. His youthful face was of someone in their thirties but his hair was white with age, and then there were his clothes from a different era. I have described this man's demeanour and manner to you so that you can envisage for yourself how he appeared, but I have not yet described to you how his energy felt.

In the time he was with us I was expecting passers-by to enter into view or to approach via the entrance path but there were none. There was a strange hush in the gardens as he spoke. It may sound a cliché, but it was as though time had stopped.

There was a dream-like unnatural feeling to his presence. Then there was the man's energy – total serenity, calmness and compassion, yet powerful.

I have met many lovely and not so lovely people in my life, but I have never met anyone who I could openly state did not have a single bad thought or bad word about them. This man was *without corruption of any kind*. He permeated peace and wellbeing. We could both feel it in the air as we stood there and chatted. I knew immediately that this moment was important and yet I did not know why, and I still do not. Perhaps it is enough that it happened.

The strangest thing of all was the warm glow that seemed to emit from this stranger. This is hardest of all to explain. The man's attitude put him from a different place entirely, his clothes suggested a different time, and yet he also gave off a soft warm glow all over that I can only describe as his positive aura and energy being so powerful that it was almost perceptible to the eye. Anyone who has ever used filters for photographs on social media platforms will understand what I mean by this 'soft warm glow.' A natural observer of people, I was taking all this in while he spoke to mum and then just as suddenly, he was gone. He had told us that he had, 'Travelled here this morning from St Albans,' which I found most unlikely because as I have already mentioned, his clothes were perfect and oddly he didn't tell us with whom he had travelled, seemingly being alone.

His parting was just as strange as his sudden appearance. Mum and I had been early into the gardens that day. We always liked to be the first ones in so that we could enjoy the gardens before a crowd arrived. Yet this man, rather than stay and look around the gardens which hadn't long opened and to which he had purportedly travelled right across the UK to see, instead made his way to the low wall and onwards past the pond to the exit. While I can barely recall anything else that this enigmatic man uttered that afternoon, the St. Albans comment stuck with me as the name of this UK city had been yet another one of my 'words' from my subconscious and I have wondered ever since if it is of some special significance.

Mum and I looked at each other and breathed out, suddenly both realising that we had been silent and tense in a strange, serene kind of way. It was as though we had both just experienced something profound and beautiful intentionally presenting itself as the everyday. Despite events to the contrary, mum remained a non-believer in the supernatural, in the spirit world or in angels. Yet still oddly in awe of what had just occurred, she immediately said that she thought there was something very 'other-worldly' about this man.

I glanced to my left and clearly saw the departing man's immaculate panama hat slowly bobbing along just above the low wall height as he made his noiseless exit. Something in me made me want to chase after the man. I had no idea what I was going to say if I stopped him to chat, but I quickly said to mum, 'Wait here!' and I dashed the short five metres distance to the wall to set off in pursuit.

Between me seeing his panama hat over the top of the wall and setting chase took two or three seconds. The man on the other hand had to traverse some twenty metres of pathway with no exit point except other than the entrance gate at the far end. I turned the corner of the wall expecting to be almost on top of the man. The pathway was deserted. There was no-one. I didn't want to leave mum alone for long as she was quite ill by this time, but I dashed off anyway to the entrance gateway to look. From there you could see the pathway all the way to the tearoom and car park beyond and yet, aside from some old ladies exiting the tearoom and now enjoying the sunshine, there was no-one. The man had vanished.

I checked the tearoom. He was not there. There was no way that he could have reached the exit so quickly without having broken into a sprint. His slow deliberate walk and the rhythmic bobbing of his panama hat over the garden wall told me that he was in no hurry to leave. And yet he had vanished. To his right had been the garden wall and to his left was the pond, so where had this man vanished to?

I write this now many years after the event and I still recall the details precisely, except for the man's youthful face. I discussed it on a number of occasions at the time with my equally bemused mother and we came to no conclusion other than something supernatural occurred that sunny day in that beautiful garden. I feel privileged to have been permitted to have been there that day. The man's avoidance of my gaze suggested to me that he was *intentionally* avoiding me as I was not a party to this seemingly important conversation with my mother who was now in her last few months of life. I felt that he had been sent to check in on my mother and speak with her so that she was prepared for when she saw him again one day, perhaps when in her passing from this dimension to the next.

Our destiny is long since plotted out for us before we are even born, and it was my destiny to have the experiences that I have had in my life and subsequently write them down amongst these pages. By my presence being permitted at this meeting between this messenger and my mother, it has allowed me to report to you the events as I saw them and that I now present to you here. Was this a messenger sent to assuage mum's fears of dying? Who was this messenger? His energy was one of peaceful and compassionate love and serenity, and while I leave you to draw your own conclusions, I believe that we received a visitation from an ascended being – or 'angel' if you prefer - that day in a sunny walled ancient monastery garden.

Chapter Fifteen

Astrology

Clockwork of the Gods

*Some people are a cake, others are a sandwich.
Which are you?*

'Astrology? That's for idiots, isn't it?' We've all heard it or perhaps said something similar. To those of us who grew up with the daily horoscopes in the national press wedged somewhere between the 'funnies' and the crossword, we became used to the common notion that astrology was a 'bit of fun' and not to be taken seriously. That was to do astrology a gross disservice and also humankind. Astrology has behind it many centuries of learned study and it endures because of its accuracy and usefulness. On my own journey I have discovered that astrology not only guides us as to world events but also as to our own purpose for being here, our destiny and our karma.

I do not profess to be a professional astrologer but of course I do have a keen interest in my own life and what my purpose is while I am here. I am guessing that you do too. I discovered that astrology will truly assist with that and I want to share this exciting truth with you. Earlier in this book we discussed that the 3D physical universe is entirely made of energy and that we are a part of that energy flow. We are, if you like, a part of an intergalactic organic supercomputer. Anyone who has ever read Douglas Adams' 'The Hitchhikers Guide To The Galaxy' will know that he was a man way ahead of his time, predicting via his comedic science fiction vision many things that we have seen come to pass. His comic suggestion that the Earth is little more than an organic supercomputer designed by well-meaning aliens to ascertain the 'meaning of life' was perhaps not straying far from the truth.

Often in fiction and film many predictions seem to come true and unsurprisingly conspiracy theories abound. The current day conspiracy question is whether we are living in a dystopian matrix similar to the film. The truth is that the physical plane that we inhabit is a low vibration recreation of the dimension that we, as energetic beings of light, originate from. All dimensions exist within the quantum field and everything that ever was and that ever will be co-exists simultaneously. This is why psychics are able to predict the future and divining and astrology are just a small part of that. We all possess the ability to tap into this energy field with creatives, and thereby filmmakers, having an especially powerful talent for this.

Sceptics will often claim that because the planets are so far apart, there can be no *known* energy or force that could possibly have any effect on us on a human scale. After many years of study there is no direct causal link between smoking and lung cancer and yet we know that smoking massively increases your chances of cancer of the respiratory system simply by the numbers of people affected. Through desperation rather than any belief I started to look into astrology in greater detail in 2016 when I was forced to sell my house and discovered that the planetary movements were having a direct influence on my plans.

A specific example was when Mercury, planet of communication and travel was 'moving retrograde' through my chart at the time that I was selling the house I had shared with my mother. A document filed by my solicitor at HM Land Registry had gone missing. In astrology, documentation and contracts are specifically covered by the planet of communication, Mercury. I had started to recognise a distinct direct correlation between the planetary movements and the events unfolding in my life.

Noticing that Mercury was retrograde, it came as little surprise that these important papers had gone missing en-route. When my estate agent called me to ask what the delay was and when would it be resolved I visited him in his office in town to speak directly. I had checked when Mercury would cease to be retrograde and noted that it would be by the Thursday of that same week. Explaining to my agent 'I knew' that all would be resolved by Friday, I received a quizzical look and further explanation was clearly required. Embarrassed, I advised that the reason for my certainty over date was because, 'That was when Mercury, planet of communication, would begin its forward transit.'

I suppose that I was a little surprised when the agent accepted this piece of information without batting an eyelid. Perhaps he had heard many strange stories and explanations in his time and this was equally as valid as any other. The knowledge of the Mercury Retrograde allowed me a degree of serenity and so I remained calm about the missing documentation when all others involved were understandably getting irate. The afternoon of the next day I received a very apologetic telephone call from my solicitor. They had discovered the documentation, unposted, 'stuck down the back of the filing cabinet' and had sent it off to HM Land Registry that day in an expedited manner.

With Friday dawning, I received a telephone call from the estate agent to tell me, with some amazement, that the documentation had been received and processed by HM Land Registry and that all was well. I suppose that I was surprised that the agent was surprised. After all, *I had told him* the likely timescale!

I was to discover that this was to be one of many occasions where through astrology or psychic means I have either known or anticipated energies and events occurring only for that information to fall on the deaf ears of others. The life of a 'Cassandra' can be a lonely one for many and a weather forecast never checked is of no use to anyone. And that is how we should think of astrology; an astrological weather forecast. Just as we might check the weather forecast to predict what the weather will be doing tomorrow and dress accordingly, we can check our own personal astrological 'weather' and prepare for what astrological energies are headed our way.

In this way astrology does not predict the future, it serves to tell you what the energetic weather will be like, and this astrological information is invaluable when making plans. It was long ago discovered that the movement of the planets activate different energy areas, or 'houses', in our personal astrological chart. We all have a personal birth (natal) chart, and every chart is unique to our date, place and time of birth. To try to imagine this chart in the physical 3D world, picture the face of a clock, divided up into twelve segments, with each segment representing a planetary 'house' rather than hours.

With the Earth and Moon spinning at the centre, now

picture not two, but seven hands on the clock face, each hand representing a planet in our Solar System, and all moving in the same direction but at differing speeds. Add the Sun into the mix and we could see in an instant which planets are in which sector of our astrological chart and be able to predict the planetary energies headed our way. Astrologers will perhaps wince at my over-simplification, but I hope that they will appreciate this easy-to-visualise metaphor.

I should briefly explain that a 'retrograde' does not mean that a planet is physically travelling backwards in the sky! All our planets move in the same direction around the Sun, but each taking their own time to complete one circuit. As one planet 'overtakes' another, the 'slower' planet appears to be 'retrograde' or moving backwards in the sky. We've all been in a moving car where the differing speeds of overtaking cars around us gives the false impression of moving backwards.

However, I shall leave the specific teachings of astrology to the experts. It takes many years to learn astrology and there are many books and online facilities out there if the reader wishes to learn more, which I recommend they do. At the very least I would solidly recommend that you get your birth chart ('natal chart') drawn up for you. To do this you will need to know your birth date, the town and country of birth and very importantly, your precise time of birth. The time is relevant as the constant planetary movements mean that in just a few minutes, the heavens will have shifted and planets moved into different 'houses.'

If, like me, you only know your approximate time of birth as say '1700hrs' then that will have to suffice. There are many able and willing astrologers out there who are more than happy to help you with your personal astrological natal chart. I drew my own up from scratch and worked out what it all meant. I was soon to find that there are now websites out there where you only need to input your place, time and date and it will produce a highly accurate birth chart for you free of charge. Once you have your birth chart you will know where all of the planets in our Solar System were positioned at the precise moment that you were born in relation to the planet Earth.

I cannot stress enough how important it is to obtain your personal birth chart. It provides your life plan, your karma and your destiny, and wouldn't we all like to know that!? It will tell you what you are proficient at and what you need to look out for. It will suggest to you to which career you would be best suited, and it will tell you where you have room for personal growth and improvement. So do not delay, get your astrological natal chart as soon as possible and then begin the journey of self-discovery through its interpretation.

Most of you reading this will be aware of what your astrological sun sign is. I am a sun sign Pisces for example. Pisces people are known to have 'one foot in this world and one foot in the next', connecting this 3D physical world with the esoteric and as such are usually interested in or proficient at all things psychic. The sun sign that we are born under only gives us a portion of the full picture. Are you, for example, aware of your rising sign, sometimes called the 'ascendant'? Your personal birth chart will reveal to you your rising sign.

Many astrologers will tell you that your rising sign is as important, or more important than your sun sign and yet most of us don't know it. I didn't know mine until a couple of years ago, simply because in my ignorance I didn't think it important. I wasn't to know that it is crucial and it is the essential missing element when reading and trying to understand our personal astrology. Once I discovered that my rising sign was Virgo, my life journey immediately started to make sense.

In addition to your sun sign and rising sign, there is your Moon sign which is also of major significance to your personal chart and thereby to your life plan. I think of your rising sign as the computer 'hardware' and the sun sign as the 'software.' This is because your rising sign characteristics are fixed for life and your sun sign characteristics are malleable and are the state of consciousness that you operate under, just like a computer program. Your Moon sign will show you your emotional make up. You may not think that this is the most important characteristic, but rather than a physical journey, you should think of life as an emotional one with a strong love in your heart and spirit as the ultimate goal.

When other people are with you or think of you, they see you as your rising sign characteristics. You may not see yourself like this at all, recognising only your sun sign characteristics. You are after all, not the computer hardware but the software that is operating it. When you are affected by emotions, positive or negative, other people will see you demonstrate the emotional aspects of your Moon sign.

We discussed that your birth chart will reveal the locations of the planets in the relative houses at the precise moment that you were born. The twelve 'houses' represent different sectors of your life, career, love, money and so on. So you will see why it is so crucial to take a long look at your own birth chart if you are to understand what occurs to you in your life and why, and how to best tackle it. You may find that some planets are in houses of your birth chart that is favourable to you and your life prospects.

You may find that others are in less fortunate placements or working in conjunction with other planets in the same sector. With the heavens around us ever moving and activating different sectors of our astrological birth chart, it becomes crucial to understand how our own chart is being affected on a day-to-day basis by these planetary movements. Every person on this planet will have an astrological chart that is unique to them, creating a unique human being having a unique life experience.

My own personal birth chart reflects exactly my personality traits, skills, emotional make up and destiny. I am all things 'Pisces'; spiritual, compassionate and emotional. Yet how was I to explain my work ethic, my preference for planning & order and my need to care for others? This attention to detail and humanitarian nursing instinct comes from the Virgo Rising aspect of my chart. Looking further into the fine detail of my own personal natal chart explains precisely how I think and feel, my values, my physical health and why I act the way that I do.

It is often said that the most difficult astrological birth chart is to be a sun sign Pisces with a Virgo ascendant, these being two sharply aspected opposite poles. The other placement considered to be unfortunate is to have your Moon in Scorpio. Well, I expect that you can guess where my Moon is placed. However, I always remember that I chose my astrological make-up as sure as I chose my parents in order to give me the necessary tools and training for the life and destiny that was to follow.

I only wish that I had looked at my birth chart many years ago, perhaps even when at school age. This would have given me the 'heads-up' on what to look out for in life and where to concentrate my attention. The child's astrological natal chart should be calculated as early on in life as possible by any enthusiastic loving parent. This astrological 'blueprint' will assist the parent in understanding what makes their child 'tick' and what the child will be interested in and proficient at. Crucially it will also help with your child's emotional development and how to guide that child into their adult life.

The birth chart should also be a critical part of any schooling in order to identify the child's strengths and work with them and identify any weak spots where the child's personal or emotional development requires encouragement or assistance. A mistake often made in parenting is to try to model your children as your ego would like them to be. This was the fundamental error that my own parents made with me. I was always told what I was and what I wasn't rather than being given freedom to be myself. With your child's natal birth chart, you will see in advance the direction of travel that your child will take in life and be able to actively engage with this and encourage them in the first steps of their life story.

A question arises of whether prior to incarnating in the 3D do we carefully select our birth chart in order to predetermine our personality at birth and set us up for the lessons that we wish to learn in our life? Or are we mere accidental bystanders when our birth chart is crystallised at the time of our birth and the life that follows is a random lottery? We have many lifetimes of experiences that shape our soul and we do not need to repeat the well-learnt and understood lessons that previous lives have taught us. So the former explanation of choosing our destiny in each lifetime rings true.

Our birth chart provides for us what I call our 'toolkit for life' (TFL). Our TFL, or personal birth chart, contains everything that we need to know about ourselves, our destiny and our skills to navigate our way through our life ahead. We are the physical living embodiment of that astrological birth chart blueprint. Every physical manifestation in the universe is of and from the same energy that is the Source, so why would we think that we are separate from the very same energy that our planets are manifested from. The universe shapes us. Once you think of your astrology as your toolkit for life you can begin to go with the flow of what works for you personally in life, stop fighting against what doesn't work and will never work for you, and look at those areas of your personality that may require some introspection, personal growth and self-improvement.

Your 'TFL' will also guide you to the kind of partner you should have in your life, or indeed whether you need one at all, it will also guide you as to your career to which you would be most suited and thereby most happy in. It will help you assess those areas of your personality that require monitoring, for example, sun sign Pisces can be highly sensitive to the energies of others and to those of the collective, so a coping mechanism may be to seek unhealthy addictions of all types with which to numb the physical reality. Once you are familiar with your astrological weak points you can be vigilant against any negative thinking or self-defeating actions. If you think of the birth chart, with planets in different astrological houses representing ingredients in a recipe, one person's astrological birth chart may result in a lemon drizzle cake and another's astrological ingredients may result in a walnut loaf. You get the point.

So, while we are all part of the human collective, we must

recognise that some of us are cakes and others are a sandwich. Life was designed that way. Does a cake take an unnatural dislike to a biscuit because its ingredients are different? That would be absurd, and so we should not judge or dislike people who are different to us. Our astrological make up results in all of us having a unique different human experience. If we were all having the same experience, what would be the point of being here?

If you are a loving and emotional sort who cares deeply for people and about the injustices of the world we live in, do not get upset the next time you encounter someone who you perceive to be insensitive or hard. It may just be their own particular astrological recipe that makes them that way. We are all on our own personal journey, we are all equally valid and we are all here for a purpose. This is why it is not our place to judge.

Our loves, hates, likes and dislikes create who we are every second of every day. It requires careful and skilful navigation to not let this negatively impact on anyone else or expect others to understand you completely. Chances are no matter how close someone is to you, they will never understand you fully because you are a truly unique personality with unique emotional needs that were gifted to you by the universe in your toolkit for life the moment that you were born.

Perhaps you are money and career-oriented and think that the world is a cold hard place, if so, do not get affronted by people who are kind and caring or who do not take life too seriously. We are on our own personal journey that we chose for ourselves before we were even born. And if you love cake but hate sandwiches, nobody is forcing you to eat one.

Still not convinced by astrology? You believe that the universe is nothing more than a freak accident of nature and that everything that occurs is entirely down to happenstance? Well, perhaps but here is a thought for you to ponder. Moon phases and eclipses are a crucial element of Earth astrology. The Moon is 400 times smaller than the Sun, but it is also 400 times closer to the Earth than the Sun. That is why we have eclipses of the Sun and Moon here on Earth. If this were not the maths involved we would not get total eclipses which are a crucial aspect of astrology and life on this planet. As a result of this unique planetary geometry, the Earth is the only known planet to have eclipses of its moon and its sun.

The placing and orbits of this and the planets in our galaxy are not random but geometric and mathematically precise. Our universe is an organic clockwork energy supercomputer. It is clockwork of the gods.

Chapter Sixteen

2015-2016 Alone

Energy shift

These two dedicated, hard-working and caring compassionate women changed my life that night. If ever you think that the world is a dark and uncaring place, always remember that there are people out there who every day make a difference.

Mum died from cancer at home in the December of 2015. I have previously written about the final moments leading up to both my mother's and my father's death and the angelic music and clearly audible spirit voices that were heard, so I shall not repeat them here. What I will mention, not because it has anything to do with the supernatural but because it is entirely to do with love and compassion, is the wonderful care that a district nurse gave to me in the time immediately after the death of my mother.

Mum died in the evening. It is often said, and many nurses will know of this, that our loved ones pass on only when we have left the room and they are alone. After a long illness our spirit is said to know the precise moment to pass and in order to relieve the stress placed on those keeping a long vigil at the bedside, we wait until we are alone, our loved ones perhaps having popped out of the room for a break. So it was that I sat at home in quiet vigil at my mother's bedside, very aware that these were her final minutes on the Earth plane. I wanted to be with my mother until the last. Her love for me never wavered in life and I would be there for her in those final unconscious moments. Those of you who have undertaken this impossibly difficult but life affirming task will know how painful it is. The time reached half past seven in the evening and I had been chatting to mum for some hours as she lay there unconscious and unresponsive.

She had been unable to eat or drink for some days and had slipped into unconsciousness two days prior. Her face was drawn, and her body wracked from the cancer that had ravaged her body and will. Her lips were parched from dehydration, unable as she was to accept water in those last few hours. I barely recognised the once beautiful, vibrant and glamourous woman who was now dying in front of me.

Speaking softly to mum, I explained that 'I was just going to get a cup of tea' from the kitchen. I got up and did so, walking down the very same corridor that the spirit of the former owner had undertaken his August visitations. At this time in my life, I seemed to be forever surrounded by death. Being the youngest son of the youngest son, it meant that almost all my family had died by the time I began my thirties. I was now in my forties and my much-loved mother was to be the last.

Calmly and quietly, I entered the kitchen, filled the electric kettle and waited, my brain on autopilot as I stared at the wall. Less than five minutes later I was back at my mother's bedside, hot cup of tea in hand. She was gone. There is no mistaking death when you see it. Even the most ravaged body has a degree of life, but when we die and our spirit departs, our body becomes an unanimated empty vessel, little more than a spent chrysalis that a pupated butterfly leaves behind on its higher journey.

It was the loneliest time, waiting for the doctor. It was a Saturday night and as anyone in the UK knows, you are not going to get hold of a doctor late on a Saturday due to this being their busiest period. I sat by the phone in the kitchen for not one, not two but over three hours waiting for a call from a doctor. In the UK, where a death occurs at home, the visit of a doctor is needed to certify the death before the funeral director may come and begin their task. I sat in the kitchen in silence by the phone.

Wintertime and dark outside, the harsh electric lights were blaring, and the room seemed clinical and the house empty. Monty my wise and knowing cat, sat some little distance apart from me, conducting his own silent vigil. The minutes ticked by. Then the hours. Frustrated, I made two or three further phone calls as no-one called me back. No words of support. No words of kindness or warmth. Just me in my solitude. I was alone now more than ever.

Eventually, at around ten o'clock, the telephone rang. It was the female driver to a senior female nurse from the hospital in the local town, a few miles distant.

'No,' she explained, 'There were no doctors available,' and my doctor on duty was at a 'black-tie dinner.' I thought caustically that it was good to know that he was being paid for being unable to attend emergencies.

Fortunately, as Senior Nurse, she explained that in these circumstances, she was permitted to sign the death certificate and release the body to the undertakers. It all sounded so mundane, like arranging the removal of your furniture. An hour and a half later at around eleven thirty pm, and some four hours after death and being alone in the house with the body of my mother, the driver and the Senior Nurse arrived. They were a breath of fresh air.

I have never thanked these two women properly. It was all over and done with so swiftly. They were kindness personified. Dignified, kind, compassionate and loving it was as if two of my own jolly aunts had arrived to help out. I am almost crying as I write this, so moving was the experience. They apologised for the long wait and understood completely how difficult it all must have been, especially to have been left alone in those final hours. I hadn't been out of the house for three months. I had been left alone to care for my mother at home, this I saw as a duty and an honour, but it was hard being shut-in for that period of time, though it got me prepared for the 2020 lockdown that was yet to come. Suddenly having two animated and caring people in the house illuminated it with love and it was transformed by their light.

I sat and waited nervously in the kitchen with Monty the cat.

The Senior Nurse returned from mum's bedroom and asked kindly, 'Would you like us to prepare your mother before the funeral director arrives?' then added, 'I think it would be nice for your mother if we wash her down and dress her nicely in clean bed clothes?'

I smiled at this immense kindness and duty of care, readily and gratefully accepting. I noted that she also recognised the need to talk about mum in the present tense, as if she were still with us, which of course, she was and still is.

These two dedicated, hard-working and caring compassionate women changed my life that night. That evening could have gone down in my memory as the worst night of my life. Instead, their thoughtful, kind and compassionate words, thoughts and actions made an indelible mark on my heart. If ever you think that the world is a dark and uncaring place, always remember that there *are* people out there who every day make a difference. I vowed then to become one of those people. I hope that when you read this book and these words that you take the same pledge to make things better. What stops humanity from a painful descent into the darkness is our ability to light the way for others with our own inner light of love that exists within all of us.

I sit and write this and I wonder 'where do I take this chapter next?' Out of dignity it feels that this should be a short chapter, bringing the life story of my mother to a close and beginning again on a fresh page. Only life isn't like that. Even as one chapter of our life or a karmic cycle comes to a close, another one has already begun or has yet to start. I had no time to mull over mum's illness and death. As is often the way, the funeral came and went quickly, the numbing drudgery of organising the closure of financial matters and the notification of the authorities was accomplished. These were the days of sitting alone in waiting rooms, waiting. Things happened, people were told, and life, as they say, went on.

Only it didn't for me. I had been made redundant four months prior, so I had no career to go back to. Christmas was only a week or so away. I had a big house and garden to rattle around in on my own and all of the bills to pay with no income. My mother had left a legacy in her will to someone other than me which I couldn't afford to pay. Mum's money was tied up in the house we'd bought together and that I had so lovingly turned into a home for us after father's death.

Mum had asked me several times to get a solicitor to come see her to change her will. She was very worried that I would be left with insufficient monies and made it very clear to me that she didn't want her money to go to anyone but me, and in the years since she had made out her will, she had changed her mind. But stupidly, in loyalty to the other beneficiary, I refused. I felt it wrong to make legal arrangements on behalf of my mother for my own financial benefit. Mum was too ill to travel to a solicitor and without me arranging for one to come to the house, I knew it wasn't going to happen. Thus, in order to pay out the legacy I had to liquidate assets. I had to sell my home.

With no job and the wrong side of forty, I had little prospect of quickly raising a mortgage to pay off the legacy. I loved my house, the home that I had created for mum. Yes, it had bad memories associated with it due to mum's illness, but I 'knew' that I could never afford to get a house like this again. Had there been an element of gilded cage to the house? Perhaps, and I was young so why should I constrain myself to living in a large bungalow. Should I perhaps move to the city? Should I travel the world? Perhaps I should take-in lodgers? There were so many options, or at least I thought there were, but my higher soul and spirit had a plan for me which has led me to be writing this for you now.

I grasped my sudden freedom with fervour and went on an exercise and diet regimen. The natural urge to find a mate kicked in and with the little savings I had left I bought a large home gym and worked-out daily in the formerly haunted garage. After three months I had lost three stone in weight and felt better and healthier than I had in years. The change was noticed by others. I am not sure if I became bipolar during this period, can you become bipolar for only a few short weeks? I had none of the 'downs' and only the highs. My energy transformation went 'through the roof' as I was filled with high energy. I knew that I looked good and despite all the circumstances my positivity returned, although my confidence was low just like always.

The energy surging through me was electric. I didn't know it then, but my aura was blasting psychic white light in all directions. My crown chakra was open wide, and friends and strangers alike were responding positively to me, even drawn to me. Drawn on the physical plane and, like a moth in the darkness is drawn to a candle flame, also on the spiritual plane. I was fully aware of the former, but the latter was yet to manifest.

It had never happened to me before and it has never happened to me since, but everywhere I went I got 'looks' and I mesmerised people and drew them in towards my aura. It was a truly bizarre time. I was always a quiet type, never the centre of attention and yet here I was, in shops, bars, restaurants and even on the street with people approaching me, smiling, and chatting or flirting – men and women. Even straight men would respond in a flirtatious manner to whatever energy it was that I was emitting.

While this must sound like an exaggeration, it truly isn't. On one occasion I was sitting in a café with friends. They had their small dog with them and the most amazingly handsome and muscular young man in a rugby player's kit entered the café saw me and made a beeline for our table, making eye contact with me the whole time, a large smile on his face. He was some twenty years my junior, we had never met before and yet he came over to speak to me. This kind of thing had never happened to me before. I was embarrassed but of course secretly delighted. My friends however, not used to me ever getting any attention, thought that the man wanted to chat about their new dog and inadvertently took over the conversation.

Another occasion I saw friends in the high street while driving in my convertible classic car. I did a quick safe U-turn in the road and parked my car right outside the café in which we had arranged to meet. It was a very busy high street and parking spaces almost never seemed to become available for me before now. It was a confusing but delightful realisation that I could now manifest simple things like parking spaces just through self-belief and positivity, a 'lucky streak' you might call it.

I leapt out of my convertible and waved to my friends as I dashed across the road to greet them, only then dismayed to realise that they were stood chatting to a policeman, the topic of conversation clearly about me. My heart fell as I realised I was about to be booked for an illegal U-turn in a busy high street. So much for my lucky streak I thought. Instead, as I approached, I saw the policeman say something animatedly to my friends.

Later they told me he'd said, 'Look at that guy, he has something amazing about him – I wonder who he is going to meet?'

To which my friends replied sheepishly, 'He's meeting us!'

The clearly heterosexual policeman was funny and delightful and rather than feel threatened by my sexuality, he was unabashedly flirtatious. It was another strange though life-affirming moment. I seemed to be emitting an energy of self-empowerment that appealed to either sex. Disarming but attractive, a psychic aura of high energy and love is something that people immediately respond to. Café waiting staff gave me freebies. Strangers approached, regularly commenting on the scent of my aftershave. Shop staff volunteered to assist me without being asked. Men and women of all ages flirted.

Suddenly people felt safe, secure and 'at home' with me, happy to stop, chat and laugh. Wherever I went over the next few days and weeks I increased the 'volume' of my energy, turning it up notch by notch. Recognising that something had changed for me, this was an experiment of sorts. Finally, one sunny afternoon I turned it up to maximum as I entered an estate agency when looking for a smaller, cheaper new house to buy to suit my financially reduced circumstances. I sat down at the reception desk manned by a young heterosexual man in an ill-fitting but smart suit. He had looked glum and awkward as I'd entered. I almost didn't go in.

Three other staff were in the agency, all female of different ages, seated at their respective desks. The glum young guy asked if he could help me and within seconds was responding to my outpouring of energy in an astonishingly reactive and positive way. The energy seemed to fill the small office and suddenly we were chatting and joking like we were lifelong drinking buddies.

Two of the women (all of them had glanced up suspiciously at me as I had entered the agency) had now left their work and their respective desks and were approaching. One woman stood behind the man, the other perched on the corner of an adjacent desk, the third not having to leave her desk as she already sat close by. I realised that all these people were now within three metres of me and all four of them were laughing, flirting and happily chatting with me about nothing in particular.

This simply wasn't me. I was the shy, reserved one at school who got ignored. I was the bashful guy who never spoke up, made a fuss in public, or got a boyfriend. Yet here I was with four adults, all seemingly unconsciously attracted to something I was projecting. I felt bad. I felt as if I was deceiving and abusing a power that I didn't yet understand. I was drawing people towards me and getting them to be nice. It seemed totally wrong and yet they were all happy, elated even. How long could this last?

So, what was going on? The astrology for this period indicated that I had Venus, planet of love and attraction, positively placed in my astrological chart and doubtless that added to my curious newly found energy 'allure.' Yet from the moment I decided that I was 'cheating' in some way and artificially attracting people favourably towards me, the energy started to dwindle. Within another week or so it was all over. This excess of high energy had abated, and people no longer looked up from their desks in shops, strangers no longer stopped in the high street to chat with me and people no longer gave me flirtatious looks or comments. The energy was fading fast and with it any attraction that I thought I had.

Had I borrowed this energy from somewhere, or was it mine to own? I concluded that I loved my late mother so much and that I put so much love and care into her wellbeing over many months and years, that when she passed away my loving energy could not just be switched off like you would an electric lamp. Instead, with nowhere to go, powerful energy of unconditional love, compassion and kindness broadcast outwards from me. Energy cannot be destroyed only transmuted into something else and I believe that my positive energy made others who came within my aura, happy. It was as simple as that. For a few short weeks I had the ability to raise other people's energy vibration. I realised that if I could do it then I could do it any time, and so can you.

It therefore follows that negative energy can also be passed on from one person to another. It is this easy transference of negative energy, especially via the creation and dissemination of fear that is the greatest threat to mankind on Earth. Only the more starkly obvious physical havoc wreaked by global warming is an equal or greater danger. You and I have a responsibility to stop the fear, stop the hate and stop the spread of negative thought and energy. The choice is ours whether we become part of the solution or part of the problem. Together we can raise the energy vibration of the planet.

Chapter Seventeen

Regency charm

The house by the churchyard

Was it just my imagination or did the area feel 'strange'?
The stone walls, the little lanes, the ancient church.
And just why was it that the family who lived there,
*didn't seem to actually **live** there?*

I looked at a few properties available to purchase in that summer of 2016. I needed a new home and yet there weren't that many houses on the market at the time and those that were didn't suit my needs or they seemed overpriced. These are the usual property buying pitfalls of course. Then there was the question of where to buy and what did I want from it? My brother advised that I should buy in the city as a single man with a sudden headwind of freedom. My heart and spirit said buy in the rural countryside. My ego centred compromising brain said buy in a village or small town.

In the end I chose what my soul needed, a home in the countryside. I found a delightful, picturesque cottage set down a pretty lane and it was safe enough for my dear old cat Monty. He loved the outdoors and would spend much of his day lounging in the garden. I loved him so much that I was buying the house as much for him as for me. It was a little more than I could afford but I hoped that they would take an offer. However, although perfect for me and Monty, it wasn't to be. At the last moment while my own house sale was still going through, the vendors suddenly reduced the asking price and it sold immediately to a rival bidder. I restarted my trawl for a new home but with even fewer fish than ever to catch in my net.

I settled on either a bungalow in the countryside that I had been given the particulars for, or a choice of two cottages which were in a far flung small historic town which I had largely disregarded due to the distance from any facilities. I'd previously arranged viewings for a couple of sensible but very over-priced small bungalows in a favourite nearby seaside town. These proved to be hemmed-in, being claustrophobic and surrounded by urban development. Having disregarded these, I set off one dank, dark and muddy summer's day to view the bungalow in the rural countryside. The estate agent's particulars stated that the bungalow was 'set in a cul-de-sac' overlooking 'glorious countryside' and only 'two miles from the nearby county town.' Not for the first time was someone to discover that estate agent property details could sometimes be misleading.

The country road became narrower and narrower and then muddier and muddier as a multiplicity of farm vehicles had churned up fields and deposited gallons of mud and cow muck over the ever-shrinking lane. Narrow bend after narrow bend followed and two miles slowly turned into four as I pressed onwards. I was now resolutely stuck behind a large tanker full of cattle slurry. Progress was minimal and it sprayed thick mud and cow dung over the road and over the hedgerows and over my car windscreen. We paused only while the tanker up ahead came face-to-face with a bus headed in our direction.

On this narrow lane this required reversing for some distance before the two over-sized vehicles could pass each other. By now I had been on the road for fifty minutes and had covered little distance. This was such a slow, filthy and stressful drive that I must have been getting hysterical. I had lived in the countryside for much of my life and was very used to Britain's narrow country lanes, yet this treacherous potholed mudbath was a lane too far. It was somewhere around the time where the lorry in front got stuck between the bus and a muddy rut that I think I had already decided that the bungalow was a 'non-starter' but nonetheless I'd come this far, and I was determined to see it.

Eventually, after some six miles and not two as the agent had promised and nearly an hour on the road, I reached the destination and was faced with a small cul-de-sac development of some six bungalows built in the 1970s to what purpose I don't know as they were in the middle of nowhere and any daily journey to work would be a turgid trek through mud, farm traffic and angry underpaid delivery drivers. It was a drizzly morning and the bungalow glowered down at me out of the mire and I could see without even leaving the comfort of my car that it had seen no maintenance for many years. The 'glorious countryside views' were out of the front windows which faced a large grassy mound opposite. Feeling ridiculous about almost being in tears of frustration after such a horrendous drive followed by a huge disappointment, I turned the car around and headed off for home and to my dear cat Monty, doubtless waiting patiently for me in the dry.

Lost now, and with only ancient wooden fingerpost signs for guidance, I tried to find my way back to town but preferably via a different route. I couldn't face travelling that same treacherous journey the six miles back again. Eventually I came to a signpost that was complete and not vandalised. Stopping the car, I craned my neck and glanced up at it through filthy car windows. I saw a familiar name of a town which was many miles from my starting point, and yet it was only some three miles away. *Had I really driven that far!?*

The name of the town suddenly conveyed to me a sunny and happy day out with my late mother when we had once visited a garden nursery situated there. Realising that I had been given particulars of two of the cottages in this town, I quickly turned my car in that direction and headed towards this new destination. I wasn't intending to buy here as it was so far out and so rural but seeing as I was this close, it made sense to put in a visit.

Things are often destined to be and spirit puts certain 'roadblocks' in our path to divert us, the dreary bungalow and the even drearier drive that morning had been just such an example. Suddenly I was very keen on seeing the cottages and saving the day, I was also very keen on having a cup of tea and a slice of cake in a local cheery and dry hostelry. It would also be a bonus to get away from these hazardous holed lanes awash with manure.

The town amazed me and the sun had come out for the occasion. Not having visited for a few years, I had forgotten how lovely and unspoilt it was. No double yellow lines or ugly local authority street furniture but lots of ancient cottages huddled side by side, greenery all around and largely unspoilt by any scourge of modernity, for example ugly plastic windows and plastic doors. I paid a visit to the estate agents in town and immediately made an appointment to see three cottages the next day.

One, a large rambling thatched cottage was reputed to be the oldest in town (all old cottages in British towns come with this claim!), another was a cute average sized cottage that had just been completely renovated to a very high standard and the last was a Regency town house which seemed larger on the inside than on the outside.

The town was very old and delightful, replete with a large historic church as the central feature, individually owned small shops for convenience and a streetscape that had been built up over centuries and not weeks. This was an ancient place and had a story to tell at every turn. Nooks and alleyways, quirky walls and doors, and glimpses of gardens behind gates and railings.

The following day arrived, and the sun was in full strength with the effect on the old pale stonework and faded grey paintwork in the town being to somehow make it reminiscent of small sleepy towns and villages in the South of France. Yet it was also the very essence of a quintessential British village and I already wanted to live here. I strolled happily alone in the town for a while as I killed time before viewing the first property with the agent.

The sunshine, the church clock carillon strike and the deep history of the town intoxicated my senses, and it was with great expectations that I nervously approached the front door of the large rambling 'oldest house in town' thatched cottage. The agent, the owner of the business and a pleasant knowledgeable man, was there to greet me personally and together we began my first viewing of the day.

I had thought that the asking price was a little expensive,

and this thought did not dissipate as I entered this ancient home. I had already noted that the thatched roof needed some urgent attention but upon entering the house it was clear that the elderly vendors had, perhaps wisely, spent much of their life's income and pension on travelling the world but very little on the essential maintenance or key updates to the property.

The agent spoke enthusiastically about the cottage, but I detected something in his demeanour which suggested that he already knew I wasn't going to buy the house. Was this in response to my own body language, or did he perhaps know something I didn't? We wandered through seventeenth century wood panelled and beamed rooms, twisting corridors, stepping over beams to enter bedrooms and marvelling at bathroom suite colours from decades gone by. This house was indeed very old, dating back to the sixteenth century, and as was often the way, it had been added onto and altered over the centuries to make a large, curious and quirky home.

The costs of restoration were ratcheting up in my mind, but it wasn't that which put me off buying this house, indeed the property was perfect for my tastes, possessing astounding history and charm and I adored the treasures that the elderly couple, clearly very much in love and adoring each other's company, had brought back home from far flung places. No, I had decided the moment that I had I walked inside the front door that I would not be buying this place. What I had sensed the moment that I entered this house, I had experienced once before. This was the experience that came with the still very raw memory of when my father lay dying at home a few years prior in that unwelcoming, thick-with-atmosphere haunted poltergeist house.

'Is this property haunted?' I asked, getting immediately to the point with the estate agent who had been waxing lyrical about the Jacobean period fittings. I was expecting a blink of the eyes or a stuttering of words, but no. 'Because I feel that it is, and it is very strong,' I added before he could respond.

He replied with considerable honesty, 'Yes, most likely it is. It *is* an ancient property, but also the husband of the vendor died only three weeks ago.' Without hesitation I said, 'He's still here,' acutely aware of the former owner's ominous male presence as soon as we had entered the building.

Clearly unhappy about our viewing of the cottage, his cottage, I could sense him close by and following us around, as tangible as if he were physically stood with us. The energy he possessed was strong. His widow was out for the day, but he had resolutely stayed behind. Not just for the day, but presumably declining to pass into the Light until his beloved wife was ready to go with him. An occurrence more commonplace than we might think.

The agent and I got into a brief discussion about hauntings and I explained that I had lived in a house with a poltergeist once before and that, even though this cottage was wonderful, I would not be putting in a bid for it. When I expressed surprise - that he wasn't surprised - at my question, he said that he had spent many years in his industry and had come across many houses with presences and 'happenings' that could not just be explained away. He understood completely and locking the front door behind us we quickly departed and pressed on to the next house. I should perhaps add that the old cottage then took several more months to sell and eventually at a huge discount. The first thing that the new owners did was to renew in its entirety the thatched roof, doubtless at hideous expense.

I had begun to get interested in astrology at around this time. At a crossroads in my life after mum had died and simultaneously being made redundant, I found myself in need of guidance as to which path to tread. The positioning of Saturn - planet of life's lessons learnt - and also of Neptune - planet of the unseen, both now showing strongly in my astrological chart, resulted in all astrological forecasts warning of something between spiritual transformation (they got that right!) and extremes of the supernatural.

'Supernatural events may occur, and some may shock you through 2016.' said one such forecast, finishing with, 'You may even have a brush with Satanic forces.' This last prediction made me shiver but I soon dismissed it, though I didn't forget it and it was to prove to be remarkably accurate. It was my preparedness for the 'supernatural' that fortified my already immense caution in my property hunt. I was determined never to share a house with a spirit again, naïve fool that I was.

The next house that the agent and I bowled up at was a small cottage in a small lane with a tiny driveway and an even smaller garden. The house had been immaculately updated, retaining the period charm and beautified to within an inch of its life. The paint colours were tasteful, the rooms were pretty, the bathroom was luxurious and the kitchen exquisite with special finishing touches. The makeover the cottage had been given was divine and something out of a homes magazine. However, right from the start it was clear that it was overlooked in all directions, that the row of neglected municipal garages next door were likely to be demolished soon to make way for a housing development (it since has been) and that there was no way anyone could get a car in and out of the narrow driveway, unless one was motoring in a 1930s Austin Seven.

One thing was clear however, and this was that the cottage was not haunted. This unspoken additional feature was a major boon. However, the original and unrestored dark and dank outbuilding which now served as the ivy clad garage had a very heavy presence. This must have once been a workshop or perhaps the village slaughterhouse in a previous existence. It exuded an air of captivity and gloom and I didn't want to remain inside for long, so I didn't. Of course, I wasn't going to live in the garage, so a haunting mattered less. What mattered more to me was that although the house had been cleverly and lovingly updated, there was something claustrophobic about its physical location. Onwards then to the next and final property.

This last property of the day had not been my favourite and as we approached it from the church path, I could see that it was a little tired and needed affection, however it had great potential. 'Pippins' was a Sleeping Beauty; it lay in a prime position in the centre of this small quaint town just waiting to be released from its spell of slumber. The front of the property was what almost everyone desires when seeking a period home. Like a typical dolls house, the property possessed a front door in the centre and large sash windows either side with two sash windows above. The whole effect typically Georgian and symmetrical and very pleasing to the eye.

To the left there was open ground and more windows to take in the view. On the other side there was an ancient walled lane or 'twittern' which led between the side of the house and the house's adjacent garden down to a row of early nineteenth century workers cottages behind. The property particulars stated the cottage to be, 'Regency fronted' with 'original Regency front door and sash windows.' In fact, the front door was a 1950s replacement, but so well done that the change couldn't be noticed at first glance.

Overlooked by the large village church at the front, which dominated the landscape in a most stunning and impressive manner, to the right-hand side was a far distant view of the countryside beyond and to the rear, the row of old cottages nestled up close to the house allowing room only for a small backyard.

Opening the charming panelled central front door to Pippins, the estate agent allowed me to enter first and immediately I was enveloped by the long dark narrow Georgian corridor which led to what was the low squat rear door. This was now the entrance to the single-storey kitchen which had been added on the rear of the property in the late Victorian period. The sitting room led off to the left and the small study and dining room to the right of the corridor. A delightful 1950s turned wooden staircase replaced the original Georgian one and stepping through a 1950s glazed door into the galley kitchen, even more space was to be found at the rear leading through a lobby and storage area to a newly fitted WC and shower room beyond. Although the corridor was poorly lit and perhaps even claustrophobic, the rooms themselves were bright and airy as only Georgian era well-proportioned rooms with large sash windows can be.

Upstairs was a spacious delightful landing with a window to the rear flooding this portion of the house with natural daylight. Here was to be found a single bedroom and large principal bedroom to the front facing the church and a generous period style bathroom to the rear. Finally, diagonally to the principal bedroom was the large second bedroom which had views high up over the town to the hills beyond.

All of the rooms, with the exception of the dining room and kitchen, were well illuminated with natural daylight and although this light also made visible the tired nature of the house and the many different paint colours used on the walls (sometimes three colours on the one wall), the overall impression was a house with 'good bones' and an odd expression came to my mind the moment I walked into the house, 'a gentleman's residence' perhaps for a gentleman writer. I had not considered writing before, at least, not since the age of about seven or eight years-old, but the moment I walked in the front door and I saw the small study replete with original Coalbrookdale cast iron fireplace and view of the church, I could see myself sitting at my old desk scratching away with a quill pen like some latter-day Dickens.

The house was devoid of many of its original features, these having been ripped out and replaced in the mid-twentieth century in some misguided modernisation. However, the squat, wide, large and heavy hardwood doors with original door furniture remained. The very old wooden sash windows, while perhaps not the original, gave the impression of originality due to their decades of use and abuse. The front door gave a wonderful resemblance of Regency grandeur being wide and low, suitable for ladies wearing crinoline dresses to enter and exit through.

The agent extolled the good fortune and beauty of having 'original Regency features' and as we walked around, I wondered what lay beneath the old, dirty and instantly forgettable 1970s carpets, hoping for original wooden floorboards ready for sandpaper and a quick wax finish. Many people had looked at the property and yet it remained unsold. I could see why; it was dated and tired, poorly finished and the single-storey kitchen roof needed replacing. Yet unbeknownst to the agent, I had already decided to buy the property before we had even looked at the quirky backyard or the separate garden, which was accessed via the twittern, complete with its original outbuilding, now a single garage and wood store.

Pippins had fully welcomed me in. Already bewitched by the strangely French feel of the town, the house itself was bright, warm and beguiling. It was a quiet day in the town, and I knew that I would have to come back again later to check how noisy the place was by night. However, the detached nature of the house and the longed-for original period features of the home drew me in like a siren singing to sailors from a rock.

I realised that there was parking for three cars available on the property if only a few changes were made to the garden. This would be very desirable as I still had my classic car as well as my everyday vehicle and the nature of the house meant that it could be locked up and left whenever I needed to go away. My only worries were not being used to living in the middle of a small town, always being a country boy at heart, and also for my dear old ginger cat Monty who was used to the rural countryside, this house being directly on the roadway, albeit a small quiet side lane.

Hindsight, as they say, is a wonderful thing. My intuition, I have discovered several times on major issues, is never wrong and I spent several sleepless nights churning my decision to buy the house over and over in my mind. Even as I slept, I was picking up severe storm warnings with the strong message coming through to not buy the house. Yes, there was the road and the fact that I wasn't used to town living but it was more than that. Was it just my imagination or did the area feel 'strange'? The stone walls, the little lanes, the ancient church. And just why was it that the family who lived there, *didn't seem to actually live there*?

The house was very sparsely furnished, and it was as though they had already moved out some time beforehand, keeping just a few sticks of furniture there to make it look occupied and facilitate a sale. I conjectured that perhaps they just preferred Minimalism. I was ever ready with an excuse to proceed with the purchase. But then, why did this town's energy feel so odd? Why did it have that French feel? And what was the strange prickly tingling sensation whenever I visited the town?

I found myself pulling up in my car at pub 'turning out time', and parking on the road in the usually quiet hour before midnight. It was a fine late summer's evening, but the sky was an inky dark blue and as I got out of my vehicle and looked up at the church, I gasped as an almost full moon broke through from the light wispy clouds behind the steeple.

The moon illuminated the church and the churchyard with its pale glow, the town was quiet and the air was warm and calm. And yet, there was that feeling again. It reminded me of my many trips that I'd made to ancient Bruges in Belgium. Just why did I love Bruges so much? A past life connection? And why did this town with no apparent connection remind me so much of that old Flemish city?

It wasn't the townscape; it was more the energy and *feeling* of the place. This was the tingling electrical energy of the frisson of excitement that you get as a child at Christmastime. Bruges always had that effect on me and yet has a turbulent and terrifying history, not that you would know it nowadays with its cafes, tourists and trundling tinkling bicycles.

This town where I was now thinking of buying my new home was also known for its turbulent history, so perhaps that was the connection. It is hard to describe a 'feeling', especially when the vocabulary does not exist to put such sensations into words, but psychics would recognise it as spirit energy. Unaware of this at the time and dismissing any idea of negative energy or anything bad, I strolled through the moonlit graveyard towards the house.

The small road outside Pippins was quiet, the public house was similarly quiet, and the town was asleep. It was hard to tell if the house I wanted to buy was occupied as the lights were off and all was calm. A result! With some relief I observed that the road and the area seemed peaceful and safe for Monty my cat. Yet there remained a strange air about the town, in particular this road and the churchyard with its path, but then surely graveyards are always spooky at night and this was, after all, a spectacularly atmospheric moonlit night.

My mission accomplished, I headed the several miles back home to my safe, warm, modern and well-lit house, which was now 'under offer' and technically sold. Monty was as ever waiting patiently for me inside and over a bowl of cream (for him, not me) I told him all about our new abode. Dismissing any apprehensions about energies or ghosts, I remembered that the house where I presently lived had endured a mysterious night-time visitation of its own each August. I reasoned that I shouldn't be afraid of moving on with my life and indeed I should be rejoicing. But something kept me awake that night and every night afterwards, my intuition screaming at me in my restless sleep.

The agent was of course delighted to receive a sale, as I am now certain were the vendors. My worries over the road and Monty proved to be correct, as was my worry about the close proximity of the rear row of cottages, the strange ancient feeling in the garage and garden and the fact that I loathed the backyard from the first moment I saw it. Stepping out into it from the kitchen back door, it was like entering a cold wind tunnel. I had put this down to air turbulence caused by the high stone walls that surrounded it, and I chose to ignore, wrongly, as it turned out, the sensation of being watched in the yard. I should have heeded the warning my intuition was giving me. Yet what did the backyard matter?

What if the lane that led to the rear of the house with its ancient stone wall gave me the creeps night *and* day? You would think that by now, with all of the supernatural occurrences in my lifetime that I would have learnt to know better. Yet I told myself what we are all told to tell ourselves when faced with the paranormal; that the creepy sensation was down to the historic appearance of the place and just my imagination. This sunny and pleasant Regency home appeared to be a delightful place to be in the daytime. Yes, in the daytime.

CHAPTER EIGHTEEN

Reincarnation Part One – Several lives in two chapters

Time after time

'Everything is going to be shipshape and Bristol fashion'

June 2020, and at the time that I write this book the world is undergoing a shift in collective consciousness on a hitherto unimaginable and on an as-yet-to-be understood level. The astrology is similar to the 1930s but this time around the establishment and the jackboot of history will not succeed in pressing itself onto the face of humanity. That does not however mean that it won't try. This time there is one crucial planet in an opposite sector of the night sky, and if we have the desire, humanity as a collective will join together and have victory over those in positions of power who seek to divide and rule, trying to impose their will over the people.

The Age of Aquarius has finally dawned, ushering out over the next few decades the Age of Pisces. Big government, big banks, big corporations, physical possessions and fossil fuels will cease to be the centre of focus and instead it ushers in an age of solar and wind-based energy and intellect based solutions for benefit of the collective as a whole. These changes take decades not weeks to happen but noticeable changes over the next ten years will occur and in only five years' time significant shifts to society and humanity will have happened leading to significant improvements for the many in the future.

That is, as long as the people do not give into the fear, anger and division being actively promoted but instead keep love in their hearts. The old decaying era of heavy top-down big government is dying. Expect it to fight back as the venomous snake always writhes the most when it's in its death throes.

So where were you in 2020? I am guessing as you're reading a book on supernatural or spiritual matters that you are already awakened or well on your own spiritual path. The collective must consider what we will be telling our grandchildren about this crucial time, of what we said and what we did. For this is a crucial time and far from the online memes where I keep seeing that 2020 is 'cancelled' or 'pointless,' this could not be further from the truth. 2020 and 2021 and beyond are probably the most important years of our lives, and we signed-up to be here for them before birth. These are the times when everything changes. We are living through history. History that will be taught and talked of for decades to come. So, where will you fit in with all these changes? How do we fit in?

I have believed in reincarnation since childhood. I have known that it exists for two years. The balance of evidence from the numerous supernatural experiences that happened to me allowed me to conclude that there is life after death. Reincarnation then seemed the only sensible solution to aide answering that eternal question, 'What is the meaning of life?' or 'Why are we here?'

Energy cannot be destroyed, only transmuted and the regularly encountered earthbound spirits demonstrate that our consciousness is a separate entity to our body. Our body may perish but our energy of consciousness does not. We either return to where we came from, to the Light, or we linger about on the Earth plane. I always considered it an illogical 'divine purpose' promoted by the old power-seeking church that humanity is born in sin and so we must repent that sin before we can be allowed back into Heaven. That doesn't make any sense at all.

We are instead here because we chose to be here, because we wanted or needed to learn and experience life in the 3D. We are divine beings having a physical journey on Earth. This difficult to navigate dimension allows our spirit to experience, develop and flourish and then return back to the 5D (the Light) for 'debriefing' before once again returning to Earth in another lifetime to begin the next stage of learning. As we complete each stage of learning we shift up a class, just like in high school. Eventually we graduate. It really is that simple.

My own experience of past lives is difficult to explain because in large part it is entirely subjective and is also based upon a 'feeling' and memories of a period of time that current day science says I couldn't possibly have lived in. And yet, even as a child I knew of at least one past life in particular, having a keen interest or obsession in a particular period of time. It is unusual for a child to be looking to the past and not to the present. These 'memories' stayed with me into my adult years and have since been confirmed by proficient psychics as coming from a past life where I met with an unfortunate end. The memories referred to here are like small glimpses in my mind's eye. Little snatches of fragrance, images, clothes, places or sound brings to life a memory that science says I cannot possibly have.

I have three past life memories which I shall mention here in this book. I am Church of England by birth-right, and yet with the first memory I have always had an inexplicable affiliation with all things Jewish. A distinct memory as a five-year-old boy was of being asked back to a friend's house after school. Even at that young age I used to walk to and from school on my own and so dropping by after school was no difficulty. So later that day, as I walked home with my new friend it was to discover that the home to which the boy had referred was an apartment above a local parade of shops near to my house. The little boy who asked me was a quiet, sensible, attractive, dark-haired child with dark jewel-like eyes and yet with a slightly sad older energy beyond his years.

I followed him up the stairs and I can still remember walking into the family's sitting room-kitchen-dining room with my friend. In this small flat a large family sat around the medium-sized dining table while the mother stood in the open plan kitchen and looked none-too-pleased at me having been invited. It was the 1970s and everyone outside was wearing bright clothing and flared trousers, but here inside the apartment, dark sombre clothing was the order of the day. I was asked to leave. I thought that I had done something wrong.

The little boy wasn't allowed to talk to me again. This was my first encounter with orthodox religions. The whole incident had an abiding memory that stayed with me, not because of the rejection by the family for me being 'different' but because of an affinity with these people and a familiarity with a past life that I couldn't possibly have had. His family were, I now realise, Jewish.

In 2017 I decided to emigrate and move from the UK to the

Czech Republic, formerly Czechoslovakia. The area to which I moved is in the north of Bohemia and has rolling orchards, fields and hopvines with a breath-taking mountainous backdrop. Prior to World War II, this area was populated and owned chiefly by German speaking people as well as Czechs, and it had been that way for hundreds of years. Following the Nazi occupation of Czechoslovakia, our local picturesque town became the Headquarters of the Gestapo with the infamous Terezin concentration camp sited just outside of the town. Many Czechs, Jews and others suffered unfathomable depravities and cruel inhuman incarceration here, however the pages of this book is not the place to discuss this Hell on Earth.

When I told my brother of my move to the Czech Republic and to where exactly I was moving, he told me that he had once been here on a business trip in the 1990s. The countryside here is a less travelled part of Europe, and so this was quite a remarkable coincidence. A stranger coincidence was his trip involved a visit to the former concentration camp. Bewildering our parents, my brother had, from childhood, endured a morbid fear of anything resembling public lavatories. Tiles, pipes, showers, cisterns, the echo of the chamber, everything and anything sanitary related where the room was cold and municipal instilled an inexplicable terror in the small child.

As a result, this profound fear had led my brother to often speculate whether, in a previous incarnation, he had been the tragic victim of a Nazi concentration camp, and this strange phobia a symptom of past life trauma. Reliving the dread, my brother now told me of the day of his business trip, and while being escorted around an outside museum, he had caught sight of the rear caboose of a historic wooden railway carriage. It was one that had been in service in the 1940s and will have looked similar to those that transported many Jews and others to their murder in the hellish death camps.

My brother said that he remembers it was a fine sunny day, with long meadow grass growing up through and around the old tracks. He had always had a fascination with railways and trains from yesteryear, even as a child. Turning and seeing the rear of the wagon, and with a shocked recollection of an event that couldn't have happened in this lifetime, the world span and went black. My brother had passed out with 'fear,' much to the mortification of his hosts.

It is a curious coincidence that both my brother and I have been to this remote part of Central Europe when neither of us has any connection *in this lifetime* to the area. I always knew about the Country when, as a child, I devoured my 1940s third-hand encyclopaedias, studying in detail the historic costumes and vernacular architecture of European countries including what was Czechoslovakia. I often used to imagine one day living in one of these exotic countries. I use the word 'exotic' consciously, as growing up in grey UK suburbia, the 1930s colour plates in my old encyclopaedias proved a stark contrast to my dull and sometimes brutal childhood existence. Later, in my twenties, when my appreciation of art and architecture grew, I bought copious books on the Art Nouveau period and they contained so many pictures of Polish and Czech art and architecture in the secessionist style.

Why would all things Jewish feel familiar and attractive to me, a boy from a secular English nuclear-family background? It was something that puzzled me. Many years later, shortly before I moved to the Czech Republic, I found myself choosing a psychic medium to sit down with at a 'psychic fair' in order to discuss problems that I was encountering with my home which are covered later in this book. I was hoping for some guidance from spirit, but I gave the medium no information at all to work with. While I seated myself, she looked into my eyes and with a sympathetic smile gave me one meaningful word, 'Sorrow!'

This hit home. A lifetime of seemingly endless difficulties and absolutely no joy had filled me with sorrow and at the time I was still grieving over the recent death of my mother. But the medium told me that the sorrow was carried over from a previous life. She told me that my life was soon to get very exciting. She told me that I was going to be a writer. She told me specifically about my ongoing domestic problem with a neighbour that I had come to enquire about. I had suspected this individual of causing troubles about my home and the medium described them accurately, right down to their appearance, demeanour and dress. Superb evidential mediumship.

Then an unsettling thing occurred. While she was still talking, I felt something circular like a hat gently being placed onto the crown of my head. I felt awkward as the medium was looking right at me as she spoke, yet instinctively I wanted to feel the top of my head to see what was there. Was someone playing a trick on me from behind? Wanting to turn around to check, I saw that the medium hadn't altered her fixed gaze, so no-one could be stood there, or she would have looked up. Yet I could sense someone standing behind me.

I forced myself to look straight ahead despite the clear sensations coming from my hair. My own gaze was unwavering, and my smile didn't change but suddenly she looked up at the top of my head and remarked, 'Your Jewish ancestors are here with you and they have just placed that round cap on top of your head.' I can attest to you now that I could feel the kippah being pushed onto my head. This allowed me to raise my hand and pat my hair but of course nothing was there, yet the feeling of this small round cap being firmly on my head persisted and lasted for several minutes.

The medium then explained to me about my Jewish ancestors from a previous incarnation and how they were delighted to be able to make contact. Two weeks prior to the reading I had been considering undergoing hypnotic regression to find out why an even earlier incarnation had always troubled me. Without knowing about this, the medium told me that I was being advised by spirit to 'not have hypnotic regression.' It was explained that to do so would 'bring overwhelming sorrow through into this incarnation.'

Again, it was emphasised that I had endured terrible sorrow in a previous life when I had been a Jewish man. Still clearly feeling the kippah on my head, I took her advice and abandoned my plans for hypnotic regression. Before I took my leave of her, she gave me the name of someone highly relevant to me from that incarnation. I cannot mention the name here as I discovered that the word appears to have some power. Perhaps it had been my own name, or perhaps it had been someone I knew.

The next day I met up with a psychic medium friend of mine called Abigail. It was a typical British summer's day and the fire was lit in my sitting room and the electric lamps switched on to counter the gloomy wet skies outside. As we sat by the fireside, I recounted the previous day's events to her and she listened in an interested manner but healthily sceptical as I would expect. I told her about the kippah and the sensation on my head and then I began to tell her about the name the medium had given to me from spirit.

As the name left my lips all the electric lights in the room dimmed and then came back on again. We laughed at this coincidence and continued with our conversation, with me repeating the name a few seconds later. As I did so, all of the lights in the room dimmed once more. This time Abigail and I looked at each other and laughed a little more nervously, and then excitedly began to discuss the meaning of the importance of the name. As a test, and not expecting anything further to occur, I intentionally repeated the name one last time. Though almost imperceptible now, the electric lights dimmed once more, and I vowed to never speak casually of that name again.

Since childhood I have had a number of 'words' filed away in my mind that are of relevance to me and yet I do not know why that should be the case. The name given to me by spirit via the medium was one of those words. 'Czechoslovakia' was also one of my words, I now live here. The place name of where I used to live and work in Dorset was another. The country and name of my partner at the time I started writing this book were two such words from my supernatural word list. Even the name of my best friend who I now live with was one of my words and therein lies another mystery. In 1987 I went to my very first spiritualist church at the behest of my then best friend. I was on holiday in Kent that week and we weren't to know that particular night was to be the night of 'The Great Storm' which swept across Britain and devastated parts of Kent.

I received a message from the psychic medium appearing on stage that night. I was later to discover that I always do receive messages at seances, the dead it seems, like talking to me. The medium was an elderly white-haired lady, typical of her generation and of somewhat terse mannerisms. On stage she told me that I worked with ledgers, I did indeed as I was a bookkeeper at that time, and she added that I had a nun as a spirit guide. There was little else given to me and it was rather a disappointment, but afterwards, as the weather drew in, my friend kindly offered to give the medium a lift home in his very ancient and faulty Citroen car. I can still well recall the drive home. Inky dark as only British winter nights can be, we swept across a motorway flyover, the gales already battering the small car and the rain lashing at us as frantic hydraulic lights flickered and warning lights illuminated across the dashboard.

The wind meant that the rain was already horizontal across the road, and I feared for our safety as my friend pressed on. Unperturbed, the medium was chatting to him the entire time and she gave him some predictions in a mildly friendly manner. This went on for maybe five or ten minutes. I was invisible in the dark on the rear passenger seat and as I was so quiet I presumed that they had both forgotten that I was there. Then suddenly, she spun around in her seat and fixing me with a steely gaze she said, 'The man you are meant to be with is called 'Adam.' And with that she was done, we had arrived at her address and tightening her headscarf against the gales she bade us farewell. I never saw her again.

Sceptics may laughingly state that if she was any good, she would have predicted the storm that night! My friend drove me home and dropped me off where I was staying. The next day it was to discover that we had lost contact as the village where I was accommodated was severely damaged by what was now being classed as a hurricane. Every single house around the village green was badly affected. Without exception every house had lost its chimney, had roof damage, broken windows, fallen trees or fences ripped up. Smashed cars and debris were everywhere. Phone and power lines were down, and in the middle of the village green was what remained of someone's greenhouse. However, our holiday house that we were renting was completely untouched as was our car parked outside.

Moving forward thirty years and I now share a house with my best friend Jonathan (John). When he and I were getting to know each other, me in the UK and he in the Czech Republic, we spoke to each other via Skype most days. I knew that John's middle name was Adam, and it was during one of these calls, on a hunch, I asked him, 'Is your actual name Adam?'

'Yes,' he confirmed, he had been known by his middle name of Adam for many years but had now reverted back to his original first name Jonathan. John is the only 'Adam' who I have ever known, and it is curious that I now live with him. It may have taken thirty years of Earth time, but the psychic medium's prediction came through.

At the time that I was regularly chatting online to my new friend John (Adam), I was encountering some pretty major and unpleasant supernatural issues in my life. I sought the advice of a local medium who I shall call Rebecca. Rebecca has since become a godsend to me and the advice she gives me from spirit is as close to 100% accurate as anyone could possibly hope. The connection that she has with spirit is so strong that it is as if she were speaking with the living - that she is instead speaking with the dead and still produces such results is astounding.

When people laugh and say to me that all psychic mediums are 'fake' I don't contradict them as their mind is already made up regardless of the evidence, however I just think of Rebecca and the evidential mediumship she has demonstrated to me over the years and I smile, knowing that I am lucky enough to have definitive proof of an afterlife and the comfort that brings with everyday struggles.

On the occasion that I sought help with my haunted house from Rebecca, the message that she received from spirit was that I needed to see a shaman and that accordingly, he and I would cross paths shortly. I hadn't really known what a shaman was prior to this but I was to discover that the haunting of my home had set me off on a new spiritual path with a sharp learning curve. Psychic mediums are often given the information from spirit in allegories, and it transpired that this was one such occasion. Rebecca advised that the shaman, 'Will have an unusual appearance and manner that would normally put you off,' but they are saying to, 'Ignore that and go with it,' and, 'He has some connection to wolves.'

Then finally, as she touched the side of her neck, Rebecca added, 'They are showing me something to do with the jugular and dragons. Perhaps it's a dragon tattoo on his neck?' she offered. Although the message was curious, it was nonetheless very specific. I was delighted that someone was in a position to help me with my haunting problem, and even if the 'wolf man' did sound a little scary, I nonetheless waited for our paths to cross. I didn't have long to wait.

A week or so later a psychic fayre was being held in a nearby local town and I decided to go along with Abigail. I paid my entrance fee and walking into the busy hall, I had a good viewpoint of the entire room of around fifty tables. I saw at the far end of the hall facing me, a man with a shock of wild white hair and not looking a little unlike the huge poster of a silver wolf behind him. This was my shaman! Apologising to my friend I immediately made my way to his table but before I got there, I recognised another medium sat at her table. It was the lady who had told me about my Jewish incarnation when the kippah had been placed on my head. I quickly made an appointment with her for later that hour and then crossed the hall to where the shaman sat.

The shaman was serious and unsmiling and not a little intimidating seated in front of his giant wolf picture. I sat down in front of him and with only a couple of words of introduction spoken, he said to me, 'You have a terrible fear of water, don't you?' Surprised, I confirmed that indeed I did. All my life I have had an inexplicable terrifying fear of water, whether that be the sea, a river or a swimming pool. As a youngster I couldn't even bear to have my hair washed by my mother or use the shower in case I got water on my face. I also couldn't then and still cannot today drink water without it making me feel inexplicably nauseous.

Before I could say anything else, the shaman told me in a continuous stream of channelling, 'Your fear of water arises from a past life where you drowned at sea in 1795. Your name was Andrew Watkins. You were a well-respected shipwright who made some of the finest vessels in Bristol. You lived from 1743 to 1795* when you were drowned on the maiden voyage of one of your own vessels when it was lost at sea. You lived at Clifton, Bristol.'*

*I forget the precise years from the eighteenth century that the shaman told me hence I have used approximate years. Similarly I do not disclose the precise Clifton address given to me in order to protect the present owners.

I had always known. Since an early age I was fully aware that I had lived in Georgian times. *I had always known.* But I had always long desired confirmation, and here it was. Perhaps in order to dissuade me from attempting hypnotic regression, spirit had revealed this little titbit to me to keep me satisfied. I received the news with a strange delight. While it explained my memories and increasing flashbacks from that time, it still left so many unanswered questions and a sadness over my premature end that had permeated through to my later incarnations. Had I been married? Had I children? What kind of person was I?

I have had a lifetime of fascination with the Georgian era, the clothes, the books, the drawings, art, houses, furniture, architecture, illustrations, culture, even the graveyards. Tall ships too and everything about them, the shape, the sails, the windows, the colours, the wooden figureheads, the sound, *all of it*. The first time that I saw a tall ship was in the early 1970s, where it was depicted on a blue and white Delft tile on my grandmother's Georgian fireplace. Only three or four years old and I was smitten, both with the tiled fireplace and with the ship. In that short paragraph I feel that I have not sufficiently emphasised what the Georgian era meant to me then and still does today.

The sights, feel and energy of the period remained fresh and vibrant in my mind as if it were a living memory from my current incarnation. Then there are the strange flashbacks to an era where science says I couldn't have lived. When watching the film 'Marie' about the life of Marie Antoinette, there is a section in the film where a black coach and horses rides away from the camera. It gave me such an unexpected jolt of recognition it made me emotional. It had reached the point that the 'noise' in my mind made me want to get questions answered and to seek hypnotic regression. Thanks to the shaman, my mind is now calmed in this matter and I seek answers no more.

You may be thinking, 'But the shaman just gave you any old pre-researched address in Clifton, Bristol.' Yes, perhaps, but I can still feel the tingling shiver that went up my spine when I did my research online later that night. Entering the address into the Google search engine I studied the map of the area and the street. The house still existed and the area seemed familiar to me. I looked at Google Earth and followed the images along the short roadway of only a handful of houses until I stopped outside the address itself. The hairs on my neck stood on end as I realised that this was the same small street, and the very same house where my friend had rented an apartment a few years prior. This was far too precise a coincidence to be anything other than evidential mediumship. This was the same friend who on the night of the 'Great Storm' of 1987 had given a lift in his car to the elderly medium. Had I journeyed with my friend long ago in Georgian England times? What had our relationship been in those times?

But back at the psychic fayre the shaman did not stop there. I had sought his help because of an unusual situation that I was encountering at home with my house. Rebecca had told me that I would come across this shaman and that he would provide answers as to my home, and she had made mention of the *jugular* and of a *dragon*. What came next was to surprise and delight me as it's always delightful to have a psychic message affirmed. It means that spirit really is watching over us, taking a keen interest and they try to help whenever they can.

After only a short pause the shaman spoke again, 'You can't stay where you live now. The house isn't right for you as you are a highly developed soul with a high vibration.' Well, that's always nice to hear, isn't it?! The shaman continued, 'You have heard of ley lines?' I nodded my affirmation, the shaman continued again, 'You have a ley line passing right through your house, but it is not a normal ley line, it is known as a 'dragon ley line' and unlike normal ley lines, these contain negative energy.'

I am sure that my jaw must have dropped open at the word 'dragon'. He continued as he wanted to explain further, 'Normal ley lines form an energy grid like the veins in the human body carry blood.' I nodded. "Well, a dragon ley line,' he said pointing to the side of his neck, 'This is more like a jugular. The energy is massive, and it is chiefly negative energy allowing earthbound spirit to travel along it like a superhighway and right through your house.'

Well, there they were! These words and the explanation were exactly what I needed to hear. Rebecca's words of 'dragon' and 'jugular' were here, and also why my house was so active spiritually and why it felt so unbearable for me to live in, whereas some visitors barely notice the low vibrational energies. I thanked the shaman, paid and got up to leave. Still pondering and reeling from the powerful revelation that my house had a ghost motorway running through it and that I was a notable drowned Georgian shipwright I moved swiftly across the large noisy and packed-out hall to my appointment with the cheery psychic medium.

My head was buzzing with excitement and gratitude over this information that spirit had given to me, resolving years of issues I'd had with all things Georgian; my love of tall ships, my loathing of water and my lifelong unwanted but strangely recurring connection with Bristol and its people, plus an inexplicable dislike of the energy of the place.

Approaching the smiling and animated psychic medium with whom I had booked my second appointment I could see that she was still busy with her last client. My mind still buzzed with images of tall ships and Georgian Bristol as I conspicuously hovered close by while she finished off her previous reading with a female client. Then, feeling elated at the powerful information I had already been given, I found myself sitting in front of this delightful psychic medium.

I had purposely chosen this medium as she was the same person whom I had consulted a few months prior and had given me my Jewish past life connection. She immediately become very excited and said, 'They have just told me to tell you not to worry because everything is going to be *shipshape and Bristol fashion.*' I burst out laughing at this quaint old British naval expression 'shipshape and Bristol fashion' which so perfectly summed up my past life reading with the shaman and presented in that humorous way that spirit so loves.

She asked if that made sense and laughingly I declared that it did indeed! It also served to dispel any doubts I had over the validity of the shaman's information. In that moment my belief in reincarnation became an absolute certainty. Again becoming excited she said, 'You're writing a book they tell me.' I replied that I was indeed as I had been writing a novel since 2016 in fits and starts. She said, 'It's going to be successful. No, not just successful, but *extremely* successful!'

I was astounded but of course intrigued and delighted. I had wondered if it would one day be published but if so, it was a long way off. Then still bouncing in her seat with excitement she added, 'Oh, they're telling me not to get so excited or reveal more as you aren't yet supposed to know how big it is going to be.' Pausing as she listened to her spirit guides, she continued, 'And there is one person in particular to whom this book is going to help and if it reaches just that one person, then that it has achieved its purpose.' With that, we talked of other matters and messages but my mind was too excited and buzzing with the events of that transformative hour.

I began this particular book long after my reading with the happy excitable psychic medium. The book that I had been writing then was a fictional novel and it seemed unlikely that a novel would 'help' anyone. It was Abigail who suggested to me during the 2020 lockdown while I was suffering financially and emotionally in my isolation that I should write a book about my lifetime of supernatural happenings, and here it is. The lockdown isolation I put to good use as I attempted to write a chapter of this book each day. I do not know which book I write is going to reach out and help others, just as long as one of them does. Time will tell but if you are that person reading this book and you take away at least one positive thing that helps improve your life, then I have completed my task successfully and I am grateful to you. You and I are connected in spirit, and you have my love and best wishes.

Chapter Nineteen

Vacant possession

Moving in day

Even the cool night air seemed reluctant to enter this house.

Moving in day at Pippins had arrived. Autumn was now well under way and winter would soon make its dismal appearance with its driving rain and gales in the southwest of England. But for the time being the mornings were dew filled low sunshine wonders of golden hues and russets and the world sparkled for a moment.

The removals team were efficient with time but careless with the furniture and a couple of larger pieces got badly broken, one of which I didn't find out about until days later where it had clearly been deliberately damaged to get it to fit into the house. I could hardly blame them as it seemed that I had underestimated exactly how small this new house was compared to my old one, or perhaps how deceptively big the last one had been. Furniture and boxes filled the house and the removals men seemed amused at what they considered the overwhelming task ahead of me.

Instead of an overwhelming task, having moved house many times in my life and being a keen interior designer, I could tell exactly where everything was going to go and that it would fit precisely. Once the floor-to-ceiling stacked boxes of books and china were emptied and the cardboard recycled, all would be well. So it was. However, not wanting to mentally revisit those last few harrowing months spent at the bedside of my dying mother, I had disposed of all of her bedroom furniture prior to moving house. I therefore needed to buy a new double bed, but on the whole, I had everything organised within days.

I was very much looking forward to getting my teeth stuck into restoring and decorating this old house and returning it to some of the Georgian grandeur that it once possessed. It was October and there were any number of practical issues that needed to be attended to. As part of the purchase deal, the previous owner had agreed to repair the electric immersion tank situated in the principal bedroom, he hadn't, and the damage wreaked by months of leaking hot water meant that the entire system had to be replaced and this now included the sodden and rotten floor underneath. This unexpected expense revealed that any prospect of lifting up old carpets and discovering beautiful original floorboards beneath was long since gone, as the worm-ridden boards had given way to modern chipboard firmly screwed over joists. With no delightful glossy antique floorboards to polish, carpets throughout was the only option.

The central heating system didn't work, neither did the new downstairs shower and I was soon to discover why the previous owner had clad in timber the main wall of the kitchen. This unfortunate discovery was made on the first day of heavy rain. Monty my cat and I stood in the kitchen and watched with increasing alarm as the rainwater made its rapid way down what was once the exterior wall of the house and was now the interior rear kitchen wall. The rain silently slipped downwards behind the recently installed wooden panelling and flowed out like a rising estuary at full tide from the bottom of the skirting board. We watched as it made its way past Monty's food bowls and out across the tiled kitchen floor. A new roof it was to be then!

It never ceases to amaze me how people can paper over the cracks – literally – and expect to cheat karma. But this was not to be the only secret that the house had to reveal that the previous owners thought they could hide. There was much more yet to come and much worse than just a damp floor.

Practical issues I could deal with. My father taught me gardening and do-it-yourself when from an early age I observed him and learnt well. So the day-to-day physical matters I felt completely at home with. I was less 'at-home' with the house itself. What was it? On the face of it, it was a beautiful late Georgian period home with lovely windows, daylight aplenty and far-reaching views. Many would cite this as their ideal home. Yet there was something not quite right. Was it the energy in the house itself? The 'feel' of the place and the atmosphere inside and also outside began to change from the day that I moved in. It dramatically altered and it festered as it grew. I had been satisfied that this house had not been haunted by anything *bad* otherwise I would never have bought it. Yet from day one I felt a creeping uneasiness in the house, day or night, but especially night-time. A sense of dis-ease, with uneasiness growing over only a few short weeks which at first was inexplicable but as certain – events – began to occur, the inexplicable became the unthinkable.

It's strange to think of it now, with the benefit of hindsight, that I didn't know from day one that the house was haunted. Of course, looking back I think I always knew. It is just we choose what and what not to feel with our intuitive perception and instead only 'see' with our physical senses, and I chose to ignore mine. The house viewing with the agent had gone so successfully, with only a light anticipation hanging in the air and a very slight gloom in the corners that gave anything away at all. Following immediately after the overtly obvious in-your-face presence felt when viewing the rejected 'oldest house in town,' the more subtle and cunning, manipulative energy that came and went within my new home had been easily overlooked at the time.

Well, I couldn't overlook it anymore. Within three weeks of moving-in, the atmosphere within the stone walls of this old house was so strong that it felt thick with tension and as though crowded with unseen eyes. There was nothing much at first, or so I thought, to indicate a definite presence here, a definite haunting. Yes, the old house made odd noises day and night; bangs on the walls, knocks and creaks of the floor, strange soft sounds that, had I not been living alone in this house I would dismiss as simply the background noise of other occupants. Yet there was background noise, the odd footstep or soft swish of clothing, and a strange cloying, claustrophobic electric sensation which I put down to power cables, or perhaps to the digital 'Smart Meter' for the electricity which was installed over the front door. Yes, I was always looking for excuses in those days. I did not want to face the horrifying reality that once again I had moved-in to a haunted house.

Notwithstanding my misgivings, I tore through the house and totally transformed it within only three months of moving-in. The rear leaking roof remained to be done plus there was a lengthy delay with the costly new carpets. These turned out to be expensive rubbish, which after a two-month manufactured-to-order wait were then 'rejected by quality control' before they even left the factory and had to be re-made with a further two-month delay and no apology.

When the carpet fitters eventually came, they lifted and removed the disgusting ancient old carpets (of which I was ashamed, even though the dirt wasn't mine) and laid down the new underlay and new carpets. They discovered not only the chipboard floors upstairs but also the 1950s concrete ones downstairs where the original flagstone floor had been lifted and removed. Not removed far however, as the backyard and the garage had original beautiful and historic flags that must have come from inside the house during this 1950s 'renovation.'

But it was when the carpet fitters lifted the old carpeting at the rear of the sitting room that a historical puzzle arose. The rear lobby and shower room were Victorian add-ons to the house and accordingly had original Victorian pine floorboards covered over by the previous owner with a selection of inappropriate and ill-fitting ceramic and oak flooring. But the rear half of the sitting room was not concrete at all, it was boarded with very old wide planks. The planks varied in width from ten or eleven inches to fourteen inches and were made of elm wood.

Prior to purchase the surveyor had suggested that the roof of the house was of mid-Victorian construction, indicating that it had needed replacement by the 1850s. The surveyor had also suggested that there was a void beneath the rear of the sitting room floor but for what purpose he could not tell, saying he had not come across anything like it before. And here it was, the carpet fitters had revealed ancient elm floorboards with a drop of several inches beneath. Closer investigation between the planks with a bright electric torch revealed a century or two, or more, of accumulated dirt and dust and who knows what else besides.

Curious as to the true history of my new home and also being aware by now that perhaps I may not be the only resident, I trotted off to the town Historical Society to check their records, old maps and census. My research concerning the property was not without success. It showed me that the house was already old and perhaps fallen on hard times by 1820 when the then owners let it out. This was distinctly odd for a 'Regency' townhouse that was supposedly built around 1830 and why would new roof timbers be needed by 1850 if it had been constructed in the 1830s?

Further research of the type of thick wide hand cut elm floorboards found in my house suggested its use right up until the late eighteenth century, after that time pine was more commonly used. I discovered that the rest of the street had been constructed – or reconstructed - in the 1760s by a well-respected local doctor and had taken his name at that time. Then I also discovered the original name of my property was 'White Ball House' – further research into this unusual name suggested it was a colloquial name given to a doctor's house. A 'white ball' was a reference to a medicinal pill dispensed by an eighteenth century doctor and was often just a white sugar ball placebo, so it seemed likely that the doctor had built – or rebuilt – my detached house for his own residence.

The architectural styling of my house differed to the rest of the street, so I could conclude that it was constructed separately to the 1760s cottages, earlier or later but further investigation of old maps indicated that the walls of my garden and the garage itself pre-dated the 1760s. The walls to the garden and alleyway had in fact once been a separate building on the site, probably farm buildings. In the eighteenth century it seemed that my house, or an earlier one on the site, had been a farmhouse and the many acres of land around were farmland and orchards. I had therefore established that my house was the oldest presence on the street, then given a Regency make over and later updated again in the 1850s which explained the early Victorian door furniture and fireplaces. What stories could my house tell? I was determined to find out and set about asking around town for information.

While my research was ongoing, I took to the (to me) exciting task of choosing new traditional paints colours and styling matters with gusto. At least I did at first. My enthusiasm for the project began to wane rapidly. I soon realised that my dream of Regency originality was just that; a dream. It became clear that the traditional paint colours that I was using, teamed with my furniture was giving a mid-Victorian look rather than Georgian. I even quipped to visitors that there was something of the 'Hammer Horror film set' to the styling as I preferred to light the house by candlelight, using original wall sconces and with Indian incense burning day and night plus other ambient mood creating methods to sooth and create calm. Soothing was needed as my enthusiasm was also being jarred by daily supernatural events.

There was also something of a rush on. My brother and his family wanted to visit at Christmas, no problem there, but my ex and his partner invited themselves to stay only a few weeks after I had moved in. Fortunately, the house was just about ready, save for the double bed that they would need in the second bedroom. This arrived with just days to spare before their arrival.

However, I had bigger worries; supernatural worries. A consequence of indifferent parenting as to assistance with any practical matters, or indeed emotional ones when I was growing up, meant that I became an overly independent type and I rarely, if ever, ask for help, usually preferring my own way or the highway. I am also used to my own company and indeed, being a hypersensitive empath, I prefer it most of the time. The energy of people and places can scatter my own energy and it has taken me many years to establish some sort of control over these psychic boundary issues. The strange energies in this house were already beginning to overwhelm me.

It is difficult to put into words, for those who have never truly experienced a powerful haunting or an active poltergeist, how the darkness slowly and inexorably takes over your life, your mind and even your physical body if you unwittingly allow it. A cancer takes a hold of the physical body piecemeal and silently until it has grown to such proportions that it can no longer go unnoticed. In the same way, a conscious egregious entity with an attachment to the Earth plane, who wishes to cause trouble, slowly envelopes you in their energy and before you know it, has engulfed you.

There is nothing that you can pinpoint exactly, not at first anyway. Eventually, over time, the spirit, or spirits occupying your home reveal themselves to you in a manner so obvious as to be an external influence outside of the subjective thinking of your own mind, that you are left with no doubt that you are being haunted. At first there are the little things. Atmosphere is the main one. Anyone sensitive and thereby susceptible to energy changes, no matter how subtle, will just 'know' that they do not feel comfortable. A logical person, I had put down these strange atmospheric influences as to perhaps power lines, or the digital equipment in the house. Yet the very house seemed saturated in psychic energy and there was the sensation of unseen beings that silently watched and judged you, their mocking eyes observing as you moved from room to room.

To blot this out I would light candles, burn incense and scented oils and play music for much of the day and night. Had the weird sensations been due to electromagnetic interference from electrical devices you might anticipate a permanent but steady background 'hum' of activity. Instead the energies in the house gradually ratcheted up until the sensation filling the house was not unlike tinnitus. Indeed, on the first-floor landing and in the principal bedroom I would often get a continuous ringing in the ears up here during daylight hours.

Superfast broadband was already installed at the house when I moved in. This was a rare thing in the UK countryside at the time and a great thing to have but unfortunately it never worked properly in my home. There often seemed to be minor faults on the telephone line, the occasional missed call or interference on the digital phone connection. I regularly used my smartphone every day to connect to friends via social media and yet I soon began to notice that whenever I was sitting down having a chat online, the messaging would suddenly stop at my end and my message would stubbornly fail to send.

This interference did not occur randomly as one might expect, instead over time I began to recognise that there was some consciousness behind the blockages as they happened only at crucial moments in a conversation and often creating awkward or comedy scenarios. It is an uncomfortable feeling to realise that someone unseen is watching and reading your personal messages and playing electronic games for their own amusement.

I continued to avoid the backyard. It was Autumn now and although they desperately needed renovation, this flagstone covered area and the separate muddy patch of ground that construed the garden could wait a little longer. Besides, there were constant cold windy flurries that blew in the small yard in two specific places. These were unavoidable perpetual breezes and I admit that I didn't like venturing out into the small yard at any time of day.

My intuition and my growing claircognizance were shrieking at me once again but I stupidly chose to ignore them, preferring to live in ignorance of what was happening. These senses had by now grown to such a degree that I was able to psychically make out rough, energetic sketches of earthbound spirit in my 'mind's eye.' But I told myself this was foolish. Surely these images in my mind were just imagination? Whether imagination or claircognizance, it suggested that there were the spirits of two men, both standing still and unseen in the backyard. One was stood near to the rear door of the house and the other stood close by. Where these two 'men' stood was exactly where the whirlwind of energy and physical air turbulence occurred.

Both men were from the nineteenth century. One had a young energy and the other, older. One was tall, the young man I believed, and the other was shorter. Both wore dark clothes from the period. There was a degree of malevolence about the energy but I wasn't clear if this was from one or from both. But surely this was nonsense?! I was making stories up in my mind now, wasn't I? I had yet to know it but my psychic claircognizance was growing steadily and this house was to prove the perfect training ground. But then perhaps that's why I had been sent here.

The downstairs shower room, newly built and installed in what must have been the old Victorian laundry, was another area of concern in the house. To be frank, most areas were of concern but the energies in some rooms were stronger than in others. I prefer taking a shower to a bath and the upstairs bathroom, while luxuriously equipped with high quality fittings and which I had thought a real boon when I bought the house, did not possess a shower. So every morning I would quickly nip downstairs to the kitchen for morning coffee, feed Monty and then pop into the shower.

Only I hated this room. Beautifully finished, well equipped, comfortable and very well heated it was a room that I determined to spend as little time in as possible. Perhaps that was because it faced the gloomy backyard and whatever it was out there that remained unseen. But the overwhelming feeling in this small room at the rear of the house was that you were being watched by many pairs of eyes. Warm, dry and pleasant, the room was claustrophobic, just as though you were walking into a packed bar on a Friday night. Inside the spacious double shower cubicle was even worse. I rarely lingered for a long soak.

It didn't take long after moving in to become aware that there were many rooms in the house where I was being watched, pretty much all of them in fact but with some rooms 'busier' than others. In the sitting room, next to a new Chesterfield sofa which I had just bought, I considered there to be a permanent male presence stood – either very tall or oddly a little height off the floor – just by the end of the sofa. This was next to my longcase clock, the only place in the house where the ceiling was high enough to accept it. This presence, although not seemingly negative, was ever-present and always hovering just a metre above ground level. Here was ground central, right at the heart of the home. This should have provided a clue as to what was going on here.

Perhaps I should explain that these spirits remained visually unseen by me and only apparent in my third eye. Our third eye, believed by spiritualists to be centred in the pineal gland in the brain, allows us to 'see' or perceive psychic images without the need for eyesight as we would normally know it. At this time I did not consider myself to be psychic to a degree where I could 'see' spirits with my third eye, yet here I was doing just that. I instead started to wonder if I was going crazy. Crazy or not, I can tell you that it is a very uncomfortable sensation to be sitting on your sitting room sofa while you believe an unseen man stands sentinel over you.

In the dining room, I was aware of what I thought were one or two female spirit entities, the energy in the room bearing a strong female quality. This used to be the kitchen or scullery in Georgian times and although the cooking range had long since gone and been replaced with a modern-day replica fireplace, I was aware of a sadness in the corner of this room by the fireplace cupboard. Many times over the following months I would smell a powerful old-fashioned scent of flowers in that specific corner and at first I would frantically open the cupboards situated either side of the fireplace, looking for the source but of course, I never found it.

Cats explore everywhere in a house and my beloved cat Monty was no exception. Yet Monty never went into this corner, preferring to give it a wide berth. I had placed a wicker armchair in the opposite corner of the room. This was the most comfortable chair in the dining room, yet I never sat in it while it was in here. Intuitively it seemed wrong to sit in a chair that psychically I could sense was already occupied.

Then there was the 1950s staircase. The bottom steps of which were situated around a metre to the right of where the original Georgian staircase had stood. The new staircase now 'turned' at two points and it was at the lower point, about a metre from the ground floor level, where I could sense a presence. Once again, surely my imagination? Yet the other side of this 1950s wall was where the longcase clock now stood and this would once have been the stairwell for the original staircase but now formed a part of the sitting room.

It seemed to me that the male energy in the sitting room who stood a metre off of the floor, was the very same man who stood on the new staircase at the same height. He was standing on a staircase that had long since been removed. It is said that animals have a far better sense of spirit than we do, not only because they have more acute senses, but also because they've never been told that something doesn't exist.

Monty was never a cat to worry about anything or anyone and was happy to take on any dog of any size. He always trotted up the stairs in that confident way that cat owners will be so familiar with, but on reaching the haunted spot lowdown on the stairs, he would squeeze over to the far edge, slink past and then continue unaffected on his journey. It was as though to move away from some invisible obstruction on the stairs itself that only Monty could see.

The remainder of the staircase itself was ok enough, though it shared the same curious background energy with the rest of the house. It was the landing at the top of the stairs that gave me and most visitors problems. The curious problem was a strange sensation of being unsteady on your feet at the very top of the stairs. This was quite disconcerting because it would have been easy to stumble and fall over the low banister. I wondered at first if the floor to the landing sloped downwards away from the wall and towards the stairwell, but a check with a spirit level (no pun intended) and a ball cat toy showed that all was as it should be. Yet every time that I reached the top of the stairs my hand would involuntarily reach out to the banister rail, even when entering the bathroom from the larger landing itself the same thing was experienced, in fact, especially then.

It was the lightheaded sensation of being intoxicated and liable to stumble and fall, but without any of the drunkenness or jollity. I became quickly used-to this odd feeling but it always took visitors by surprise. Visitors, who did not know of my suspicions about the haunting, would suddenly clutch for the handrail and laughingly joke about 'feeling like I'm drunk' and of 'nearly falling over the handrail.' I suspected that whatever spirit it was who lurked in the house he, for it was definitely a 'he', was trying to cause injury or harm and may well have been a drunkard in life. This thought was alarming. I quickly began to learn every creak and groan of the wooden staircase and of the house itself.

I had bought an antique Swedish wall-mounted clock which had a strike sounding not dissimilar to a typewriter bell. Chiming every quarter, it thrashed away merrily on the landing wall which backed onto the second bedroom. I did wonder if guests, hearing the clock striking all night, would find it kept them awake, but then again if I was lucky, it would stop people inviting themselves for a second time! All the same, there was something unnerving about this particular clock striking the hour that added to the discordant ambience within the house and guests staying over did not disagree.

The bathroom was a nicely finished sizeable room and a pleasant place to spend some time. A double-aspect room it comprised a reproduction Art Deco bathroom suite with a roll-top bath and a solid oak floor which was warm underfoot but noisy to walk on. I decorated the room with literally hundreds of reproduction photographs of Hollywood stars from the golden age and randomly selected photos of people from the Victorian period onwards. Hundreds of eyes stared down from the walls while you sat in the bath or on the loo. Looking at it now, this seems an odd thing to want to do in a bathroom and it unnerved many visitors. Perhaps it was because I jokingly called the bathroom the 'Room Of A Thousand Dead People' that it unnerved them! The overall effect was extremely chic and you will see from this that I am not by nature a fearful or jumpy person and I enjoy frivolity. My fear of living in this house only grew over time and was a very real response to actual happenings, very much based on external influences, and was not merely the inner workings of my mind.

The small upstairs single bedroom which overlooked the church to the front was warm, cosy and relatively free of overt energies. I put my single bed in this room, together with a bedside table and lamp and I installed my computer and art materials on the fitted desk. The room was jolly and colourfully modern. This was quite unlike the way in which I had decorated the remainder of the house. In here there were no antiques or original period fittings. Instead there were bright reproduction vintage advertising posters and postcards on the walls and a multitude of art materials and gadgets. In short there was nothing to suggest anything supernatural or spooky.

The only part of the room which I ventured into as little as possible was the fitted 1950s walk-in wardrobe that had once housed the fireplace. Inside this simple cupboard was a very uneasy feeling indeed, I never did get to the bottom of that, and I rarely hung around in there. However, I did spend many an hour sat at the desk. Whenever I did so, my attention was always drawn to the bedroom door which opened onto the landing. It was the same feeling every time. The feeling of being watched by a male energy, stood either in the doorway or a little way further out on the landing where the 'drunkenness' sensation occurred. Even with the door shut, the same feeling of being watched was felt strongly. It was as though a male energy was unable to enter this little room and so instead chose to stand in the doorway monitoring me.

The second double bedroom had fitted shelves and a strange cupboard affair that was quite old and once again was cobbled together from the remnants of the fireplace and which also used to be the hatch to access the attic. This was a tiny square hole that would have given me claustrophobia just attempting to put my head through, let alone any other part of my anatomy. Fortunately someone had had the good sense of installing a new larger hatchway on the landing itself. On the fitted shelves I placed very neatly, in tidy rows ready to be worn, all of my footwear, many of these items new, or shoes polished and trainers cleaned. This I mention because it becomes relevant later.

The head of the bed backed onto the rear wall of the property which was where the haunted backyard was located on the ground floor. I had bedside tables either side of the bed and the bed itself was brand new, arriving in time for my ex and his partner's stay. The large sash window to this bedroom was a particular feature having an original window seat and views over the village and countryside beyond. Many people must have sat here over the years, looking out over the view beyond which probably hadn't changed for centuries. It was a delightful sunny room and the predominant energy in here was inexplicably feminine. Monty liked this room and so did I, or so I thought.

The principal bedroom was where I originally moved into and slept when I first pitched up at the new house. It was the largest of the bedrooms, spacious and although the original fireplace had been sealed up many years before, it retained its large sash window overlooking the church which was an impressive sight as you lay in bed. As with all the rooms, I sumptuously decorated and installed new carpets, curtains and soft furnishings. The curtains in the principal bedroom were in a pale blue and taupe silk-style chinoiserie pattern as I had originally intended to decorate the room in a 1920s chinoiserie style, but by the time I got around to thinking about doing this, my mojo for the house and this room in particular had greatly diminished, more of which later.

All of the bedrooms, like the rooms downstairs, retained their original doors and door furniture. Indeed, the door to the smallest bedroom showed peeling paint when I moved-in which revealed an original early Victorian vibrant russet paint effect. By the time that I had finished the house it was a tour-de-force in interior styling and received many plaudits. It was apparent that I could do this for a living if I chose to but other less positive matters were taking over my attention.

The downstairs front facing study was a strange room. It retained its original fireplace with surround and was fitted with many bookshelves which I filled to the brim, as indeed I did with the fitted bookshelves in the sitting room. Into this small study I squeezed my late parents glazed Georgian style display cabinet which I also stacked with antiquarian books that I had collected over many years. My father's old wooden desk I positioned in the window giving a stunningly beautiful view of the church to the front. I had perhaps grandiose dreams of sitting at this desk and writing frenetically like Charles Dickens, burning the midnight oil as I did so. In the end I never used this room. Probably one of the most charming rooms in the house, it felt extremely uncomfortable to be in. There was a cloying close feeling of being trapped inside a small box and watched by something as ever unseen.

Whenever and wherever you were in this tiny room, you were conscious of someone always just out of view, perhaps stood looking over your shoulder, or watching from the corner. I felt that a previous occupant was still visiting this room and indeed, the room had a sweet sickly scent that I never did get rid of, despite the total repaint, new flooring and soft furnishings. The electric lights were recessed into the ceiling and while practical, were perhaps too modern for the house. However, they couldn't be used because if you sat in this room any longer than a minute or two, the unseen occupant of the room would let you know their dissatisfaction by making the lights flash on and off. An electrical fault you suggest? Perhaps, but if you commented out loud that it is 'like a bloody disco in here!' more often than not, the lights would – temporarily at least

– immediately cease flashing on command.

While all this was going on, the church carillon rang its tune every quarter and a full strike on the hour. I am sure that just like me, any stranger or visitor to the town would be delighted to hear such a joyous and melodious tune sounding out from the bells in the very English church tower. One of the major attractions of this small town was the very beautiful setting of the church in the heart of the community and my new home faced the church directly and looked upwards at this ancient religious site. In moving to this house I knew that I was getting the full benefit of the magnificent church and its peel of bells.

Those who have lived next to a busy roadway or a train line will know that we can get used to any regular noise. As a child I lived next to the railway and the trains that ran past the house every ten minutes or so never bothered me. Our brain tunes-out background sounds after only a short while – perhaps this is one of the very reasons that children see and hear spirit and adults do not. So just three short weeks of having moved-in, during daylight hours I had pretty much stopped noticing the church clock strike every quarter. Night-time was different.

I chose to sleep in the principal bedroom which faced both the road and the church. Most nights my cat Monty would sleep on the bed with me but strangely for him he too would more often than not be restless and move about the room in the dark, finding a way of jumping up onto the windowsill, pushing his way through the curtains to look out into the inky darkness across the churchyard at mice and bats and at goodness knows what else lurked there.

By now it was autumn and cold nights followed cool damp days. But nights spent in that principal bedroom meant stifling.

It's not that the room was warm, or even the bed hot, but the room somehow seemed airless, yet the old draughty wooden sash windows leaked like a sieve. The air in the room felt charged, as if by electricity. Ever looking for a logical explanation, I quickly figured that the electricity supply cable entered the property on the corner of the house just outside this room and that must be the issue.

Having settled satisfactorily on this explanation, my clever theory was soon blown apart when it transpired that this was not the electricity supply cable at all, but only the much lower voltage telephone cable. This was a fact that I found out only after weeks of poor telephone and internet connectivity to the house which had led me to call the telephone company. They confirmed that the telephone wiring to the house was from the 1950s and they very efficiently turned up and changed not only the entire supply cable but all of the telephone wiring in the house.

The result was absolutely no difference, my internet continued to drop out at the most inconvenient moments and all of my telephone calls to my wired telephone (not a hands-free device where low battery levels may affect performance) were plagued by noises on the line. In particular, clicks, crackles, fizzing and poor volume levels that ebbed and flowed could be heard during conversations at both ends. These curious noises often led callers to jokingly ask whether 'MI5 were listening-in?' Yet this interference could scarcely be possible as this was a completely modern digital connection.

Then the scratching started. Even from the first few days of moving-in to the old Georgian house, it was difficult sleeping in the principal bedroom. This was in my honeymoon period with the house, innocent days if you like, before things started getting nasty. Monty was free to come and go as he pleased and so I always left the heavy old bedroom door ajar so that he could enter and leave at will. He could then access the downstairs litter tray and food bowls during the night. To not leave the bedroom door open would result in a scratching and meowing that would disrupt any slumber. I knew my old cat Monty well and he me, and I knew his soft footfall on the carpeted floors and on the stairs in particular.

Yet it wasn't Monty's scratching to which I refer. After a long arduous day of painting, decorating, unpacking boxes and moving furniture, my routine would be pretty much the same. Dog tired, I would feed Monty the cat (no pun intended) and then shower and retire to bed, often very late. It would be true to say that I was already a little unnerved by this point in the day as showering in a small room where you feel observed by many prying eyes is not a pleasant experience, and just before bed is unsettling when hoping for a good night's sleep.

Switching off the electrics downstairs, I would slowly make my way up to the pretty principal bedroom, pausing only on the dimly illuminated landing so to gather my bearings against the drunkard sensations. Monty, more often than not, would come trotting along behind me, knowing that it is bedtime.

Sitting up in bed I would often do some social media, read a few pages of a book, or watch a film on the small television that I had set-up in the corner of the room. Then, I would switch the bedside light out and try to get some sleep, with Monty as ever lying at my side on the bed. However, in this house things were different and very unusually for Monty, it would not be long before he was stirring and moving about the bed in the dark, seemingly unable to get to sleep, or more annoyingly, moving about noisily in the room.

I began to nod off myself just as the town fell quiet, the people leaving the public houses having finished walking home along the street outside my front door. More often than not in those first few weeks I was awoken by the quarterly strike of the church clock, but I knew that I would soon get used to it. My reliable longcase clock downstairs had suddenly seemed reluctant to work, perhaps affected by whatever lurked there, and so the only other clock strike to be heard was the Swedish wall clock on the landing tinging away on the hour.

Silence settled over the house and in the darkness you could hear the metaphorical pin drop. There would be the occasional knocking noise which I took to be wood settling down, particularly in the bathroom where the oak floor expanded and contracted from the heat of the central heating. Then there would be the odd rustle or sound of subtle movement somewhere deep in the house but nothing that would alarm most quiet-minded people.

Only then, just as I was about to nod off once more, and it was *always* just as I was about to nod off, came the scratching. It was clearly high above my head, somewhere to my right as I lay there in the darkness. This was somewhere between the corner of the house facing the road and the chimney breast behind my headboard. I switched on the lamp, expecting to see perhaps a giant spider or a mouse, but there was nothing and the operation of the electric light somehow stopped the noise.

Off went the lamp again only for the sequence to be repeated several times. Each time the lamp was turned-on the noise would stop and each time I extinguished the lamp, the scratching began again. It reminded me of something. Yes, it was reminiscent of that little cottage I had rented all those years ago when I had heard rustling newspaper in the wardrobe that responded to the light being turned on.

Mice, I decided. Mice in the attic, or worse, I had read about Deathwatch Beetle and its nocturnal noises – but in October? I lay there on my back in the dark, staring up at the black ceiling in the inky darkness of the room. I could see nothing, and I settled on checking out the somewhat creepy attic the next day to look for signs of mice or beetle infestation. I did so the next morning, making a thorough inspection and with relief finding nothing but also disturbed as to what had caused the noise. But that was the next day and for now it was still night-time, and the bedroom was humming with electricity and it was stifling to breathe.

I got out of bed, leaving the lights off lest I be seen naked, and crossed to the vast sash window to open it to get some fresh air. It was stuck fast. I struggled with it for a short while and eventually it gave an inch or two but allowed in an unsatisfactory amount of air. Even the cool night air seemed reluctant to enter this house.

This pattern repeated itself every night for many weeks. At that time, I was still more fearful of woodboring beetles eating my home from the inside out than I was of nocturnal supernatural entities. That was soon to change as the manifestations gained power from my slowly increasing sense of fear. Fear is a most powerful energy, and we should always be cautious of those who seek to invoke it.

Chapter Twenty

In the bleak midwinter

The turn of the screw

Just when I thought that it had gone quiet, another specific creak or groan told me exactly where the night-time visitor was on the stairs. One thing was certain, whatever was on the stairs was ascending. Then silence.

The days moved by quickly. I was not yet seeking work, choosing instead to restore the house as part of my therapy following the long illness and death of my mother. I was living off my capital but at that time it was considerable, and I was in many ways in a fortunate position. Nonetheless an uncertain future worried me and like most people I find uncertainty unnerving.

Because I didn't know better, I didn't then have faith in the universe that when we follow our true life path, we are always in the right place at the right time for what we need to experience and learn on our journey. Now that I am used to this concept, my spirit guides help show me the way through life's intricate maze and have done many times, although they always make sure to leave invaluable life lessons on my path.

In the house there remained finishing touches to achieve and the downstairs shower room still needed renovating but by the time my ex and his partner came to stay that winter, the house was very much together. This was only a few weeks into my tenure at the address but by then I had already concluded that in all likelihood, the house was haunted. While I thought that my almost completed home was looking pretty amazing, I received no compliments from any of those who I knew.

Social media with its anonymous populace was a different thing altogether with positive feedback abound. What was this telling me? Perhaps my ego shouldn't have been searching for external positive affirmation, and while this was due to unhealed childhood wounding, the absence of any positive comment was nonetheless unavoidably noticeable. I had become so used to an absence of positive input from all of the people I held close in my life, especially my parents, that this was completely the norm, and I didn't question it.

I have learnt that this was one of my karmic life lessons and when I discovered this, it made perfect sense of something that had become bizarre. While strangers would always love my creative and artistic abilities, those people whom I had chosen to be close me were always cold in their response. It had not occurred to me that either a jealousy, resentment or a personal dislike could be the reason. I had very little confidence in my capabilities, having been taught from an early age that I was an unremarkable child and that it was undesirable anyway for a child to seek attention.

I have discovered in recent times that this abandonment of my basic childhood emotional and developmental needs was as a result of a jealous and emotionally detached narcissistic father and my enabler mother projecting their own insecurities. I also now know that I am an accomplished interior designer, a creative, a writer and more besides, but as is often the case, the child that lacked recognition and acknowledgment grows up to become the adult with the inner child still seeking the same recognition from the same types of people who are also unable to provide it.

I wasn't expecting any complimentary words of approval from my ex about the house, and I wasn't to be disappointed. However, I was surprised when he complained bitterly the next morning of the bedroom, the bed and how he'd slept. 'But it's a brand-new orthopaedic bed!' I exclaimed, more in distress at the cost of the bed relative to its performance, than any feeling of rejection of my hospitality. 'The room was stifling, and I barely slept,' he complained. I knew that this wasn't completely true as through the bedroom walls I'd very clearly heard my ex snoring loudly throughout much of the night, as I had been lying awake, unable as always to gain a restful sleep in this stifling house.

'I tried to open the sash window but it was jammed and there was no air,' he said. The complaints went on for a while but soon settled down after breakfast. That evening, not finding anything satisfactory in the fully provisioned kitchen to eat, and sensibly not relying on my cooking abilities or lack of them, we got takeaway fish and chips for dinner and sat, for the very first time, in the restored dining room which looked delightful but was less welcoming than its graceful appearance might suggest.

Takeaway supper or not, I wasn't going to let this inaugural moment in the dining room pass lightly and I had the finest porcelain china out together with the silver cutlery and a lit candelabra. Anyway, we found it amusing to use the finest dining materials for such a humble dinner. By night the dining room glowed by candlelight, and it looked pretty in the reflective glass and metal.

However, I was uneasy. I never did like this room and my ex's strange insistence on keeping the curtains open as he said the room 'felt claustrophobic' made matters worse for me. An intensely private man, I can't bear the thought of being watched by unseen eyes, alive or dead, and yet my ex was happy to have his back to the darkness outside the window.

The sash window to this room overlooked the alleyway that ran between my house and my garden and was used by the people residing in the cottages to the rear. They often came and went but there seemed to be no-one about that night, however I had a powerful feeling of dis-ease at being watched through the window the entire time that we sat and dined. Could I sense sarcasm and loathing from beyond the window that night, or was this just paranoia?

My guests must surely be feeling the same overwhelming sensation of being watched, and perhaps this was causing the sensation of claustrophobia. Suddenly, my ex got up from the table, turned and announced that he was, 'Closing the curtains as it's like I'm being watched.' I didn't disagree as he anxiously tugged them together swiftly and tightly.

Their visit was a short and not an entirely pleasant one for me or I suspect for my ex's partner, who was probably wondering why on Earth he had been brought here in the first place. We tried to engage in conversation a few times but he was a quiet man and I felt an understandable sense of reluctance, or resentment, on his part. It's always difficult engaging with your partner's ex, and so I let it go, feeling 'less than' and thinking, like I always did back then, that this lack of engagement was my fault.

After they had departed I felt a sense of guilt and shame that perhaps I could have made a greater effort in some way as my ex had made it clear that he had not enjoyed himself or liked the house. Yet despite all of this, no mention was made of the potential for the house to be haunted. Unusual, as my ex was very interested in all things paranormal and I should have thought would be actively seeking evidence of a haunting in a house this age. I considered that perhaps I was imagining the whole thing and maybe I was spending too much time alone.

However, as I waved them off in their luxury top-of-the-range hired car, my ex's consistent gripes was interpreted by my unhealed inner child as stinging criticism, and this left me not only feeling belittled in some way but also grateful that I did live alone. I turned and looked up at the house which was beginning to dominate my life in ways that I hadn't anticipated, and I trudged reluctantly back inside the home that should now have felt very empty after their departure but instead felt abuzz and mocking.

The colder nights drew in and I had the woodburner in the sitting room going at full tilt and incense, candles, tea-lights and oils being burned at an alarming rate. I prefer ambient lighting to heavy overhead electric lights, so the entire house was lit by a warm embracing glow of table lamps and oftentimes candles. I had filled my home with art, antiques and books. Music was always playing, and the house was a cosy hygge embracing paradise of warmth, scent and colour, at least this is how it appeared to a casual visitor.

As for the actual energy and feel of the place, well that remained an entirely different atmosphere ranging between a stifling electric anxiety and a thick intoxicating opium den soup.

These feelings and sensations, known so well to sensitives who have experienced other people's energies and/or the energies of earthbound spirit, are so very difficult to put into adequate words of description. But at the core of everything was the question; is this all in my mind, or is this really happening? If I needed clarification on this point, I wasn't to be disappointed as matters were about to intensify considerably.

In the daytime, the house now seemed dark, grey and gloom laden but to those who know of the British weather in wintertime, you will be unsurprised to hear this. By evening, with the fire lit, exotic incense smouldering and restful music playing, I would sit on the Chesterfield sofa in my sitting room with my dear old cat Monty and you could be forgiven for thinking that I was residing in the very idyllic home that I had always planned and that many people would give their all to be living in. Yet I began to dislike this house immensely.

The people too were slightly odd I thought. Living in the rural peaceful southwest I was used to exchanging a 'good morning' or a 'hello' with a friendly smile to passers-by, almost always receiving a jolly acknowledgement. But here in this pretty and idyllic looking small town, everyone seemed so unhappy and often just downright unpleasant. I was very lucky if I received any acknowledgement at all from walkers or pedestrians and if I did it was likely to be a nervous 'hurrumph' with a sharp glance of the eye or a muttering of breath as they passed.

Was I imagining this? I needed to stay objective, so difficult when dealing with a subjective subject. I often had the front door to the house open, in order to let the rare British sunshine in and also to allow the beautiful sound of the carillon bells of the church echo through the house. It was in this way that

I would often hear passers-by talk and sometimes mention my house and me as the new occupier. I learned quickly that I was not well-liked or wanted by some in this small town. I was everything from a wealthy mum who had moved from London merely to get my kids into the local good school, to a promiscuous gay man who had a string of men calling at my door. I should be so lucky, by this point aside from carpet fitters and plumbers I'd only had four visitors in total. Perhaps this was just a small-town attitude?

Maybe, but the open hostility upset me a little, though I was to discover that the people running the local Historical Society were both knowledgeable and delightful. The man 'in the know' kindly called at my house to inspect it and give me a little more detail about its history. Only he couldn't. He admitted that my house had been overlooked in its historical importance for many decades, although I did learn that the flagstones that once adorned the interior of my house and were now re-laid, somewhat disrespectfully I thought, in the garage, were several hundred years old and likely to be from the local abbey that was torn down on orders of King Henry VIII.

My enquiries of the local Historical Society did mean that I discovered that my house had probably fallen on hard times by the late Victorian period, which by then appeared as a 'boarding house' in the 1891 census with 'salesmen' and 'travellers' staying that night. My surveyor had told me that the house had a 'never-seen-before' chimney arrangement and a beam installed into the sitting room wall which he said indicated a large opening had been present at one time. Further research showed that there was some kind of extension to the house on that side, strutting out into the street and probably a wooden glazed Dickensian period type of shop front, which was now sadly long gone and mysteriously the land that it had stood upon was now under the ugly tarmac and ownership of the local authority.

So, it transpired that the house had a rich history yet not always an illustrious one. I found out that a previous owner of the house, who had lived there in the 1930s when she was running an art gallery in the town, was not only still alive and well and in her nineties but was living in the very next road in a warden-assisted old people's home. I decided to pay her a visit. She proved to be very happy to chat about the old days, though I didn't tell her that I was curious as to if the house was haunted when she owned it, I mean, you wouldn't, would you as she might refuse to meet me. We settled down in her warden assisted apartment over tea and biscuits and chatted about the layout of the house and the town back in the 1930s.

She must have been a relatively wealthy lady as she told me that she owned a 'Standard' motor car and kept it in the tiny garage, which she said, always flooded when it rained in those days. Motorcar ownership in the UK in the 1930s was then the preserve of the more prosperous middle class and above. She described to me the then layout of the house and it was evident that since her time, the stairs had indeed been moved to the right by a metre or so and with a wall removed entirely in the sitting room so as to make one large open room, the centrally placed fireplaces in those rooms having been done away with completely and replaced with one large new fireplace against the outer wall.

There was little else that she could tell me apart from the ancient history of the town and its connection to monks and nuns at local dissolved priories and abbeys, but I did ask her, with a light laugh, whether she thought that 'the house was haunted?' She rolled her eyes and guffawed stating that such things were the manufactory of the tourist trade in the town. As a result I felt a little foolish for asking but then she paused and thinking about it, she added that she, 'Had a little dog back then,' and that, 'It was an odd thing, but now you mention it, whenever he used to go up the stairs, he always got a short way up and moved over to the far edge before continuing – always at one particular spot.'

She went quiet and her eyes glazed over. I could see that there were some long forgotten memories now returning and that perhaps she was rethinking her position on hauntings or even recalling spectral events at the house, but then the subject changed, and we chatted a little more before I sensed that she had become weary and so I bid her farewell and left. So, Monty my cat was right to edge to one side when ascending the stairs. Animals do indeed have a far greater visual spectrum than humans.

While it was nice to meet up with a former resident, little was discovered that day about the true history of my house, or more pertinently, who was still occupying it. Nonetheless, this rather grand old lady's recollection of the entity on the staircase was the first corroborative evidence, no matter how tenuous, of anyone else experiencing something supernatural going on in the house. It also exactly corroborated my own experiences.

When I got back home, I attempted one more time to sit in the small downstairs front study. It was a lovely day and the short walk back home had inspired me. The sunlight streamed in through the sash window and the view of the now beautifully illuminated church never ceased to impress.

Doubtless the church clock must have struck the quarter or the hour and looking about the room (I was always looking over my shoulder in here) my eyes caught sight of my antiquarian books that I kept preserved in a glass fronted display cabinet. In particular, I was attracted to a vellum covered journal which had belonged to an early nineteenth century parson and later by his ecclesiastical son. I often peruse this old book as it makes me feel closely in touch with the past, with spirituality, and with the two men who wrote of their ecclesiastical travels within its pages. The journal must have been very important to both men and travelled with the parson and then later with his son at all times. Unsurprisingly it therefore has a strong energy with it. While I have always felt this energy, I was always uncertain whether that energy was good or bad, just interpreting it to be 'energy'.

Returning the book to the shelf, I wondered who else I could speak to in the town about my house. Glancing about the unsettling little room, I studied the beautiful old door with its period door furniture. I still gained much pleasure from the remaining original features of the house and this room preserved the best of them. You could clearly see where the 1850s door furniture had replaced earlier simpler Georgian door handle mechanisms, the holes for which having been long since covered over. The door frames were equally beautiful, being hand carved with elegant grooving though now very worn away and under two centuries of paint.

Sitting in the sunny but strangely hypnotic tranquillity of this room, a thought came to me that to finish the house off nicely, wouldn't it be a great idea to pin little blue ribbons, like those worn to commemorate important events, to the left side or to the top of each door frame. I had absolutely no idea where this thought had suddenly come from, and it was certainly nothing that I had thought of or done before. Blue I could understand as it was my favourite colour but why ribbons and why on Earth should I desire to pin them to the door frames!? I sat there bemused. What a ridiculous idea and yet what a lovely finishing touch it would make.

The idea in and of itself seemed charming if a little odd, yet the energy that came with the thought felt disturbing. Was I unsettled by the curious notion or was it because of the dawning realisation that this thought wasn't my own. Maybe the idea of blue ribbons was perhaps a protective one, akin to sprinkling salt at access points to a house in the old days for protection. Suddenly I felt unnerved. This idea was alien to me and was not mine. Who had put it in my mind and why? And if there was nothing in this house to fear, why did I need to protect myself from it with little blue ribbons?

It was shortly after this time that my new next-door neighbours moved in. The row of cottages behind me was a mixed ownership of empty holiday-homes and occupied houses. The cottage immediately behind mine was only some five metres across the rear yard from my kitchen door, the end wall of the terrace making up my rear yard boundary. The young couple who had been occupying this house had moved out several weeks prior, leaving the cottage empty and shut up and available to rent.

With the house being so close in proximity to mine and also to the other attached neighbouring houses, all of us were delighted to be told that the couple soon to move-in were a 'quiet older couple in their sixties.' Little more was said on the matter, nor need it be until the new tenants moved in. However, I did worry somewhat for these future tenants as the vacant cottage set off my 'spirit sensing alarm bells', as did one other empty cottage in the row next door but one. And just why were these cottages empty? I thought that I knew the answer.

Next door to the vacant property soon to be occupied lived Terence. Terence was a recently divorced man in his late fifties. Tall, masculine and charming to speak to, he lived alone and was dating Jane, a demure and delightful woman who was always a pleasure to chat with. The next two cottages were empty and then at the far end of the row lived Edith. Edith was a retired teacher of the 'old-school' type who gave free car rides to those in need and did a lot for the community at large, although that did mean that she 'knew' about everyone and their movements and made sure that they knew that she knew. Terence and I agreed however that this different type of 'neighbourhood watch' saved on a burglar alarm.

Nonetheless, I installed around the house, garden and driveway some wi-fi controlled day and night security cameras that I had brought with me from my previous home. These were triggered by heat and movement day or night, and the recordings uploaded to the internet with a warning message sent to my smartphone about any recorded activity.

It was approaching Christmas and I couldn't get a satisfactory paint colour in the downstairs hallway. It was dark with the front door shut but at the top of the stairs it was bright with daylight streaming through the upper windows. With the wall colour stretching all the way from the front door to the upstairs landing it was difficult to get the right tone of paint. What was perfect in the dark of the ground floor hallway looked too bright or colourful in the uncompromising glare of sunshine upstairs.

After two failed attempts at different blues (one famous brand of period house 'blue' paint in fact turned out to be an emerald green) I settled on another famous brand of period paint colour. This however proved to be horrendous to apply, required several coats, all of which had to be applied without stopping or it would dry up patchy with noticeably different shades. I also observed to my dismay that until it was bone dry it had a heady aroma of cat poo. Monty was outraged at the smell, but I braved it and the very dark blue in the downstairs hallway gave way to a beautiful Indian indigo colour as you ascended the stairs into the light. But to make the hallway appear more spacious, and in the absence of coving, I decided I needed to add a hand-painted gilt frieze along the top of the walls, just below the ceiling.

Christmas was approaching and I was feeling seasonal. After all, this was to be mine and Monty's first Christmas in this house. Indeed, this was to be my second Christmas alone. For the written frieze itself, I settled on the beautiful lyrics to the very much underrated Christina Rossetti's 'In The Bleak Midwinter.' A favourite since childhood, I began to paint the words in illustrated medieval style script to the upper part of the downstairs hallway walls with a nod to the Arts & Crafts movement.

To make things more Christmassy and brighter, I played songs on the hi-fi as I worked, 'In The Bleak Midwinter' being a favourite to work to. This may sound very jolly and cheerful but in fact the intoxicating and strange atmosphere of the house, and in particular the hallway, gave a powerful sensation of being watched with disapproval while I worked.

The ground floor hallway was actually my least favourite part of the inside of the house. This I put down to the strange acoustics in this long dark ground floor passageway. When all the furniture was removed for decorating, there was a very unusual acoustic 'dead spot' in the exact centre of the house, right at the very heart of the home. With the corridor bisecting the ground floor into two, standing dead centre of the house any noise had a curious short reverberating tinny echo. Move one metre either side and the audio effect could not be appreciated. The only other time that I have experienced such a sound was much more recently when we dug out a very large pond in the garden where I now live. Before the pond was completed and filled, if you stood dead centre at the bottom of the symmetrical dish of the excavated pond, the same curious aural effect could be achieved. In a dished pond you could explain this sound effect easily due to the reflective aural qualities of a dish. In the middle of a Georgian town house with an open staircase to one side, it made less sense.

The painstaking application of the gold paint by hand to the upper part of the hallway walls was unexpectedly the creepiest part of the renovation of the house. The words of 'In The Bleak Midwinter' are uplifting and religious in flavour, speaking of angels and the Christ Child and I also had inspirational Christmas music playing as I worked. Yet the entire time that I worked my way around the walls balanced atop a small stepladder, the overshadowed energy I experienced in that enclosed space were actually frightening.

How to explain this sensation of fear is difficult when there was nothing *physical* present for the human senses to detect. If you were inside a dark cellar, with no means of light and believing yourself to be quite alone, a sudden shuffling noise over in a far corner would be extremely alarming. Now imagine that same feeling of dread of something unseen, but you are very much in the 'now' and stood under a harsh electric light, day or night, in your own entrance hallway. It doesn't make sense, does it? Of course, I had to dismiss these feelings as imagination.

Sleeping in the front bedroom had never been easy. The suffocating and intoxicated feeling at bedtime particularly in this, the principal bedroom, was unpleasant enough but my waking in the small hours and feeling stifled was causing some sleep deprivation, though not yet enough to cause ill health. Fortunately as I wasn't working at this time I could please myself as to what time I started my day, so I often had a small lie-in, perhaps starting my day an hour later than most people.

The nightly disturbed sleep was still often accompanied by the scratching noises of what I had originally thought to be mice or woodboring insects. I felt as though unusual occurrences were more frequent now and as my fear grew, they seemed more profound and intimidating. With the nights turning colder I no longer needed the bedroom window open at night, a good job as all the sash windows in the house seemed to have a mind of their own and jammed to one degree or another.

It was also a narrow noisy road with on-street parking, and which connected two public houses, so people departing the pubs late at night thought nothing of chattering loudly outside your window at 1am before starting up their cars. You could always hear their footsteps in the road as they approached and departed, and with a high stone wall opposite my house which formed the boundary to the cemetery opposite, the echo of the feet on tarmac was accentuated. I quickly got used to this nightly disruption and I usually slept through it. But even when slumbering, the sound of a lone night-time dog walker or an early-morning jogger making their way past the house stirred me from my sleep.

When I look back at that time, I can see that as my fear grew this gave the necessary nourishment to the entity or entities that haunted my house and by extension haunted me. Was this haunting personal? Yes, you can be sure that it was, and the screw was turning ever tighter. With the weeks passing and plenty of time alone to consider such things, I had to decide whether I was encountering another difficult and malicious haunting, or whether it was just my mind playing games and I was in fact becoming unhinged. Neither solution seemed favourable.

However, the answer to that troubling question came soon enough one night, around midnight and in total darkness. It was that time when I had just put down my bedtime reading, switched off the electric bedside lamp and I had started to drift off to sleep. The act of switching off the lamp would sometimes cause the scratching to begin in either the corner of the bedroom ceiling, or above my head. However, this night was to be different.

My eyes flickered in the dark. Was that a sound in the hallway downstairs? I was familiar by now with all of the creaks and groans that the floorboards made and I could pinpoint precisely which step on the stairs made which noise, each one making their own particular creak or squeak underfoot. Only I lived alone and so who was this stealthily ascending the stairs in the dark? My heart raced; a burglar! No, surely not, Monty perhaps? Monty was deliciously plump but he wouldn't be so heavy as to make the floor creak under paw, yet all the same I reached out a hand in the darkness and felt Monty asleep beside me on the bed like always.

There was very little noise from whoever was on the stairs, save for the creaks and groans of the floor. I heard no movement of clothing and no breathing. But those of you reading this that have experienced similar hauntings will know what I mean when I write 'you don't hear the ghost moving about, but you *hear* the ghost moving about.' It is similar perhaps to when someone is secretly observing you and your senses just know it. You can feel the presence of their energy watching you. Similarly, when a ghost is moving about in the darkness of the house you can sense their energy moving around rather than necessarily hear an audible noise of clothing.

Nonetheless, lying in bed in the darkness I dismissed the whole thing as settling floorboards and yet listened even harder, holding my breath as I did so. It is amazing the power of the physical senses in the darkness. Just when I thought that it had gone quiet, another specific creak or groan told me exactly where the night-time visitor was on the stairs. One thing was certain, whatever was on the stairs was ascending. Then silence. Finally, the creakiest part of the stair was the top step and the landing itself made a 'bonk' sound. Muted but very definitely present, the familiar noises came. The visitor was perhaps only eight metres from my bedroom door which I had left ajar for Monty.

Craning my head off the pillow I peered into the darkness. There was a small echo of light coming through the gap around the door from the illumination of streetlights some way away via the rear landing window. As my eyes accustomed themselves to the darkness you would expect this light to get a little brighter but instead was it my imagination but was the gap around the door getting darker? Was someone stood outside my door blocking out the light? I didn't have long to wait to find out.

You instinctively know when you are sharing a space with someone, even in the dark. Everyone, alive or dead, has their own energy and in the darkness of night, it is perhaps the easiest time to detect someone else stood in the gloom watching and you can even accurately pinpoint their location in the room. The darkness around the doorway lifted, as if smoke had cleared, but it had not gone away and had instead, without the door opening, entered the bedroom. Squinting into the inky dark I could sense it stood briefly at the foot of my bed monitoring me and then it crossed the room towards the bedroom window. At this point I switched the lamp on.

Brightly illuminated the room was now empty except for me and Monty. Only it wasn't of course. We often read 'and then as the light was switched on the ghost disappeared and the room was empty.' No, the ghost hasn't gone anywhere you just can't see it anymore! This new night-time visitation then occurred on and off for some weeks. Not always that obvious, sometimes subtle, just a feeling that someone had entered the room in the darkness, either as I was just getting off to sleep or sometimes when I would wake in the hours just after midnight.

The church clock would often wake me, or so I thought,

at 3am. I was used to the strike of the clock by now and so I couldn't fathom why I would wake up at this hour, even when I was in a deep sleep, with the sound of the bells slowly dragging me back to consciousness. Was this a curious type of insomnia or had something roused me, and if the latter then what. It was the same each time. I would be deeply asleep when the church clock would start to strike the hour. In my slumber I heard its carillon tune before it struck the full hour – almost always 3am. Waking slowly from my heavy sleep, I would half hear the sound of the church clock carillon playing its tune but as though it were muffled.

I experienced several nights of this and I concluded that the church authorities had thoughtfully muffled the sound of the bells so as to allow locals near to the church to sleep soundly. However, I wished they hadn't bothered as the muted noise it made was disquieting and muffled in a most unsettling way. The unusual sound would actually drag me out of my sleep as assuredly as if someone was shaking my shoulders. Then there was the strike itself, always the same every night. As the clock finished its muffled carillon, the hour would be struck equally as muffled, as if underwater. It was quite an unpleasant sound and the muffler on the bells made it appear as though the bell was striking the hour backwards. Horrible!

Anyone who has ever heard The Beatles clever use of backwards music, particularly in amazing songs like 'Strawberry Fields Forever' will be aware of what this backwards sound is like. From a church bell it was extremely eerie and at that time of night usually seemed to herald some kind of psychic activity in my bedroom that was to follow.

Those who have had a baby disturb their sleep in the night

every night will know all too well what this sleep disturbance does to your overall mood. Being dragged out of a deep slumber by the backwards muffled church clock became such a depressingly regular nightly event that on one occasion I even shouted out loud in the darkness, 'For God's sake get that f****** clock fixed.' I had finally decided that such a discordant noise couldn't possibly be by design but must instead be a fault. In the daylight hours the clock was never faulty like this, so it must be a night-time muffling device which was making the clock play up.

That however didn't explain the sensation that came with the muffled noise, such an awful eerie sensation when half asleep that was akin to experiencing a bad trip. I have never taken LSD but I doubt it has anything on what it was like when I was awoken at 3am during those times. The discordant sound of the church clock would bring me round from my sleep in a horrid and fearful manner. The atmosphere in my head, let alone in the room was of an alcohol and drug-induced terror. The result was I awoke in a sweat or in a sensation of total despair felt through psychic fog. It was truly horrible and I wouldn't wish the experience on anyone. Eerie scenes from the 1960s film 'Rosemary's Baby' will give you some clue as to the semi-conscious mind-altered state.

The night eventually came when an event occurred that made me decide to move out of this large pretty bedroom and into the smaller spare bedroom across the hall, the room where my ex and his partner had stayed so uncomfortably. It was just before 3am and once more I was awoken by the faulty church clock. I slowly came around from my sleep with the muffled discordant carillon of the bells playing deep within my head, the backwards staccato sound of the hourly strike calling me back to consciousness.

One ... Two ... Three ... I was awake and lying in the darkness. No sound in the room or elsewhere. Something else had woken me again, but what?

I glanced at the soft glow from my electric bedside clock and saw in the darkness it was again 3am. There was a yellow glow entering through the bedroom curtains which came from the streetlamp across the road. All was quiet. Nonetheless, something I was sure had awoken me. Fearful, I was used to my night-time visitor by now, imagined or not, and I lay in bed for twenty minutes listening keenly in the darkness. There was not a sound. Yet it was like a game, I knew that he was there in the darkness watching me, and he knew that I was awake and listening. I could feel his energy.

Then, just as I was about to relax and go back to sleep came the noise. It was nothing amazing, just a loud cough; a single cough from a man clearing his throat. The cough, distinct and clear in the silence, came from immediately outside my house in the road. More worryingly than that, it came from outside my front door below my bedroom window and under the Georgian portico. *But for nearly thirty minutes I had heard no footsteps in the road.* Any sound at all and I would have heard it, after all I had been lying in the silence intensely listening. My heart leapt to my throat. Why was a man stood in the entrance porch to my front door, and why for so long and at that strange time of night!?

I was fearful of the darkness, but I knew that I couldn't switch the bedside lamp on as I wanted to see out of the window into the darkness beyond. Naked, I slipped out of bed and across the bedroom to the sash window. Pulling back the curtains carefully I looked out to the street below that was softly illuminated by orange streetlamps. No-one was there! I waited for a while but there were no more noises and there was no-one about. Quickly and silently, I slipped downstairs and looked first out of the study window which faced the roadway and then out of the sitting room window. There was nothing. There was no-one about.

I simply couldn't bring myself to open the front door, although I stood there for ages and considered it, listening all of the time. I peered out through the bullseye glass panes and unless the coughing man was only five feet tall or crouched down on the doormat it was easy to see that there was no-one outside. Had anyone have been there and walked away I would have heard them do just that. The small town was totally silent by night, and I have explained how you could hear all footsteps approaching or departing along the narrow lane. I returned to bed that night vowing to move into the second bedroom the very next day. I would not and could not sleep in this room again.

Chapter Twenty-One

Reincarnation Part Two

A game of snakes and ladders

*If at first you don't succeed, try, try, try, try, try, try,
try and try again*

I wasn't to know it, but the personal allure of all things British Georgian and the strange familiarity of things Jewish was just a small taster into my past life incarnations and more was to follow. Very few of us are here on Earth for the first time. Like me, many of you reading this book may have had a lifelong enduring sense of being an 'old soul' and others will feel that they are 'farm fresh.' Most of us do not need to know about our previous incarnations as they are not relevant to our present journey. We remain veiled and our prior lifetimes remain unseen for the duration of our current incarnation, only to be revisited when we once again pass back into the Light. It is only recently that I have become conscious that spirit afforded me the insight into my past lives not only because of my curiosity but chiefly because it is pertinent to my spiritual life purpose this time around.

The energetic pull and emotional awareness of my Georgian and Jewish past lives was always powerful and so I decided that some less intense 'memories' of other eras and places were nothing more than a keen interest in a people, place or time.

For example, I have a long-held fascination for the culture, music, art and zeitgeist of the 1920s and 1930s, devouring Wodehouse and Agatha Christie books when in my twenties. Since childhood I have been drawn to the vibrancy, sound and colour of traditional Indian culture and sounds as much as I am to the Jazz Age and the Bright Young Things.

Growing up in predominantly white British suburbia I had absolutely no cultural reference point for Indian culture but even as a child I had an immediate love of Indian music from the moment I first heard it. When I became a huge Beatles fan in my teenage years, it was to group member George Harrison to whom I naturally gravitated and his exquisite Indian inspired pop songs. Today, when I meditate it is Indian music that I first turn to.

I had not considered that I might have a past life connection to a lifetime on the Indian subcontinent. So when I discovered last year that I have, I was thrilled and another missing piece of the jigsaw of my past-life memories slotted into place. I have mentioned elsewhere that I have familiar powerful 'words' and placenames that have a hidden subconscious programmed meaning for me. Two such words or placenames are 'Monte Cassino' and 'Egypt' and I thought that these came from childhood.

The Egyptian connection I could explain easily because when I was very young, my brother was fascinated by archaeology and being a member of a book club, he collected glossy coffee-table books about Ancient Egypt. From an early age I therefore learned about Ancient Egypt, its pharaohs and astounding architecture. My mother had spent a part of her childhood in Egypt when her serviceman father was stationed there in the

1930s and she would often tell me of her childhood memories from this time. Indeed, by the late 1990s I fulfilled a life-long wish and as an adult, my first proper holiday abroad was a week spent travelling the Nile in Egypt.

My father had spoken many times and with much enthusiasm about the Second World War to the younger impressionable me, and for this reason I logically concluded that this was where I must have picked up the place name Monte Cassino, though intuitively this didn't make sense. Because the place name 'Monte Cassino' was familiar to me, yet despite knowing little of the area, I have always wanted to visit there and I'm sure that one day I will. In 2012 I named my much-loved and much-missed rescue cat 'Monty' after Monte Cassino and also after the Second World War Field Marshal Bernard 'Montgomery.' Montgomery was commander of the Eight Army in the North African Campaign and in the Italian Campaign – a further synchronistic connection. Then, two years ago, I discovered that both Egypt and Monte Cassino may have played a significant role in a prior life, the strange discovery of which I shall now tell you.

Sometime in the early 2000s I had an occasion to take my elderly mother on a daytrip to one of my favourite UK cities, the beautiful Chichester. We had previously been there a handful of times with my father, but it was a long distance to drive and on this particular day he was feeling too tired to travel. I wasn't to know it, but this was the last time that I was to go to Chichester and I haven't seen its magnificent cathedral or picturesque streets since. I first discovered Chichester, West Sussex when I was in my twenties with 'Chichester' being another one of my placename 'words' and I was inexplicably drawn to travel there. I even desired to live there at one time but it proved too expensive as it is a very desirable place. On the final occasion I visited Chichester it was a fine summer's day and my mother and I set-off on the long car journey with high hopes for a lovely day out.

We were to be sadly disappointed, by the 2000s the city had, like many English towns, begun to change and I considered that it had started to get over commercialised and cloned. Car parking was now frowned upon and near impossible to find and when we did finally stop and sought refreshment it was to discover that the beautiful Arts and Crafts 1920s panelled restaurant where we always used to dine had been 'modernised.' This meant the destruction and removal of most of the original features, replacing them with something intended to make it look up to date, but actually just made it look tired and tacky. The town was bustling but with seemingly busy and anxious people rather than the happy slow-paced shoppers of my memories. Perhaps I was just getting old.

Despite all the anticipation and jollity, the day had not been a successful one on the whole but with the long drive home ahead of us that fine summer's evening, I knew that I had to first refuel my car. I hadn't long driven past the famous Chichester Theatre when, opposite the old army barracks I pulled into a service station to fill up with gasoline at the self-service pump. After, I went inside to pay and stood in the queue. When I returned to my car, it was to find my mother in an excited mood as she told me that I had been, 'Stood next to (the famous actor and heartthrob) Nigel Havers in the queue.' I am ashamed to admit that I hadn't noticed, but when I turned to look I could see Mr Havers getting into his rather nice motorcar and driving off.

Indeed, Nigel Havers was appearing in a production at the Chichester Theatre that week. Perhaps it was this unusual event that made what my mother said next stick in my memory. These synchronicities happen for a reason and so you should always seek to remember them when they seem particularly relevant or make an impression. Perhaps you may think this incredible, but I wonder if we were meant to see Nigel Havers at that very moment in order so that what my mother told me next would stick in my mind, only for it to become relevant many years later and it appear in this book.

Although we had been to Chichester a few times, my mother had never mentioned that she had lived there as a girl. Seeing the Army barracks she said, 'Your grandfather Sidney was stationed there just after the War,' and followed up with, 'I think we lived here in Chichester too for a while,' referring to her younger siblings and her mother. Well, this was a revelation to me as my mother rarely spoke about her late father or her UK childhood, though I knew that she had been in Alexandria in Egypt as a girl when, as I said, her father was stationed there during or just after the War.

I always suspected this reluctance to talk about her childhood was because it was not an entirely happy one. Then, as we drove along the road exiting Chichester, out came the next memory, 'Your grandfather was in the Sussex Regiment so I suppose that's why he was here.' Chichester, I should explain for those not familiar, is the county town of West Sussex. 'Why hadn't you told me this before?' I questioned, but all that my mother could add was that she didn't know why the memory had only just then returned to her.

This may all sound rather unimportant, banal even.

Nevertheless, it was one of those random conversations that stuck in the mind, yet I didn't know why that should be. I didn't then, I do now. My mother was meant to remember her father being in the Sussex Regiment and I was meant to remember our conversation, and as a result I can easily play the whole seemingly unimportant petrol filling station forecourt scene in my mind. This was an important signpost moment destined for an event I couldn't possibly have imagined happening in a distant future.

I now move forward to the summer of 2019 and to me sitting down for my annual psychic reading with my favourite and trusted psychic medium Rebecca. My reading lasted for one hour and as usual Rebecca was completely accurate on all counts, not only in detail about things that I had been discussing that day and that week with friends but also about my future plans and information about my deceased loved ones. On this occasion my maternal grandfather Sidney was the main 'speaker' together with my spirit guide, a military-decorated Roman in traditional dress, which as psychic medium Rebecca said laughingly 'was a bit of a cliché.'

In the background to the conversation were my late father and doubtless many others. Despite all the many spirit circles and readings that I had attended with psychic mediums, I had never before 'spoken' with my late grandfather Sidney. I was aged about ten years old when he died and didn't know him at all well, so I wasn't expecting to hear from him.

Rebecca asked me with surprise if I was going bald. It was a Skype reading and I appear face-on to camera and in photos as enjoying a full head of hair. She remarked that she doubted the information being given to her as she could see that I have a 'full head of hair.'

I explained that, 'Yes I am going bald, and it had been a recent matter of discussion with John.' I live with my best friend John and that very week my rapid hair loss had indeed been a topic of conversation and a matter of personal tragedy to me! Rebecca joked that my maternal grandfather apologised to me for this genetic disposition as he had been bald too.

Rebecca couldn't have known this, but my maternal grandfather was the only member of my family prone to baldness. 'Once it's gone, it's gone,' he said to me via Rebecca. Rebecca explained that when he was younger Sidney had long unruly hair which would get caught in the wind. I confirmed that this was correct as I specifically remembered my mother talking to me about this when I was younger, her father's refusal to control his unruly locks coming as something of an embarrassment to his straitlaced daughter.

Rebecca then asked if I had any connection with India as she was being shown an Indian soldier in British Army uniform. I explained that I had no connection. Rebecca said that what she was being told was 'amazing' and that I may perhaps think she was crazy for what she was about to say, and she explained that my grandfather said that he had known me *twice in his own lifetime*.

Sidney went on to explain via Rebecca that he knew me as his grandson in this lifetime but that he also knew my soul in my *previous incarnation* when we had served in the British Army together. Rebecca said that she was being shown an Indian man with a big dark beard and an upturned moustache. She said that the man was wearing British Army uniform with puttees. 'Puttees' is another one of my 'words' stored away in my subconscious for this lifetime. I can still remember playing with my brother's toy soldiers as a child and being weirdly fascinated by the puttees that some of them wore. I should also perhaps explain that in this, my present lifetime, I am dark haired with a large beard and despite an upturned moustache being considered comical by today's standards, I had often considered experimenting with an upturned moustache – this is how strong our past life memories truly are.

I had just been discussing with Rebecca and my spirit guide that my energies get easily scattered and I must protect my energy field, with the requirement that I need a lot of 'alone time' to meditate and recharge. My grandfather now explained that when he knew me as an Indian man I needed a lot of time alone then too, often going off to meditate and recharge. My spirit guide then cut in to explain that was because I am a 'highly developed soul' who is thereby very sensitive to external energies and accordingly I must protect myself. Intuitively I'd already known for many years that what I was now being told was true, my sensitivity and psychic spiritual awareness setting the agenda for my life. Not that I had ever spoken to anyone about this because no-one, not even other psychics, likes to hear a person declare that they are a 'highly developed soul'!

My grandfather said that he and I were very good friends when serving in the British Army together and that he'd had high respect for who I was as a person. Unlike the rest of my family, my grandfather was a heavy smoker and for several months prior to the reading I had been smelling cigarette smoke around me. Rebecca had introduced my grandfather to me by telling me that she could feel a very sore mouth and throat and told me that this would have been acute when he died.

When a 5D spirit comes through via a psychic medium to Earth's lower vibrational frequency, it is usual for the very last physical sensations of the deceased to be re-experienced as he or she enters the 3D physical world once more, the psychic medium then experiencing this physical discomfort themselves. Although I was young at the time of his death I recalled well that he had died of mouth and throat cancer, doubtless on account of the cigarettes he smoked daily. When he became ill, my mother used to make the long journey by train to visit him and her mother in Southampton some many miles distant.

Two years before my grandfather passed away from cancer, I was taken by my mother to meet him for the first time. I was aged about nine years and I well remember my mother and my grandmother chatting happily in the front room of the small two-up-two-down Victorian terraced house in Southampton whilst I had been ushered into the bare back room next to the small add-on kitchen. This little back room contained a 1960s dining table and two dining chairs. One chair was empty and the other occupied by a smiling bald-headed elderly man in stripy pyjamas who regarded me happily. This was Sidney and I was left alone with him, knowing him to be my grandfather but feeling all of the awkwardness and shyness that a small child does when meeting an adult.

More than that though, this was another defining moment – an important memory that stayed with me always. I had never met this man before and yet he looked at me as if meeting with an old friend, his expression was a mixture of curiosity and delight. In the following years I was to replay this moment over in my mind. A grandfather seeing his grandson for the first time would have been an amazing encounter, so surely his reaction was natural, wasn't it? Yet there seemed something more and it troubled me for years.

But the years of unanswered questions were about to be cleared up. My grandfather explained to Rebecca that upon meeting me when I was aged only nine, he suspected immediately who I was because he 'recognised my soul.' Rebecca wasn't to know but that explained precisely my memory of my grandfather being overwhelmed with happiness at seeing me 'again' for the first time in 1979. My grandfather had suspected that his grandson was his reincarnated wartime pal but this belief was only confirmed to him as correct once he had passed into the Light.

Sidney then told Rebecca that when I was growing up, he had known that I was struggling with being my own person. My parents were strict with rigid and outdated ideas and were endlessly trying to mould me into the son that they wanted, rather than the son that they had been gifted. My grandfather said that despite seeing me struggle, he had done nothing about it. He said that he deeply regretted this. I was told that it had upset him then and it still does.

We carry forward our regrets from unresolved issues from the 3D physical reality into the afterlife. Rebecca explained that he is around me a lot and he needs me to know that he is there and that I would 'smell cigarette smoke or see a flash of light.' I experience both these things regularly and so I always try to acknowledge him when I know he is present.

Our deceased loved ones visit us often. To some this can be a comforting experience and to others, scary. There is the added difficulty for many of us to differentiate between our crossed-over loved ones coming to visit us, and the irritation of being 'haunted' by an earthbound spirit who has not passed into the Light. Those who have crossed into the Light will never seek to intentionally harm or aggravate us. They visit us out of love and interest in what we are doing. Often they try to grab our attention and this can sometimes mistakenly be taken for a haunting, when it is not.

If you are uncertain as to the identity of the spirit who is around you, the advice is always to *not make contact of any kind*. There is nothing wrong chatting with your deceased loved ones. Indeed, they love the acknowledgment. But unless you know what you are doing, do not seek to identify or engage with spirit activity in your home or surroundings. This is because if you do have an earthbound haunting, you may empower it and you never quite know what you're dealing with.

Spirit does not follow the linear concept of time that humankind has created on Earth to keep track of our life. There is no past and no future, only the 'now.' How often are we told to 'live in the now'? It is quite possible for our soul to incarnate more than once at any one particular 'time', and so as you read this book, another part of your soul may well be enjoying its own unique experience in some other part of the globe. And that, in and of itself, is a very good reason to never be unpleasant to anyone!

The more that we seek to grow, the more incarnations we may have, passing back the learning to our soul as it grows in knowledge and experience. It is an uncomfortable concept to process and accept. I had some difficulty with it as my ego fought with the idea that there could be more than one of 'me' in existence! When we understand that we are all connected and that we truly are all one, screened only by the 'veil', we begin to lose that firm grasp on the egotistic concept of the individual and instead we firmly embrace the beauty of a diverse shared humanity.

I have written of my certainty that in a prior life I have been of the Jewish faith and told as much by a psychic medium. The soul has the ability to reincarnate more than once in a linear timeline. For example, one could reincarnate as a Jewish man or woman in occupied 1940s Czechoslovakia and simultaneously be an Indian soldier fighting in the Italian Campaign in war-torn Europe. With multiple incarnations, it is no wonder that the world's population is now so vast! Imagine *how few of us there may actually be here on Earth*.

I am ashamed to admit that I was quite disheartened by what I considered to be this obvious mistake on Rebecca's part. I *knew* that my grandfather Sidney had never been to India, so how was it possible that he could have known an Indian British Army soldier? Yet Rebecca was certain, and she had never before been wrong in any of the psychic readings that I had enjoyed. I regret now that I thought that Rebecca was mistaken, especially as this tiny doubt in her abilities started to bring into question everything else that she had previously told me. Losing faith in the spirit world, I dismissed the whole thing for several months. I wasn't to know it, but I was being tested. Later I was to find out that Rebecca was not only correct but also that she had told me something about my family history that I was yet to discover for myself.

It was one sleepless night during the 2020 pandemic lockdown, and on a hunch while sensing my grandfather's energy (& cigarette smoke) around me, I remembered Rebecca's reading clearly. With time on my hands, I went online to do some research. I didn't know much about my grandfather but the strong memory of the conversation I'd had with my mother outside the petrol station in Chichester, told me that he was stationed in Chichester around the time of the Second World War. I also remembered that my grandfather had been in the Sussex Infantry Regiment.

Online, I now looked up 'Chichester Barracks' and yes indeed, my grandfather's Sussex Infantry Regiment was based there from Wartime until about 1960 when it closed. No surprise perhaps, but nonetheless I felt a sudden thrill that I was on to something. My grandfather *had* been posted there and my mother had been correct.

My heart raced when I read that during World War Two the Sussex Infantry Regiment had been posted to Alexandria in Egypt. This again confirmed my late mother's tales of her childhood in Alexandria. It was when I read that The Sussex Infantry Regiment was *stationed with The British Indian Army* in Egypt during the North African Campaign that I felt a shiver run down my spine. And not only stationed together but unusually the two regiments actually *served in action together*. It was indeed probable, or inevitable, that my grandfather would have known and worked alongside Indian soldiers from the British Indian Army. They may well have fought side by side in battle.

I next looked up the uniform of the British Indian Army and the old black and white photographs showed me that it was exactly as described by Rebecca right down to the puttees plus the turban and big beard with the upturned moustache being part of the standard appearance. Rebecca had said to me that my grandfather liked my present-day beard because both he and I had had one before. I know nothing about my grandfather having once had a beard but chances are in the operational battlefield in the desert this would be likely. I had always wanted a beard and I grew one at the first opportunity, though that opportunity didn't arise until after the death of my parents, who were so strict and controlling that such things were fiercely disapproved of.

The next step was to look up online which battles the British Indian Army had fought in during the War and I was rewarded with the information that they had been *exclusively posted with The Sussex Regiment* (my grandfather's regiment) to fight at El-Alamein, Egypt and later, despite no doubt being exhausted by their experiences, to Monte Cassino, Italy. 'Monte Cassino', 'Alexandria' and 'El-Alamein' were all amongst my 'words' stored somewhere in my subconscious since childhood.

There was no way that Rebecca could have known any of this information concerning my grandfather as not even I knew any of it! One often hears explanations of psychic mediumship as being an exercise in 'mind reading' which, aside from being just as unlikely as messages from spirit, cannot be the case when the sitter isn't even aware of the provable facts being given by the psychic.

It was so strange to look at all those old black and white photographs of Indian soldiers in the British Indian Army because it occurred to me that perhaps one of the men in the photographs, now long since dead, could in fact be me. It is strange to think that in this way we are all time travellers. I don't know when I died (my incarnation as an Indian male coming to an end) as that bit wasn't told to me by spirit. Perhaps I enjoyed a happy retirement back home in India. Perhaps I had been posted to Chichester in the 1940s or 1950s, hence my fondness for the place. Or perhaps I died on a foreign battlefield.

Maybe I will visit Monte Cassino one day and the memories will come flooding back. Whatever my end, it seems likely that I was dead by 1969, the year in which I was born – if you know what I mean - and reborn as my wartime best friend's grandson. Now, how amazing is that? Particularly when you consider that this makes it likely that I knew of my own mother before she gave birth to me.

This was the most convincing piece of evidential mediumship yet, but there was more to come. A year later my grandfather Sidney came through once again at my annual psychic consultation with Rebecca. He explained that he had wanted me to have inherited his 'brass telescope' so that I could study the night sky and he said he was upset when it didn't pass to me on his death. There is no light pollution where I live in the mountains and Sidney accurately described this wonderful aspect, stating that 'you will be surprised at what you can see in the night sky.' It seemed probable that the brass telescope to which he was referring was an early twentieth century military telescope which my grandfather would have been issued with when a serving soldier. When I served alongside Sidney in the British Indian Army had I coveted his brass telescope? Had we shared the use of it on military reconnoitres?

As part of my Georgian past lifetime hangover I had always wanted a brass telescope, being fascinated with the instruments. As a shipwright I would undoubtedly have possessed one of my own in that timeline and Sidney would doubtless now appreciate this fact. Rebecca explained to me that my grandfather Sidney was so keen for me to have had his brass telescope that

I should 'not be surprised if one comes across my path' in the near future.

Six months later and I was in an antiques shop in Poland. Via Rebecca, my spirit guide had indicated to me that I was soon to meet my 'divine counterpart' and that the area being shown to her by my guide 'Put her in mind of Poland.' It was explained that this would happen, 'By the end of April.' The last day of April came and went, and I openly berated my spirit guides for having misled me. Of course, this was one of their jokey tests which psychic mediums will be all too aware of, because the next day, the first day of May, I was approached online by a very lovely guy who just happened to live in Poland, the only problem being that this is many miles from where I now live. So, this is how I found myself in an antiques shop on vacation with a lovely Polish guy in his home country.

Curiously, I'd had a strong sensation that during this week's holiday I was likely to come across a brass telescope just as Rebecca had predicted. I had only noticed the one antiques shop in this town and it looked the pricey kind. Nonetheless after walking up and down outside a couple of times I bolstered up the courage to enter the shop and I began a long and enjoyable browse of the antique china and furniture.

I had looked at everything twice and had baulked at the prices so I decided that there was nothing here for me and to leave. I was about to turn and head for the door when a small inner voice said, 'Look down.' As I did, I felt something heavy roll and tap against my shoe and looking downwards, there literally at my feet, lay a small telescopic brass telescope.

Bending down to pick up the heavy item the first thing that I noticed was the price tag. It was the only affordable thing in the shop! Upon opening the telescope up the second thing that I noticed was that this was a military telescope issued to British Army soldiers and used in both world wars, this one proudly declaring that it was 'Made in England.' This was it. This would have been precisely the same model that my late grandfather Sidney would have used when a serving soldier. It was his gift to me from beyond the grave. I felt such a thrill of excitement combined with a shiver that ran down my spine that lasted for a good half hour.

Beaming, I took it to the cash desk to pay and as I looked behind the shop assistant, I could see a handmade ceramic figure of Archangel Michael staring down from the wall. It was naively made and yet accomplished with so much love that it possessed a very beautiful positive energy. Knowing that this too was meant for me, I purchased both items together, feeling very happy that I was being divinely guided that week. Besides, who is to say that this wasn't my grandfather Sidney's very own Army-issue telescope that had somehow, many years before, found its way to Poland just for this very moment.

Chapter Twenty-Two

The haunted lamp

Electrickery and a ghostly pilgrimage

Just before coming to a stop outside their cottage grounds, I caught sight of a hunched-over plump white-haired elderly lady wearing a long dark skirt, puffy white sleeves and a black shawl. She was facing away from us as she made her way laboriously on foot up the hill past their cottage. A second glance told me that she was gone.

It was a long dark wet winter; British winters often are. My brother and his family came to visit and my brother stayed over, sleeping in the guest bedroom before I had moved into it. I didn't tell my brother about my belief in the house being haunted, this was not because he may have thought that I was crazy, instead it was because I reasoned that if I were wrong, the power of suggestion might make him imagine things. I also wanted to see, unintentionally cruelly, whether he would report experiencing anything.

Just like my ex had reported, my brother also claimed that the sunny and fresh looking second bedroom proved to be strangely claustrophobic at night and that the atmosphere, especially on the landing with its cheery chiming clock, was 'intense.' He also said that there was something about the house that made him uneasy, but that was about all. Certainly there was nothing that you could claim as 'corroborative evidence.' However, I couldn't have anticipated what would occur later with online video calls with my brother, who had retired to Cyprus with his wife a year before, but more of that later.

With hope for a better night's sleep, I abandoned the front principal bedroom with its night-time aural manifestations and the visitations of the 'shadow figure' and I relocated diagonally across the hallway landing into the second bedroom. This sunny room had the new double bed and a single sash window with amazing views over the garden and the countryside beyond. Looking down out of the window you saw below the long stone walled alleyway that led to the row of little cottages behind and looking right, the church tower with its clock dominated the landscape.

I was hoping that in this new room the church clock with its pretty daytime carillon would disturb me less by night when the faulty night-time striking mechanism usually stirred me from my sleep in the early hours. I don't know why I thought that this might be the case as the magnificent church tower was just as close to make no difference, but I had to try something.

Week after week the faulty church clock woke me at 3am from a deep slumber. A few times the clock would strike the hour correctly and I would either sleep-on or wake in the night, still expecting to hear the now familiar sound of muffled bells and the backwards peel. At other times the bells sounded correctly but as if being struck a very long way distant rather than just a few metres from my bedroom. But more often than not I would be woken at 3am, slowly coming around with the discordant corrupted sound of the carillon deep inside my head, and then just as my consciousness came online, the sound of the hour, one ... two ... three ... muffled, unnatural and impossibly struck backwards.

Daylight hours brought with them not only the sun but also the relief of the clock performing impeccably, and I presumed that the church authorities only operated the muffling device by night. Eventually, after several weeks, I decided that the church clock was broken. The random nature of the muffling, sometimes working and sometimes not made no sense, after all why would they make the strike of the clock sound so absolutely hideous by night?! It truly was an awful and discordant noise, as though my head were underwater.

The sound reminded me of an event in 2012 when following some botched dental work I got a deep abscess and an inner ear infection so severe that it painfully filled with fluid. Repeated visits to the dentist and to my doctor were futile and the infection spread across my sinuses to the other ear. Eventually the untreated infection became so bad that it led to sepsis. I was in agony and unable to move, hear or speak. My body began to shut down and only the correct antibiotics at the last hour saved my life. Yet it was the memory of the sound of my ears filled with fluid – the sound of drowning - that now came back to me, as night after night I woke in my bed at the muffled strike of the clock, backwards, haunting and indistinct.

I was pleased to discover that the phenomena of the faulty clock mechanism affected me far less in the fresh and sunny second bedroom with its delightful views. While bright and fresh in daylight hours, by night the bedroom did suffer from a pall of gloom which strangely chiefly affected the wall which the double bed faced. This wall comprised a curious small Victorian door, like something out of Alice in Wonderland, which was set high in the wall and led to the original hatch to the attic.

For now, this small cupboard made for a useful space to store my linens and towels, and if I were so silly as to leave the door ajar, it also housed Monty my cat, cats always preferring fresh, clean linens to sleep on! I never got to the bottom of why I disliked this particular wall of the bedroom but then this unusual house was filled with pockets of strange energies and unexpected zones of unpleasantness.

From my viewpoint of lying in my bed, to my right I had my wall of shoes, all neatly arranged in pairs on what had been floor to ceiling fitted bookshelves. This neat and practical solution to shoe storage appealed greatly to my Virgo Rising aspect. To my left was the cheery sash window with its picture window seat and pale ochre floral linen curtains which gave the room a bright breezy 1950s feel. Sitting here amongst the scatter cushions you could soak up the sunshine and read – or at least you could if you were able to sit there for longer than a few seconds.

Personally, I always found this window seat (there was another one immediately beneath the bedroom in the equally disagreeable downstairs dining room) to feel highly uninviting, despite its pretty looks. Then there was the draught. Contrary to what my ex and his partner had discovered, the sash window in this room worked well and it could be opened at the top and the bottom, though I admit that it was in the habit of dropping without warning. Fearing for broken glass, or worse, a broken cat, I usually wedged it tightly open with a sash window jamb.

Monty was a very clever and very sensible cat, but he gave me a scare in this room on two occasions which resulted in me never again leaving the sash window in here completely open. It was fortunate that I was stood in the room at the time. He had come trotting slowly into the bedroom, ignoring me completely, having seen something at the window and without warning and in a single bound he made a sudden leap up and onto the window seat and made to jump straight out of the first-floor window, almost certainly to injury or to his death below.

I had never seen reckless behaviour like this from him before, nor since, and I only just caught him in time as he was – literally – about to fly out of the window. After the second incident I decided to keep the window shut or opened only an inch or so. Birds never perched on the windowsill and we were too high up for roosts in trees. It was as though he had seen something, or someone, just outside of the window and had made to leap out at whatever it was that beckoned. Yet we were up high and there was nothing outside to obstruct the view.

Night-time was a different matter, and I now always removed the wedge and kept this window closed tight shut. A curious thing however was that the sash window made a restless squeaking noise. Even when I used to try and sleep in the principal bedroom this sound would disturb me and I would often get out of bed in the night to check on the window in this bedroom. I say 'squeaking' because it was as though the window was speaking or chattering to itself.

That sounds silly I know, but the noise was soft and subtle but also endless. I reasoned that a draught was causing one of the sashes to rattle slightly in its frame and this gentle movement was enough to make a whisper as wood rubbed against wood. Wedging the window tightly, I would walk away, only to have to return later in the day, or worse by night, and repeat the fiddling about with the frame to stop the incessant whisper.

This curious noise of scraping and whispering was often unnerving in an otherwise 'empty' house. Sometimes there was no sound at all and at other times the window would chatter away busily to itself for long periods yet with no visible movement. The sound was soft but incessant, and although I refused to admit it to myself at the time, it was also other-worldly. Even when there wasn't a puff of breeze on the stillest of days or nights the sound would start up or cease without explanation. My inability to settle on a logical explanation led to me to consider alternative reasons for the window to chatter. Of course, as soon as I was permanently ensconced in this room the noise from the window by night became the new irritation, taking over from the faulty church clock mechanism or the apparent threat of scratching insects in the attic.

Therefore, I immediately bought several rubber sash window jambs and jamming them into various crevices it stopped the noise for much of the time, allowing me the opportunity to catch up with my sleep. However, the window jambs would on occasion become ineffective and I would wake to once more discover the sash squeaking and chattering softly in its frame. Why was this sash so 'alive' with a seemingly perpetual vortex of breezes concentrating its efforts at the window? Was this just a movement of air, or was there something else swirling around outside?

Despite, or perhaps in-spite of, the all-new broadband cabling connection and equipment, my smartphone continued to encounter difficulties with the home internet connection. This situation continued to be only encountered at crucial moments when chatting online with friends or with potential new online dating partners. The intermittent break in internet connection, which often caused embarrassment due to the long pregnant pauses it created, seemed to be perfectly timed with an apparent mocking conscious intelligence behind it.

Similarly, despite the new cables, the landline telephone was continually interrupted with fading audio, clicks, pops and howls. In the pre-digital era it may have suggested a crossed line but this was a new all-digital connection to the nearby digital telephone exchange. Neither was this a cordless phone with a battery that could fail, so it wasn't that, but mistrusting the device that I was using, I replaced the telephone itself however the problem gradually got worse rather than better. The electric overhead lighting in the small front study also continued to flash on and off whenever it felt the need to, this chiefly being when I was in the room, though fortunately I chose to light the house by table lamp.

Having reconnected with my brother before Christmas, I was now talking with him via Skype on a fairly regular basis. My laptop I had set-up permanently in the small upstairs front bedroom which I used as a study as well as housing the single bed. I hadn't used Skype that much before. I used to keep in touch with my ex-partner via Skype and rarely on occasion my former boss when I had worked for him, so I wasn't that used to its foibles. One thing I wasn't expecting was the interference that came with the audio but I presumed it was normal even though I'd not encountered it before. I say 'interference' however what I actually mean was 'crossed-line' in the old-fashioned sense, yet this is not possible with Skype as it is digital data streaming, not analogue.

Yet as my brother and I chatted, at my end of the conversation I would hear loud illegible conversations going on in the background. This was all very irritating and sometimes actually scary when the distorted and ethereal male chatter got so loud that I could no longer hear what my brother was saying. On occasion there were clear one-word comments and affirmations responding to something that I or my brother had just said. Was this just a coincidence? I took a gamble and I asked my brother if he too could hear the disturbing noises and conversations. To my relief but unsettled surprise he confirmed that he could, although it was not as loud at his end.

My fear was that the earthbound spirit(s) in the house were behind this somewhat creepy and intrusive background noise and chatter. As I sat at the desk and talked on Skype, I would often look nervously over my shoulder towards the bedroom door and into the darkened hallway beyond. Perhaps I was anticipating seeing someone stood there and watching. When I began to Skype my new friend John, who I now live with, the same noisy occurrences happened, only whereas my brother could hear the noises, thereby corroborating my experience, John said he could not. John used Skype regularly for his work and suffered no difficulties of this kind.

Yet since I moved to John's house in Central Europe, on the rare occasions that I do use Skype, which includes speaking with Rebecca my favourite trusted psychic medium, this background chatter continued. This was a clear indication that spirit listen-in to our online conversations, their own comments and dialogue somehow impossibly being picked up electronically by the laptop. In recent times I have spoken to clients via Skype in a different (UK) location but with the same results. Chattering and comments on the 'line' that I can hear but I am certain that the other person cannot.

When during one particular conversation the interrupting voices became so pronounced that I wanted to record them as to demonstrate to friends what I was experiencing. I quickly switched on the recording facility of my smartphone as I chatted. However, when I later played back the conversation it was to discover with a chill that although the interference was apparent the loud voices in the background were missing from the recording. I would have questioned my own sanity if it weren't for Rebecca and my brother having previously heard them.

Less frightening and oddly comforting was the optical interference that simultaneously influenced my Skype calls. This began a short time after I had begun to regularly Skype my brother. I always sat in that little upstairs front bedroom, and we chatted away late into the night. Behind me, the bedside lamp appropriately situated on the bedside table was always switched on in preference to the stark overhead lighting. This did not then explain the 'light energy build up' that occurred behind me during our Skype chats. Whenever the conversation became high energy and I got energised and enthusiastic, the video image on the laptop screen would show a steady build-up of warm bright light behind me in the room. This light grew in intensity from a place somewhere behind my back so that I could not pinpoint its source.

Rather like a bubble of white light, it expanded with a pulsating flashing action over a period of around five to ten seconds until it looked as though I was sitting in a disco. Suddenly as my own energy would drop, the bubble would 'pop' and the light immediately dissipated. This process would then repeat itself several times but only when the energy of the conversation was high vibration and could only be observed on the laptop screen and not actually in the room itself.

Was the laptop camera picking something up in the room behind me that was not visible to the human eye? Happening on many occasions, the overall feeling was one of support and high positive energy rather than anything scary. My brother, perhaps less certain as to the benevolent nature of the light source, regularly commented on it warily 'it's happening again' he would say as he indicated that I should look over my shoulder. This was an important corroboration that it could be clearly seen on his own laptop screen hundreds of miles away in his home in Cyprus.

Logic dictated that I search for a rational answer and suggested that the light interference was caused by my strange broadband connection. But moving home and location made no difference to the phenomena. Much more recently I began to use Skype to chat with clients. Some of them also witnessed this energetic light build up on their screens whenever we spoke. Equally as strange is that one or two clients did not witness this brilliant light show or they chose not to mention it. Occurring only when energised, enthusiastic and high-vibration I began to see the light display as a manifestation of my own psychic energy, which I am told is strong in fluorescence. However, I now am given to understand that both the light and the sounds are indeed caused by spirit and spirit guide manifestation through me as a psychic medium. This is how I am writing this book right now, on my laptop but with the constant companionship and aide of my guides.

Back in the days when I was resident in the haunted Pippins, I knew very little about spirit guides and psychic channelling and so I therefore theorised that the light interference could be caused by earthbound spirit. This particular room was not as strongly affected by the haunting occurring each and every day in the rest of the house. There was something comforting about this little room, perhaps this was the result of decorating it in an unintentional but delightful fashion of a child's bedroom. This look was the result of colourful artist materials, period posters, postcards and other ephemera covering the walls and on the fitted white bookshelves and across the fitted white desk.

Without intention, the fun colours and objects had recreated a facsimile of a cosy 1970s childhood bedroom and there was a clear sense of this being a boy's room. Perhaps I had done this on a subconscious level for myself, or perhaps for another resident of the house – a little boy maybe? From the start I had the sensation of the energy of a small playful boy being in that room. I dismissed this as the residual energy of this smallest bedroom probably often having been a children's room over the years. I could easily imagine children spending many hours over many changing seasons staring out the upper floor sash window across the churchyard to the church beyond and watching with keen interest the comings and goings of the townsfolk below.

Then there was the bedside table lamp. I have explained how I always lit the entire house via table lamps, preferring the more ambient light these provide to stark overhead light that is more commonplace. In my little upstairs bedroom where I used to spend many hours Skyping friends or my brother, the table lamp in here had once been my late mother's, formerly in use on her bedroom dressing table. The lamp was in fact now situated on a low chest of drawers used as the bedside table. These drawers had once been my late father's and in turn these sat beside the small single bed.

Every night before bedtime I would walk around the house and switch off all the electric lamps until the house was in total darkness and Monty and me would then curl up to sleep. Around Christmastime, after I had begun to use the small bedroom as my study and Skype chatroom, the lamp took on a life of its own. At first it was sporadic. Now settled into the second bedroom, I would stir in my sleep and through closed eyes would see a glow of lamplight coming from the landing.

The first time that it happened, I blearily got out of bed in the middle of the night and treading barefoot across the carpeted landing it was to find that the bedside lamp in the small bedroom was switched on. This was curious. Had the lamp been on when I turned my own bedside table lamp off in order to sleep, I would have immediately noticed the light. No, it was definitely off and so somehow it must have switched on in the night.

Beneath the lamp were to be found separate framed photographs of my late Uncle Gordon and his late wife Joan plus one each of my late mother and father. Could it be that one of them was trying to get a message to me, maybe to let me know that they were watching over me and protecting me? Dismissing the idea as fanciful I checked the lamp operation thoroughly the next day, finding everything in order. I even took the electric plug apart twice and checked the operation of the switch. All was fine and I put the whole thing down to a fault or forgetting to switch off the lamp before retiring for bed.

However, the next night was the same, and the next. It

became a sporadic but regular event, sometimes switching itself on in the morning and sometimes during the night, but always the same I heard nothing and I sensed nothing but woke in the night or in the early morning to find that the lamp was once again illuminated. This curious and slightly unsettling occurrence continued for many weeks, with the lamp more often than not switching itself on in the night.

My laptop was only a year or so old. Waking one night it was to discover that there was a cold blue glow coming from the same small upstairs front bedroom and I presumed that it was the bedside table lamp once more. Dragging myself out of bed and entering the landing I could immediately see from the open doorway that the lamp was off and that the glow was coming from my laptop screen which was in full operating order. I presumed that the laptop battery was not fully charged which had caused it to restart, or perhaps there had been a software update in the night.

Shutting down the laptop, I went back to bed. But this was just the first instance of what was to become yet another unexplained regular nightly occurrence. From then on, the laptop went through a period, lasting for several months, of being switched on every night. Even when on occasion that I would sleep in this small bedroom, the laptop would still switch itself on disturbing my slumber and on a couple of occasions, the bedside lamp would also be illuminated as I woke next to it. At first this scared me. I considered it another manifestation of whatever was troubling this old house.

While the disturbing nature of this seemingly random event has never quite left me and remained a mystery for many years, I now recognise that it was my deceased mother trying to let me know that she was with me and everything would be ok.

Two or three weeks passed and the manifestation of the activated lamp and laptop continued unabated. After being woken one bleary-eyed night I asked my late mother out loud to stop the night-time lamp and laptop activity. The result of this was that it lessened considerably but didn't stop completely. Indeed, many months later, long after I had moved to where I now live, my laptop continues on occasion to switch itself on but only during specific relevant days. However, I no longer have any issues with the bedside lamp. Once or twice when I chatted openly to my late mother, that same night, I got a confirmatory laptop switch on.

At other times the laptop will operate by itself on special occasions such as on my birthday and on my late mother's birthday, Christmas day and the anniversary of her death. This gave me the confirmation that I needed that this phenomenon was at the behest of my late mother and not earthbound spirit. When I have been sad or lonely, the laptop will once more turn itself on in the night, offering comfort of sorts, as if to say, 'I am with you.' After a gap of nearly one year and while editing this chapter of the book on the very same laptop it was once more switched on in the morning of Saint Valentine's Day, only two days ago. I had spoken to my late mother the night before.

Strange events in the old house continued to increase as did my levels of mental distress. My mother was clearly around me and protecting me as best she could, even if only from the small upstairs bedroom. My brother, now aware of the scale of the haunting at Pippins, believed that he was being goaded into action by our late mother or father as he too started to receive regular night-time visitations of his own many miles away at his house in Cyprus.

Over Skype he explained to me how he and his wife had both seen a 'shadow figure' in their house and that they had started to experience strange phenomena on a regular basis. This culminated in loud crashes and bangs along with a shadow figure being seen by the both of them in their bathroom. This did not sound like our parents, but rather an earthbound spirit or entity causing trouble.

When I later flew out to stay with them for a week's break, I could certainly sense that their cottage had the energy of a spirit present, although I did not experience anything. Their separate guest cottage was a different matter, however. The guest cottage was adjacent to their home and within the grounds. Unlike their ancient cottage, the guest house was a relatively modern conversion and it was here, early one morning that I distinctly heard footsteps coming up the open-tread wooden staircase to my mezzanine bedroom. I knew that this was not my brother or his wife, sensing immediately that a spirit had just entered the property. It was already a bright sunny morning and I lay in my bed with my head propped up staring at the staircase opposite.

The spirit had made its way to the top of the stairs and in this small room must have been stood at the foot of my bed. I could not see anything however and there was no malevolence with the energy. My brother later disclosed to me that the cottage where I had stayed had been renovated by the previous pop star owner for his own use as his bedroom, he having sadly passed away elsewhere only two weeks prior to my stay. It seems that morning he had returned to visit the cottage where he had once lived and loved.

When I had arrived in Cyprus following a long flight and then a long drive from the airport, it was night-time when my brother's car finally pulled up at the gates to their Cypriot cottage. I experienced something which at the time seemed mundane and normal, but I was to discover was anything but. In the darkness our car swept up the steep dusty road through the village which was to be my home for the next week. Just before coming to a stop outside their cottage grounds, I caught sight of a hunched-over plump white-haired elderly lady wearing a long dark skirt, puffy white sleeves and a black shawl. She was facing away from us as she made her way laboriously on foot up the hill past their cottage.

Alighting from their car, I glanced up the hill and thought it was a charming sight, to see people still wearing traditional dress in this pretty rural mountainous area. A second glance told me that she was gone and without thinking more I presumed she had entered a cottage further up the lane. It was such a pleasant and normal sight that I didn't say anything about it until later that week when my brother and I went for a walk along the same route. My brother was keen to show me a historical landmark of a small stone chapel which sadly a recent earthquake had ruined.

Walking up along the same steep slope it occurred to me that there were no houses up here save for one long-derelict old building, the dusty lane leading only to fields and to the ruined chapel. As we trudged up the hill in the 40c afternoon heat my brother commented, 'This has been a site of pilgrimage for hundreds of years. This old lane must have been walked by thousands over the centuries.' I could well believe it as the entire area seemed steeped in history and the energy of many lives lived.

It reminded me to ask my brother where the elderly lady that I had seen on the night of my arrival would have been walking to so late at night. My brother stopped abruptly, exclaiming, 'Oh, you saw *her*!' He then explained that what I had seen had also been seen by him in the past and by many others locally. It was the ghost of an elderly lady, presumed to be a pilgrim, making her way to the chapel. To me it had looked very real and yet I now realised that she had made her way in complete silence, catching my attention one moment and gone the next. My brother clarified that when we arrived home there had been no-one else in the lane that night.

Chapter Twenty-Three

George

'She told us she'd seen it'

Drawing close in his seat, he leaned forward conspiratorially and whispered, 'The thing is, she told us that very night that she'd seen it.'

Home again at Pippins after my trip to Cyprus, I decided to see whether I could talk with a local who knew something more of the history of my property, not just historical information but I also wanted to ask about hauntings. The town was renowned for its old houses with resident ghosts but no-one I asked knew anything about mine, or perhaps they just didn't want to say. Enquiring further about 'the history' of my house, the local historical society put me in touch with a rather lovely old chap who when a child in the 1930s had lived in one of the terraced cottages immediately behind mine. He happily agreed to come and meet with me at my home and have a chat about the old days. He and his wife were 'very keen' to see what I had done with the old property as they 'remembered it well.'

George arrived alone the next day, exactly on time as one would expect of someone of his generation but sadly without his wife who was unwell at home. I gave George my good wishes to pass onto his wife of many years and I chattily gave him a whistle-stop tour of the old house. He was very polite about what I had done with the property but I suspect it was not to his taste!

He told me how he well-remembered the house as it once was and of course none of us like things that we are fond of to change. When I say 'as it once was' I am not referring to his 1930s childhood as disappointingly he told me that he never saw the inside of my home back in his childhood days. Instead I was surprised when he revealed to me that he was a regular visitor to the house in more recent times. Indeed, this was in the period immediately before the last owners' occupation, some four years prior.

Sunlight streamed through the large sash window which faced the church as we sat in the comfortable sitting room, he on the corner of the Chesterfield sofa, and me facing him on my late mother's favourite well-upholstered floral armchair. Monty lay happily at our feet, his little ginger legs in the air as he took in the warmth of the sun's rays, the ambience of the room that day was delightful, and you would never guess that this house had such a dark secret.

George had very kindly brought me a pile of old books to read, they all were concerning the town's history and included one that he himself had written. I promised to read and return them to him as soon as possible. I liked this old chap, his sense of warm generosity and yet teenage mischief still shone through despite his years.

George talked animatedly of his youth spent in the town. He told me about the people who lived in the street back in the 1930s. His memory was razor sharp and indeed, he listed off the surname of every single occupant of each house in the road back then. I greedily took in this information and with his agreement I made copious notes while he spoke. He told me about a serious crime decades before that had occurred in one house in the street that would have had lasting repercussions for those involved.

He then told me that back in the 1930s there lived an elderly couple in the cottage immediately behind my house. George was referring to the cottage at the end of the terraced row that backed onto mine, explaining that the man 'was not very nice at all' and 'a bit of a brute to all the children in the street.' He described the couple as both being quite short, both stout and the woman having white hair and the man balding and slightly hunched. I didn't know it, but this was to become important knowledge for much later in my story of this curious old place.

With a shudder, I learnt from George that this was the street in the town that was always considered the poor area and that young delivery boys would 'run from one end of the street to the other' on account of it being a 'no-go area', even by the relatively modern 1930s. He went on the explain that across the road and parallel to what is now the attractive church footpath, ran a row of slum cottages of eighteenth-century origin or earlier which suffered from no exterior space and considered to be the poorest houses in the town where the 'worst of the worst' lived and died.

What those poor individuals must have endured and suffered over the centuries is anyone's guess. He told me that the houses were so terrible and their reputation becoming so bad, that they were demolished in his lifetime. The end wall of the end terrace of demolished houses now served as the garden wall to the public house in my street, the cleared area serving as a pleasure garden for weary pedestrians to sit awhile. Within this garden now stood a wooden gazebo and I had myself sat in there on a few occasions, even as I visited the town prior to buying Pippins. It had a good viewpoint of the house and it had been a good place to sit and watch the comings and goings while I decided if this was a town where I wanted to live.

I did think at the time that it was an odd place to have a public garden, wonderful though it was for the local authority to provide such a facility. You see, the garden was mostly in the shade of some very large and gloomy fir trees and also of the church building itself. Being on the shady side of the churchyard it was predominantly dark and damp which never makes for an ideal situation for growing flowers. It wasn't a great place to sit either, possessing a lovely church path wall, but which when seated gave the impression of being hemmed in. The shade of the garden gave way to utter gloom inside the gazebo itself, which was of a round pavilion type construction, beautifully designed and lovely to have, but perhaps in the wrong place.

While it was nice to have this spot just off the churchyard, I disliked it very much and by its lack of use I guessed that the townsfolk thought the same. There was a gloom pervading every leaf and every stone of the garden and while I put this down to it being poorly situated on the dark side of the church path my intuition told me that there was something more. Were spirits still loitering from whatever had once stood here or even perhaps from the graveyard opposite? Was I just being fanciful? Now that George had explained to me the type of buildings which had once stood on this site and the lives of those poor wretches of the parish who had to endure living in these long-demolished damp slums, then those psychic sensations and my intuition began to come into sharp focus. I was building up a picture of a seedy past to this part of town and a past that must have contained some very unhappy people - and unhappy people make for unhappy earthbound spirits.

George's memory really was quite superb, and I was grateful to him for his ease of recollection. However, as yet, there wasn't much said about my own house. So, when I asked about my house back in the 1930s he explained to me that a 'very strict' old lady used to live here and that it used to be a sweet shop. He told me that she 'used to sell sweets to the children from a side window.' He couldn't recall whether it was the sitting room side window or the dining room window which faced the narrow passage running along the side of the cottage.

I suspected it was the former, the sitting room interior wall having been removed at a later date confusing him as to the layout. The children he said, had to line up in an orderly queue outside the window, or the old lady would get annoyed. He didn't think much of her it seems, suggesting that she was an embittered old woman with perhaps many of life's regrets. I was later to discover that the old lady's name was, appropriately enough, Miss Sweetland.

George's tales of life in the town during the early twentieth century made it apparent that some of the long-gone former occupants of the locality had perhaps not been the most uplifting of people and many would have been wisely avoided. A long-since deceased former occupant of a cottage behind mine was a prime example having many decades before spent time in gaol after he committed a terrible crime during the early part of George's life in the town. But it wasn't just the people that I learnt about, it was also about the practical appearance and function of the town and its buildings. For example, the reason that I had a very high old stone wall attached to one side of my cottage was because it this once comprised part of the blacksmith's yard which George told me all about, including the life of the former blacksmith many decades prior.

My own digging about in the parish archives suggested the wall was originally a part of a building, or farm structure either before my house was built, or from when it was a farmhouse during the eighteenth century. The entire street had a long and rich history attached to it and it was no surprise that my house would be haunted. Perhaps it would be a bigger surprise had the house and the town not been haunted given the history and age of the place.

George spoke at length and in most interesting terms about the town and townsfolk as it once was, but I was thirsty to know more about my house. In response to my prompting George revealed, 'Yes, my wife and I were very dear friends with Miss Tomkins who used to live here.' Delighted to be finally talking about the recent history of my home I shifted to the edge of my seat but tried to not appear over keen. However, I could not have anticipated what was about to be revealed. 'She used to live in the small front room. She even slept in there,' he explained, telling me that Miss Tomkins spent her entire life in the one room.

'What, the downstairs front study!?' The door to the sitting room was open and from my vantage point I could clearly see into the little room.

'She always greeted us in there and we chatted in there, dined in there and did everything in there.'

I considered it very odd that this former occupant of very

recent times, only some five years before I moved-in, had spent her life in that small room. Perhaps it was easy to heat, but presumably we are also talking about summertime and not just winter. What possesses a woman to eschew the rest of her spacious house and instead choosing to live and sleep in the smallest room, with the busy street right outside the window, people and vehicles passing by day and night? Having experienced the upstairs bedrooms by night, I suspected that I already knew the answer.

George continued to chat happily about his and his wife's friendship with the late Miss Tomkins. Suddenly he threw something into the conversation that stopped the flow of jollity.

'We were the last people to see her alive.' he said.

'I'm sorry?' was my inadequate response.

George looked sad and eager in equal measure as he explained, 'We had been invited over for a chat, for drinks and for dinner. As usual we met and spent the whole time together in the little room.' referring to the study. He continued, 'It was only the next day that we were told that very sadly she had died in the night. She had been found still sitting in her armchair where we had last seen her.'

If I was stunned, I was horrified at George's next revelation. Drawing close in his seat, he leaned forward conspiratorially and whispered, 'The thing is, she had told us that very night that she had seen *it*.'

My eyes must have widened and George went on to explain that Miss Tomkins well knew that the house was haunted. He described some of the experiences that she'd had over the years which corroborated my own. But the inference was clear; she had, after many years of occupation, finally *seen* the ghost and perhaps as a result, she was dead only a day or so later. George speculated whether she had seen it again that night of their dinner and maybe this time it had frightened the poor woman to death. I didn't doubt it.

Though difficult to satisfactorily explain, the night-time visitations in this house were very dark and very scary indeed. Doubtless my face must have given my thoughts away. George could see that his parting shot had hit home. Was I also to see the spirit? Was it soon to manifest? Would the same awful fate befall me as it had the former occupant?

George bade me farewell and we agreed that he should return with his wife when she was better. They never did return, given the knowledge of what was in the house, I could understand his wife's reluctance.

So, what was I to do? Many times I had wondered if I had merely lived alone for too long and my imagination was causing me all this grief. No, here was actual corroborative evidence that my house was very haunted indeed and that it was not only in my head. The former occupant had not only regularly experienced the haunting, but she had actually *seen* the ghost *and* she had died soon after. The fear in me was expanding and fear fuels the negative energy that earthbound spirit hungers for.

George had been unable, or unwilling, to describe to me how the haunting had specifically manifested for his friend. Incredibly, he admitted that he had forgotten to ask what the ghost looked like! I was amazed by this lack of foresight, particularly from a man with a memory still so sharp. Perhaps his reluctance to engage with the finer details had nothing to do with an absence of mind but much more to do with a surfeit of fear. All the same, this left me with little to go on, but even if

I knew what to expect, what would I do with that knowledge?

The atmosphere in the house continued to be alarming both by day and by night. Please do not think that just because I was engaging in jolly chats in my sunny sitting room in any way meant that I was feeling settled or secure in my home. Quite the opposite was true. I was putting on a brave face for all outsiders, yet behind my closed front door, the negative atmosphere continued to slowly build. Night-time bangs, creaks and knocks were just a small sideshow compared to the heavy atmosphere, the footsteps on the stairs, or the strange sensations of being drunk on the landing. And it was on the landing that I had hung a recently acquired antique oil painting of boy of around ten years in age, dressed in medieval garb and holding white lilies to symbolise purity.

One day when passing the portrait, I paused and jokingly asked out loud what his name was. Immediately 'Thomas' came to mind and so I decided to call him by this name. I observed however that 'Thomas' seemed to better apply to the energy of the little boy who I had long suspected still occupied the small upstairs front bedroom. I glanced into the small room from where I was still stood on the landing. It was as though he had answered my question which I had addressed the portrait.

Yes, I am fully aware of how crazy this all sounds when I write these events down into cold, hard black and white text on paper, yet crazy as it may appear, I can only write of the energy, feelings and events of that time. Things however were about to get crazier – and more frightening.

Chapter Twenty-Four

Do you want change?

Become the change

'To get angry at the actions of another person, is like that person has baked you a cake with poison inside and knowing this you then agree to eat it.'

It is part of the human condition to want change for the better, but we more often than not expect that change to come from outside sources, 'well if only *he* would do this' or, 'why can't *they* just do that.' The 'he' or 'they' are on their own journey of discovery in life and however regrettable it may be, they have no obligation to you to change. If circumstances or others' behaviour won't change to suit us and the behaviour or actions offend us, then it is for your own ego to adjust to that. While we cannot alter how others behave towards us, we can alter how we respond to their behaviour. When we speak of 'they' it implies that 'we' are not part of the greater '*they*' and yet of course every one of us make up the collective whole. Ask of yourself honestly, 'How do others see me?' Perhaps others look at you and they also think to themselves, 'If only *they* would change, then my life would be better.'

You may think that you do not need to undergo any degree of self-improvement but there lies the problem. There are billions of people in the world who earnestly believe that they do not have any need for further spiritual growth or self-improvement. But if that were the case then how does humanity's longing for a change for the better arise and where do all the people who need to change come from?

Our ego is superb at self-deception. It creates a metaphorical wall of protection around our sensitivities and our hearts and daily reinforces this protective construct. This is to the very detriment of our own spiritual and physical wellbeing. A heart that is so protected that it cannot be wounded in love is also a heart that cannot be loved and feel love given by another.

Each time that we encounter those who offend us or who behave in a toxic way towards us, we remember that hurt and carry the wound with us so as to learn from it and ensure that it never happens again. The wall that we build around ourselves is therefore not constructed of bricks but instead is built-up of our judgments of people we have known. With each personal sleight or unpleasant encounter, we build resentment and with the passage of time we can begin to approach life with the 'victim mentality.'

We become attached to our viewpoint, believing it to defend our position and thinking wrongly that to have strong opinions makes us a powerful minded person, and even a leader of men. Instead, being unable to empathise with another person's viewpoint, which has probably come about through their own life's journey and similar emotional wounding, is a weakness that demonstrates an endless requirement for the ego to be pampered.

Anyone who dares to contradict our tightly held viewpoint can upset us, and we have created our own imagined world built around beliefs and constructs that may not be true or be the complete picture. Ultimately, we bicker, fight and fall out with friends, family or lovers and then we crawl away to lick our wounds, only to make up later when love once more establishes the equilibrium of the heart. We may consider ourselves to be a victim of others behaviour but that just makes us a sore victim of our own ego. It is therefore not how others behave towards us that is crucial to how we feel but it is how we choose to respond to their behaviour that can make for a quiet mind.

Do we want to remain a victim to circumstance our whole life? Of course not, but most of us do not want to take any degree of responsibility for the things that happen to us in life. When people ask, 'What have you been doing with the four years that you've spent at your retreat in the Czech Republic?' I respond that I have been doing 'my inner work' or 'healing the wounded inner child' as I think of it.

Good mental health can come from good spiritual practice and spiritual housekeeping, and it is therefore invigorating to see that many people these days are taking up practices such as meditation, yoga and other forms of self-care. We should all do some degree of spiritual practice and inner work on a daily basis. The western world's frenetic mantra of 'more is more' takes us far away from the place where we can quieten the mind to achieve any level of inner peace and sanctity.

The first step is to meditate several times a week, even if it is only a few snatched minutes here and there in your day. 'But I need a quietened mind to be able to meditate in the first place!' people have complained to me. Yes, we can find ourselves in a chicken-and-the-egg situation, for example when I am unwell or encountering one of life's more stressful days or weeks, I can find it very difficult to settle my mind enough to meditate.

There will always be days when we don't feel able to meditate and that's fine. Just like there'll always be those days when we stray away from the healthy food option and sink into the welcoming toxic arms of junk food, we don't have to be tough on ourselves all of the time. But a healthy physical body comes from regular maintenance and good natural food and in the same way good mental health and good spiritual health comes from the same degree of tender loving care.

For those who have not tried meditating, I would recommend a guided meditation and see if that works for you. Many of these can be found online, some good, some not so good, therefore find something that works for you and stick to it. Alternatively anything that helps you to relax can be done while meditating; listening to relaxing music or taking a bath, all help.

If you are one of those people who, like me, wake early and then lie in bed worrying about the day ahead or have those annoying 'internal conversations' about 'what was said yesterday and to whom' then stop those negative thoughts as they occur by switching over into a positive meditation practice mode as you lie there. There is no better place to meditate than when lying in bed and no better time than first thing in the morning as your day is about to begin.

We are trying to do the inner work and change for the better, but what about that bully at the office, or the neighbour from hell next door? Well, we cannot just ignore other people's abuses, but we can forgive them and when we do the inner work, we start to find that they affect us less and less. This comes about as we heal old childhood mental wounds and thereby become more self-empowered and less triggered by other people and their behaviour.

When faced with an unusually discourteous or perhaps downright rude stranger, for example a check-out operative at the supermarket, rather than get irritated I first try to repel the anger which is being unintentionally or even intentionally directed towards me. This can be done internally or with a big smile and a positive response. Always pause before reacting and first remember that the person may have had a particularly difficult day, or even a difficult life! Perhaps they have just been berated unfairly by their boss, and, unable to retaliate lest they lose their job they take out their inner frustration on the customers. Maybe they are deeply in debt and about to lose their home or knowing that they must return to an abusive partner that evening. Or maybe they are just an obnoxious, rude person.

Whatever the reason for their negative energy, why let it affect you? You are the bearer of your own internal light and you do not need to allow others to dim it. *To do so is to give away your power.* You do not need to react to another's negative behaviour, it is your ego that is reacting and in doing so it takes on the other person's energy.

A very good friend of mine once said to me that he keeps himself in his 'own whirlwind.' He explained that he considers everyone to be in their own whirlwind and the trick is to not allow other people's whirlwind to affect your own. I like this analogy as it illustrates what is energetically happening with our own personal energy field whenever we encounter others. Some people seem to surround themselves with the lightest of summer breezes and others a full-blown hurricane. Whatever the energetic weather, always be prepared for a storm not of your own making.

In the longer term, does it truly matter to you when a stranger in a shop or elsewhere is rude? Consider why you are getting angry at that person who angrily pushed their way in front of you in the queue. Why are you adopting *their* anger and negative energy? The quote 'to get angry at the actions of another person, is like that person has baked you a cake with poison inside and yet knowing this you then agree to eat it' is apropos. The only power that another person has *over you* is the power that you are prepared to allow them to *take from you*.

Have you ever noticed how negative or toxic people seem to dump their problems? Whether that be the angry customer in the queue at the Post Office, or that one friend you have who is always moaning about their lot in life. The one thing that they have in common is that they are spreading their own particular negative energy around. Some people have the ability to walk into a room and light it up with their positive energy and vibes, while others seemingly can do the opposite until the whole room is miserable and you can feel a palpable change in the energy. This is energy being passed about. This is a reminder that we are all made of energy, so don't give yours away by becoming needlessly embroiled in other people's whirlwinds.

'Toxic' is today a very over used expression to describe someone with undesirable personality traits, it is also a very unpleasant one but I'm sure we've all felt justified in using it at one point or another. In this book we have considered how we are all on our own life journey and our own life path and our soul learns and grows through experience. However, there is nothing in the rule book that says you have to sacrifice your own empowerment for the benefit of someone only too willing to take it from you. 'Ah, but I like to help and I'm a kind person.' Well I am sure that you are, after all, you're unlikely to be reading this book if you were not already on a voyage into personal and spiritual development but be on the watch for that toxic person in your life, we have all had one.

They can be readily identified as the friend or work colleague who always has moans and issues that are seemingly insoluble. No matter what you suggest, offer or do for them it's never quite enough and there's always a counter argument as to why their lot is so much worse than anyone else's or why they are unable to change things for their betterment.

They have engaged with the negativity in their life to such a degree, and over such a long period of time, that they have reprogrammed their brain and their body on a cellular level to respond to negative input. This is rather like a junkie getting a fix. Dopamine is released when the brain associates an activity with pleasure. This can be anything such as food, shopping, sex, getting angry at the news or even moaning. This repeated cycle of negative emotional thoughts then becoming words, triggers the release of these relaxing chemicals into the bloodstream. This is in just the same way that any other stimulant operates.

The person wants their dopamine fix and to get it they want discord not harmony as only upset and negativity now works for them on a cellular level. This is why they will reject your compassion, empathy and love but this does not mean that you have to share in their negativity, nor does it mean you should be their dealer of choice. Empaths and compassionate loving people are sensitive types who can all too readily be taken advantage of by less caring individuals.

I was reared by my parents as 'a fixer.' Both of my parents were on the narcissist scale and I was therefore trained from an early age to respond to the needs of others. This has been a blessing and a curse, but mostly a curse. It was hard for me to accept this aspect of myself which I only discovered when doing my own 'inner work' healing my wounded inner child, and I recognised that I had few, if no boundaries and I was all too willing to accept the responsibility to 'fix' the other person if I felt that they had a need or something lacking in their life. Yet who am I to assess someone else's needs.

It is not our responsibility to fix another person, even if they are a close friend or family member. The responsibility for that repair work, if any is needed at all, falls to the person concerned. Offer love and compassion by all means, but to offer them your own time and your own precious energy to 'fix' them relieves them of that duty and may leave you with a lack of time and energy for your own personal development. If you attempt to help out and heal that person when they are not ready or not willing to make the changes that they themselves need to do, then your kindness will fall on deaf ears or worse, they will come to resent you for your interference.

I have had friends who are warm and beautiful people, and yet they seemingly revel in the misery that they perceive their life contains. They have become addicted to their own negativity narrative on a cellular level. Some may also become addicted to the receiving of kind and warm energy from empathic friends and family. Each time they speak about their perceived troubles, they give voice to them and it reinforces the narrative in their mind, this is how we program the brain. At the same time the dopamine rush they receive programs their body down to the cellular level to respond to the rush of chemicals. As with any drug, the body then craves a repeat dose, and the cycle perpetuates.

When you become intertwined with someone addicted to their own negative thought patterns, you become part of the problem and not the solution. Additionally, you are giving your energy away. You don't believe so? Why do you think that there is the old British expression of 'a problem shared is a problem halved?' That toxic person in your life whom you arrange to meet for coffee once a week has set out that morning with the express purpose of dumping their negativity onto you.

You still don't believe me? Well, has no-one ever said to you after such an emotionally fraught coffee date (we've all had one), 'Oh, I feel so much better now!' and with a cheery 'Goodbye, see you next week,' they depart the café in which you two have been chatting together for an hour or so. Yet even before the ink is dry on the bill, you assess how you feel by contrast and realise that you feel dreadful, and certainly much worse than when you came in. That negative energy of your lunch date has been shared with you *'a problem shared is a problem halved.'*

A good guide whenever you meet with a friend, an acquaintance or a family member is to ask yourself immediately afterwards 'How do I feel?' If the answer is always 'meh' then you have the beginnings of a shortlist of people who should not be in your life. Remember that it is always acceptable to walk away from relationships that are 'toxic.' Many people in our lives are 'karmic relationships' and once you have learnt the lesson that you agreed to learn with this person prior to birth you may acknowledge it and then walk away.

Then there are the narcissists and people with narcissistic tendencies. The psychological narcissist will seek out empaths and compassionate people in order to manipulate them. This is a whole different topic for another chapter or book. Having suffered from narcissistic parental abuse as a child, it followed that in later life I became the unwitting 'victim' of a clinical narcissist. This is a common pattern that follows from being an empath with few boundaries. These were all my undealt with issues from childhood that I am ever in the process of healing from, but in general if we recognise and resolve our own issues, then a manipulator is unable to manipulate us.

Once healed from our own personal traumas we begin to identify toxic traits (or 'red flags') in others that we simply wouldn't have seen before, and the healed empathic person is now able to confidently put up the appropriate boundaries with little effort and with no guilt. That is not to suggest that we become thoughtless uncaring people, quite the opposite. But you must learn to fill your own cup first before you have enough to allow anyone else to drink from it.

As I healed from my traumatic childhood, instead of being the people-pleaser that I once was, I began to realise that I was everybody's friend except my own. My advice to all readers is to say that it is never selfish to be your own best friend and to love and honour your own energy and soul. No-one is coming to rescue you; *you are that person*. Begin the rescue today.

Chapter Twenty-Five

The most haunted house in town

Blue ribbons

'My daughter wouldn't even enter this small downstairs reception room as she said there was something extremely unsettling about it.'

The same afternoon that George had visited, I sat down and began to read through the pile of books that he had kindly loaned to me. My neighbour Edith had also loaned me some books on the town and its history, while the elderly lady I'd visited who had once lived in my house in the 1930s had given me a fictional book based on the town. Settled in the comfortable armchair by the sash window which overlooked the church I began to read, perusing the books and trawling through the pages one by one.

Most were about daily village occurrences, who said what to whom and when and accentuated wartime goings on. In fact, much of the material was a little pedestrian in nature concerning who and why, rather than when and how. The fictional book was an as to be predicted amusing diversion about a romantic tryst between a nun and a monk, high spirits but not the kind that I was seeking. Then, finally there was the book that I had saved until last. It was the most recently published being only a couple of years old and was about the town and its ghosts, purporting to contain specific details. I was intrigued though George had said that there was nothing in here relating to Pippins my house, but perhaps there was something that might help.

The book was informative, well written and illustrated containing page after page of the most renowned hauntings in the town. There were quite a few, including a girl in a white pinafore dress, presumably late Victorian period, who had been spotted all over town by various people over many years. Seemingly the little girl was able to come and go as she pleased and seemed quite happy to do so. Most of the reports were restricted to a bump or a knock in the night or perhaps to a rare sighting.

While all these occurrences were thrilling in their own way, my heart started to sink as I realised that I was running out of book without having discovered anything about my own house. None of these hauntings sounded as profound as what I had thus far experienced in my own home. Perhaps this whole thing really was all in my head? Was I going mad? Had I imagined the inexplicable noises, the terrible stifling vibrating atmosphere and the dark shadow figure? Then I remembered the late Miss Tomkins and knew that there must be *something* to all this.

Finally, there was a story about a holidaymaker and his family, plus a mention of other holidaymakers before them who 'some years before' had stayed in 'a cottage in the town' hoping to enjoy a relaxing week or two away in rural peace. Unusual for the book, no name was given to the house but something familiar immediately rang true about the details. It was said to be a cottage, next to the church and near to the public house and possessing its own driveway and garden.

My interest immediately piqued, and I sat forward in my armchair gripping the book tightly, a strong fascination mingled with a tingling fear which prickled down my back as I read each word. There was the mention of driveway gates; my house had none but I was aware that there had once been some. The name of my street was clearly given, and I knew that there were only three or four houses sited immediately next to the church and near to the public house. Pippins was the only house in the street with a driveway *and* garden. Could it be that this holidaymaker was referring to *my home*? Perhaps they had just forgotten the name of the house and referred to it as a 'holiday cottage.' I read on, thrilled to perhaps have found something at last.

'Upon entering the property there was a peculiar atmosphere.' Well, so far so good I thought, I've certainly got plenty of atmosphere. 'There was a small room immediately off the front door which served as a reception for the self-catering guests where you completed the visitors' book and could browse through the selection of tourist attraction brochures.' The layout as described was exactly like my own house and the reception room precisely matched in description the little room where Miss Tomkins had sadly died, and which was now my study. It also eliminated the only other house in the street to which the book could be referring, as this other cottage did not have a small front reception room. Yes, the book was most definitely referring to my house.

'Throughout the house was an extremely creepy atmosphere that is very hard to describe in words,' and 'My daughter wouldn't even enter this small downstairs reception room as she said there was something extremely unsettling about it.'

This was it! This was my house! The book continued, 'It really was a very strange small room, with an eerie atmosphere and the owner had inexplicably attached blue ribbons to the door frame. Then we noticed that throughout the house the owner had attached little blue ribbons to all the doorframes.' *Little blue ribbons*! I had been *sat in that very room* when the strange idea had come to me of attaching *little blue ribbons* to the doorframe and to the doorframes elsewhere in the house!

I felt a little nauseous. What was this?! What the hell was going on here? Although I had eventually dismissed the idea of attaching little blue ribbons to the doorframes, partly because my mind told me that it was a crazy idea and partly because I found the idea inexplicably creepy, the point was *I had thought of it*. Here in black and white it stated that a previous owner also had the same idea and *had carried it out*. I noted with fascination that the holidaymaker who was interviewed had thought the blue ribbons significant enough to talk about them for a book on hauntings.

This apparently benign act of attaching small blue ribbons to the door frames had unsettled the holidaymaker enough for him to make specific mention of it in this book. I understood fully what that holidaymaker had experienced as even thinking about these little blue ribbons had made me fearful, yet I knew not why. The blue ribbon that the holidaymaker had first spotted was also in the very room where I had come up with the same idea and which I had thought was my own. This was crazy! *Am I going nuts?*

The interview with the holidaymaker and his family proved a fascinating read and of course no longer having the book in my possession I have had to paraphrase. The astonishing moment of validation that I had from finally reading about my house in a published book was however a memory that I shall not forget, and there was more to come. I do not know how the book author was able to obtain the interviews but there were further unnamed former holidaymakers who also gave their accounts of the supernatural happenings in the house. In *my* house!

They explained how they had settled down for their first evening in the holiday cottage only to find that they were extremely disturbed by the strange ever-encroaching atmosphere in the property, recalling that as night fell this became worse. I knew this atmosphere well and I realised that this was accurately describing my very own home – the same haunting had been going on for many years and may have affected hundreds of different people staying in the property.

I have explained how hard it is to accurately describe the cloying vibrating atmosphere in the cottage. It was something akin to being drunk, scared and perhaps on some narcotic opiate all at the same time. I was alone in the house yet feeling intoxicated and as though the cottage was filled with people, like so many strangers at a party. Yet you were an uninvited, and crucially, unwanted houseguest.

Anyone who has ever watched the popular cult television drama 'Twin Peaks' will know the type of creeping supernatural atmosphere that this house brought about in people, especially as night fell. The holidaymakers continued to explain how at night in bed the house felt warm and 'claustrophobic' and the air electric as they tried unsuccessfully to sleep. One holidaymaker explained how he got out of bed and tried to 'open the sash window' which overlooked the church, only to discover that it refused to open more than an inch. This was indeed my house.

The interviews continued about this unnamed house in much the same vein. Disturbing atmosphere. Stifling. A feeling of being watched. Unsettling. But which house was this that had affected so many people? I was absolutely certain. It was mine. The practical descriptions given by the people interviewed for the book were so accurate that it could only be my house in that street. Mine was one of only two detached houses and the only one facing the church with a garden, driveway and sash windows. It was also the only house with a small front reception room just off from the front door.

Then, just when I thought that was everything there was to discover, this crucial chapter ended and I turned the page for the final chapter of the book, expecting it to be about some other property in the town. The confirmation that followed was to leave me bewildered and not a little frightened.

The new chapter summarised the entire book by explaining how they had discussed the most famous haunted houses in the town. What I was about to read next I should perhaps have been expecting but strangely it still took me by surprise. 'Perhaps the most haunted house of all in the town is one that isn't mentioned much or known about by locals. This is a house called 'Pippins'.' Hairs down my neck tingled and my stomach lurched. *My house*!

Here was my house not only being included in the book by name as being haunted but as the conclusion to the entire book as *the most haunted house* in this most haunted of towns. What followed accurately described the ghostly experiences from the previous chapter but now the house name had been revealed.

Perhaps the author had not realised that this was one-in-the-same house, possibly because the name of the property had been changed back and forth in the preceding years.

Here in this last section of the book, the *very people from whom I had just bought the property* were interviewed and stated that their teenage children had experienced any number of ghostly happenings and sensations, knocks and noises, feelings and strange atmospheres with specific mention made of 'electrical gadgets', particularly the teenagers' 'mobile phones' inexplicably failing to work at specific moments. It was a pyrrhic victory for me to finally establish that I was not going mad and that my house was haunted. Not only haunted but considered so active that it was given the label of 'the most haunted house in the town.'

When buying the house, I had specifically asked the vendors if the house was haunted and they had confirmed via the agent that it was not. Yet here, in print, they were fully aware of the haunting, having experienced it themselves at first hand. It suddenly made sense why there was so little furniture in the house when I viewed it, the vendors perhaps having already partially moved out. Indeed, when I moved in to the property the neighbours advised me that the house had been empty for some weeks and inexplicably the downstairs front sash windows facing onto the road had been left open in all weathers. Another unsolved mystery.

This was not only the most haunted house, but the owner prior to the last vendor had also seen the ghost herself and had died alone in her room soon after. As I closed the book and put it down, I sat for a while in silence and then it came to me that I was also living here alone. Could it be that I was soon to suffer the same fate?

Chapter Twenty-Six

Dark forces

Archangel Michael moves in

Occasionally I would catch one or the other of them taking a sneak peek through the dining room window, trying to see past the stained glass panel of Archangel Michael. I had no blinds or net curtains, but I thought 'What harm could it do? They are just a nice elderly couple.'

British winters are when the nights draw-in, the days grow colder and the evenings wetter. At Christmas it is said that the veil between this world and other realms is at its thinnest. This was undoubtedly the case for me one afternoon in early December. It would be true to say that the 'goings ons' at Pippins could have reduced me to drinking wine in the evenings just to relieve my ever-increasing anxiety, however I remained a fairly moderate drinker.

This particular afternoon I had been teetotal all day and was feeling bright and fresh which made what was to come unfathomable. The night was already settling in and therefore so was I, sitting on my chesterfield sofa with my cat Monty. Doubtless he was happily washing himself, the lamps, candles and incense were lit and the woodburner burning away, providing much needed ambience and warmth for the inky black night to come.

After a relaxing afternoon spent indoors it was now dark and cold outside, in fact quite forbidding and I chose to snuggle down and do some social media on my smartphone with the curtains tightly drawn to keep out the winter. I am not a fan of television and so as usual, I had my ancient hi-fi playing music in the background and I began to enjoy some relaxation. The word 'hygge' would probably sum up the scene that late afternoon, with no ghostly disturbances or outside world interruptions to speak of.

Then something very strange happened to me physically. It was exactly 5pm, I remember checking the time on my phone. My smartphone had pinged to alert me to two new followers who had suddenly joined my social media account. Checking, I discovered with some alarm that both these new followers were self-proclaimed 'Satanists.'

Having people choose to follow you on social media who perhaps may not wish you the best is not unusual. Satanists and other misdirected people of the 'Illuminati' had followed me before and my usual action was to block their accounts without a second thought. This particular afternoon was different as a bolt of warning shook me as I quickly blocked these two new accounts.

Within seconds, my head span and I was suddenly overwhelmed by a wave of fatigue. 'Fatigue' understates the force of the tiredness that hit me as I sat motionless on my sofa. I felt that I was falling into a chasm of darkness which was teamed with a tsunami of sleepiness that washed over me, my solar plexus drained of energy. My hackles rose with my senses on high alert. I wasn't to know it, but I was under psychic attack.

I had never knowingly encountered a full-on psychic attack before, indeed I had never really thought about it. The alarm caused by the two blocked Satanists wouldn't subside and this gave way to fear as my physical body came under attack, and fear is a powerful manna for dark energies. My inexplicable drowsiness increased. Monty was relaxing on the sitting-room carpet as I staggered to my feet. I only knew that I had to get to bed immediately!

There were candles to extinguish, the hi-fi to switch off and burning incense to attend to before there was any question of going upstairs to bed. It was only just after 5pm! What the hell was going on!? Hell ... yes, that was it. I remembered many months ago reading the 2017 astrology forecast for my astrological sign recalling it advising that there will be 'many frights this year' of a 'supernatural' origin and indeed even 'encounters' with something 'Satanic.' I had scoffed at this at the time and yet here I was under a full-on psychic attack. Was this attack connected to satanism? Or had the spirit entity in the house smelt fear and seeing a chink in my psychic armour was trying to drain my energy and take me over? Were there more than one entity working together as a collective negative consciousness? My head was foggy, I needed to sleep *now*!

I cannot here tell you how I managed to walk around the lower ground floor extinguishing candles and electric lamps before heading upstairs. Indeed, I have no memory of climbing the stairs at all. It was as though I was under the influence of alcohol or drugs, or both. Somehow, by a little more than two or three minutes after I first felt the sudden onslaught of apparent narcolepsy, I know not how but I made it to my bed in the second bedroom, climbing in semi-clothed and falling into an immediate deep sleep.

I woke-up several hours later. Not untypically when you

fall asleep at a strange hour, on waking I had that momentary sensation of not knowing where on Earth I was, what time and day it was, or even who I was. Something had woken me. The room was now completely dark, a New Moon and a cloudy sky adding to the blackness. I glanced at my bedside alarm clock, it was exactly midnight. What the hell was going on!? I had been in a deep sleep for nearly seven hours! Yet still I felt drowsy and what had woken me?

I didn't have to wait long to find out. There it was again, a slight scratching sound from above my head. It was the same noise that I used to hear in the principal bedroom. I lay in the dark, rigid, silent, holding my breath as I listened with all my ability. The scratching continued and as it did so I could 'see' in the darkness above my head something inky black form on the ceiling. The room was entirely in darkness and yet the blackness that was now forming was even darker - a total absence of light. Surely an optical illusion?

I blinked repeatedly as the black mass slowly increased in size until it was easily the proportion of a grown man, suspended but spread across the ceiling in the corner above my head. Then in seconds it slithered like a scrambling mass of black smoke moving diagonally across the ceiling to the opposite corner of the room nearest the bedroom door. The bedroom door was ajar for Monty but neither he nor any light from the streetlamp entered to assist me in my lonely plight. Fear had by now turned to an immeasurable terror.

Many other things were to happen to me in this house over the coming months and many things have happened to me before and since, but in all my experiences of the supernatural, I have never outside of a nightmare felt such a feeling and sensation of a malignant evil that now filled my bedroom with its dark energy. Whatever this was, it was not human and probably never had been.

Lying in silence, I realised with an inner cry for help that the darkness that had made its way across my ceiling was not yet done. Now arriving over the bedroom door, I had somehow expected it to continue its course until it reached the opposite diagonal corner of the house in the principal bedroom where the scratching usually started. Instead, stealthily and steadily, it spread down the walls like black oil being poured. Spreading quickly, it was with horror that I realised I could no longer see the opposite bedroom wall, the mass spreading out like a black fog and engulfing the entire wall. The wall now only blackness, the bedroom was vanishing in an absence of light as this dark entity made its way across the room towards where I lay in my bed.

I did what I had forgotten that I used to do as a child when in fear of psychic visitations; I envisaged the room flooded with the white psychic light and love of the Source and at the same time I began to pray to the Holy Trinity. Whatever was in my room was concentrated evil and an absence of the Source and the Light. I had never before nor since experienced anything like it but if it represented everything that was furthest from the Source, or God, then the pure white love and light of the Source would surely resist it.

I was surprised and relieved in equal measure to discover that it did. The black mass not so much moving away from me, or out of the door, but rather like smoke dissipating very quickly until it had vanished. I switched on the bedside lamp, relieved by the modernity of its electric glow, my heart pounding, my eyes bulging, my breathing quickened. It was gone. I could feel that it was gone, the fear and terror which I thought had been mine was almost completely shifted in only a few seconds. If it had all been my imagination I would surely still be gripped by fear, wouldn't I?

My head remained heavy and spun with tiredness. My smartphone pinged. Unexpected at that time of night it would have made me jump if I weren't already rigid with adrenaline. Welcoming the smartphone's outside world intervention into my sudden loneliness I picked it up to check and discovered that I'd had several new social media followers while I had been asleep. Not Satanists this time but as I glanced at my total number of followers I saw with a start that it had just turned 666. This was a synchronicity too far and remembering the two Satanists from earlier, I lay in bed and pondered if there was a darker connection to that night's fright than just a passing earthbound spirit.

I am not normally one to fear the number 666, I know of its origins and many misinterpretations and myths, nonetheless I also knew it is intended by some to represent the entity that is the deepest terror to humanity. Surely it was no coincidence that after what had just occurred in my room at exactly midnight my social media account should now reach 666 followers. Was I being warned, or I was being deliberately scared, maybe both?

I had no-one to speak to about these experiences. I had only a few friends and none of them had any belief or shared any desire to talk about the spirit realm. I could talk with my brother but what I needed was guidance or professional assistance. It was therefore soon after this latest spooky occurrence that I sought help from the local spiritualist group in a nearby town. They met twice a week and making contact I was invited to attend one of their open groups or 'spirit circles' as they are more accurately known. I don't know what I was expecting but what I discovered was a group of very pleasant down-to-earth people, all with very different backgrounds and lives but with one ability in common; they spoke to dead people.

Unfortunately, I didn't really get the opportunity to fully discuss anything that was happening to me at home. This was because to ensure evidential psychic mediumship, we were encouraged to not speak of our private lives. If we were to reveal to the others much more than our names and where we lived, it might give the 'heads-up' and reduce the evidential value of the mediumistic work that we were doing.

There were occasional titbits to pick up, however. When one woman at the weekly circle discovered in which town I lived and specifically in which street, she expressed sudden surprise exclaiming, 'Oh, that whole place is known to be very haunted!' She asked me exactly where I lived and although she didn't recognise the name of my house she said, 'I wonder if that's the same house I know of where there were teenagers suffering problems with a haunting, strange things happening and weird electrical interference with their smartphones and stuff.' I wondered too.

I cannot explain how, it is a condition of being claircognizant, but I will write here that I had by now an idea of who was haunting my house. In my 'mind's eye' I could 'see' very vaguely an impression of the main protagonists. I write in the plural because by now I had worked out that there was more than one spectral visitor to my house. I felt that there were at least two men, both from the nineteenth century, one from an earlier period than the other, this being the younger male. I had a distinct impression of the younger adult being tall and the older short, the taller one being slender, even gaunt, the older well built and wearing a hat, perhaps a Bowler. Writing this now I can flesh out these impressions I had with ease. The older male was dressed in late Victorian or early twentieth century dark working men's clothes, boots, trousers, jacket, waistcoat with watch on a chain. The younger one I could 'see' wore a high-necked shirt with a white cravat tied around his neck. This was a popular fashionable look in the late Georgian/early Victorian period. I had the impression that he wore a long dark overcoat or jacket of some kind and unusually for the period, wore no hat, an indicator of poverty at the time.

I wasn't able to make 'contact' with the older man to see what his face looked like, although I 'knew' he had a moustache. The younger man I knew had a thin, mean face and a countenance of anger blended with youthful sarcasm. I chose to not make any psychic contact with him, being fully aware that it was most likely he who was causing the majority of the haunting problems within and around the house.

It was at the spirit circle during my second week when the woman who had commented on my haunted town and perhaps my house, stood up to present her evidential mediumship abilities to the circle and brought forth one of these men. The psychic would usually be expected to turn to face the person who the spirit message was for. Facing me directly, she explained to the circle that she 'had someone with her, a male.'

I immediately connected via my claircognizance and knew that the spirit message was for me. Asked by the circle leader to describe the man, her face creased with anxiety and she said, 'Oh! He's showing me a frightening face.' Gesticulating she described him, 'He is very gaunt with hollowed cheeks and a terrible wide sneer.' She went on to explain that his face had the same appearance as the then popular 'Guy Fawkes' masks, with her emphasis fixing on his 'awful sneering smile.'

It was immediately apparent to the leader of the circle that the visiting spirit was a low vibration earthbound ghost and not from the Light. The leader immediately instructed the woman to dismiss it from the circle which she did quickly and successfully. 'I don't know how he got into our circle,' said the leader, 'He must have followed one of us in here.' She didn't look at me directly when addressing this to the group, but I felt shame for having brought him in with me. We then continued with that day's meeting as if nothing untoward had happened.

I knew exactly who the spirit was the moment the psychic medium had made contact with him. I felt ashamed that I had brought a dark entity into the circle with me, and guiltily I said nothing. He never returned to the circle, but he'd tauntingly made his point about how powerful and aware he was. Two things concerned me in that moment, firstly this trapped entity knew more about me than anyone else in my life at that time and secondly, had he travelled with me in my car?! I had not wittingly let this earthbound spirit into my life, so how had he become attached to me?

The night-time scratchings from above my head in the corner of the bedroom continued over the coming weeks and months, not occurring every night but often enough to keep up the pressure. The scratchings necessitated a further five visits into the attic and there was absolutely no insect or rodent infestation of any kind, nor bats or birds. Reluctantly I had to admit that the scratching had supernatural origins. I hope that readers will appreciate my logical and pragmatic approach when I encountered these matters.

My first inclination was always to ascertain if there was a logical explanation for the events unfolding. I am fortunate to possess a questioning mind and there was no greater sceptic than myself at that time, the reason for this chiefly being that I did not want to live in a haunted house. Certainly not one this haunted with a taunting, clever, manipulative, energy sapping and atmosphere-altering spectre who I felt sure would soon make his visual debut, as he had done with the former owner who had passed away in the house.

Many people seem to take delight in the idea of a haunted house, even desiring such a thing for themselves. I would emphasise extreme caution, as we should be careful as to what we wish for. The cold, hard reality of sharing your house with an unseen psychopath is not for the faint hearted or weak of mind.

Since childhood I have been fascinated with the enduring and empowering image of Archangel (Saint) Michael slaying the Devil. This, and the similar image of Saint George and the Dragon has always caught both my eye and my imagination. It is one of my favourite spiritual images and it represents to me pure love and light giving humanity victory over the one who represents all evil in the physical universe. What's not to like?

There are many who are drawn to the darkness and wish ill upon others, yet they are also suffering in the physical realm. We can change our heart and mind at any time and welcome back-in the healing love of the Source, becoming a warrior of the Light with love as a weapon, rather than hiding in the shadows and expecting the warmth of the sun to ease our coldness. Although I may not have known what it was, I knew from day one that I had a divine purpose, as we all do here on Earth, and I always knew that I was a warrior for the side of love and truth.

With a haunted house and only a large ginger cat for company, I often found myself in town, surrounded by the bustle of people and the noise of cafés as I people watched over coffee and cake. One day, somewhat short of cash, I strolled into a favourite local antiques store, only intending to 'window shop' and maybe burn an hour or two. It couldn't be said that I was enjoying my time at home and any excuse to remain out was beneficial.

Immediately that I saw the exquisite stained glass panel I knew that it was serendipity and that I had to buy it for the house and for me. Over a metre high, it depicted Archangel Michael slaying the Devil in beautiful red, white and blue individually cut stained glass. A lifelong fan of the beauty of stained glass, I am fortunate in this incarnation to have grown up in Great Britain with its rich heritage of stained glass long being used in ecclesiastical sites.

The previous year I had bought a small blue topaz symmetrical cross in an antiques store which I have worn around my neck ever since. The acquisition of this piece of antique jewellery came about via another act of serendipity when I was accompanying a friend searching for an antique Art Deco ring to buy. I had been looking for something fitted with blue stones for ages but had been unlucky in my search. Then, as I patiently waited in the jewellery store for my friend, I saw it behind a glass screen where it had been expecting me.

The shopkeeper was much more interested in selling an expensive ring to my friend and so when I casually enquired about the cost of the cross, without even making eye contact and with a wave of a dismissive hand, I was told that I could have it for a bargain price. My friend and I therefore left the store without the ring but I was wearing my new cross. I didn't know it at the time but blue is the colour that represents Archangel Michael and also the throat chakra. At my annual psychic reading with Rebecca, she spotted the little blue cross and asked me if I had found that my 'life had changed' after I had bought it.

I did not have to think long about it, confirming with confidence that, 'Yes, it had.'

'It will give you the ability to speak up.' was all she said.

Only a few days after I bought the blue cross, I was in the same little seaside town and, in an art gallery window, I saw a small badly tarnished silver-plated badge of the Lion of Saint Mark. A memory of something that I had long ago forgotten from my childhood came rushing back to me. My late mother had an identical piece of jewellery to this when I was a small boy. I stood looking in the shop window and wondered if perhaps it was the same piece, somehow finding its way down through the years and across the miles into this storefront.

A fanciful idea perhaps but then I have had stranger things happen to me. I stepped inside the gallery to buy both the silver badge and also a limited-edition print of a Jewish work of art in blues and greens which I instantly fell in love with, and this, long before that I was told that I was Jewish in a prior incarnation. At home later, I polished the tarnish away from the badge and I remembered that my late mother's brooch had

had a dark velvet backing. Studying it closely now, I wondered why I had such a strong recognition of the Lion of Saint Mark, which is the symbol of Venice, another prior life connection perhaps? Turning it over and looking at the rear I could now see that there were traces of a dark-blue velvet backing just visible.

This was identical to the brooch that my late mother had owned in the early 1970s, maybe even the very same one. Yes, perhaps it was just a 1950s tourist piece from Venice manufactured in the hundreds, but what serendipity to find it in this little gallery in the same little town where my mother and I used to regularly walk. I am certain that my late mother was with me that day and directed me to find and buy the little lion and I shall treasure everything that it symbolises.

When I got the large stained-glass panel of Archangel Michael home, I of course wanted to see what it looked like illuminated. Not wishing to attract unwanted attention from passers-by, I couldn't sit it in the front windows because these faced the street and so I, somewhat reluctantly, placed it in the side window of the downstairs dining room. I say 'reluctantly' because I felt that whatever was haunting this house paid particular attention to the alleyway that ran directly outside this window and along the side of my house.

It may sound a curious thing to think but I was living in a curious house and I believed that it was possible that by placing the glazed panel in this room, any 'holy' or 'spiritual' positive energy it had might be diminished or damaged by unseen negative entities. You may consider that this sounds crazy, but at the time it seemed a perfectly plausible theory and indeed my intuition was fired-up.

The stained-glass panel remained on display in that room

for a number of days while I decided what to do with it. In the end I affixed it to the 1950s internal glazed kitchen door which led from the downstairs hallway. This transformed it from a dated and tired entrance to a magical and colourful gateway, the daylight from the kitchen shining through and illuminating the hallway.

Prior to this my new neighbours were moving into the little cottage behind mine which abutted my rear yard. They passed up and down the alleyway alongside my house carrying in their possessions piecemeal. Occasionally I would catch one or the other of them taking a sneak peek through the dining room window, trying to see past the stained-glass panel of Archangel Michael. I had no blinds or net curtains but I thought, 'What harm could it do? They are just a nice elderly couple.' Yet curiously my hackles rose whenever I caught sight of them, my senses already on high alert.

This couple made me feel anxious, there was something 'not right' about them or their energy, yet I had only seen glimpses of them up until now. I told myself that maybe the haunting was just making me jumpy and tried my best to go about my daily business in this strange unwelcoming house. But once again I was ignoring my intuition at my peril.

Chapter Twenty-Seven

Judging others

Life is a hill of beans

> *Angels wouldn't compare themselves by*
> *'who has the most feathers.'*

Self-empowerment, or self-confidence if you prefer, comes from within. True personal empowerment will never come from reducing or taking away someone else's power, though we may do this every day in our thoughts and sometimes in our behaviour. Most of us are familiar with the passage from The New Testament 'Let he who is without sin cast the first stone' but few of us heed the deeper meaning of keeping our thoughts non-judgmental.

Our ego is always on the lookout for a potential threat or for a comparison that makes the ego feel powerful and it does this by judging others. Those others can be anyone; people at work, in the street, on the television, in the news or quite simply wherever there is social interaction. It could perhaps be something as simple as the colour choice of someone's clothes through to their sexuality, skin colour or political affiliation. No-one escapes the judgment of our ego.

We may think that we are being masterful in our judgment of others, but this judgment is merely the projection of our own wounded ego; what we dislike in others is usually what we dislike in ourselves. By judging someone we are not looking inwards as we should be, spending time on inner self-reflection and self-improvement which we all surely need, but instead we are looking outwards at others, assessing their life journey and what we perceive as their mistakes, even though we may have little or no knowledge of their life journey.

Why do we do this? Partly from learned behaviour in childhood and partly habit but chiefly we do this in order to feel better about ourselves. As humans we spend a lot of our time avoiding the essential need to look inwards and engage with our shadow side, it is lazier and much easier to look outwards and judge others. When we do this, what we are actually looking for is to 'find' someone whom our ego considers to be inferior and thereby make the ego feel better about itself.

Yet to judge others is to set ourselves above one another. We are guilty of creating a hierarchy in our minds based on prejudice or snobbery. Importantly we are also side-stepping the ever-present need for personal growth. When we attend to the wounded inner child within and begin the long and sometimes painful process of self-healing work, we can slowly become the person that we always intended to be and we no longer need to compare our progress with others; our self-pride coming from a place of healing and love for ourselves and no longer from the corrosive fake empowerment of comparison.

We have all known someone who judges another by an essential difference. Yet there is more that binds the human race together than separates. The problem is that so many of us feel disempowered by forces beyond our control that we revel in the faux power that comes from believing we are superior to another person or group. It is not unusual to encounter one beleaguered minority of people single out and 'pick on' another. I am a gay man who grew up through difficult times and when such things were taboo, so it truly astonishes me when, for example, I encounter gay people who are prejudiced against someone based upon the colour of their skin. This example of a minority feeling disempowered by the prejudices of the majority, so that they then in turn seek out an even more disempowered minority to judge harshly is perhaps one of the silliest games that humanity ever invented.

Empowerment by the disempowerment of someone else is nothing more than bullying in the playground, and that's where it should have stayed. There is no space for childhood ego trips in adult life but for many of us our egos remain stuck in the developmental stage of childhood, particularly in relation to emotional development. Unhealed children make for unhealed adults. Harsh words and harsh life events cause our still developing young ego to become outwardly angry and inwardly overprotective.

When adverse things happen to us, as they must, we either grow stronger from our struggle or, some of us hide the hurt and seek only to regain our empowerment by venting our rage on others, either openly or through passive aggressive behaviour. Those 'others' are people perceived as weaker; the compassionate, the sensitive carer, the kind person, the empath. Yet it is these beleaguered people who have weathered life's storms and have survived stronger and more loving than ever. The carers and the compassionate empaths are the true strong ones.

Political leadership that takes humanity into war and genocide all begins with the unhealed wounded child within. It is time for humanity to grow up, come out of the playground and start to recognise that we are all one collective. There is no place for the unhealed psychologically walking wounded in positions of leadership, so stop voting for them.

I have written elsewhere about my experiences with spirit and how I was helped by people with psychic abilities, but even in the spiritual world I have come across the strange phenomena of one-upmanship. Psychic people are gifted in the same way that someone who can paint or play piano is gifted, but of itself being psychic does not automatically mean that they are 'better' people. Many may consider that psychic people must by definition be of a higher vibration than most. Yet my experience is that this is not necessarily the case. People are just people with all the human frailties, and some happen to have psychic abilities.

I have found that some psychic people, by dint of their stronger connection to the 5D, consider themselves to be chosen or special in some way. This is an unhealthy way of thinking about spiritual practice as all of us have our shadow side and we all have a requirement to do inner healing work each day.

Traditionally, many of those in organised religions over many centuries have considered themselves to be 'closer to God' simply by being a member of the particular religious club that they were in. Instead, good spiritual practice requires looking inwards and being honest about whether we are of a good heart and spirit, not looking outwards from the pulpit to judge others.

Even today, many who turn to organised religion or who begin a journey of spiritual and psychic discovery can be judgmental and discriminatory. Having discovered the secret, as they see it, they feel that they are in a higher position that gives them entitlement to judge. They are of course wrong. Goodness is about thoughts and deeds. It is not about who is the most spiritual. Angels wouldn't compare themselves by who has the most feathers.

Why do we tend to be critical of others, or judge them for their way of life or for their own particular journey? Often it is to distract ourselves or others from our own faults and to avoid the need to look inwards to establish those areas requiring personal development. Concentrate your reserves of energy not on others' perceived faults but on looking at yourself and your own life and seeking to make positive changes where they are needed. If you do this, you are guaranteed to become a more content person, because someone who is at ease with themselves is also at ease with others, even if those others are a right pain in the butt.

At the time of writing, the globe seems ever consumed with major political clashes between people sharply opposed on one side or the other, a political tug of war. Whether this is caused by the strange astrological weather or a deliberate 'divide and rule' policy of political movers and shakers is uncertain. What is clear is that it highlights a major problem currently afflicting humanity of how we disagree, argue and ultimately clash over opinions rather than just accept someone else has a different opinion and move on. We may fail to understand how someone could be so 'stupid' in their political affiliation or viewpoint. We get exasperated when an acquaintance fails to understand our own point of view. It is only when we look at why and how we are here in the physical 3D world that we begin to understand that we will never all see eye to eye and therefore the only logical solution is to agree to disagree.

There are two main factors. One is astrology; each of us, at the moment of our birth, is assigned a specific astrological toolkit to work with for our entire life. If you study your own natal astrological birth chart you will clearly see which talents and which blindspots the planetary line-up has gifted to you. The planetary alignment was carefully selected for us at birth to give to us the psychological blueprint required to have the experiences and undergo the lessons that we set out to learn. These astrological 'toolkits' are unique to the individual and our soul must work within the strict parameters of the tools available.

Our ego or personality for our physical presence on the Earth for the time that we exist in this incarnation is restricted by the parameters of those supplied tools. This is where the problem with the human condition comes in and why humanity is incapable of seeing eye to eye on all matters. We are designed to experience and perceive life differently according to our own journey. If you are fixing your car and need a spanner, it's no good getting angry at a passing electrician if he can only lend you a screwdriver. Similarly, it is no good getting angry at someone who disagrees with you politically, a disagreement which is based upon their own life experience and within the confines of their astrological toolkit.

The second factor is that we are all at a different level of soul growth. Some of us reading this book will be debuting their first incarnation here on Earth. Raw, energetic and ready for all of the life experiences that the physical world can offer. Others, who have been here and incarnated manifold times before, may appear worldly-wise, sage and even unenthusiastic for the physical world. The newbie may get exasperated by the lack of energy or the delicate nature of the older spirit, 'Why are they so slow and dull?' or, 'Why are you so sensitive?' they may ask. The older spirit may smile aghast at the naivety and impetuousness of the younger spirit, 'Why are they so headstrong and quick to temper?'

No matter what the person's *physical* age it is to the age of their *soul and the number of incarnations* that will be evident. We all know of the pensioner who is 'young at heart' and we all know of the newborn child where everyone who looks and coos into the crib declares the child to be an 'old soul.' We presume that because someone has physical age behind them, that they are mature or wise, but this is not necessarily the case; the young adult who has incarnated many times over may be much wiser and of a higher vibration. Whatever the age of their physical body, both headstrong juvenile soul and worldly-wise old soul may clash and disagree on many topics. We are high vibrational energy beings of love who incarnate here to experience and to learn, we should therefore ignore the ego and remember who we are, only ever holding space for love-based opinions and humanity-based political decision making. The politics of hate, greed and envy have no place here on Earth.

I have discovered that it is good to remember that often when we feel that we are being judged by others, we are not being judged at all. The other person may have their own problems at home, at work, or just having a bad day. They may feel shy, or awkward or suffer from an anxiety disorder that impairs their social skills. They may not have noticed you at all and an apparent rebuttal is nothing of the sort.

A well-spoken friend of mine told me of an embarrassing

occasion in a British supermarket. After many years abroad, he had only just arrived in the UK and travelled straight from the airport to a supermarket, remembering that he hadn't eaten at all that day. Hungry, as he stood in the checkout queue waiting his turn, he saw the many cans of baked beans on the conveyor belt that belonged to the customer in front. Suddenly nostalgic for the canned food that he'd not seen for many years, he spoke excitedly about them to his accompanying mother who had collected him from the airport. In that moment this humble foodstuff looked delicious and brought back fond memories.

It was therefore with some surprise when the young woman, to whom these tins of beans belonged, turned around and started to shout and yell at him, 'My food isn't good enough for you?!' adding some expletives and angry gestures. An avoidable and embarrassing 'scene' occurred. The customer had presumed, wrongly, that my friend was judging her by her choice of food. Instead, he was just excited to be home in the UK and see all the familiar foods again.

Unknowingly the woman was judging herself. It's a common mistake we all make and it is our wounded ego at play again. It was she and not my friend who was judging her choice of dinner to be something 'less-than.' She felt an irrational sense of shame that she thought she was being judged by the 'stuck-up' customer behind. This said so much more about how she thought about herself rather than what anyone else was thinking. If we didn't judge ourselves then we might stop judging others.

Chapter Twenty-Eight

The beguiling of Merlin

Chop chop

*Staring at me she hissed 'Don't you EVER say that to me again!'
then louder, 'I am NOT kind! I am never kind!
DON'T YOU EVER SAY THAT WORD TO ME AGAIN!'*

I went away for a week's break. I was however very worried about my dear old cat Monty. I couldn't bear the thought of him going into a cattery for any length of time, let alone a week. He was a rescue cat and a smart one at that, so I didn't want him to think that he was being abandoned once again. Additionally, he always had a furry meltdown on any car journey, which made the idea of travelling with him to a cattery unthinkable.

The vet suggested that this was likely because car journeys brought back bad memories of his abandonment and trip to the cat rescue centre. Whenever he went into a car it always resulted in my proud old boy messing himself only a few minutes into any drive. Trips to the vet were a nightmare! I therefore hired a pet firm to come into the house twice a day while I was away and attend to Monty's needs and play with him to his satisfaction.

The pet care guy came to my home in advance of the holiday so as to check out the likely routine for Monty's requirements.

I showed him Monty's feeding regimen, handed over a set of house keys and explained to him about my wi-fi cameras that I had recently set up about the house and garden. These were a godsend as not only could you remotely keep an eye on your house from your smartphone but, and perhaps more importantly, you could keep an eye on your pet when you were away. These little remote-controlled devices would be triggered by movement or heat and had night vision.

I had these cameras installed at my previous home and they were very reliable in that they were not easily triggered by a false alarm. It was therefore with dismay that I quickly discovered that the camera I had installed in my rear yard, which faced the rear door to the kitchen would be activated several times day and night. These false triggers seemed to occur in flurries of activity and I would receive instant messages on my smartphone to advise me that the camera had been activated. Ten seconds of video footage of whatever had triggered the camera was then relayed to my phone. In these instances the footage showed nothing apparently untoward at all, so what was triggering the camera?

Until this house I had encountered no issues at all with these cameras, an animal larger than the size of a cat was needed to trigger the devices, or a bird flying close to the lens. Insects rarely triggered the cameras which I presumed was because they were heat as well as motion sensitive. So what was it that repeatedly activated the camera in the rear yard? This spot was the same place where I was convinced that the two spirit men stood and where a curious vortex of air occurred.

One of the spirits was standing sentinel as if watching and guarding the house or perhaps guarding the other spirit. The taller malevolent spirit who I believed to be causing most of the issues in and around the house was not grounded and being fully mobile only stood in the rear yard when he chose to be, or perhaps when the older spirit guarded him. Was it these two who were triggering the camera? If so, I was expecting an orb or some kind of spirit mist to appear on camera but nothing like that had yet occurred. However, there was nothing physical present to indicate what had repeatedly switched on the camera either.

What did happen was the supernatural phenomena of sudden battery drain. This is believed to occur when an earthbound spirit is attempting to draw energy from any available source in order to manifest. Surrounding air may suddenly lose heat and batteries in any device in an operating mode with an active circuit are a likely target. In normal service the camera batteries usually lasted for some three weeks or more, but I soon discovered that the batteries in my cameras, whether activated or not, now only endured for up to three days when the spirit activity in the house was high.

While the remote cameras did later record a curious white glowing object in the rear yard, I decided that this evidence was inconclusive as to whether it was a spirit manifestation or merely a small object such as an insect close to the lens. I was to be luckier elsewhere in the house and garden, though while I say 'luckier' I was actually hoping to not record any spirit activity. The first recording of an orb occurred just before I went away on my holiday.

I had discovered from my research at the historical society that a small house had once stood on the site of my driveway. This dwelling was described as 'condemned' in the 1901 census and with a single 'hermit' occupant. Whether my driveway camera captured the spirit orb of the poor man who once occupied that house or whether it was the spirit who presently tormented me in my home I don't know, however one night my smartphone 'pinged' and checking it I discovered that the driveway camera had been motion triggered.

The ten seconds of footage clearly showed the camera switching on in night-vision mode to an empty driveway, a full one second of nothing and then an orb quickly and clearly headed towards the camera on a collision course. The moment that the orb hits the camera lens full-on, it malfunctions and static appears as the video ends abruptly, the camera shutting down.

Perhaps this was to be a one-off incident. While I was away on holiday all the cameras operated correctly and perhaps my absence calmed the spirit activity in the house. Or conversely, perhaps my presence in the house provided the energy required for the spirit to manifest. Whenever the kitchen or sitting-room cameras were triggered it was only ever to the pet guy entering the house to attend to Monty, or more rarely Monty himself strolling past the camera and I noted with sadness that he was looking a little bit lost without me.

However, all was 'normal,' quiet and serene until one day of my holiday I was sitting and relaxing in a café when my smartphone pinged. Watching the security camera video playback recorded only three minutes prior, I could see that the camera in the sitting room had been motion activated. It was sunny and bright on my holiday but back in the UK it must have been a gloomy day because the camera which I had placed above the cast iron woodburner in the sitting-room fireplace had automatically switched to night-vision.

While daylight was coming in brightly through the large sash window and everything could be clearly seen in the room, it wasn't enough to switch on daytime vision. With the camera activated I was expecting to see Monty, feeling a little thrill of excitement that, as I sat hundreds of miles away sipping coffee in my tourist destination, a miracle of modern technology meant that I could simultaneously watch my dear old friend Monty trot about the house.

However, Monty was nowhere to be seen and instead what I watched was an orb enter the sitting-room door coming from the hallway in a sharp right-turn and then make a direct beeline downwards towards the camera some several metres from the doorway. Just like a bee it travelled straight to its destination, but unlike when a flying insect is caught on camera there was no insect shape or suggestion of light reflecting off its body. There was only a moving sphere of semi-translucent light. At the moment the orb hits the camera the image is immediately lost, static appears, and the camera shuts off.

The uploaded video had taken only seconds to travel from my home via the internet to my smartphone where I was on holiday. The spirit was inside my sitting room at that very moment, and it wanted me to know. It also demonstrated admirably that it knew what the cameras were for and how they functioned. This spirit was a powerful consciousness and extremely clever. In demonstrating his knowledge of technology, it also showed that he understood the year in which he now existed. He was proving to be quite some adversary.

What makes this evidence all the more compelling is that the distance from the sitting room door to the camera was some five metres. The cameras are small, perhaps the size of a packet of cigarettes and dust particles do not activate them. In night-vision mode a small red LED illuminates when filming but in daylight this is certainly not bright enough to attract any insect, though it would easily attract the attention of any human, alive or not.

The orb had also been travelling along the hall corridor at waist height, turning right into the sitting room before angling downwards and heading directly towards the small camera in one smooth motion. Finally, the camera shuts-off at the precise moment that the orb hits the camera, suggesting electrical interference or power drain. Alarmed, I hated the thought of Monty being alone in the house with this spirit entity and reluctantly I wanted to be back in the UK and with him once more.

I hadn't seen much of my new neighbours as they began to gradually move in next door. Over several weeks they brought their furniture to the tiny cottage by themselves, all loaded into the back of their new small hatchback car. I had begun to improve the small backyard, planting nursery-bought mature climbers and shrubs and introducing many planters for spring colour.

At the front of the house I installed period looking lead-style planters and inside these I grew roses, redecorating the front of the house and the front door, making the many necessary repairs where needed. The house had come out of a long dormancy of neglect and it began to look beautiful. You would never know, unless you were psychic, what was going in within.

With the onset of spring, I excitedly turned my attention to the main garden. This is what I had been waiting for. A relief to be out of the house, gardens being my first love, I had hired a local jobbing guy to remove an unwanted hedge which the previous owners had mysteriously decided to plant right across the middle of the driveway. With this gone, I was able to start on the garden proper. I had all of winter to make my plans for the small walled plot and I began in earnest that February, marking out on the muddy lawn where my new flower beds would be.

The previous owners had left a wooden summerhouse which was a real boon as Monty would spend most afternoons in there sunbathing whatever the weather. There wasn't much in the garden by way of mature planting but there was an old hawthorn tree which was a true delight, though the top had died back, and my elderly neighbour Ethel kept telling me that I needed to 'cut the tree down' which I had absolutely no intention of doing. I believe that trees are sacred, and hawthorn in particular has a lot of ancient lore surrounding it. Woe betide the person who chops anything off a hawthorn tree without asking first, and anyway I liked my tree.

The long winter conceiving the lay-out of the garden meant that I had the entire plot dug, manured, gravelled, planted and completed by myself within two cool but sunny days. The summerhouse was kitted out with my late parents' comfortable old wicker chairs and cushions and my antique garden bench was now situated under the low clay tile hung arbour surrounded by large terracotta pots filled with plants and bulbs sat atop pea gravel.

The once bare and patchy driveway I re-gravelled and planted up around its perimeter with cottage garden plants. In a newly created centre flower bed I planted roses, cottage garden flowers and a couple of small trees. The ancient walls of the garden, the old stone garage behind and the beech hedge provided privacy from prying eyes and the only garden to overlook it being the small end of terrace cottage next door, but as yet I still hadn't seen much of the new neighbours who had just moved in.

I admit that it is possible that I may have gone a little over the top when I placed my vintage stone column centrepiece in the middle of the garden plot. I had bought this a couple of years before for my late mother on the anniversary of her and my then late father's wedding. To this I affixed to the top an antique metal statue which I later discovered was the god Hymen who celebrates marriage, another wonderful synchronicity. Sentiment is one thing and good taste is another, but I decided that I had fallen just on the right side of good taste and everyone agreed. Except that is for my neighbour Terence, who having been a professional garden designer I valued his opinion and he said, 'It looks very nice Rob, but no more.' My garden was complete.

Time spent in the spring sunshine creating with my hands in the soil was good for me and very grounding. It was also a pleasure to be out of the house. While the energies of my garden, the alleyway and even the driveway and garage were all a bit 'weird', they were at least easier to tackle than being inside the house. I often looked up at the tall building from the safety of the garden and felt that it was looking back at me, or something was.

Being in the garden might have felt better than being in the house but it was it was immediately clear that the energies of the garden were not ever at rest, the energy of the driveway was in some way one of sadness, with the alleyway feeling the same as the inside of the house did whenever the entity had put in a visit. As a result, there was nowhere to go to get some inner peace, with even the apparently warm comforting summerhouse leaving me feeling unable to settle, though happily Monty could, much preferring it to inside the house. This necessitated the need for me to install a cat-flap in the side of the wooden summerhouse for his exclusive use.

It was a sunny day in early spring when I met and spoke with my new neighbour June for the first time. On my hands and knees in my garden I was weeding and planting out some young tender plants when movement caught my attention, and I looked up. The garden next door which belonged to the end terrace cottage and to my new neighbours was some metre or more lower in ground height than mine, with steps up into my walled plot.

With me crouching on all fours and my neighbour standing, our heads were at the same height. I'd had the sensation of being watched by someone in the same way that a predator might watch its prey, perhaps waiting for the right moment to pounce. It is instinctive that we know when we are being looked at and intuitively, we look up. My claircognizance alerted me to subtle energies of amusement, inquisitiveness and cunning, and something else too, a jealousy born of anger.

Moving silently and slowly, my neighbour was now only two metres away as she seemingly emerged from the hawthorn tree to my left and approached alongside the ancient stone boundary wall. A slow and deliberate approach, I glanced up again and saw that she was looking straight ahead as though she hadn't noticed me and with the deliberate walk of someone sleepwalking. She wore a curious smile on her face.

Partly visible, she disappeared in and out of view through the lush sunlit greenery. A distant memory from childhood came immediately to mind and which I now know was put there by my spirit guides as a warning. It was a scene from a BBC children's television programme from the early 1970s. This was a televised book of 'Lizzy Dripping' which British TV viewers of a certain age will well remember. What had frightened me as a five-year-old is where Lizzy Dripping meets the old woman. As I now crouched on the ground one word came immediately loud and clear into my mind and that word was, 'WITCH!'

It was this single word 'witch!' that was later repeated to me by a psychic medium that I consulted just a few weeks afterwards. The moment that I had sat down with the psychic for this consultation she immediately pulled her mouth into big gurning toothy smile and said 'witch!' As I nodded my head in enthusiastic recognition, she went on to explain that this was a dark hearted woman who not only 'wore a silver spider around her neck' as a talisman but who also wore a fake smile to conceal her anger, seeing herself at the centre of a web of her own creation. This was superb evidential mediumship as my neighbour wore a large silver spider pendant and had proudly boasted to me of her 'big smile' that she said disarmed others but that didn't reflect her inner thoughts.

Back in my garden and flashing across my consciousness, the warning of WITCH! was clear and loud. It was as though the woman could already hear my thoughts as she suddenly feigned recognition of my presence.

'Oh hello!' she exclaimed, welcomingly and jollily, a big smile on her face. Her voice may have sounded jolly and her face broken into an expression of welcome and sincere interest but her flashing eyes told their own story.

'Hello.' I replied with my usual open but embarrassed awkwardness.

My politeness instructed me to enquire how she and her husband were settling in to their new home but before I could she added, 'Lovely day, isn't it?' I acknowledged the beauty of the early spring sunshine but then she near took my breath away with her next question.

Now looking directly at me and still with that fixed smile she asked, 'Are you the Grand High Master?' she laughed out loud, as though she had said something hilariously funny. It was a laugh with which I was to become all too familiar, a sudden loud mirthless laugh which came from a cold place and always ended with a sharp cut off, as if to be mirthful for too long was unacceptable.

'I'm sorry?' The surprise in my voice and the look on my face was all the answer and the weakness that my questioner needed or wanted to know.

There have since been times since when I regretted not saying 'yes' to that question, the following weeks may have been much easier as a result. But back then I didn't know what a 'Grand High Master' was. I do now and having been honoured and fortunate enough to have since had my spirit guides partially reveal to me just some of my incarnations and my purpose in this life, in many ways my psychic energy would have appeared to her as that of any Grand High Master. However, I do not follow 'the left-hand path' as it is referred to in western esotericism, and while it is not mine to judge anyone's personal journey, I am very much of 'the right-hand path.'

Regretting my stupefied response, I could see that my reply in the negative to her enquiry was met with a mixture of disappointment and after the briefest of pauses, malicious amusement. 'No, I wasn't a powerful witch,' she thought, I was an amusement much as a cat may discover a new toy to play with. I didn't know it then, but this cat and mouse game was to become my reality over the ensuing weeks. Later I was to discover that she could easily read people's auras and that she used this to her advantage. People often say one thing while their emotions are saying quite another. To be able to see the human aura gives the unscrupulous an insight into people's true feelings.

My own psychic energy is strong, and I am told I have a bright crown 'chakra' connection to the 5D. This she could clearly see and made her question whether I was a magician or witch. At this time in my life, I was plugged in but I was not switched on to the divine. The divine works in mysterious ways and while my supernatural experiences thus far had given me good coaching in supernatural awareness, it was as a result of her future actions that gave me the greatest gift of all; a quest to harness and use those energies correctly for my and the collective's highest good. She would have hated that.

It is sad to say that I was to discover that my neighbour was not using her own abilities for her highest good, or anyone else's for that matter. She asked me again, perhaps just to make sure and when I replied that I was not a 'Grand High Master,' and, 'No, I am not working for the dark side,' she laughed, that same cold mirthless cackle and said loudly and proudly that she considered herself to be, 'A friend of Satan.' My face must have looked a picture as she quickly went on to tell me that she was a 'witch' and extol the fun that could be had, at least as she saw it, by working for the dark side.

I was new and naïve to the esoteric world but from birth I was fortunate to have had a built-in intuitive knowledge of the correct path to follow. This has guided me throughout my life and enabled me to achieve my life purpose. I immediately felt a pang of sorrow for her in that moment but also fear in my heart. I had been a bullied and unhappy child and my solace had come from retreating into a world of books of fantastical tales of witches, warlocks, dragons and wizards. Somewhere deep with my inner child the fear of the supernatural remained within me, and perhaps more importantly, she could see this and use it.

Satisfied that I was of no threat and introducing herself properly, June began to chat about the weather, her new cottage and very quickly the topic turned to my house. Pippins, it seemed, was what she really wanted to talk about. June told me that she and her husband Charles had been keen on renting the house next door for 'some months,' having looked at the vicinity long before Christmas, in fact around the time that the haunting in my house really took off ....

She said that while their new cottage had still been occupied by the previous tenants, she knew that she wanted it and that it would be hers soon. She explained that she had seen me moving-in to my home and that she had taken a keen interest in my house and my belongings which she had spied admiringly through the windows. She explained that it wasn't so much the house that she wanted, it was the energy of the area and, in particular, the 'energy inside my house.'

My ears pricked up. At last, someone recognised the powerful energies centred within my home. June began to gain my trust as she explained that she'd thought that I was a 'Grand

High Master' because of the spirit energy that surrounded me and was drawn to me and my home. She asked me if I had experienced the spirits that occupied and surrounded my house, and I replied in the affirmative. I was not taken by surprise by her apparent knowledge of the earthbound spirits that were at home in my property, my own intuition already told me that I was speaking to a knowledgeable and powerful psychic medium.

Indeed, despite her creepy declaration that she 'wanted my house' because of its energies and spirits, it came as a relief to finally have at least one person who could see and understand what was going on inside my house. I felt that in some way I now had an ally, if perhaps not one that I could openly trust. It had not occurred to me at that time that June could have been activating and encouraging spirit activity inside the house for some weeks.

June explained a little about her life and I was told that she and her husband had once been wealthy but had suffered a recent 'financial setback.' I could tell that this had taken its toll and she said that her health had suffered as a result. The conversation was left standing there and I returned to my gardening with a lot to think about. June went back indoors but it was only a day or so later that another chance meeting was engineered by her, and I was soon to find that this was to be a regular occurrence.

What had struck me from our initial conversation is that intuitively I did not trust the woman one little bit, indeed all my red flags were waving and warning bells sounding. Doubtless my spirit guides and ancestors were all hollering at me too. In the meantime, my rational mind, the brain that thinks so logically in the physical but is practically useless to us when dealing with the supernatural, told me that this woman not only understood my plight more than anyone else but was a friendly neighbour with whom I could have a good chat over the garden wall – literally. However, I should instead have relied upon my intuition.

Springtime, and I found myself in the garden a fair bit. There is nothing I like more than a visit to a local plant nursery, stocking up on new plants and investing time and effort in my garden. I was soon to discover however that a walk into my garden meant more often than not an encounter with my new neighbour. After a short while she no longer made the pretence of an accidental meeting but instead would come outside specifically to see me.

It was therefore one beautiful spring morning while being serenaded by birdsong and surrounded by emerging fresh spring foliage that I was cordially invited to sit and chat with her. We sat down to two cups of tea which I had made in my own kitchen, and this somehow amused her though I did not then know why. Her husband had only recently positioned their garden table and two chairs immediately outside of her front door and so we sat drinking tea and chatting while she also ate pork cocktail sausages from a large plastic container.

Being a vegetarian, I declined her offer to share and she found it highly amusing to talk about the suffering of the 'little piggies' that had given their lives for her lunch, making little oink noises as she ate and chuckling to herself. 'Chop chop,' she kept repeating like a mantra. I found this distasteful but chose to say nothing and was grateful that I hadn't when she went on to explain, somewhat incredibly I thought, that as part of her chronic illness she was, 'Only able to eat pork meat.'

This curious nibbling of pork cocktail sausages then became a regular event at our later meetings. Each time June would mutter 'chop chop' and cackle to herself in sinister amusement. The purpose of this macabre habit was to become clear to me only when researching for this book, more of which later.

June began to tell me about her youth spent in the surrounding area and also of her more recent past. She talked of her family's genealogy and their eight hundred years in the locality, including a long tradition of witchcraft. She explained proudly that she believed that she had been a witch here before in this small town and then with a knowing look that I still recall today she tilted her head quizzically on one side and laughing made the curious comment, 'Perhaps we have met before here in this place?'

Was there something that she knew about a past life that I didn't? Then I remembered Bruges and that I had discovered from the Historical Society that this town had a connection in trade with that ancient Belgian city dating back to Medieval times. I remembered the familiarity and similarity with this place and Bruges on my visits to this town before I had bought Pippins and decided that yes, perhaps June and I had met here before. I wondered in what circumstances.

I heard that she and her husband were once wealthy and had lost it all due to an unexplained unfortunate set of circumstances. I did not pry further, especially as she openly made it clear that by contrast, she saw my apparent wealth very irritating. June changed the subject and told me that she was raised in a strict Catholic household which held no space for anything supernatural. A psychic child, this must have been very difficult with her grandmother identifying early on that her granddaughter had 'the gift.'

The result was that her parents sent her to a Catholic school with the hope and expectation that anything psychic would be schooled out of her. For 'schooled' read 'beaten.' It seems that June must have fought back as it became soon apparent that she was an accomplished psychic medium with additional honed abilities that she was most proud of. Finally, she told me that she had belonged to a local coven of witches for some time but had been 'asked to leave.' This stuck in my mind and I didn't have the nerve to ask why she had been asked to leave the coven, though I well imagined that it was not for any good deeds that she may have done locally.

All the same, whilst I was mistrustful of my new friend, she was entertaining, funny and at that point in my life, the only contact I had with anyone in the psychic world outside of the spirit circle. She was also my nearest neighbour and therefore a seemingly pleasant distraction from my haunted house. The people in the spirit circle were lovely but I felt that I had come late to the party as a clique of friends had already formed. I was also one of only two men present each week and I admit that I felt a little bit of an outsider as well as a bit of a fraud. I wasn't yet fully accepting or open to my psychic abilities and I certainly didn't understand them. This reluctance on my part meant that I misunderstood just how strong my connection to spirit is.

The purpose of the circle was to evidence and prove the existence of an afterlife. There was therefore little prospect of getting to know anyone in the circle on a personal basis as we weren't meant to know much about each other's lives in order to evidence any messages that came through with personal details and specifics. I therefore cut rather a lonely figure as a psychic, and indeed I did not think of myself in those terms at all. As far as I was concerned, I was just an ordinary guy who was being troubled by an extraordinary earthbound spirit.

I soon formed a bond with my neighbourly witch. She took great delight in proving to me her various psychic abilities by being able to accurately tell me where her husband was in the town at that precise moment. Whether he was 'walking down the church path' or just about to turn into our little shared Georgian alleyway, she was always right. 'He's ten minutes away,' or, 'He'll turn the corner in two minutes,' was always met with an accurate arrival of her husband Charles. Neither of them possessed smartphones and so any notion of her using GPS was not in question. Whilst my host was short and pleasantly plump with purple hair, her husband was similarly endowed but without the hair. They were a good match physically, mentally and karmically. I suspected that they had travelled together many times before.

One thing that her husband didn't share with his spouse was her supposed liking of me. Indeed, the expression 'if looks could kill' always sprung to my mind whenever I saw him looking at me. As he approached, his face would look like thunder or worse and his brooding silence was telling. No man wishes to return home from work to discover their wife chatting away to an apparently idle younger man in his own garden. I think that I would be a little irritated myself. I was still not working at the time, and this too seemed to irritate him. The fact that, like many, I had worked hard all of my life for what I had, seemed to evade them.

Oddly, after each initial hostile greeting, he always seemed to warm to me. Eventually one day telling me that he was, 'Glad that his wife had a new friend as she now seemed much happier,' (with me around) adding that he, 'Hoped I would stay to keep her happy as others had gone away which had left her depressed.' This was rather a heavy burden to place on anyone, let alone a relative stranger. It also raised more questions; why had they gone away and what was to be my fate?

The appearance of a very large black rubber spider in her downstairs front window one day caused a little local eyebrow raising and over tea at her garden table June proudly showed me her large silver spider necklace, cackling that she 'loved spiders' as they reminded her as being at the 'centre of a web.' I recall that a little chill went through me as I imagined her pulling everyone's strings and orchestrating events and happenings simply for her own entertainment. There was that laugh again.

She suddenly looked pointedly over my shoulder along the alleyway. I had noticed that while she was talking to me, she had kept glancing over my shoulder. I presumed wrongly that she was watching people passing by in the road at the end of the alleyway. Instead she said, 'Can you see it?'

I turned to look to where she was indicating. I could see nothing.

'There is an outline of a man there against the wall,' I followed her line of sight as she had not pointed, perhaps thinking that by pointing she would make whatever apparition she was staring at vanish.

I turned and looked again along the ancient stone wall and saw nothing. June insisted that I gaze at the spot in question but still I could see nothing. The 'spot in question' was directly outside my dining room window and my rattling and whispering bedroom window was above. I had not told my neighbour about the specifics of my haunting, or where I slept, or where the spirit had been entering my bedroom by night. For me this was the first affirmation that I had correctly sensed the correct location and access points for the malevolent male spirit, for I was certain that it was he that she was referring to.

Where she now indicated was the very same spot where I had recently painted the outside of the dining room window. Quiet and alone in the alleyway I brush painted the window as quickly as I could. I was not overlooked by anyone here, yet I cast the occasional furtive glance over my shoulder feeling that I was under the watchful gaze of an unseen presence. My neighbour had now confirmed to me that all my instincts were correct and that the spirit of the man had stood at that spot, looking over my shoulder as I had decorated.

'He's often there,' she said casually. 'Not fully formed as an apparition but often around the place.' 'He's gone now. He was listening to us,' she added. Then without another word she rose, left the garden table and walked slowly and silently to the open back door to my rear yard. She was looking for something. My dislike of my backyard had not dissipated with time, the strange vortex and currents of moving air continued whatever the weather and the two male spirits were I was sure, still loitering.

June peeped around the corner of the yard doorway. The yard itself, surrounded by ancient stone walls was now resplendent in climbing roses, magnolias and clematis all just coming into full leaf. The sun shone and the birds sang nearby in the hawthorn tree. It seemed like a paradise where nothing bad could happen, yet all the while I had an unsettling feeling that everything was most certainly not alright.

Before she had even returned to her chair, she said to me, 'He's in there now,' referring to my backyard. 'He's stood by the kitchen door, a tall thin young man. There is another man stood nearby, older, shorter and in dark Victorian clothes with a hat.' *This description perfectly matched* exactly my own claircognizant 'envisaged' scene, even down to the positioning. She went on, 'The older one is there to keep an eye on the house and on the younger man. The younger man is not … pleasant.'

Once more she had confirmed my suspicions and my fears. Now returned to her seat she made no suggestion as to how to get rid of the spirits in question, instead she gazed up at the sky and the church tower.

'Can you see them?' she asked. I looked up to where she was staring.

'See what?' It was broad daylight and a delightful day and yet I already knew what was coming next. A memory from childhood and of sitting on the sofa at the age of ten years old, reading Charles Dickens' 'A Christmas Carol' and in particular, the passage where Scrooge looks out of his window to see the dispossessed throng of unhappy spirits, bound in chains, flying past and wailing at their failure to lead honourable, caring lives.

She gave another one of her laughs, an appalling cackle of malice and jollity combined. She was truly enjoying herself now. 'The spirits,' she said, 'are up in the sky around the church tower, lots of them.' Finally adding, 'They are always there. It was one of the reasons I wanted to live here.'

Peering upwards into an empty blue sky I pictured these earthbound spirits flying through the air in a ghostly vision. It was at a much later time that I began to understand the relevance of lost spirits travelling along this energy line, how it pertained to my house and why she wanted to live here.

Doubtless June was enjoying the puzzled look on my face but instead of elucidating on the sight she had just laughed about, she instead explained how her husband had been 'furious' with her at their last house when he had seen an earthbound spirit in their bedroom. 'It frightens him,' she said. Having met him, I doubted that anything could frighten her husband, but I chose not to say.

June explained that their last house had been haunted and both having seen earthbound spirits there, she said that her husband had become quite 'angry' with her because her psychic abilities seemed to attract them. June further explained that one of the reasons that they had chosen their current cottage next door to mine was because she had assured him that it 'wasn't haunted' whereas in fact she knew that it was. She cackled that laugh again and gaily admitted that she had chosen her present location precisely because the entire area was very much haunted, adding 'not to tell Charles what she had just said.' He had apparently forbidden her to involve herself in anything supernatural ever again. I wondered what she had been up to and mused to myself that I wouldn't be telling her angry husband anything that might upset him.

Several more garden table meetings were to occur like this. Me drinking tea, or eventually, sharing wine and she eating cocktail sausages from a plastic container whilst laughing at her mantra of 'chop, chop.' Neighbours would pass us by on their way to their cottages and glance at us smiling, saying 'hello' or passing the time of day, but over time as our laughter grew ever stronger and more raucous, their look soon changed to one of disapproval at our alfresco meetings. I could feel a change within myself when I was with this self-proclaimed witch. I felt that I was under the influence of a narcotic or alcohol, even when I wasn't drinking.

Yes, June's company was intoxicating, and I began to greatly look forward to our daily meetings. Not dissimilar to the curious sensation of intoxication that accompanied the male spirit who came and went as he pleased in my home, June's energy added a soupcon of sweetness to the mix, a toxic pleasure of low vibrational laughter and hilarity. Eventually, we would find ourselves drinking wine and sitting under a moonlit sky, the moon and stars high above the church tower as it struck the quarters. The peel of church bells is supposedly to disperse any negative energies and entities but here in this town they struggled in their task.

'Dinner' was suggested, and we dined outside at her table, as always under the night sky. Fish and chips were ordered from the local takeaway and June, her husband and I dined off my dinner plates, using my silver cutlery, which seemed to amuse my host greatly. The three of us talked and drank wine, her husband very kindly and unexpectedly producing my favourite wine from inside their house. Much was made of this gift, and I was aware that there was a hidden shared joke that I was not a party to.

The laughter got louder and more raucous as the evening went on and I got ever more intoxicated. June became ever more pleased by the scene unfolding. Her husband appeared confused by the jollity but happy that his wife was being entertained and kept amused. The passing neighbours were not so happy, but they stayed silent on the issue. I relaxed and enjoyed

June and Charles' company to the full. After all, their hilarity was just well-meaning neighbourly banter, wasn't it?

I should add here that this was most unlike me. I am a solitary person and I always have been in this life and, so I am told, in others. Hilarity, jollity and raucous behaviour is something that I have often envied in others but never felt able to partake in myself. I am a dull sober sides, but I wasn't at that moment. A couple of glasses of wine would not produce the mind, body and spirit altering affect that I was now encountering as we sat under the shade of the hawthorn tree. I knew that I was being bewitched and yet oddly it didn't bother me.

I suspected that the use of my crockery and cutlery together with the sharing of food and wine had enabled an enchantment to take place. But to what purpose? I dismissed the suggestion of bewitching as superstition at best and ungrateful at worst. Feeling guilty at my suspicions I continued to sit in their company and under their hospitality.

'Thank you so much for dinner, it really is very kind of you,' I said by way of ending the evening. The scene at the table froze.

In a second her look changed from one of jollity to that of thunder. Her husband went quiet. Staring at me she hissed, 'Don't you EVER say that to me again!' then louder, 'I am NOT kind! I am never kind! DON'T YOU EVER SAY THAT WORD TO ME AGAIN!' Unusually for me I don't think that I apologised like the English always do when they've done nothing wrong. Instead, I looked dumbfounded, or perhaps just dumb and silently raised a quizzical eyebrow at this totally unnecessary and unwarranted outburst.

This woman is either unhinged, or she is exactly what she says she is; a witch who has darkness in her heart. This is what went through my mind, sitting now a little uncomfortably in their company. Suddenly, as if a cloud had moved away from the moon, she gave a little laugh and her face switched back from stormy skies to fair weather, and changing the subject as if nothing had just passed between us, she looked up to the rear of my house and asked politely, 'So where do you sleep?'

Even in my apparent drunken state, her insane outburst had *finally* alerted me that not all was well in this woman's mind and so I mumbled feebly something about 'somewhere at the back of the house.' Following her gaze, I could see that she was looking precisely at the wall where the headboard of my bed backed onto. Why on Earth would she need to know that unless she was going to cause mischief, I asked myself. I suspected that as a direct result of this curious interaction I would be getting a night-time spectral visitor once more in my bedroom. I was not to be disappointed.

Chapter Twenty-Nine

Manifestation

You will listen and you will learn

'It was the smell of damp wood, mouldering stonework, festering old books, earthy moss and creeping rot. Strong and overpowering now, the message was clear – 'DO NOT LET THAT BOOK OUT OF THE HOUSE!"

Still troubled about what kind of person would consider being called 'kind' as a terrible insult, I woke the next day feeling ungrateful and a little guilty as I pulled back the curtains and let in another beautiful spring day. It had been a further night of unsettled sleep and regular waking, listening and trying to ignore the scratching at the bedroom ceiling, something on the stairs and the rattling whisper of the sash window.

Adding to my list of nightly woes was the faulty church clock, which after a few days off was now striking backwards once more, alerting me throughout the night to its nocturnal activities. I had lain in the darkness not thinking of the time but instead remembering June's words about lost spirits flying around the church belfry. After the exchange of words the night before, I was not expecting to hear from my neighbour for some time. It was therefore with a little surprise to discover a smiling June waiting for me outside in the alleyway later that morning, catching me by 'chance' and asking for a quick chat.

This time she seemed alarmed.

Flustered and a little out of breath June once again invited me to sit down at her garden table as she explained what had just happened to her. As it was such a nice day, she had strolled into town returning home via the churchyard footpath. I was not surprised when she confided that she 'never went inside churches' though inwardly I speculated why anyone would have an aversion to a House of God.

'Today I felt drawn to walk up the church path and go inside,' she said and finding herself alone inside the church she began to have a look around the ancient and magnificent interior. She explained that suddenly she became aware of the sensation of no longer being alone. No-one had entered the church, of that she was sure, the old massive wooden doors being very loud in operation. Yet, as she stood there alone and listening, an unseen presence made itself known in a loud and commanding voice, 'YOU *WILL* LISTEN, AND YOU *WILL* LEARN!'

Whether she questioned the unseen speaker to what she should be listening to I don't know, instead she described how she fled the church in terror, reaching the large ancient doors in quick time but finding the door handle unyielding. Realising with horror that she was locked inside the church with the disembodied voice she began to panic. Repeated attempts at the door mechanism met with a determined force to prevent her leaving. Suddenly the door handle gave and yanking open the door she dashed home to where I had only just discovered her.

After the previous evening, my first thought was that she was inventing a story to scare me, adding this to the mix of the ghostly goings-on at home, my house facing directly onto the church. However, the look of fear on her face which she unsuccessfully attempted to hide from me suggested otherwise. Now speculating about who or what it could have been, she declared that it was a haunting of sorts sent to frighten her. Only now, some years later, I realise that this was in fact the work of her spirit guides.

Our spirit guides watch over our affairs constantly and are always waiting to be given the opportunity to intervene in our lives for our highest good, to help us and aide us throughout our earthly life, keeping us on course for the life that we chose for ourselves. Free will and our ego may get in the way of our divine purpose and as such our spirit guides cannot and will not intercede on our behalf unless we specifically ask or invite them to do so.

This old woman had many years ago decided that she was not 'kind', her heart had become blackened and her manner dark. She relished chaos, upset and causing fear in others and she used her innate psychic abilities to bring that about and to gain a degree of control over people. Her 'guides' to whom she was listening daily were likely to be not of the Light. June was a necromancer, this is a magician or witch, who, through the practice of dark arts, summon earthbound spirits to do their bidding. These were usually of the lower vibrational orders of conjured spirits, and just like her only in it for what havoc they could wreak.

In short, she was a foolish woman who was to be pitied; the karma that such meddling actions incur would have to be balanced out eventually. Her true spirit guides would have been well aware of what she was 'up to' with regard to me and my home, even if I was not at that stage, nor was I knowledgeable about necromancy. The situation was dire and far worse than I had realised, thus they had to intercede.

The question for them was how to reach June and speak with her directly when their daily attempts to get through to her were always repelled. It was a question of reaching her by first closing her off from the darker low vibration entities that clamoured around her and who she considered her own 'spirit guides' but were anything but. He, for it was a male voice, did this by encouraging June to enter the holy and sacred site of the church where such negative entities that clung to her would temporarily be unable to gain access.

Free from them in this holy space, her true spirit guide was able to get a clear message through to her, '*You will listen, and you will learn.*' She had previously boasted to me that she had been incarnated in this town many times and each of them she joyfully believed as a witch working for her own material gain. I say 'joyfully' because she made it clear that she believed that she was getting something 'over' on her guides and on the Source by having repeated incarnations of malevolent badness.

By repeating the same karmic pattern and in the same location many times over told its own story. She was not free at all but simply on a treadmill of karma that she refused to make any attempt to get off. Her spirit guide was clearly trying to bring her to her senses and get her back on course. By her own admission she had readily veered away from her true path and from the Light, drawn into the darkness for short term gains while living a human existence.

So unused was she to sensing and hearing from her own true spirit guide, a being of the Light, that when she did it terrified her. Just for once she was not the spider at the centre of her own web as she saw herself but instead for a fleeting moment understood that there was a loving force greater than she who controls our reality. Fleeing from the safety of the church and back out into the darkness of her home she soon regained her composure, however.

I was not truly spiritually awakened at this time and only now I understand that the events at Pippins were intended to shock me awake to my psychic path and abilities. This it did most successfully. Unbeknownst to me Spirit was trying to awaken me, curtail June's activities and simultaneously rescue trapped earthbound spirit. The scope, foresight and power of our spirit guides and higher vibrational beings is truly amazing. Knowing none of this at the time I instead theorised that June had received a visit from my own night-time spectre. She nodded and mumbled, 'Yes, perhaps,' but for the first time I saw that this woman was perplexed and not a little worried.

She suspected now, exactly what this visitation had been and what it meant. I didn't know that she was a necromancer working closely with the spirit that haunted my house, and in doing so she knew that it wasn't him. Within a few minutes she was once again self-composed and almost back to her usual jolly demeanour. Rather than make her feel repentant about her malicious activities against me, instead her spirit guide intervention only served to make things worse.

The church was nearly one thousand years old, very beautiful inside and rich with history. Like all ancient churches it had that peculiar musty scent that pervades damp stone and wooden structures of antiquity. With the town seemingly rife with earthbound spirit, I speculated that perhaps her church visitor had been a former reverend of the parish and I was suddenly reminded that I had in my possession a small vellum bound journal which had been lovingly handwritten by two gentlemen of 'The Cloth' from 1811 all the way through to the late Victorian era.

In what seemed a coincidence, at the spirit circle only a couple of weeks prior, my late father, who had entrusted me with this journal ten years before, came forward via one of the psychic mediums and describing what the little book looked like told me that I, 'Have a small journal,' adding that, '*I must keep it safe.*' When he was dying, I had promised my late father that amongst many other duties, I would always keep the journal safe and well looked after. The medium's message seemed at the time to merely be a good example of evidential mediumship. I wasn't to know that it had a more profound meaning.

The journal therefore lay amongst my other antiquarian books in my possession. This was in a glazed bookcase in my front study, the same small room where Miss Tomkins had died and where I had wanted to place blue ribbons on the door frames. I don't know what possessed me to suggest it but by way of lightening her mood after her fright in the church I said to the old witch, 'I have a journal written by a clergyman, would you like to see it?' She looked keen and nodded her head in affirmation and I rushed off inside to fetch it like an obedient puppy.

As soon as I had mentioned the journal, I knew intuitively that this was the wrong thing to have done. Her grasp over my reason and thinking was a powerful one. She was indeed the spider at the centre of a web of her own making. Readers may think me totally credulous, but it was only now, when her power had been temporarily diminished that morning, that I was finally suspicious of this woman and her intentions. As I headed to the little study along the downstairs corridor, the scales suddenly fell from my eyes and a toxic spell of control was broken.

Perhaps my spirit guides in their frustration were shouting their message to me. I paused and thought. I had made the promise to show her the little book and I would feel foolish or rude if I now returned outside and said that I had, 'Changed my mind.' After all, what harm could it do? So, I continued along the hallway to my study, turned left into the room and stopped in my tracks. The room smelt different.

There was always an unusual, sweet perfume odour in here that no amount of redecorating and cleaning could remove, but it never smelt bad. This time not only did it smell different, but it was a powerful and unsettling odour. There had been no suggestion of any scent elsewhere in the house, yet in this tiny room there was a strong smell and furthermore it was growing. Before I had even reached up to the large, glazed cupboard to reach for the small bound vellum book which was now in sight, the smell became intense. '*What was that smell?*' I pondered and the answer coming back to me by return. *It was the smell of churches.* It was the smell of damp wood, mouldering stonework, festering old books, earthy moss and creeping rot. Strong and overpowering now, the message was clear – 'DO NOT LET THAT BOOK OUT OF THE HOUSE.'

The words of my late father's message at the spirit circle seance suddenly came back to me, '*He has a small bound journal, tell him to keep it safe.*' At the time I had taken that to mean that my father just wanted me to look after the book and to not let it get lost or damaged. Instead, he was specifically referring to just this very occasion, that such a book written by two clergymen was holy and spiritual in purpose. It was also something dear to me. If I were to let the witch who considered herself to be a 'friend of Satan' hold the journal, even just for a glance, it could either alter the energy of the book in some way, or give the woman even greater control over me. I finally got the message and I stood in the small study and said so out loud. 'I understand'.

Quickly I returned to my neighbour whom I found sitting still at her outside table, waiting unusually patiently for me to return but deep in thought as if listening to something, or someone. I had wondered what excuse to give to her to explain my empty-handedness and instead I told her the truth about what had just happened. I could see her thinking and she surprised me by saying, 'Perhaps it's best,' adding, 'Obviously I wasn't meant to see it,' and that was that.

June then went on to claim that while I was indoors fetching the book, she had seen the spirit of a little girl in a white dress walk about my garden. June told me that she had often seen it about town and although I doubted her claim that the ghost had been in my garden, now understanding that she was just trying to frighten me, I knew from the book that George had loaned to me that this girl spirit in the white dress was indeed often seen about town. With that day's conversation over, I made my excuses and left.

I will never be able to claim that I got used to the events that unfolded daily in my home, but they had become a background noise to my life. The nightly visitations, the feeling of being watched by day and night, the sweet sickly scents, inexplicable movements of air, feeling of 'otherworldliness' and a sensation of the house being crowded all persisted.

The stairs and the landing still creaked by night, my laptop and bedside lamp in the small front guest room continued to turn themselves on by night only, my brother still reported psychic poltergeist activity in his own house in Cyprus, my cat still dodged the same spot on the staircase and that wretched church clock still hadn't been repaired.

Adding into the general mix of supernatural phenomena was now the cupboard under the stairs. I am not particularly fond of any claustrophobic space (who is?) but I do not have what would be classed as a 'phobia.' My stairs cupboard had a modern and bright appearance both inside and out and yet it gave me the creeps, feeling cramped and leaving me with a strong sensation of being watched whenever inside. Many weeks after moving-in it suddenly began to smell of soot.

This was inexplicable as there was no chimney near to this spot and there never had been, and yet every time that the door to under the stairs was opened, perhaps to retrieve a shopping bag or the vacuum cleaner, my nostrils were assailed by the ever-strengthening aroma of soot or coal. I tried to persuade myself that coal must have once been stored in this cupboard. I knew however this not to be true as the floor and walls were spotless. In the greater scheme of the haunting this did seem to be an unimportant matter, nonetheless it bothered me.

I continued to attend the weekly spirit circle and also travelling to the once-a-week public demonstration events held in a nearby town. Whilst I learnt nothing new to help me with my haunted house, I did receive messages every week from deceased loved ones and even from a former work colleague who had only recently passed on. This came as such a comfort at this most difficult and lonely time. My father came through twice. Once I had been rushing to get to a psychic event on time and feeling guilty at leaving him alone for the evening, I placed three bowls of food out for Monty plus a saucer of cream, whereas I then grabbed a shop-bought plastic container of salad from the refrigerator and dumped it unceremoniously onto a plate before digging-in.

An hour later at the séance my father came through and commented to a ripple of laughter, 'That cat eats better than you do!' On a separate occasion my father commented about all my shoes spotlessly presented in neat pairs on the bedroom book shelves (which I have mentioned earlier in this book) and I confirmed this was completely accurate to a laughing audience. My father's brother Uncle Gordon also came through at a séance, and the contents of my desk was accurately described, down to the paintbrushes and the fact that I was, 'Writing a book which will be very successful.' No-one, except for me, had been into the small bedroom study since I had finished decorating it, and this was a crucial example of evidential mediumship.

However, I was alone in the world and jobless plus my home did not feel safe or the haven like it should. I had also finally come to realise that my elderly neighbour and her husband were actively operating against me, using what I now believe to be necromancy as their weapon of choice. Yet because of the supernatural tactics involved, should I have discussed this with anyone else they would surely think that I was delusional or mad. Even the couple running the spirit circle seemed less than willing to engage in such a difficult conversation.

I have a deep-rooted fear of spiders, but I was fortunate in that an unintentional consequence of the house timbers and floors being treated for woodboring insect was that I never once saw a spider at Pippins. That is until one night, when pulling back the covers to get into bed it was to discover a huge black hairy spider on my pillow. A spider just like the silver one that June had around her neck as a talisman. Coincidence? I never saw another in the house, let alone on my pillow.

Spring was turning into summer and my hard work in the cottage garden was now paying off. It looked beautiful and this was just the first year. I was pleased with the results but one man's hard work is another's target of envy and so it was with my neighbour. June and her husband suddenly began to make 'improvements' to their own garden, adding items of domestic indoor furniture to the outside space and this being intermixed with items of litter such as brightly coloured plastic bottles, tins and other items not intended for outside use.

'My husband is a fantastic gardener,' I was told which was closely followed up by complaints that my own garden was encroaching onto theirs. When I asked to what they referred I was shown some strands of ivy on my own wall, which although it was doing no harm, I cut away to keep hostilities at bay. The 'fantastic gardening' skills proved to be the addition of several bags of multi-purpose compost tipped directly onto the top of concrete flagstones and some colourful shop bought bedding plants pushed-in and left to their own devices.

Our other neighbours secretly laughed at the naivety and brashness of what was going on and I refused to be drawn into any negative comment as I had once thought of them as friends. But as the accumulating household junk, the boxes of car boot stock, furniture, trash and an old rug were left out in all weathers the neighbour's mirth soon turned to irritation and later to anger. The witch's garden was to the front of the row of cottages and her neighbours therefore had to walk past this eyesore whenever they came and went, as well as look at it from their front windows.

My neighbours spoke to me whenever they could about this eyesore, perhaps expecting me to 'have a word' about the accruing mess. I think that I must have a longer fuse than most as I tried to not let the state of their garden affect me but after many weeks of this, even I began to dislike the gaudiness and downright trashiness of what I had to look at every morning when I opened my curtains.

'Enjoy your soup?' my neighbour asked me one day as she accidentally bumped into me in the alleyway. How did she know that I had just made and eaten soup for lunch, I wondered? Later I peered upwards out of my kitchen window and decided that if my neighbour leaned out of her ever-open upstairs bathroom window, it was perhaps possible that she could see right into my kitchen. Immediately I rushed out and bought a kitchen blind, determined to believe that she had been spying on me through her window rather than face the awful prospect that she possessed psychic skills sufficient to allow her to observe me in my home.

Since the incident with the vellum covered journal and a sudden awakening that I was in danger, I had been trying to avoid June and her husband for several days when one morning the front doorbell rang. I looked through the peephole and nobody was outside. Opening the door to double check, it was to discover my diminutive neighbour June stood on the doormat with that all-too-familiar smile on her face that even she admitted was deliberately false, just as the psychic medium who had said the single word 'Witch!' to me some weeks prior had warned. June asked about some unimportant matter that was an obvious pretext to intimidate. I had rumbled her, and she had rumbled that I had rumbled her.

She took a step forward, as if I had asked her to enter my home, I hadn't. This I suddenly realised was odd behaviour and noted that she retracted her hand as if it had touched something hot. I had invited her into my home many weeks before and each time she had declined most firmly. I had not thought anything of this at the time, presuming that she was shy. I now knew better than that and it was curious after our hiatus in communication that she was now keen to gain entry. June stepped forward again and gently rubbed the large cast iron door knocker before I could object, but then what could I say to that seemingly inoffensive action?

I wondered if this meant anything as far as hexes were concerned and resolved to seek protection of some sort.

Alerted by her strange behaviour, it was with alarm when later the same week she once again just 'happened to be passing-by' while I was gardening in my rear yard. I had left the gate from the rear yard to the alleyway propped open. 'Oh, what a wonderful old bell,' she said as I looked up from planting some bedding in a container. I hadn't heard her silent approach. She was already caressing the ornate antique brass bell that hung by my back gate. Why was she touching and caressing objects around my property?

A few days later I had my classic car out of the garage and parked on the driveway. It was time for a summer polish and preparation for the hoped for good weather that lay ahead. With dismay, I discovered that once again she just 'happened to be passing by' although to my certain knowledge she had never walked up the road in that direction before now. Seeing my car, she crossed over cautiously to it and asked a very odd question, 'Would you mind if I touch the bonnet?'

The answer should have been a resounding 'No!' but before I had the opportunity, her hand was already gently stroking the car's hood. Later that same week the engine seized.

Coincidence? With no job and diminishing savings I was dismayed to find that the engine which had served me well had suddenly failed without any warning. I was therefore obliged to pay a specialist garage to insert a brand 'new' restored engine to the car. When I eventually collected the repaired car with its as-new engine, it was to discover that it seemed low on power. The new engine was not happy. I returned the car to the specialist, and they stripped it down twice to discover what the problem was. Several weeks passed with the as-new engine at first being repaired and then finally being rebuilt but all to no avail. The company that had supplied the engine refused to take responsibility and the costs kept mounting. The engine never did work properly again, and I was forced to sell the car just to recover my costs. I wondered had June cursed the car, and was that even possible?

'Can I borrow a baking tray?' June had knocked at the front door again, standing there with her familiar fixed cold smile. I lent her an old non-stick baking tray but ensured when it was returned that it did not re-enter the house. It sat in the rear yard for a few days before I reluctantly placed it in the trash. Yes, things really had got that bad.

'Oh, I'm returning the crystal vase you lent to me,' June said one day when 'passing by.' I had not lent it to her at all, she had in fact taken it into her home for 'cleaning' after I had placed some roses in it for an alfresco dinner. I made sure to leave this outside too and when a medium friend later visited me, she claimed, 'Oh, that vase is shooting out energy in all directions.' Therefore, the vase went into the bin too.

I couldn't risk giving it away to charity and have it emit negative energy in someone's home. Anyone unaware of the situation would understandably feel that my behaviour was irrational and that this was a harmless old lady who just wanted to make friends. I was therefore unable to speak of what was occurring to anyone. However this was not a harmless old lady, this was a self-proclaimed Satanist with a declared intention to take my house from me. Whether you believe in witchcraft or not is somewhat irrelevant, what is important is that the intimidation was subtle but constant and worked on both a psychological level as well as a supernatural one.

The ongoing haunting and the sense of dissatisfaction with the neighbourhood and my troublesome neighbour, made me decide to move on. I had a private meeting with an estate agent to get a valuation which was very satisfactory indeed. They loved what I had done with the house and I had a good idea of what price I could achieve. But what of the ghost? Could I really sell my home with the ghost still resident? My conscience told me no.

Private meeting or not, news travelled quickly, and I was stopped by a complete stranger on the church path one afternoon who demanded to know to where I was moving. Astonished, I received the same question from my witch neighbour and her husband who had also heard on the grapevine that I was thinking of selling. I made up the story that I was going to live with my brother, but she then suggested that I let her and her husband live in my furnished house rent free as they would, 'Look after it for me.' Was this woman utterly insane, casting a spell, or both? I batted away any such suggestion but thanked them for their 'thoughtful' offer – I made sure that I did not use the word 'kind' this time.

They pressed the point, stating that they, 'Used to have money and a nice car,' and that, 'They would look after the house very well for me.' Even had she not been practised in the dark arts, having experienced at first hand the state of their garden, I doubted this very much. I declined their offer again.

June stood back a little and staring at me, she angrily snapped, 'Your aura is grey. You're scared!' Hardly surprising I thought to myself resentfully, but I denied it and making my excuses I re-immersed myself into the darkness of my haunted abode.

I sought advice from the spirit circle on how to deal with this troublesome woman and her husband. The leaders of the spirit circle advised me that what she was doing was normal procedure for witches who practice dark arts, explaining that this was how they operated. I was told that the witch chooses an individual who they felt they could manipulate through witchcraft (or psychological pressure, you take your pick) with the aim of obtaining material advantage, usually their property, from them. The chosen individual would preferably have no close relatives or heirs who would interfere.

It was explained that the only option available to me was to close myself off completely from my neighbour, leaving no room for any discussion, contact or interaction. This I was doing but it clearly wasn't going down well with either her, or her husband. On the face of it I had offended an old couple by making friends and then ignoring them. Or had I instead thwarted their plan to get my home and control over my assets?

If I thought that the psychological build up had peaked, I was to be sorely mistaken. My newfound animosity towards my witchy neighbours only served to aggravate the haunting in my house. I suspected now that the two were closely connected. Skype conversations with my brother in Cyprus were now almost inaudible due to the voices 'on the line.' The bright flashes of light continued to occur behind me on-screen much to my own and to my brother's amazement. The bedside lamp and my laptop in the small front bedroom now switched themselves on several times each night.

My sleep was disturbed as I trudged into the bedroom to switch off the laptop or the lamp, but it would have been anyway by the scratching, the creaking and of the whispering of the window. Someone or something was desperately trying to get my attention. How much more of this psychological pressure could I take? My savings were depleting rapidly, my neighbour who it seemed was always working against me was now hell-bent on ramping up the harassment both physically and psychically. It hadn't been long since I had suffered the loss of the two most important people in my life and I had no-one to talk to about my problems. My own persona was altering as I began to crumble under the assault.

Then, finally one night, what I feared the most occurred, a full ghostly manifestation. It was a dark and cool night but as usual it was stifling in my bedroom when I unexpectedly woke in the small hours. I had become so used to the church clock striking the hour that it rarely woke me now, and when it did, it still regularly struck backwards during the long dark hours before dawn. This time was no exception but was it the church clock that had woken me or something else? I lay in my bed in the dark, unable to see I strained my ears to listen for any sound at all, no matter how miniscule. I didn't have long to wait. The sound came again and I suddenly remembered what had brought me out of my slumber, it was that scratching again.

Once more it sounded high above my bedhead in the corner of the bedroom, in the corner of the house. There it was again, a rhythmic scratching and scuffling. The sound of a mouse making a nest but inside my bedroom and up near to the ceiling, scratchy, scratchy, scratch. Scratchy, scratchy, scratch. Just why was the noise so rhythmic? Manmade surely and intuitively I knew that this was my ghost. This was the male entity that had haunted my house for two centuries, a restless spirit which took pleasure in its teasing and slow psychological torture of its chosen victim. For how long had this earthbound spirit been tormenting residents of this house?! My heart raced as I waited in dark silence.

Somewhat like a frog that places its hands over its eyes in an effort to stop its hunter from seeing the prey, I stupidly imagined that the darkness shielded me from sight. Ghosts don't have eyes and they do not need daylight to see. He knew that I was lying in my bed staring upwards at the ceiling and unable to see him. He knew that I had heard him, as that was his intention. The scratching noise quickly subsided and I waited for what I knew would happen next.

I have said before that only those who have suffered a 'shade' in their home will understand what I mean when I say that in the inky darkness, something even darker moved. Not for the first time I could 'see' in the blackness a long dark mass move slowly, from the corner of my bedroom ceiling above me, across to the opposite corner. In doing so, the mass passed right above me. The size of the black shape was human in proportion, and it noiselessly made its way. I knew that he was doing this as a psychological weapon and that he was looking down at me, hoping to fill me to my core with fear. He was not disappointed. I lay there frightened although not completely terrified as I had been once before in that bed under similar circumstances. Perhaps I was getting used to these night-time visitations.

Those who have experienced such hauntings and poltergeist phenomena will know what I mean when I say that there was no sound but that my mind heard the movement of the figure as he made his way above me. It is as though you 'hear' the energy move. He finally reached the opposite corner of the room and with the black mass dissipating I realised that he had made his way out of the room through the ajar bedroom door and into the hallway landing beyond which was also in total darkness. Mistakenly, I thought that this meant his sideshow was over with. It was therefore with horror that I found it was far from over.

My uninvited but persistent guest had one final trick up his Georgian sleeve as while I looked into the blackness of the night, the gap around the doorframe of my open bedroom door became dimly illuminated by a greenish grey light. The flash was so very dim but unmistakable in the dark. As though someone standing outside the bedroom door had lit a cigarette with a match, but instead of a warm welcoming yellow glow, it was a ghost light that I saw that night. Yes, my spirit had manifested on the landing just outside of my bedroom.

In country house hauntings, one traditionally reads of a 'grey lady' or a 'green, grey' spectral light emanating from a spirit. Understandably, people therefore suggest that the spirit they've seen was wearing grey, white or green, whereas this is merely the glow of energy that a manifesting spirit emits. I now remembered back to my days at the bungalow only some two or three years prior where I had seen a greenish-grey light flash outside of my bedroom window, believing that the previous owner had manifested in spirit form.

Now however I was absolutely determined that I was not going to be audience to any manifesting horror on the landing. I knew well that this ghost had appeared to a previous owner and that she had died in the house the same week, perhaps from fright. I was not going to be his next victim! I quickly switched on all the electric lights and leaping out of bed, dashed into the hallway. The landing was of course empty, at least to my eyes.

The next morning I was to discover my laptop and my bedside lamp once more switched on in the bedroom next to mine. My late mother had, it seems, once again visited me, doubtless letting me know that she was around me and protecting me, or at least wanting to afford me some comfort. My mind buzzed for much of the day, I was unable to shake off the very real possibility that the spirit was growing stronger and now able to manifest at will. What would happen this night coming? Was the witch assisting the spirit with his haunting? Witches practising dark arts are able to conjure spirits at will and make them do their bidding. My mind whirled.

Nothing, as it transpired happened that night. Instead, it was worse than that as my spirit was to manifest in broad daylight.

Waking in my bed the next morning after a surprisingly good night's sleep considering the circumstances, I remembered that as usual my bedroom sash window had squeaked and rattled for much of the night, but I was by now used to this. Doubtless the church clock continued to malfunction and strike the hours after midnight backwards. Now however, the strong early summer sunshine shone through the bedroom curtains, birds were singing outside in the garden and as it was a mild morning, I realised that my leg was sticking out of the bed, protruding its entire length from under the duvet. I felt rested and relaxed.

Suddenly, and without sound or warning and as I looked down at my leg, I felt the fingers of one invisible hand grasp around my ankle. I could see nothing. It was with disbelief rather than fear that I felt the grip of a man's hand. A firm but soft grip, the sensation was that of a tingling electric shock. Where there would have been fingers wrapped around my ankle, each finger was replaced by an electrostatic shock. As one might caress a lover, slowly and deliberately the unseen hand moved higher and higher up my shin until it eventually reached my knee. While I felt utter amazement, I did not feel horror.

Eyes bulging, I stared at my leg in disbelief as this could not be happening in broad daylight. It is odd to say but I was by now so used to this spirit's games, that I was not as frightened as you may expect, or indeed as the spirit might have expected. When the invisible hand began to move above my knee and make its way up my thigh towards my genitals, I realised that this spirit was definitely playing games. I had been unfortunate enough to live cheek-by-jowl with this spirit for many months, so doubtless he knew that I was a gay man. This was what could be construed as a sexual assault from beyond the grave. Sleeping naked, the unseen hand reached the top of my inner thigh before I finally took action by leaping out of the bed and this time I thundered with rage at the ghost. The final straw. Something had to be done. Standing and shouting with anger, I told him that he was not welcome and that he was to, 'F*** off!' amongst other expletives.

Hurriedly I washed and dressed and later I was to be found outside of the house looking up resentfully at my bedroom window where the latest incident had taken place. I was livid. The fear of the haunting and of my witchy neighbour had been replaced instead with rage at this intrusion into my life. This was my home and I was under attack. I had already been through so much trauma in my life without having to put up with this intrusive and pathetic crap.

June was conspicuous by her absence that sunny morning as I gardened with Monty at my side like always. But I found no relaxation in this activity and I could not put my mind at rest. I couldn't face going indoors just yet and so I decided to wash my car on the driveway. It was there that my neighbour Abigail found me when she was walking past with her dog on their way for a walk. Abigail was one of only two residents to have welcomed me to the town when I had moved in some months earlier. We hadn't really chatted properly at all, and I didn't know her well enough but the look on my face as I furiously washed my car that morning must have been enough for her to stop in her tracks and ask me, 'Is anything wrong?'

Rather than brush it off as I usually would do, saying in the false cheery English way that 'everything is fine thanks', instead I said forcefully, 'No, I was touched up by a ghost in my house this morning!' and then briefly explained what had happened and that these events had been going on for some time. Abigail looked unmoved. It was a relief to finally get out what had been troubling me for months.

I now expected a shocked embarrassed silence and something like a muffled, 'Well, goodbye and I hope your day improves.' Instead, without surprise or fuss Abigail briskly said, 'Right, well I'll just put Oscar my dog away and I'll call 'round your house in ten minutes.' I cannot tell you what this simple matter-of-fact response to my long cry for help meant to me in that moment. Abigail did not bat an eyelid at my odd tale and she was prepared to listen and to help. There is a lesson there for all of us and help she did.

Chapter Thirty

Compassion for the self

Learning from experience

Let the negative emotions of the moment pass through you like sand running through your fingers

How often are we told that happiness is the benchmark for a good life and sadness, or anything less is undesirable? It is OK to feel what you are feeling. It is a natural part of the human condition and the experiences that we have incarnated here to have. You should not try to bury and deny your feelings as they are valid and are there for a purpose. When we encounter anxiety or depression then there are issues within our psyche that need to be resolved, but we should never feel 'less-than.'

Experience your sadness. Take it, hold it and own it. You have incarnated here in this time to live a life of experience, both positive *and* negative. Allow yourself time to process the emotions that you are encountering. This is not to allow yourself time to wallow in your feelings, as that will only lead to festering energy which over time will affect you in the physical. Instead, let the negative emotions of the moment pass through you like sand running through your fingers, do not let them linger.

By allowing any negative emotions to engage with you and then move-on through you, you will not permit these emotions and experiences to define you as a person. Do not hold on to negative events, thoughts and resentment, if you do you will find that your mind will recycle and replay these toxic thought patterns until one day you will become them. We program our brain every moment of the day by the thoughts and experiences that we have.

Regurgitating negative thoughts over and over in our mind, they become a part of the program. In the same way that a virus in dodgy software infiltrates the operating system on a computer, replayed toxic thoughts and emotions will lead to preoccupied overthinking and our minds spinning. I speak from a place of knowledge, having experienced my own negative programming over a lifetime.

Be kind to yourself. We often blame ourselves for the part we played in any negative scenario or experience. Though we all do it, replaying the role we played and the conversations we had will not help you. Often we think of the things that we 'should have said' in a past hurtful scenario and berate ourselves later for not being quick-witted enough to have spoken up in the heat of the moment. Remember that you are here to experience everything, both good and bad. Accordingly, there are no 'mistakes' in life, there are only life lessons.

The trick to living a life well-lived, is that once we learn a difficult life lesson, to not then repeat it. All of us involve ourselves in toxic situations from time to time. For example, many of us will experience unfaithful relationships, or have a lack of personal boundaries, addiction problems or co-dependency issues. It is normal, it is human, it is part of the experience.

Whatever the hurtful situation, we must *learn from the experience* and choose never to repeat it. The universe is very adept at checking back-in with us from time-to-time and seeing if we have indeed learnt all that we needed to learn from a particular episode in our life journey. Eventually the astrological weather will repeat over the passage of time and certain scenarios will replay themselves at some point in your life, often with different characters but always the same storyline. This has happened to me so many times, particularly with financial and boundary issues.

When you reach a certain age as I have, you begin to recognise these repeated life cycles. Often I have said to myself 'I'll never let that happen again' and then a few years later I do just that with the same dismal results. I have learnt to recognise when I am being tested by the universe. You can even speak out loud to your spirit guides or to the universe and say, 'Ok, I have learnt that lesson, there is no need to repeat it, I get it now and I understand it fully.' Once the universe has understood that you get it, those negative lessons will either not repeat, or you will be ready for them next time and nimbly sidestep them.

Support and love yourself and if the healing takes a little longer than you anticipated, or the upset comes back after you think you have healed and it bites you on the butt, then do not criticise yourself. This is a recovery process, so be compassionate with your mind, body and heart. Think of yourself always as someone you love. If this was a close friend or family member who was suffering would you ever choose to speak harshly to them? Of course not, so why won't you be kind to yourself? In the same way that you would be there for a friend in need, be there for you too. Always hold a space of compassion and love for yourself.

CHAPTER THIRTY-ONE

The rescue

This man had been haunting the house for two hundred years!

'He's here.' Nothing had changed. The room was still filled with sunshine, I felt very calm and the atmosphere was peaceful, unusually peaceful. 'He's coming in through the window now.'

I returned to my house and waited. Abigail was a lifeline being thrown to me. Alone inside Pippins I had no idea what to expect and so I experienced the same feeling of anxious positivity that comes from an imminent rescue from an emergency breakdown vehicle while you sit by the roadside in your broken car. It was unusually silent inside the house, as if the building itself knew what was coming.

The subtle pleasant sounds of springtime could be heard outside but inside the only thing to disturb the peace were the clocks recording the passage of time as I sat and waited. I didn't have to wait for long. As promised, only a short while later there was a ring of the front doorbell and Abigail was stood on the doorstep looking calm and in control as if she did this sort of thing every day of the year. Perhaps she did.

'Thank you so much for coming,' I smiled. Abigail was blonde, petite and with a kind face that belied her years as she is one of those people who retain their youthful shine. And shine she did. Welcoming her inside it was with only a hint of nervousness at being in a stranger's house that she popped off her shoes and together we began a tour of the property, starting in the sitting room. What she began to tell me exactly fitted with that which my own long-ignored psychic senses had perceived. It was incredibly empowering to have my psychic perceptions validated by an independent source.

'Your clock has an attachment,' Abigail said, already looking away at something else while gesticulating absentmindedly at my longcase clock. I had bought the eighteenth-century clock online a few years before and right from the day of delivery I would stand and stare at the clock, convinced that there was a strong male energy staring right back at me. This confirmation brought a degree of comfort difficult for me to now explain. 'There's an old woman who sits here,' Abigail said. Abigail had walked over to the sitting room side window where the old villager George had told me that he and the other children used to queue up and buy sweets through the window from the strict and appropriately named Miss Sweetland way back in the 1930s.

Head on one side, as though listening to voices Abigail said, 'She used to sell sweets from this window,' then adding, 'She was quite a hard woman.' All this fitted the facts perfectly but could Abigail simply have known the local history of my house? No, even the historical society hadn't known anything about Pippins, *so how could Abigail know*?

I was surprised that the sitting room was so quickly concluded, and we moved to the small study where, surprisingly, Abigail didn't pick up on much psychic activity. Moving into the dining room and pointing to my favourite cane armchair where curiously I never liked to sit, Abigail immediately said, 'There's an old lady who sits here. This used to be the kitchen, and this was her domain. She doesn't want to move on as she likes it here in this house. She protects the house, and she doesn't like to see any changes made. She is of no harm.' This was at least some comforting news!

Looking over to the right-hand corner by the fireplace where the original old stove would have once stood, Abigail stared at the wall where the sad cold spot existed. Monty and I disliked this corner, which often smelt of perfume and Abigail added, 'A maid or serving girl stands there. She was very unhappy in life, and she keeps herself to herself. She is quite aloof and won't speak with me and she doesn't interact with the other spirits here.' Confirming Abigail's psychic reading of the dining room I explained my own reluctance to go near this corner of the room, even to switch the table lamp on, and I advised that there was often a strong sweet scent here. Privately I felt alarmed at Abigail's words '*other spirits here*' – there were more!

Satisfied that there was nothing else to 'see' in the dining room, we moved onwards to the kitchen, passing the staircase. Abruptly Abigail looked left and said, 'There is a man here,' and with her arms held out parallel she indicated a place to the left of the staircase and about a metre from ground floor level. 'He is not actually stood on the staircase itself but hovering and partly in the wall.' This was truly amazing. Abigail could not possibly have known that *the original staircase was exactly where she was now indicating*.

Long since incorporated into the sitting room, part of the space for the old staircase was now where the longcase clock stood, and the new mid-twentieth-century staircase now swept upwards to the right. The spirit of the man was ignoring the present-day staircase completely, instead preferring to stand on a step where the old staircase had once been, half of him on the stairs and the other half in the sitting room.

I explained to Abigail that this was the same spot where my cat Monty avoided on his way up the stairs, and I also recounted the story that I was told by the old lady who lived here in the 1930s about how her two dogs always kept to the side of the staircase in the very same place. This area was dead centre to the house (pun intended) and would be a good place if you were a spirit to monitor household activity. Abigail nodded in a matter-of-fact way and added, 'He is in Victorian clothes, and he protects this house. It used to be his house.' She did not say whether he was of any harm to me, so I clung to the word 'protects.'

The tally of earthbound spirit in my home was quickly adding up! We moved into the kitchen where Abigail stayed silent. On the way through to the downstairs shower room we paused as I opened the rear door so that Abigail could see into the small rear yard. I wasn't expecting her to say anything much but she announced, 'There are two men here.' This corroborated my own intuitive thoughts and also what June the witch next door had said. We stepped outside. 'Can you feel that?' Only a few feet from the doorstep, Abigail now moved aside so that I could stand where she had been.

The sudden breeze was chilly and circled all around me. I had noticed these air currents many times. The constant movement of air made it cold out here and despite my inviting garden furniture I never hung about for long as there was always the feeling of being 'watched' by unseen eyes. 'There is a vortex just there (indicating to where I now nervously stood) where one of the men stands.' Moving to another spot some two metres distant she added, 'And this is where the other man stands, I think this is the same man as the one on the stairs. He (the man on the stairs) stays with the other man, who is much younger. This older man is protecting the house and watches over this younger spirit who has a darker energy about him.'

Now we were getting to the nitty gritty of the haunting! 'The older man is still here but the younger one has just left.' It seemed that my younger spirit, who was causing all my troubles, had popped off into hiding. We returned inside and onwards into the final room of the ground floor which was the small shower room. Abigail and I squeezed into the room together, closing the door behind us to make more space. This was a modern fitted washroom with a new solid oak floor, but Abigail was about to reveal the reasons behind my dislike of showering in, or of even entering this room.

'This room is very busy,' Abigail said as she stood in front of the large shower cubicle. For the first time I saw Abigail look surprised and she explained, 'There is a soldier in World War One uniform inside your shower and he has his horse with him. There is also a pig!' No wonder the shower room felt uncomfortably busy! Back to my mind came that unpleasant expression from my other neighbour, 'Chop chop!' Laughing, Abigail explained that her spirit guides will often place earth-bound spirits who need rescuing in a prominent place inside a home that is about to be cleansed. Well, you couldn't get more prominent than fitting a horse inside a shower!

Then came some shocking news, 'There's a portal in the shower and this is where spirit is entering your house. There are three portals in this house, one is good and two are bad.' Still reeling from this surprise, Abigail suddenly asked spirit to bring forth the Light, and very quickly the soldier, his fallen horse comrade and the pig were rescued, and the portal was closed permanently. Of course, I cannot verify all that Abigail told me, but I hadn't told her of my sensation of being in a crowded room of watchful eyes when in here. Neither had I told her that in the eighteenth century, my walled garden had been a piggery for the farm. What I can tell you is that from that day I never again felt claustrophobic or nervous in the shower room.

We moved upstairs. On the way Abigail paused at a large oil portrait of a twentieth-century monk which I had hung halfway up the stairs. She said, 'In life he was very sad,' adding, 'He used to like a glass of whiskey.' Reaching the top of the landing Abigail paused again and her face took on a more intense look. 'There is something here,' she said, adding, 'There is a feeling of being unsteady,' now grasping the stairs handrail, 'It is as if the floor is uneven, and you may fall.' I nodded expressively and confirmed that she was exactly right. This was the same spot where many visitors to the house, including me, encounter a strange feeling of being unsteady on their feet as though about to take a tumble through intoxication.

Now it was Abigail's turn for surprise as she hadn't encountered anything like this before. We stood there a while testing the floorboards under our feet which were rock steady. Underneath the carpeting the original floorboards had long since been removed and replaced with modern chipboard. We walked up and down until we were both satisfied that the floor was level and even. However, the curious heady sensation of unsteadiness persisted.

Peeping around and into the bathroom, Abigail did not sense anything in there but said that my historical portraits on the walls were adding to the energy of the house. We moved on and into the large principal bedroom which I had long since abandoned. I believed that this room was a hotspot for the haunting activity. Standing now in silence in the middle of the bedroom floor, Abigail smiled and asked, 'Can you hear that?' I listened intently. I hadn't truly noticed it before, but it had been there all along, a noise like faint tinnitus.

'There is a very high-pitched buzzing sound,' she said with surprise and as though this explained everything that had been occurring. Impressed but confused I asked what did that mean? 'I don't know,' she replied honestly, 'But there is something here.' I well knew this already of course and whatever it was, it chose to stay unseen. Before we left the bedroom, she turned one more time to look around the room. Staring at my wooden monk's bench used as a window seat she said, 'There's a monk sat on that piece of furniture. He likes to look out at the church from the window.' I felt rather uncomfortable at the idea of a monk in my bedroom but advised that the item of furniture in question was indeed called a 'monk's bench.'

Back on the landing, Abigail paused at a small Victorian oil portrait of the small boy that I had christened 'Tom.' Without saying anything about it we then entered the smallest bedroom at the front of the house. This was where my laptop and bedside lamp regularly switched on and where I believed the spirit of a man stands in the doorway but doesn't enter when I'm in the room. 'There's a small boy in this room,' she said. 'He sits in the window. He likes this room as he feels safe in here.'

I said that I wasn't surprised he liked it as it was cheerfully decorated like my own bedroom as a child. 'He says his name is Thomas and he used to work for a chimney sweep.' With yet more surprise, I told Abigail that the name 'Tom' was what had come to me earlier that week when addressing the portrait of the boy on the landing. It seemed that I had psychically tuned in to the earthbound spirit boy. Confirming that the boy was no harm, Abigail advised that he was earthbound because his Victorian chimney sweep master was also still earthbound and wouldn't let the boy cross into the Light. As a result, the little boy was quite frightened whenever the man was around.

Abigail explained that the boy felt safe in the cheery small bedroom, which in someway explained why I did too, and it also perhaps explained who the older male energy was who stood in the doorway glowering at me whenever I was working in this room. Maybe negative spirits couldn't enter this room? The table lamp and laptop that were being repeatedly switched on were in this room. Were they being operated by the little boy as a joke? Or perhaps it was indeed my late mother protecting this small enclave from the more negative spirits and energies.

NB In Victorian Britain, children from poor families or orphans were often taken-on and 'owned' by chimney sweep masters. Little more than property, the children were made to climb inside chimneys in order to sweep them. They suffered the most terrible hardship and often died prematurely from diseases of the lung.

Leaving the little boy, we crossed the landing and finally moved into the large second bedroom that I was presently using to sleep and where the incident with the ghostly hand on my leg had happened that morning. Silence again as we stood together a little way into the room and I followed Abigail's gaze as we looked out the sash window and out across the fields beyond. I hadn't told her about the fluttering scratching noise above my head in this room or of the noisy window.

Urgently, Abigail asked, 'Can you hear that?' I knew exactly to what she was referring. The sash window, locked shut and tightly chocked with a window jamb, was squeaking and whispering to itself like it always did. Walking over to the closed window, Abigail did not touch it or inspect it for faults as many might have done, instead she turned to me and softly announced, 'That's where the other negative portal is,' indicating the window with a sideways nod of her head.

'That's where your spirit is entering your house.' I was shocked, each night I lay sleeping and vulnerable right under this bedroom window but suddenly everything fitted. That very morning, my leg had been poking out of the duvet directly under the window. In turn, the window was directly above the place in the haunted alleyway where June had claimed she had seen the spirit standing. The whispering and squeaking of the window was not caused by currents of wind but instead by ceaseless eddies of spirit energy from the portal. This was a vortex of negative energy right inside my home that allowed negative entities unlimited access.

I lifted the sash and looked out the window directly across to the church clock tower standing proudly only a few yards away. It was a delightful spring day and a quiet had descended over the town with the only sound being birdsong. Nothing bad could happen here, surely. Then I remembered what the witch next door had said about earthbound spirits flying high above and encircling the church tower by day and by night.

Little wonder then that one or more of them had made their way into my window which acted as a portal.

My memory was stirred and I was reminded of a scene from the 1970s television series 'Salem's Lot' which had terrified me as a small child. Thinking that he is safe in bed at night, a vampire comes beckoning at a boy's first floor bedroom window, scratching at the glass to be let in. Well, this was no vampire, just a stubborn malevolent earthbound spirit. Wondering what was next, I didn't have long to wait to find out as Abigail was proving to be someone who didn't waste time.

She had already sat down on a small wicker chair in the corner of the bedroom near to the window and indicated that I should sit on the bed. I perched anxiously on the edge of the soft divan. Monty my cat, hitherto nowhere to be seen, suddenly made his appearance in the doorway. I said that I would take him outside before we started, but Abigail exclaimed her delight that he was present and said, 'He knows what is happening as animals can feel the energy.' That energy, it seemed, was building as Abigail quickly became anxious looking herself, very different from her previous relaxed self-assured charm.

Quiet and peaceful in the small town there was an occasional twitter from a bird in the garden and the sun shone warmly through the window. A benevolent hush descended over the house and the energy felt very good indeed. Monty promptly sat down at Abigail's feet and quickly fell asleep. Monty never slept when there was anyone other than me in the house. I later found that he always came in and made a fuss of or slept near to Abigail whenever she visited in the coming months. 'He feels the energy and he feels safe in here,' was all Abigail said. I had to agree with Monty, I felt safe too with this complete stranger in my home, far more so than with my spectral guest. It felt so good to have someone who believed me and on my side.

'I am going to go into trance. I need you to make sure that I don't go too deep. If I stop talking, then I may need to be brought back. You'll need to start talking to me and call my name if I go into a trance too deeply.' I agreed to these terms and Abigail took two or three deep breaths, her eyes closed and hands neatly placed on her lap, feet flat on the floor. I realised that we had begun. I didn't have long to wait. Monty snoozed when Abigail suddenly said, 'He's here.' Nothing had changed. The room was still filled with sunshine, I felt very calm, and the atmosphere was peaceful, unusually peaceful. 'He's coming in through the window now.'

My eyes darted nervously to the sash window. I saw nothing and I heard nothing, but I didn't doubt it, the energy was intense. 'He's here. He is young. He has quite a frightening face.' Abigail visibly recoiled at the appearance of the spirit with whom she was now communicating. 'He has sly eyes and a very long sharp nose, but it's his sneer that is quite frightening. He looks like one of those Guy Fawkes masks.' A thrill of excitement, this was him! This was the man who had been haunting me for months, with the very same description of the spirit who had travelled with me and broken through at my spirit circle some weeks before.

Continuing Abigail said, 'He has one of those high collar shirts and with a white cravat or scarf tied at the neck.' Immediately I knew that we were talking about the male dress of the early nineteenth-century, probably Georgian and matching the rebuild date of my house. This man had been haunting the house for two hundred years! 'His smile is very sinister. He knows what he is doing and has been watching you, deliberately affecting you. It amuses him to upset you.' There was a pause and then Abigail said, 'He's showing me where he died. It was a dark night and a damp place, with high stone walls either side, like a narrow alleyway.'

Instantly I knew that the spirit was describing the alleyway that ran along my house – *outside my dining room window and just below this very window where he had just entered*. In modern times my Regency house had been rendered and painted but when it was built it had a stone façade like the remainder of the houses in the street. The alleyway was wet and unlit by night even in these modern times, I could easily imagine that two hundred years prior it would have been even darker, and anybody killed here would not have been discovered until daylight.

'He says that he was taken by surprise and set-upon by some people in the town who he knew. His friends. They killed him in cold blood there and then and he is angry about that and never passed. He saw the Light come for him but he had led a bad life, so he chose to stay. He was as bad as the people who killed him and he would have done just the same thing given the chance, and indeed he may have done, so he was frightened when the Light came for him.'

For the first time, I felt sadness for this young man who had been making my life hell. What had his life been like? What sadness and hardship had he known? I thought about those long-demolished slums by the churchyard that George had told me of.

'I don't know that he'll go to the Light,' said Abigail. For the first time anxiety set in and suddenly fearing that I may be stuck with my tormentor for years to come. 'He says that he won't go.' It seemed that matters were quickly progressing as Abigail explained to me that the Light had come for the spirit and that two other male spirits 'like policemen' had stepped forward from out of the Light to take him through. 'They are standing either side of him, but he is refusing to go.' There was a pause while this struggle of wills continued and then Abigail said, 'He says won't go with the men if they make him. He says he will only go with them by his own accord.'

A slight pause and then, 'His mother is here. She has stepped forward to greet him and tell him everything will be alright. To tell him that there is no judgment and no punishment. He is stepping forward. He is entering the Light with his mother.' Abigail stopped talking. I realised that she was going deep into trance. Was it all over with? I called her name two or three times and slowly she began to respond and return. Looking relaxed but tired, Abigail woke and smiled and again expressed alarm at the spirit's disturbing facial features and also with the dark, damp place he had shown her where he had been murdered and spent his final moments alive.

'That's done then,' said Abigail, getting up smartly. Waking at her feet, Monty got up as if this kind of thing happened every day and trotted off downstairs for a snack. Abigail and I briefly discussed the matter, then it was all over and we bid farewell, but not before Abigail told me two things; that my spirit would give me a sign that he had arrived safely in the Light and send thanks for his rescue, the other thing was that I was not to think about him at all, and if I were to, it was to only to send him healing love. Otherwise, my thoughts could create an energetic link and encourage him to return.

I closed the front door as Abigail made her way home and I made a cup of tea and sat on the sofa with Monty. I ruminated whether what had just happened had actually happened and if so, would if work? If so, we had both just been rescued that day.

CHAPTER THIRTY-TWO

Visitations

The end of a cycle, the beginning of a new

This was it. This was my ghost saying thank you to me in a light-hearted and ironically funny way.

It was later the afternoon of the spirit rescue that the doorbell was pulled, and I responded to the tinkling bell by opening the front door to admit Abigail. The low setting sun still shone brightly through the sitting room window and a relaxed and cheery Abigail was soon sitting in my late mother's favourite chintz armchair as we chatted about the curious events of earlier that day.

'I was guided to bring this for you.' 'This' turned out to be a large rock that Abigail was now retrieving from her tote bag. It was in fact a very large piece of uncut rose quartz crystal, about the same size as a grapefruit. 'You should place it somewhere in the house where you feel intuitively guided,' she said. Abigail then produced a random selection of small, polished crystals of many different colours. She explained that these were being loaned to me as she felt drawn to bring them with her as she had left her house.

I gave Abigail a proper tour of the house again and she commented that it was so nice to, 'Have such a beautiful view of the church,' from the principal bedroom window, where I was reliably informed my monk was sitting down once more. The second tour of the house afforded me the opportunity and time to discuss thoroughly the numerous manifestations of the spirits that had occupied my home. It was such a relief to finally be able to tell someone about the various scratchings, sensations, shadow figures and noises.

When we were once again in the comfort of the sitting-room, the church clock struck the hour and Abigail remarked about the time. I had probably bored her with my endless ghosts-related phenomena, but she also seemed pleased to be able to share her thoughts on the supernatural, especially with someone who wasn't going to immediately baulk at the topic. The bell strike reminded me of my disturbed sleep, and looking for a topic of conversation I absentmindedly asked her, 'When were they going to fix the church clock?'

Abigail looked at me confused, 'Fix what?' Expressing surprise that she hadn't noticed, I explained that just prior to my (freshly despatched) ghost making known his nightly presence I was usually first roused from my sleep by the church clock discordantly striking the hour. Abigail looked curious and I told her that the bells were muffled with the effect that they peeled backwards.

'Just like a Beatles song played in reverse.' She looked at me bemused, as if I had said something quite ridiculous which was quite funny when you consider what we had only just been talking about.

'There's nothing wrong with the clock, other than it loses a few minutes each month,' she advised. At this I insisted that at 3am I often heard the strange muffled underwater sounds of the clock striking backwards but Abigail insisted that the clock was fully operational and that she had 'never heard' it play backwards or muted in any way. Finally it dawned on me what had been happening. I think that my jaw must have dropped open, the spirit manifestation and the church clock striking backwards were connected! What if my ghost had made the strike of the clock sound to me only, muffled, eerie and apparently backwards? This was done to unsettle me and rouse me from my slumber each night, thereby heralding his ghostly nightly arrival in my bedroom. What a peculiar but magnificent haunting accomplishment!

But why muffled and so disturbing a sound? It was obvious that he would want me to be frightened as fear is where negative energies source their power, but then a shocking truth came to me. My ghost had been murdered right outside my house in the alleyway some two hundred years prior. Was the ringing of the church clock at 3am the last sound that he heard?

In his day assailants would be armed with fists and perhaps with knives. How to commit such a cruel and awful crime without the prospect of being caught? A premeditated crime without weaponry would take time, there would be a struggle and the culprits were likely to be caught, even on an unlit night, due to the probable noise. More likely they had set upon the helpless man in the dark, overwhelmed him in number and stabbed their victim. Perhaps an alcohol or drugs fuelled fight about money?

I pictured the poor man, lying in the cold, dark and damp alleyway and unable to call for help. His final moments would have been spent alone and in fear, doubtless wanting his mother. As I have written elsewhere in this book, I know well that feeling of despair, having been in fear of my own life some years prior, alone in a country lane and thinking of my parents. Could his last sad memory in his physical body have been of his own blood, filling his mouth and sinuses, his hearing becoming muffled by the fluid as the church clock struck the hour of 3am? Was it this dreadful experience that I had been repeatedly haunted by most nights at that same hour?

These were gruesome thoughts, and I did not then convey them to a smiling Abigail. 'This is my favourite chair,' she remarked about the chintz armchair of my late mother's as she tapped the arms. She looked happy and relaxed as Monty lay in her lap purring contentedly. Monty never did this with any other house guests! She then explained that the reason for feeling intoxicated whenever the ghost had been around, was because this was how he had spent his adult life, and because I was psychic, this energy was affecting my own.

Abigail reiterated that for the next three weeks I was not to think of my adventures with the now released and free earthbound spirit. If I did so, she had been guided to warn me that my energy may draw him back from the Light. Abigail and I chatted like the friends we were to become, and after a most enjoyable couple of hours spent together, she left, and Monty and I were once again alone. Or were we? I picked up the large lump of uncut rose quartz that Abigail had loaned to me, and I walked slowly upstairs, uncertain what to do with it or why I had been guided to have it in the house.

As I passed the leaded window halfway up the stairs, the guidance came to me in a flash. I was to place it in this window. This made perfect sense. I knew that Rose Quartz radiates the energy of love. Love is the only energy that will always defeat hate and fear. This small stairs window immediately faced the side wall of my witch neighbour's house. Could it be that spirit was guiding me to place the large crystal there in order to protect my home from dark energies and hateful thoughts? I made a space and carefully placed it in the window, along with two glass tealight holders. Each night from then on, I would burn small tealight candles in this window and enjoy the protection that the crystal gave and the love that it emanated outwards, to my own house and to others.

I went to bed that night not, I must confess, entirely convinced by what had just happened in my home. After all, my logic told me that Abigail was a stranger who could quite possibly have just made-up a story about being a psychic medium. These thoughts churned over in my mind, but I remembered that she precisely pinpointed the exact same places in the house that I also considered to be haunted hotspots. She also suggested the name of Thomas for the child, a coincidence perhaps? What about the chair in the dining room that I wouldn't sit in? How did she know of Miss Sweetland who served the people of the town from my sitting room side window? How did she know about the creepy scented corner in the dining room where the sad maid stands? She also successfully noted the place on the stairs, the issue with my longcase clock and identified the two men in the rear yard and their positions. Nobody else knew of these two men and their description except for me and my neighbour the witch.

Paranoia suddenly washed over me, could it be that Abigail was also a member of the same coven that my next-door neighbour self-proclaimed witch belonged to? Was Abigail's passing by my house this morning all part of an elaborate plot? My God! This is what a severe haunting does to you, your reason and scientific logic departs on the first bus out of town and what remains is the unthinkable.

That night I was not as you might envisage with a more relaxed mind but instead in a heightened state of vigilance. I feared that Abigail's cleansing might not have worked, I knew so little about her and perhaps she was just a misguided amateur who winged it. Could it even be that she and the witch next door were in cahoots?

However, I needn't have feared as the next morning I awoke refreshed and bathed in sunshine that poured through the drawn curtains. I had slept deeply and without disturbance of any kind from spirits or from the church clock. Now I questioned whether this new situation would last. Heeding Abigail's warning, I ensured that I did not think of my former ghost, and I got out of bed to prepare for the day ahead.

It was not long before I bumped into my neighbouring witch later that same morning. On my way out of the house, I had paused in my rear yard to notice that the atmosphere had changed. No longer was there a movement of air or the vortex by the rear door. I had paused too long however, the moment that I opened my rear gate to cross the alleyway into my garden, June was already waiting for me.

I had of course kept Abigail's visits to my home private but someone – or something – had tipped-off June. Keen to find out what had been going on inside my house the day before she openly questioned me without any shame. Psychically she already knew that something had happened, and I presumed that her 'guides' had informed her. It would also have been the case that she was no longer in communication with my former resident ghost who had perhaps been doing her bidding by dint of necromancy.

What awful karma was June creating for herself by employing legions of the dead to create chaos and havoc in innocent people's lives? Short-term gains in the physical world and yet long-term repercussions for her own soul with a merry-go-round of repeat incarnations trying to learn the same lesson over and over.

I explained to June that I had received psychic help from a neighbour. I did not want to name Abigail in case she too fell under a hex similar to that which had befallen me. But even as I told her what had happened, June looked into the distance and along the street towards Abigail's house, as though a little voice had just whispered in her ear who was responsible for ruining her fun and where this new enemy lived. Ignoring that, I told her about the rescue that we had undertaken in my house and that the spirit of the man who had been troubling me and many others before me had finally gone to the Light.

She cackled a loud mirthless laugh and her pretence fell for a moment. It was apparent that this news irritated her in the extreme. It was as though a favourite game she was playing had been spoiled. 'Ah! You two are dispatchers,' she said. 'I line them up, you sniff them out and *she* sends them to the Light.' The word 'she' was almost spat out. This was the first admission on June's part that she had anything to do with the extreme quantity of spirits haunting Pippins. I noted that she spoke in the plural and remembered that Abigail had commented on how 'crowded' my house was with the sheer number of spirits occupying such a small space. My former resident ghost had also a considerable arsenal of spirit activities to his spectral hand. Had this witch been empowering the supernatural activity in my home? It would seem so.

Then, with a sly smile she looked at me and said, 'A man is arriving this weekend.' I was beginning to recognise now when she was hearing information from her lower vibrational 'guides' as June temporarily looked as though she was eavesdropping on a conversation going on elsewhere. The weekend was the very next day and I had indeed invited my new boyfriend to stay with me for the first time. He lived some distance from me and was due to travel down to where I lived the next morning.

This was a personal closely guarded secret, I had told no-one, and short of tapping my phone, she couldn't possibly have known this any way other than supernatural. I didn't deny it. June suddenly found this visit highly amusing, and my anxiety grew, but I told myself to not be foolish, after all what could this woman do to someone living at a distance?

Standing outside her cottage, June suddenly turned away from me. Something else had been whispered in her ear by her low vibration spirit 'guides' and she was now looking towards the end of the alleyway and out onto the street. Following her gaze, we both suddenly saw Abigail walking past with her dog. I muttered something to June about being very busy and having things to do. Secretly I wanted to have a chat with Abigail, and I also needed to get away from this troublesome woman.

The witch suddenly burst out angrily, 'That woman again!' and then contemptuously, 'She's one of the Love and Light brigade, what a load of rubbish!' June obviously knew that it was Abigail who had helped me the day before and that it was Abigail who had thwarted her plans. There was obviously no longer any need for pretence and so I departed hurriedly and chased after Abigail. Abigail agreed to wait for me, and I put on my walking boots so that we could go on the long dog walk together.

Warning Abigail that the witch had worked out that it was her who had helped me, she seemed utterly unconcerned. Instead, Abigail explained to me that her spirit guides had told her that the witch had been encouraging the spirits within my house by feeding them the energy required to manifest. Why would June do that? Mischief perhaps, but also her desire to occupy my house. I told Abigail about the witch's suggestion that I move out of Pippins and rent it to them free of charge. In return, they said, they would, 'Look after it for me.' Abigail laughed at the idea, though I felt less like laughing, and she simply said, 'The woman must be mad.' I agreed that yes, she probably was.

I wasn't ever to tell Abigail, but secretly, when alone at home, my paranoia about the synchronicities grew. In the cold logical light of day, the only way that June and Abigail could possibly know so precisely about the spirits and supernatural activities in my house was because they were working together in cooperation. Was I being duped? No, I simply couldn't give this negative way of thinking about my new friend any mental space, to do so would open up a ghastly rabbit hole. The only acceptable explanation was that both women were extremely good psychics, one working for the darkness and one working for the light.

At no point in this strange battle between light and dark did I ever consider that I was anything but a casual bystander caught up in a maelstrom of psychic activity. The truth however was to be slowly revealed to me by spirit over the following years. I was a much larger part of this than I could ever have imagined.

The truth was literally staring at me in my face when every day I passed by the ever-present figure of Archangel Michael slaying the Devil as portrayed in the stunning stained glass panel that I had 'stumbled across by chance' and brought home and affixed to my kitchen door.

The days and nights passed without a further visitation from my former unwanted spooky occupant. Although I was aware of spirit presences in the house, these were benevolent background energies that did not try to negatively impact my life. I knew that the old lady and the young girl remained in my dining room and that there was the former owner and protector of the house on the stairs, not forgetting the small boy who liked to be in the upstairs small bedroom. But was the silence from the malevolent entity a coincidence, or had Abigail truly ridden me of this troublesome 'guest'?

I noted that the church clock now struck properly and no longer woke me in the night. Could it possibly be true that the ghost had manifested this audible malfunction, or had the clock been repaired that very week following many months of being faulty? The questions in my mind grew rather than dissipated. There was a frightening prospect that I was now faced with of neighbours with an irrational hatred of me cooperating together to force me out of my home through psychological warfare. The alternative was that I was embroiled in a psychic war and shared my home and my reality with unseen forces. Neither option seemed favourable and neither left me feeling comfortable in my own home or was good for my mental health.

Adding to this paranoia was when my boyfriend messaged me at the last minute to tell me that he was unable to come that weekend after all. Without any warning, he had suffered from a suspected heart attack. It had occurred around about the same time that I had been speaking with the witch in the alleyway where she had revealed that she knew about his forthcoming arrival. This was a shock, but tests carried out later that day showed that he was fine but needing to rest. He had never encountered anything like this before and so it had come as a complete surprise. Obviously I didn't tell him that 'a witch next door' had seen him with her third eye! Was this yet another coincidence or had she hexed him too? Whether this was paranoia on my part or whether there was something more to it, either way I had a major problem on my hands.

On two or three further occasions the scratching noises from the ceiling above my bed occurred. Only this time the noises did not herald any significant spirit manifestation or my departed spectre. It was caused by 'other spirits' I told myself but as they left me alone, I left them alone too. I also thought it highly probably that the witch was actively continuing in her efforts to introduce further earthbound spirit into my home. Also continuing unabated after Abigail's rescue was my laptop and bedside lamp still switching on by night. I had tested the electrical plugs and sockets but all seemed well. Sometimes this curious event occurred every night and then sometimes several days would pass between incidents.

Some few days after the cleansing had taken place I woke once more in the sun filled bedroom to find Monty asleep on my bed and all seeming well. Only I knew something was about to happen and I lay still and silent waiting. I didn't have long to wait, the sound of something dropping and rattling across the solid oak floor of the bathroom came from across the landing.

There it was again. The same noise repeated. What was that?

Rat ... rattatattat ... then one final time, unmistakably it was the sound of something small and wooden being skidded across a solid wooden floor. Rat ... rattatattat ... it wasn't Monty as he was on my bed, so what was making the very loud and very clear noise? My first thought was that something or someone was inside the house. An alarming thought! It was very clear that the sound emanated from the bathroom, this being the only wooden surface on the first floor.

Swiftly I got out of bed. Perhaps Monty had brought a mouse into the house overnight. Wary of what I was to discover, I peered around the door into the bathroom. It was to find nothing. This was more confusing than finding something in a place it shouldn't be. The sound was loud, clear and obvious. With nothing on the bathroom floor to explain the sound, I spent the next few minutes checking under the bath and all around the toilet and elsewhere to discover nothing.

Later that day I was to chat with Abigail about it and she was immediately told by her guides that it was the little boy, Thomas. He had been playing with the old fashioned type of wooden pegs and had been skimming them across the bathroom floor. Ghost pegs! Of course .... The energy of his 'ghost pegs' had created a sound which I could hear clearly as a clairaudient. It was an entirely real sound and there was no way that I could differentiate between it and something created in the physical. Abigail pondered whether the boy needed to be rescued but she was unable to ascertain anything further as the little boy was scared and wouldn't be contacted.

Some three weeks or so after the rescue of my troublesome ghost had taken place the most wonderful and amazing thing happened that even today makes me happy. In fact, there was not only the one wonderful thing, but two wonderful things to occur. It was obvious that spirit preferred to capture my attention during my waking or slumbering moments and this particular occurrence was to be of no exception. I woke early on yet another bright and sunny morning to the sound of my bedside iPod alarm clock making a noise.

I had set it to go off at 7am that morning and as I slowly roused from my sleep, I imagined that the clock had developed a fault. I had set the wake-up call to switch on music from my old iPod, and yet what I heard was a strange faint whisper of a noise coming from the loudspeaker close to my ear like nothing I was used to hearing. I turned over in the bed and peered at the clock through bleary eyes. It was 6.50am. The alarm couldn't be going off yet. I could see that the alarm was still set, and that the iPod screen wasn't illuminated as it would be if the alarm had been triggered.

While I had never experienced the sound before (or since) from my alarm clock speaker, I had heard the tune many times. The tune was the very same one that the church clock carillon played when striking the hour. But as it wasn't yet 7am and the device was switched-off, where was the sound coming from? My hand reached out from under the covers and hit the 'snooze' button, but no amount of fiddling could silence the noise coming from the loudspeaker.

The faintness of the sound was similar to that which you hear when tuning-in to a distant radio station in some far-flung country, yet I never deployed the radio on this device and it was switched-off. Quiet it might have been but distinct it was too and loud enough to wake me from my slumber. As the carillon tune playing through the loudspeaker finished, it heralded the striking of the hour. I had already guessed that this was no ordinary music, this was spirit sound yet the vibes in the bedroom were feeling amazingly good and positive.

Was this my recently departed spirit trying to haunt me once more? Was the strike of the hour to now be played backwards through the clock speaker? The strike came, bong, bong, bong, bong, bong, bong, bong. The strike was normal! Like tiny jolly little peeps for bell sounds. Then I remembered what Abigail had said. Always in spirit rescues, the rescued spirit who travels to the Light will send a, 'I made it safely and thank you,' message. This was it. *This was my ghost saying thank you to me in a light-hearted and ironically funny way.* It was from this moment that I started to like my nemesis.

This was incredibly clever, incredibly exciting and incredibly welcome. After months of misery, the spirit who had so cleverly manipulated the sound of the church clock each night at 3am, was now manipulating my alarm clock to replicate the church strike in a strange tinny digital way, the notes thin and electronic. It made me realise how much energy earthbound spirit has to its ghostly fingertips to utilise when manifesting and how puny the energy is when spirit in the Light is trying to contact us through the veil. No wonder we miss the cues from our angels and spirit guides so often. *You really have to be listening to hear*!

I lay in bed marvelling at what I had just experienced, was this house never to cease with its surprises? Then the clock suddenly hit 7am and the iPod burst into life and played a song at the usual volume as it normally would do. The church clock, always three minutes out then joined in. I leapt out of bed that day very happy and I couldn't wait to tell Abigail that the rescue had been successful.

But that wasn't all. Only a couple of days later I received yet another morning visitor. Once more it was to a delightfully sunny bright and fresh morning and as the sunlight blazed through my closed curtains, something in my room woke me. It was the weekend and my alarm wasn't set. I had been asleep and lying on my left side facing the window. As I opened my eyes for the first time that day, it was to immediately focus on a pink glow.

It was the size of a grapefruit and the same beautiful colour as rose quartz. It was also the same height as my face and only a metre from it. The strangest thing was that it was behind the curtain, and yet glowing so brightly that I could see it through the fabric, even though the sun was already up. It was as though whatever, or whoever it was, in some naïve way was trying to hide its presence from me by keeping behind the drawn curtain.

This only lasted some five joyful seconds. Rather than be a frightening experience, the entire sensation was one of peace and love – literally love and light. Instinctively I knew that whatever or whomever this visiting being was, it was immeasurably good, kind, loving and caring and that I was indeed blessed in that moment. It was as though it had stood watch by my bedside as I slept, in the same loving way that a mother would watch her child sleep.

Upon my waking, it had tried to hide itself from view. Was it my late mother who had been standing there behind the curtain? Had it been an ascended being or perhaps an angel? Whatever or whomever it was, I knew that I was loved and protected and that I had been so fortunate to have had such a visitation. That soft and gentle light emanated love and is such a wonderful positive memory that it will stay with me always. I am truly blessed, and I am truly grateful.

CHAPTER THIRTY-THREE

Universal adapter

Piousness

'Take no thought for the morrow, for the morrow shall take thought for the things of itself' Matthew 6:34.

An everyday reality for those on a spiritual journey of self-discovery and self-love is to encounter prejudice, suspicion or ridicule from those at a different stage of their personal growth or on a different life journey. Many of us resist healing our own wounded inner child or resist the soul's desire for the spirit incarnate in the physical body to operate at a higher vibration. We all do this at some point in our development and it is merely projection of the ego, because in truth we all wish that we too could summon the effort required to begin a new spiritual journey.

I have struggled with my weight for much of my adult life, and I have always found that the most difficult part of the journey to good physical health is the first step of taking action towards a wholesome diet and regular exercise. So it is with good spiritual health, the ego resists transformation lest it become threatened by any positive changes that may come about through self-realisation and spiritual growth.

When you experience mockery of your spiritual path, wherever you are along it, do not be affected by or listen to other people's negative attitudes directed towards you. Remember that you know what is best for your own personal growth. When you are on the path always bear in mind that you must take baby steps along the way and that there is no rush to an imaginary finish line. As with life, it is the spiritual journey that is to be savoured and not the destination.

What is less spoken of is a sometimes 'holier-than-though' attitude that you may encounter from those who are also on a spiritual or religious journey and should thereby know better. Perhaps I shall make myself a little unpopular for raising this topic, but we may sometimes find ourselves on the receiving end from those who consider themselves 'more spiritual.'

It is such an honour to be spiritually aware that it is understandable that the excitement can lead to a strong need to share the knowledge with others. This desire to spread the good news about the divine and the meaning of all things can sometimes come across as sanctimony. It is easy to fall foul of the ego and consider that we are morally better placed than others in terms of spiritual advancement, whereas we are merely cognizant of divine knowledge or bestowed with gifts that others have yet to experience.

Merely because we have enjoyed a head-start leading to a better knowledge of spiritual and religious texts, or because we are in clearer psychic contact with Spirit does not make for superiority. There is no superiority, everyone is equal, and we are all little sparks of the Source enjoying a unique physical experience as desired by our soul.

A spiritual life, and the quest to raise our vibration as we pass from incarnation to incarnation is not a competition. All of us are on the very same conveyor belt in the universe's spiritual supermarket checkout, only we are at differing points along it. A packet of cornflakes being scanned by the cashier at the head of the queue would not smirk at the toothpaste further down the line – everything will end up in the divine shopping bag eventually.

There is simply no need to be pious to anyone who we consider has not yet awoken or reached our own level of spiritual learning. Each and every one of us on our own unique spiritual journey is doing so in our own predetermined timeframe. It is not our place to judge or act in any way superior over another still learning; and we are always learning.

My own experience of 'organised' religion and also of the esoteric world is that because it is by inception open to everyone, naturally not everyone is always of the highest vibration. You don't have to be 'high vibe' to be psychic, but it helps. Once you begin to tune in to it, your 'higher self' or intuition will tell you whether someone is genuine in heart. This applies not only to the psychic medium, the tarot reader and the shaman, but also for the officially recognized religious minister, some of whom may be up to many a shenanigan behind their congregation's collective backs. When the appointed religious cleric, of whatever religious denomination, has an unhealed shadow side their ego may seek to hide behind or use the sanctity of their office to promote hate speech dressed-up in religious clothing.

When equal marriage rights for the LGBTQ community was first mooted by the British government, I well recall the opening piece by our rural village vicar in the monthly parish newsletter. It was a thinly disguised liturgy of intolerance – though for 'intolerance' read 'hate speech.' Pretending to be a plea for the protection of the sanctity of the Church of England the article thundered, 'Where will it all end?!' Presumably with equal rights for all, I thought.

It is unlikely that Jesus would have advocated one rule for one section of society and another rule for those who didn't fit-in to a predetermined man-made patriarchy. But the (male) vicar was far more concerned with exclusivity rather than inclusivity, with some mistaken religious folk often demeaning their faith to little more than championing one football team over another.

I do not desire to put off some readers by making any overt political statements within these pages. However, human rights are everyone's affair and with the Source viewing all humans as equal it is always inequitable for some people to have fewer rights than others. On the subject of 'gay rights' could I suggest that as a test, the next time you come across a media article calling for the slow down, or reversal of, equality for LGBTQ, you mentally delete the word 'gay' and instead swap it for the word 'black' or 'ethnic' as you read. The results may shock you.

Few healthy-minded people would disagree in the twenty-first century that all humanity, regardless of skin colour, should have equal status. Yet by swapping around the word 'gay' with 'black' as you read, you may be horrified to realise that you have been reading 'hate speech' dressed up as 'freedom of speech.' You may also be saddened to realise that without having swapped these words, you wouldn't have even noticed the hatred in the article at all. This will give way to the sudden realisation that such toxic propaganda is commonplace and unwittingly accepted as normal and acceptable.

While our spirit guides may rejoice when we eventually rediscover the life path that we had intended to follow at birth, for those of you who have 'awoken' in recent years, try to avoid pressing your newfound spirituality on others who are not as yet ready to ascend. While it is always laudable to offer help to someone to cross the road, it is polite to ask first as it is often met with offence if we insist that someone crosses over the road when they are not yet willing or able! We are all part of the same collective and we are all on our own separate journeys, with everyone eventually 'getting there' given enough incarnations.

Even those who have enjoyed a misspent youth and who are now reformed characters have at one time boasted to friends and others about their 'unholy' exploits. Once they tire of hedonism, they try spirituality, like it, and having taken it up as a new hobby they now boast about how pure of heart they are and compare themselves favourably to others further back down the spiritual conveyor belt. Please don't compare, instead please extend love and acceptance to all, no matter where they are on their journey of discovery called life.

Tree of Knowledge – Anxiety Is The Fruit of Knowing

An animal does not fear its future. It does not know that it has one. The concerns of an animal relate to food, sleep, shelter and reproduction. Humankind is different as we have an additional awareness above the survival instinct. Adam, in the Garden of Eden took a bite from the fruit of knowledge and in that moment irrecoverably changed from peace of mind to one of self-awareness. Adam hadn't been concerned with pension annuities and health insurance and there was no knowledge of guilt from 'not doing the right thing' or anticipating that a future day may come without food, shelter or sex.

Suddenly becoming aware that he had a past and a future and that the things he needed and wanted might not always be available, he became worried. He became anxious. The story of Adam and Eve is of course an allegorical one but at some point in human development we became conscious that we should seek to control our future by planning ahead.

Collectively, our ego misled us into believing that it was capable of controlling future outcomes. We saw that we could mould our life and those of others by thoughts turning into actions. By *believing* that we could anticipate, plan and foresee all eventualities, an outcome and an end result could be expected. Or so we thought and, in that way, anxiety began because as we know, the universe is chaos with a billion differing factors at play.

We became self-conscious too. A baby is not self-conscious. A baby remains deliciously free of all expectations and conditions placed upon it until that child reaches the approximate age of seven years. By the age of seven the ego is formed, and it is our ego which seeks to protect at all times.

To do this the ego collects the 'data of disapproval' received from our parents, family, friends and peers in order to coordinate a tactical response to these incoming threats to our sensitivities. We must have the right education. We must get a decent job. We must have the right house, the right car, the right 'lifestyle'. We must have our hair the right way, we must wear clothes which will make us stand-out from or blend-in with the crowd, we must be smart in appearance, we mustn't be ugly or speak strangely or grow old. The list of anxieties grows swiftly, and it is a strong mind that can withstand this onslaught of learnt faux rights and wrongs.

Panic sets in and by our teen years we begin to read 'lifestyle' and fashion magazines which tell us what we need that season to 'fit-in' and be accepted. Into adulthood we read slimming and beauty magazines to learn tips to make sure that no-one secretly laughs at our middle-age spread. When did we become so self-conscious? *Just why are we so worried* about getting the right job title, owning our house or having the right car, the right toys for our kids, the right Christmas?

I would be prepared to wager that right now you are anxious about some development in your life, or indeed, lack of development of some sort. Yet we are constantly reminded by the world's religions to not fear the coming day. In the New Testament, Jesus is quoted as advising us to 'take no thought for the morrow, for the morrow shall take thought for the things of itself' Matthew 6:34. He was telling us that the Source already has our anticipated future taken care of, for good or for bad, and that we are exactly where we need to be. So, ignore what your ego is currently making you fret over and enjoy every moment that comes and worry not about the physical things in your life.

The religion and way of life Daoism also contains this philosophy at the heart of its teachings. 'Wu wei' is Chinese for 'non-doing' or 'doing nothing'. This doesn't mean not acting, rather it means 'effortless action'. In this way we can be at peace even when working frenetically. We are not in a state of resistance and instead we go with the flow of the universe.

The Ego Actually Creates Problems Not Solves Them

It is part of the human condition to think that if we do not allow our ego centred brain to resolve problems, then things will get worse for us. 'The Law Of Unintended Consequences' often comes into play here. When we work against the natural order of things in the physical 3D universe, believing ourselves to be somehow separate from it, the more we create trouble for ourselves. The more that mankind tries to eliminate problems, the more problems he/she creates. Sometimes mankind would be better placed accepting and adapting to restrictions in the physical universe rather than trying to change the physical universe to suit.

When the gasoline powered internal combustion engine was created, it had a peculiar problem of 'knocking.' The knocking was caused by erratic combustion and long term this could cause damage to the engine, as well as an unpleasant noise. The cylinders in the engines also needed lubricating to prevent overheating and sticking. How to resolve this? A very bright scientist came up with the solution which was to introduce Tetra-Ethyl Lead into the gasoline. Leaded petrol was born and the problems with gasoline engines in the twentieth century were resolved and awards for the solution were given.

Only the solution came with unforeseen problems. Lead is a heavy metal, highly toxic to the human anatomy and brain. What then was the solution to the lead in gasoline? The solution proved to be unleaded petrol and a redesign of car engines. The problem with unleaded petrol is high levels of extremely carcinogenic benzene. So, what was the solution to benzene in gasoline? The solution was the promotion of diesel fuelled cars, with better load lugging capabilities and the ability to travel further on a full tank of fuel producing less pollution. Only they don't. Diesel particulates, the microscopic particles of partially burnt fuel, together with highly noxious greenhouse gasses, are still poisoning us on a global level. The solution to this?

The latest solution is electric cars powered by several large powerful lithium batteries. This will solve the issue of pollution at road level. Lithium batteries are extremely versatile when stored and used correctly. In the event of a rupture however they can become lethal. The energy to recharge them also must come from industrial scale power-plants. Lithium is also a finite resource.

Can you see a pattern emerging here with mankind's problems and solutions? Did I mention that the same scientist who came up with the solution of Tetra-Ethyl Lead in gasoline also solved the problem of flammable liquids in early refrigerators by the creation of chlorofluorocarbons, better known as CFCs. We all know where that one ended.

I am not a luddite, but we must recognise that humanity needs to begin to work in sympathy with the physical universe that we are a collective part of, rather than seeing ourselves as individual consciousness's separate from the creation that surrounds us. We made a mistake when we set ourselves up above the plant and animal kingdom. Having eaten of the fruit, Adam believed he was separate from everything around him. God was saddened because Adam thought himself *separate* and *above* the universe, and the universe is God or Source. The Bible was in fact teaching us in allegorical terms that we are *part of* the Garden of Eden (the universe) and *not separate from it*. We are *of* the universe; we did not come *out* of it.

Chapter Thirty-Four

Saved by the bell

Divine protection

'Hello?' I said, holding the ancient receiver to my ear.
'Is June there?' the female caller enquired.

Abigail and I continued to meet up regularly after all that had happened, becoming good friends. We often went for long walks with her dog or for day trips out together to nearby towns and scenic places. This allowed us to spend many hours talking of spiritual topics and to relax in the company of someone who was prepared to understand the seemingly impossible.

Occasionally our travels would bring us into contact with an earthbound spirit requiring rescue, a memorable example being on a day trip to a seaside town in Dorset. Here, inside a church, Abigail came upon a woman in spirit who had in life devoted herself to the Church. Unlike Abigail, I could not see the spirit of the woman and in vain I blindly followed Abigail's pointing finger.

We were in the town as tourists and I had been taking digital photographs, so I had the idea of getting a snapshot of the area inside the church to where Abigail was now indicating. Abigail's hand moved upwards, advising me that the spirit of the woman was now high above us. My camera is equipped with an automatic focus feature. Pointing it in the direction that you want to photograph, the camera does the rest for you, the powered lens moving in and out to achieve focus. This is a pretty foolproof operating system, and it always focusses on the object nearest to the lens.

There was, to the naked eye at least, nothing between us and the far wall of the church which was some thirty metres distant. Yet, when I pointed my camera over to where Abigail was now specifically indicating, somewhere high up in the corner of the church, the camera immediately sprang into life and electronically focussed on something nearer to us rather than the far wall which remained blurred. This had never happened before and as Abigail continued to indicate where the moving spirit of the woman was, I followed with my camera.

Each time that I pointed the lens in the direction shown I achieved the same result with the camera electronically focussing on something nearer in the foreground that the camera could see but the human eye could not. The only disappointment being that there was nothing in the photographs to indicate any kind of spirit activity. Abigail was unsurprised but pleased that the camera could so easily detect the presence of the spirit of the woman even if I could not.

I repeatedly tested the camera elsewhere in the church, but it did not 'malfunction' in this manner again nor has it since. The rescue of the woman was short and simple. Abigail sat down for a while in the church as if in prayer. The Light came for the woman high up close to the central stained-glass window and the spirit passed quickly and willingly into the awaiting love beyond. It is always an honour and a joy to be able to help people find their way back home into the Light.

Back at my house things were less joyful. My neighbours,

aware that they had been rumbled became increasingly annoyed at my cutting all communication with them and by doing so severing all energetic ties. This was following closely the advice from my spirit circle and on the face of it seemed a highly anti-social and 'un-English' thing to do, especially so far-in to the 'friendship.' However I reminded myself that she had openly stated her purpose and intention of filling my house with spirits and in doing so, getting me to vacate so that she and her husband could move in.

I am reminded of the internet self-help meme of 'when someone shows you the first time what they are really like, believe them.' June's annoyance at my refusal to further entertain her games of amusement soon turned to outright anger directed solely at me, but only when no onlookers were witness. This is how the narcissist or psychopath operates. I consoled myself that had my neighbours been innocent and ordinary in their intentions, they would have been disappointed or saddened by the rift between us, not filled with rage that misguided plans had been spoiled.

I was often cornered in my garden, the alleyway, the street, or even in the supermarket many miles distant. June's clever ability to know people's precise 'comings and goings' was a powerful weapon in her armoury of intimidation. I realised that my energetic tie-severing needed bolstering.

The 'coincidental' supermarket meets were the oddest. The supermarket I frequented each week was a large twenty-four-hour superstore that remained highly busy at all hours. However, on two separate occasions when shopping at a very busy time of day I found myself in a mysteriously deserted aisle. Suddenly I heard that all-too-familiar voice behind me and spinning around it was to discover and be greeted by the wife and husband combo of June and Charles now beaming at me and purring with their own cleverness.

I admit that it spooked me that they had managed to be in the same place at the same time and in a cleared aisle located in a supermarket, miles from where we lived. I knew that my ashen face must have told its own story. Had they followed me here? The words that passed between us in public were always polite, as if nothing had happened, and yet as soon as socially awkward husband Charles strolled away, June's mask would quickly fall to be replaced with obvious open hostility aimed at me with each word spat out through snarling gritted teeth. Yes, she really was that angry with me.

Each time we 'happened to meet each other' June would enter my personal space and try to tap me on my chest. This had happened once before many weeks prior and because I was wise to this witch now, I comically reversed slowly while still engaging in smiling conversation. Someone may affectionately tap you on the chest while talking to you, but if they are being aggressive then the same action has a completely different connotation or purpose.

Abigail, calling 'round one morning, came to tell me that she had asked her spirit guides for more information about my neighbours. She was told what I already knew; that they were both 'mentally ill' and gripped in a constant battle of wills with each other. A karmic pairing that no doubt had reincarnated over and over until their lesson is learned – 'you will listen, and you will learn.'

More worryingly was when Abigail told me she had been warned that my witch neighbour was 'capable of anything' with a strong inference that June had, at least on one occasion, already carried out the 'anything.' In response to these palpable dark negative energies being directed at me and my home I began to keep Monty indoors as often as possible. I also began a three times a day cleansing of my house using white sage smudge sticks and a Tibetan singing bowl which I had recently acquired for the purpose. The purchase of the bowl was a happy one as I had always been drawn to the beautiful sound that they give.

I also bought many crystals that were for protection work and after charging them with their duties, I placed these at specific points around Pippins. These included all entrance points to the house such as doors and windows and even the chimneys. Of course I constantly had to assess whether this was all in my imagination. Perhaps Abigail was deliberately frightening me, or even a part of the conspiracy to get me 'out of my house.' These are the toxic seeds of paranoia that are planted when you come up against such dark madness. Whether you believe that the battle from my neighbour was a psychic or a psychological one, what was clear to me was that I needed to keep a cool head.

Now fully convinced that I had been under psychic attack for some weeks I realised that I had to protect myself spiritually. This was all new territory for me, and I was guided by my psychic medium Rebecca to meditate and cleanse my house every day, one room at a time, and fill it with love and light. I did so, sending out love in response to the hate that was being directed at me which is easier said than done.

I perhaps should add here that when faced with dark energies being directed at you, whether that be through spell work such as was the case here or even jealousy and dislike, you should always use love as the response. It must be genuine love coming from a heart-centred place and well-intended. While I do not doubt that love can be a tricky thing to muster and send to someone who wishes you ill, it is the only defence against negative energies where you do not wish to incur karmic consequences. And none of us should desire negative karmic consequences!

If you fight hate with hate, then your result will be adding gasoline to the flames. Water extinguishes fire, more fire does not. When sending genuine love to a person who is sending you dark energies and ill wishes, there is a potential prospect of those dark energies rebounding on the original sender. So, do not 'weaponize' your love, instead send the energy of your love in an open, *unconditional* and heart-centred manner. This will not then create any karma for you. The consequences remaining the ownership of the ill-wisher.

I wasn't aware of this at the time and whether my love bombing was working or not I could not say but June still attempted to re-engage with me and reconnect her energies to mine. Calling at my front door with no pretext one afternoon her unsmiling opening question was a simple, 'Are your crystals working?' I hadn't told anyone about using crystals around the house for psychic protection. Only Abigail knew that I had acquired crystals for protection work. Either June was able to psychically see into my home or Abigail had told her. I don't know which prospect would have been worse. The paranoia was deepening.

Perhaps the crystals and the sending of love was indeed working because it was at this time that June and Charles' campaign switched from the psychic to the physical. Every time Charles walked along the alleyway by my house, he would clear his throat and cough loudly as he passed the dining room window which you'll recall was directly beneath my bedroom window. This was unfortunate because he set off to work at 5am and this occurred *every* time in *exactly the same place*, so it soon became apparent that it was a deliberate action to create irritation.

Then during daylight hours he would cough outside of my sitting room window as he passed by and he would now always park his car directly outside my house. This might all seem rather petty, and indeed it was. Charles would spend many hours each week loading up his car until full and then unloading it again, putting in and then taking out many old random bits of junk. Each item had to be carried from their house to the road and then back again, much of which ended up littering their garden. I presumed that his strange behaviour was at the direction of June, psychically or otherwise, but his curious behaviour seemed to enrage her all the more.

I invited Abigail around to witness this odd behaviour of coughing outside the windows. Explaining to her that she wait and watch, I asked her to listen out for the cough as Charles walked past the windows. I think she perhaps thought that I was exaggerating but this scepticism soon turned to laughter when on cue, Charles walked past the dining room window and gave a loud clearing of the throat. Giggling, we rushed as quietly as possible to the sitting room to hear Charles cough out loud when passing the small front study window and then again when he reached the sitting room window.

This would be laughable in any other situation but it was quite apparent that it was being done to annoy as it happened every time and over many weeks, by day and by night. Abigail was informed by her spirit guides that June kept Charles closely under her psychic control and had been creating spellwork to get her husband to cough on cue. He perhaps did not even know that he was carrying out this curious behaviour which may also go some way to explain the repeated loading and unloading of his car outside of my window.

The strange behaviour and actions of June and her husband to keep up the pressure on me by whatever means did make me realise that I was not paranoid. Abigail had witnessed the same curious behaviour that I had, and whether you believe this to have been psychological or psychic warfare, it was nonetheless warfare. I said to Abigail that whether or not her spirit guides were correct about the state of June and Charles' mental wellbeing, Charles probably just couldn't bear to be inside his own house, preferring to spend hours in the roadway tinkering with his car.

I already knew that their house had ghosts of its own. You may recall that earlier in this book I related how June had told me that their previous home was haunted and that this had angered her husband as he was, somewhat understandably I feel, scared of ghosts. June was not scared of ghosts and doubtless she had encouraged them for some nefarious purpose. June had also told me that she chose the little cottage simply because it was directly next to mine and thereby the next best thing. I still didn't understand the significance of this statement at the time.

Tellingly, June laughed when she joyfully told me that their new cottage was also haunted and that she knew this before they had moved-in despite reassuring her nervous husband that there were no ghosts present. June explained how she had seen the spirit of an old white-haired lady sitting in a chair in her cottage on two occasions. But it was the spectre of a 'short, bald man' glowering at them at the foot of their bed which had so frightened her husband, Charles. Twice the poor man had woken to see this angry ghost who was dressed in early twentieth-century clothes and who made very apparent his annoyance with his home being occupied by June and Charles.

No wonder then that Charles didn't wish to spend much time indoors. Knowing that the description of these two spirits exactly matched George's recollection of the couple who had lived in the cottage in the 1930s, replete with the angry short bald old man, it was apparent that June was telling me the truth on that occasion.

The strange campaign to gain access to, or ownership of, my home continued unabated with June catching me unawares when entering my garden one afternoon. I had mistakenly thought that she was out for the day. It was getting rare now when I could freely go into my garden without her interference. 'I've noticed a mark on my sitting room wall where there was a door,' she said as her opening gambit. I looked quizzically at her and wondered how this information was relevant to me. 'There must have once been a doorway from my house into your rear yard,' she added by way of explanation. I started to see where this was going. 'I believe that your rear yard is actually mine. I think that I need to look at the property records to see who owns what.' This woman was completely mad.

'Either way, I'm going to ask Charles to look into opening-up the doorway again.' I struggled to hide my irritation. June was trying to bait me and get me angry plus she was absolutely serious about her plans. I made it clear that not only was there no sign of a doorway on her external wall in my yard, but that I had seen the property records dating back centuries and that there had never been a doorway there, her house having been built many decades after mine.

She reiterated her claim, and annoyed now, I suggested that perhaps she would want to ask her landlord before knocking a hole in the wall. How this woman thought that she had any claim or right of ownership over her rented property eluded me. It was clear now that she was crazy but also there was something about my house, even if only in the rear yard, that she desperately wanted.

Meanwhile the litter continued to accumulate in June and Charles' garden. When I had foolishly been on good terms with my neighbours, I had agreed to shampoo a large rug of theirs outdoors in their garden. Having had new light-coloured carpets fitted throughout my house when I had moved-in, the electric carpet shampooer I bought was a godsend when dealing with muddy cat paws.

On hearing that I had such an electric device, June asked if they could borrow it to clean their large wool rug which was rolled-up in storage. I didn't want to lend my new shampooer in case it got broken, so I suggested that I do the shampooing myself one sunny afternoon, unfortunately breaking the machine in the process. When the rug was unrolled it was so incredibly filthy that the shampooer, while it finished the job, did not survive and I was forced to abandon it.

However, my neighbours didn't then dry and use the now spotless rug as I had expected. It should have told me something when instead they rolled it up and left it outside in the front garden in all weathers. Here it began to rot and added to the eyesore. This apparent deliberate snub was doubly irritating as my cat Monty would now sit atop the rolled-up rug in their garden much to the curious delight of June.

Like all cats, Monty had the occasional cat flea, but I kept him regularly treated and so this had never become a problem in the years that had him. Yet it was during this time period when he would go outside to bask in the sunshine lying atop the abandoned rotting rug that he caught the worst case of fleas that I have ever seen. Much fumigation and endless vacuuming were to no avail as Monty would spend each day sunbathing atop the rotting rug. To resolve the problem, I had to request that the veterinarian visit my home, at considerable expense, to give Monty anti-flea shots.

June once more appeared at my back gate, ringing the brass bell that hung there to summon me. Stepping out into the rear yard, I stuck my head around the gate to see what she wanted this time. Even I was surprised when she blasted me with her anger, calling me several insults without any provocation and hissed at me that my house was 'a filthy flea infested hole.'

Nobody knew about the cat fleas except for Abigail and the vet. But then I suspected that the pet fleas had come from the dirty rug deliberately left lying rolled-up in the hot sunshine. Before I knew them, June and Charles had previously owned three small dogs, all of which she had told me had tragically died within a short period of time of each other. Where there are dogs and cats there are inevitably pet fleas and flea eggs in soft furnishings. Monty didn't come into contact with any other animals and had never suffered from cat fleas until now and he never suffered from them thereafter. There was nothing supernatural about their behaviour, it was just sheer bloody-mindedness.

June had previously boasted that Monty had been spending 'a lot of time' in her house and this hugely annoyed me, although I didn't let her see it. Remembering that this woman was apparently 'capable of anything' I did not consider Monty to be safe. I now understood where Monty had been disappearing to, and June went on to brag that he 'liked it in my house' and that she had been 'encouraging him upstairs.' What lay 'upstairs' for him I shuddered to imagine but ignoring the supernatural, this type of sneaky pet theft where a cat is encouraged to swap homes is just plain cruel and should actually be illegal.

June had never made any secret of desiring my 'familiar' as she called Monty. He was a supremely clever cat and I was later to discover he was much more besides, sent to me for companionship and for more mystical reasons. June wanted Monty as her own and she made no pretence otherwise, so I decided to keep him indoors as much as possible. I thought this was for his own good, but I was soon to discover that it was exactly at this time when he contracted a strange virus and a bacterial infection that eventually took his life only a few months later.

There was no let up in pressure. The same week as June insulted my home at my backyard gate, I experienced a sudden plague of blowflies which suddenly appeared in my kitchen. There was no explanation for the flies. They miraculously appeared one day when the doors and windows had been closed. I had returned home from town to discover hundreds of them but their sudden arrival was met with an equally sudden departure.

A knock came at the front door. It was, of course, an angry June. She cackled that I was 'living in a fly blown house.' Had she seen the flies swarming in my kitchen? I think that to be very doubtful. This time I hadn't even told Abigail as the infestation had come and gone so quickly that I hadn't had the time.

Some years prior I had been visiting an abandoned haunted house. The reason for my visit was work-related but I still remember the overpowering negative feeling inside that house and upon reaching the top floor, the two attic bedrooms had been infested with large black flies. Hundreds of them buzzing on the windows and blacking out the daylight. This was years before all the supernatural occurrences at Pippins and I suspected then that dark energies were at play in that house as the horrific scenario put me in mind of the story behind the Amityville Horror.

Now it was my own kitchen that had suffered a plague of flies and once more I suspected dark energies at work. As I have mentioned elsewhere in this book, I am a sufferer of the commonly occurring health condition Obsessive Compulsive Disorder (OCD) and I prided myself as a necessity on keeping my home immaculate, including sometimes ridiculously high standards of hygiene. There was simply no possible way that hundreds of blowflies could suddenly appear in my kitchen, a kitchen which faced directly onto June's own home. Any sufferer of the OCD condition will tell you that a household invasion of any pest will cause extreme levels of anxiety, likely to even make you want to leave your home.

Perhaps June's campaign against me had worked after all because I was desperate to get away from this place. Except for meeting Abigail, the events since I had arrived in the town had all been of a negative nature. On a regular visit to my psychic medium Rebecca, I was just leaving her consultation room when she stopped me and said, 'You need to move from that house. If you stay in that energy, you'll dry up like an old orange.'

It was this message from spirit as well as the manifold other events that made me place my property with a local real estate agent to be marketed for sale secretly. Just one such manifold event was when June approached me outside looking worried. June told me that she was alarmed that a house of 'a friend' of hers had 'spontaneously burst into flames' shortly after she had 'paid a visit.' I had thought little of it at the time, but in hindsight ….

Those of you reading this who have done spirit work, where you connect as a psychic medium with deceased loved ones, will know that we feel physical sensations in our body when the spirit comes close to give their messages. Usually these are the last sensations that the deceased experienced in their life. When I was working and training with the spirit circle, each one of us in turn would be called to stand up in front of the others in the circle and wait for a spirit or deceased loved one who wished to connect to step forward. Feeling an imposter, my expectations were low and when I did this for the first time, I was anticipating failure, despite the host's complete conviction in my abilities.

Standing awkwardly and feeling shy in front of the seated others I suddenly felt an intense heat behind my back. This feels not dissimilar to standing with your back to an open fireplace. 'There's someone with you now,' the spirit circle host would say each time, talented as she was to be able to see the energy of the spirits that came in close to us to impart their messages. The spirit would indicate their gender or which side of the family they were from, maternal or paternal, by positioning themselves behind one or other of your shoulders. When it was a spirit guide or higher being I was advised that your entire back would heat up, though I did not experience these higher beings while at the circle.

I mention this to you now in order to explain the following event. A bright, warm day and the garden was looking delightful, my cottage garden flowers and roses that I had planted that spring were now in full bloom and had a vibrancy and freshness that is synonymous with early summer in a warm and rainy Britain. There wasn't a lot of maintenance work to do in my garden, at this time of year it mostly looked after itself, so I pottered happily amongst the flowers with Monty ever at my feet. I loved his company, as he did mine, not that he would ever admit it.

I remained watchful for June. Her sudden appearances were always disturbing though I hadn't seen her for a few days, and I wondered if she was unwell. June's neighbour Terence was in his garden directly the other side of hers. He could be easily seen toiling away in the sunshine clearing out his large garden shed where he had been storing boxes of belongings and old books. June would normally have appeared in her garden by now on some pretext or other to have a 'chat.' On this occasion she remained nowhere to be seen and seeing that the coast was clear I exited my garden through the gate and into the alleyway to go have a talk with Terence.

Terence had previously shocked me only a few weeks prior when a discussion we had about the past revealed that he used to live in the same small yachting town where my brother and I grew up. He had gone on to reveal that he had been schooled at the same high school as my brother and at the same time. Terence still drove the several hundred miles back there once a month to visit his elderly mother. This tiny town only has a small population and the chances of my close neighbour Terence also originating from there were miniscule, and yet here he was. It seemed to be clear evidence of karmic relationships where we travel with the same tribe of people in repeating incarnations.

A delightful coincidence though this was (I had experienced manifold coincidences since I had moved into this house) this was such a strange one that it fed into my paranoia. Only a few months before, the celebrant who had conducted my mother's funeral, chosen by me entirely at random from the internet, had revealed at the service itself *that he too* had originated in the same small town and had gone to school with my brother. We were now many hundreds of miles from that small town. Here was one synchronicity after another occurring.

'Hello, having a good clear out?' I asked somewhat obviously as I approached. Terence glanced up from his labour and cheerfully confirmed that he was indeed clearing out old stuff and began to tell me one of his interesting tales about his life. Terence then went on to tell me that he had been hearing noises day and night coming from the empty cottage next door to his. Terence was not a man to be easily spooked and when I suggested that this was just the house settling, he claimed that for over a week he and his partner had been hearing loud bangs and footsteps.

Perhaps this spirit activity was why the house was empty. It seemed that this whole bloody street was haunted! Was June's necromancy also behind this haunting? It seemed possible as only two weeks prior, Terence had been involved in an argument with June and Charles over the accumulating piles of junk in their garden. The subsequent week to my meeting with Terence in his garden, and after further arguments with June and Charles over the rubbish, Terence mysteriously and suddenly fell ill one evening and an ambulance was called. Terence was in agony and spent a few days in hospital suffering with kidney problems, necessitating three weeks off work before he recovered. When I next saw him, he was gaunt and clearly had suffered greatly. He told me that he hadn't had any such health problems before, and he looked a broken and nervous man. I rarely saw him after that last meeting and he put his property on the market for sale soon after.

I continued to keep a close watch out for the witch as Terence and I chatted in the warm sunshine in his small garden. As he talked, Terence continued with his sorting through piles of open cardboard boxes spaced out on the lawn while I idly stood about. When June didn't appear I became more confident and presumed that she was out for the day with her husband as their car wasn't directly parked outside my sitting room window where it usually now resided. As we talked, I began to glance at the covers of the old books that were piled up in the open cardboard boxes. There, right on the top of the pile, as though I was intended to see it, the title of the book froze me in my tracks.

Terence carried on nattering to me, but all I could focus on was the title of the book, my eyes staring. It was a large hardback book about the history of dark witchcraft in Britain and the practice of the dark arts. It was as though I had been intended to see it amongst the hundreds of other books. There was no reason why anyone would have such a book unless they were a witch themselves, or highly interested in the subject matter. Terence caught me gazing hard at the book and paused, he knew about our witch neighbour and a tiny bit about my struggles with her, and he instantly felt the need to explain.

'My ex-wife came from a family of witches,' he said, 'Though she wasn't a witch in that sense,' he laughed at his own joke. I did not laugh, but nervously smiled. Terence explained that his wife was descended from a famous coven of British witches hence her interest in the subject matter. That would perhaps explain why he now owned a book on witchcraft, but there was something about the distorted reality of living in this town that had become a little too 'Wicker Man' for my comfort. I felt ill. My head prickled. It was a warm day and I had been stood talking in the sunshine for several minutes. In another 'Rosemary's Baby' moment, it suddenly felt as if the whole world was closing in and against me.

I think that I could be excused for my paranoia this time. I already knew of an active coven in this area. Most covens do not permit dark works but doubtless there were always rogue witches just as there are rogues anywhere. Could it be just a coincidence that June and Terence had moved in next door to me? Could they be witches acting together? Could Abigail be a witch too? After all, she was a gifted psychic. Who was to say that she wasn't working with them and against me? I had only her word to say that she was working with and for the Light.

The synchronicities, coincidences and odd happenings had been mounting over the weeks. Too numerous to simply dismiss, there had been many others that I have not mentioned in these pages. One expects coincidences to occur all the time. But most days and every week? My brain was spinning and so I didn't notice June quietly slip out of her front door and make her way across her garden and into Terence's.

By the time that I saw her it was too late, she was only some five metres away. Hearing her all too familiar laugh and a comment about books, I spun around. Had she known about the witchcraft book now lying on the surface of the box? Could she have even been somehow supernaturally responsible for this book of all the books to be on the top of the many piles and in the box nearest to me? It was quite a coincidence. The book had captured my attention for just long enough to keep me there like a fly in a spider's web, while I failed to notice her silent approach. She was beaming at me now and rather than stop some two metres away from me like she always did, she carried on approaching slowly, talking to Terence as he continued with his work. Terence muttered under his breath at June's unwelcome intrusion, but her eyes remained fixed on me and held a purpose. That sinister smile again ….

Terence made no secret of his irritation that this woman had entered his garden without asking, and I think he couldn't have wished both of us further at that moment. He remained polite as always and answered as briefly as possible the chatty questions put to him by June. But all of the time I knew that it was me that she had come to see. I felt the warmth as soon as I had seen her. I imagined at first that it was the heat of the day but curiously it was only my back that was heating up. The witch inched towards me as I faced her, the heat behind me intensifying, yet my face was in the sun and my back in the shade.

Immediately I understood that my spirit guides were here. The heat was across the whole of my back and so I knew that it was caused by my guides or higher beings, known as 'ascended masters,' rather than by a deceased loved one. They had come close in order to protect me. I had not truly felt this level of heat from their presence before. They were *very* close. I knew from the spirit circle that when spirit comes in close to a psychic medium's energy field, the heat gets more intense the closer they get. Comforting and in no way painful, the powerful presence of my spirit guides alerted me that June's approach meant danger.

The witch didn't seem to notice as she continued to slowly inch her way forward, very slowly as though testing the water until finally she started to intrude into my personal space. She was coming so close now that I wondered if she was going to whisper something. Remembering how she had touched my classic car and from that moment on it had been faulty, I knew that I couldn't afford to let her touch me. However I stood my ground.

Suddenly, something made her change her mind. Halting her slow approach but now within touching distance, June continued with her banal conversation with the disinterested Terence, only now she tried to bring me into it. However, I had other ideas. She was stood between me and the exit to the garden and she knew it, but I quickly made my excuses and dashed off, leaving a surprised and probably irritated Terence to speak with her alone.

I retreated into the cool darkness of my house and pondered this latest curious event, thanking spirit for their intervention and help. Intuitively I knew that if my guides hadn't been with me in that moment, she would have touched me on some daft pretext, just like she had with the cars, and in that way place on me some dark magic. It was only later when Terence became seriously ill that I wondered if she had instead placed her magic upon him.

Only two days later a fresh attempt was made to connect with me, a ring of the bell at my backyard gate indicating that a friendly neighbour wanted to talk to me. My gate only led out onto the private alleyway leading to the cottages at the rear, so this bell was only ever used by my immediate neighbours. Ethel, the retired schoolteacher who lived in the cottage at the end of the row often liked a chat and to make a fuss of Monty, and so I anticipated it was her as I had seen her pottering about that day. I wasn't expecting June as she had made her anger and jealousy towards me perfectly clear, so the last thing that I was expecting when I went out into the yard was her angry but smiling face.

The air turbulence was long gone since the spirit rescue and the yard, filled with flowers and climbers, was now a pleasant place to sit awhile. Happily I unlocked and opened the wooden door to the alleyway expecting to see Ethel or Terence. Instead, the witch stood smiling that smile yet as always with a look of sheer rage in her eyes.

'Yes?' I couldn't even be bothered with the pretence of polite neighbourliness. When your neighbour has been seething in your face and called your house 'a flea infested dump' diplomacy eventually dries up.

She began some odd explanation as to why she was calling, to which there was clearly no point, and all the while was gently fondling in her right hand the antique brass bell that hung by the gateway to alert me to callers. Turning her full attention now to the quirky antique brass door knocker which adorned the gate itself, she touched it briefly, as though to test it. The knocker had an impish face and inside I had secreted a blessed and protective crystal. She quickly took away her hand as if the knocker itself were hot. I made a mental note to later cleanse both the bell and the knocker of any dark magic.

Unexpectedly, June suddenly took a step forward though she couldn't have gained access to my rear yard as there was a step-up and I was blocking the entranceway. However, I got the clear impression that she was testing the entrance to whether it was protected against her magic. She seemed satisfied that she was safe, or perhaps that I wasn't, and she visibly relaxed her shoulders and began talking about why she had called. Many words poured forth and I said little but nonetheless she continued, laughing at her own witticisms.

Something was going on here, why the sudden change in her demeanour and approach? Why the unexpected charm? Was I being mesmerised? It was at this very moment that my elderly neighbour Ethel, having seen June stood by my gateway chatting, quickly approached for a chat of her own. Ethel lived alone and did many good charitable works in the town and was rather old fashioned in that she seemed to come from a different, gentler age. She was however loud and often without tact. Like a school gym mistress from the 1930s, her voice boomed out, cutting across my witch neighbour.

Interrupted, June did not turn her face towards Ethel who was now addressing her. Instead June tacitly acknowledged the interloper's presence but refused to engage in conversation, keeping her eyes firmly fixed on me. Was June just ignoring

Ethel, or had Ethel interrupted some new dark spell that she was performing? This rudeness was not even observed by our neighbour, as Ethel remained undeterred and merely stood behind June, looking at me instead and talking loudly of the weather, the state of the gardens and that week's waste collection.

While Ethel could not have seen June's face, I most certainly could. It was disturbing but also amusing to watch the rage rapidly swell within my witch neighbour. June's eyes became slits of anger and her mouth set in a firm line as though it was taking all of her might to hold in the anger she presently felt for Ethel. It was clear that June had an express purpose in her visit to my backyard that day and Ethel's innocent interruption had thwarted her carefully laid plans.

Innocent interruption or divine intervention, I wondered? Whatever the purpose was, she was up to no good and it would likely be to my detriment. Ethel, oblivious to the unspoken communication going on between me and the witch, continued talking jollily and loudly. June's eyes were now rolling angrily in her head, and through her teeth she seethed words of anger and uttered oaths.

I wondered if she was cursing Ethel in that moment. Certainly, for the coming two weeks Ethel was unwell and housebound. A coincidence perhaps, but in that moment and mid-sentence, the old lady suddenly broke off, and without pausing, said her goodbyes and quickly walked back to her cottage. Something had made Ethel feel the urgent need to return home. Damn, I was alone again with the witch and I had little to protect me.

June began to speak once more and internally I requested

divine intervention from my spirit guides and I received it immediately. Now ringing out clearly through the open rear door of my house was my recently installed antique 1940s telephone in my sitting room. It was a long way to the sitting room from where June and I were standing but the sound of old-fashioned tinkling telephone bells was unmistakable.

'Oh, do you hear that?' I asked.

'No. What?' June testily replied, peeved at another interruption.

'Saved by the bell!' I jokily laughed and added, 'I'll be right back.'

June began to talk again, presumably hoping that I would linger but it was no good, I had nipped off indoors to answer the telephone and leaving her speaking mid-sentence.

I shut the kitchen door to the backyard and realising that I had left the yard gate wide open and that my witch neighbour could enter the yard and perhaps even the house, I quietly locked the back door and dashed down the long corridor to the sitting room where the cream Bakelite telephone was still ringing. I wondered who could be calling me.

'Hello?' I said, holding the ancient receiver to my ear.

'*Is June there?*' the female caller enquired. To say that I was taken aback would be an understatement. The caller was asking for someone with the same unusual name as my witch neighbour. Shocked, I queried the caller.

'*Is June there please?*' she repeated.

My mouth opening and closing like a goldfish I explained that, 'There was no-one here of that name and that you must have the wrong number.'

The caller however was not giving up. She was most adamant

that she had dialled the correct number for June.

"I want to speak with June!"

Something told me that she was quite right and had indeed dialled the correct number, but at that moment my request to spirit had resulted in her call being diverted through to my telephone in order to save me from whatever it was that was about to occur at my backyard gate.

Spirit had once more rescued me and they wanted me to know. Saved by the bell I repeated to myself and laughed after I had hung-up. Bells are excellent vibrational tools for the removal of negative energies. The statistical odds of receiving a rescue telephone call for someone of the same name in that very moment must be quite small. The caller didn't call back, presumably getting through to the correct number on her second attempt. The spirit realm is truly amazing. Miracles can and do occur every day, and I was learning that you should never believe that all we see, feel and hear around us as 'real.'

Reluctantly I returned to face June at the backyard gate, but instead of finding my witch neighbour stood waiting for me as I had anticipated, she was nowhere to be seen, nor did she reappear. This was very odd as she was not a woman to give up. Looking about the deserted alleyway briefly, I closed the yard gate and locked it thoroughly. I wasn't to know it then, but I was never again to encounter any further face-to-face confrontation from either June or Charles.

Had I won? Had spirit done something in that moment to keep her away from me once and for all? Or had June slipped into my rear yard as I went to answer the phone, as was likely, and placed spellwork here? The next day I thoroughly spiritually cleansed the backyard, including the touched rear yard bell and door knocker. But with both Ethel and Terence falling ill within days I wondered if June had overstepped the mark with her dark magic. My spirit guides close by me in Terence's garden and the curious intervention of the telephone call indicated that I was being strongly divinely protected.

Chapter Thirty-Five

Sooty and Sweep

All packed up and nowhere to go

'The energy is massive, and it is chiefly negative energy allowing earthbound spirit and entities to travel along it like a supernatural superhighway and right through your house.'

Since the departure of my unwanted spectral house guest, the more alarming spirit activity at Pippins had subsided but curiously the smell of soot from under the staircase intensified. It wasn't an entirely unpleasant smell, and I was used to strange things manifesting in this house so I chose to ignore it, even when the aroma started to appear in other rooms. At first the sitting room was affected which I had put down to the chimney as you naturally would, even though the stack was sealed with a woodburner.

Then the dining room on the other side of the house was similarly affected and there was no fireplace in here.

Finally, the small front study began to smell of soot blended with an alcohol scented manly odour. It was this that at last made me curious because previously, try as I might, it had proved impossible to remove the scent of women's perfume in here. The scents in all of the rooms came and went at random but it still hadn't occurred to me that the smell of soot might be spirit energy.

Synchronicities came thick and fast at this time of my life. In a nearby town, I had become a regular customer of a vintage antiques shop, getting to know well the two women who ran the small premises. When I was originally furnishing my cottage, I was often to be found in here purchasing vintage fabrics, pictures, fittings and occasionally a larger item of furniture. It was around the time that I was encountering the strange smell of soot in my house that, as a gift for a regular loyal customer, the women kindly gave to me a gift of a room scent spray called 'Library.'

I hadn't discussed any of the ghostly goings-on at my house with the two women and I certainly hadn't thought to mention the smell of soot. When I reached home later that afternoon and unpacked my purchases, I came across their thoughtful gift and opening the box I gave the sitting room a little test spray from the glass bottle. It transpired that for 'Library' the creators had chosen the scent of sooty fireplaces! It was actually a very pleasant heady aroma, though my cat Monty wasn't too keen and when Abigail next called 'round for a social visit she seemed just as dubious as I shall explain.

Those of you familiar with psychic work and dealings with spirit will be aware that our guides often communicate with us via synchronicity. Looking back, it seems that spirit intended the room spray to be gifted to me, not only as a present but as a prompt to rescue another earthbound spirit in my house. Like me, Abigail had noticed the aroma of soot in the hallway a few times and also like me she had put this down to coal perhaps having been stored under the stairs in the past, although as I have previously written there was no evidence for this. But it was on this particular day that Abigail paused in the corridor by the stairs and gave the air a sniff. 'Can you smell that?' Without needing to ask to what she was referring I nodded and said that it was strongest under the stairs. Abigail opened the cupboard and sniffed inside. She was confronted by a spotlessly clean interior with no suggestion of any coal having ever been in here.

I wasn't to know it, but Abigail had a hunch. Only later, when we were seated in my sitting room drinking tea, with Monty as ever on her lap, did she comment on the overpowering smell of soot in this room too. I remembered the 'Library' room scent and tested it for her. Rather than expressing delight at the fragrance, instead this seemed to have confirmed something in her mind for her. 'The little boy from the small bedroom upstairs is in here now. He is sitting over there in the corner of the room,' Abigail indicated to where my gym equipment was located. I could see nothing, but I didn't doubt the talents of this remarkable woman.

Abigail then chastised herself for forgetting the chimney sweep that the boy had mentioned many weeks before. 'The boy cannot cross into the Light because his chimney sweep boss won't let him.' There was a short pause before Abigail indicated that the Light had now come for the little boy. A rescue had begun. It wasn't clear if the little boy had crossed into the Light because at that moment the chimney sweep arrived to stop the rescue. It was the sweep who had been creating the strong scent of soot in the house and suddenly it made sense why I could also smell alcohol and male scent in the study. 'He is furious. He says he owns the boy, and he won't let him go. The boy, he says, is his property.'

A short battle of wills ensued, and with the boy apparently gone, the Light came for the chimney sweep. It seemed uncertain if the child and the sweep had crossed into the Light but Abigail reported that they were no longer present in the room although one or both may not have passed. Sceptics may rightly question the evidence that these two spirits existed at all and if they did, whether Abigail rescued them and sent them to the Light. By this time of my tenure of Pippins, my own sceptical mind had taught me that there are things beyond which we can tangibly feel with our physical senses and to have faith, don't resist, and 'go with the flow.'

What I am able to confirm is that the smell of soot and male odour vanished from the house from that day and there was no further manifestation of the child's energy in the upper rooms. Something had palpably changed. I believe that once again spirit had cleverly created a sequence of synchronistic events that resulted in two more successful rescues.

Earlier in this book I explained how a shaman that I had consulted at a psychic fayre told me about a previous incarnation when I had been a shipwright in Bristol in the eighteenth century and in doing so he had successfully cleared up a close-held conviction that I'd had since childhood of having lived in the UK in the Georgian age, also explaining my intense fear of water and the sea.

Rebecca, my regular go-to psychic medium had told me to look out for a 'shaman' with, 'Some connection to wolves' and that he will have, 'An unusual appearance and manner that would normally put you off,' but they are saying to, 'Ignore that and go with it.' Then finally, as she touched the side of her neck, Rebecca added, 'They are showing me something to do with the jugular and dragons. Perhaps it's a dragon tattoo on his neck?'

I didn't know it then, but spirit guides often 'speak' in analogies and that 'a dragon tattoo' on his 'jugular' was shorthand for what was to come, the symbolism making it instantly recognisable when the event actually happens. Occasionally some of the information provided by a psychic medium can be ambiguous and misinterpreted, only for it much later to make perfect sense with the benefit of hindsight. I believe that this is often intentional in order that spirit does not influence our life choices, with just enough detail provided so that we later recognise we made the right choice.

Only a week or two after the psychic reading with Rebecca, I had found myself seated with the shaman at a local psychic fayre. He had a large mane of white hair, not dissimilar I thought to the huge photograph of a wolf behind his chair. This, I realised with excitement, was my wolf man. This was also the man that I was told would help me with the haunting of my house. I sat listening to him enthralled as he told me about my previous incarnation as a Georgian shipwright which had caused so much angst in my present lifetime.

Then, after he had finished speaking about that prior incarnation, and without stopping to ask me any questions, he went on to tell me about my house. 'You can't stay where you live now. The house isn't right for you as you are a highly-developed soul with a high vibration.'

I nodded my head. Well, I wasn't going to disagree with that rather flattering account, was I?

'You have heard of ley lines?' I nodded again. 'You have a ley line passing right through your house but it is not a normal ley line. Instead it is a 'dragon' ley line. Unlike normal ley lines, 'dragon ley lines' only contain negative energy. Normal ley lines form an energy grid like the veins in the human body carry blood. With a dragon ley line, this is less like a vein and more like a jugular,' The shaman pointed to the side of his neck and drew his finger downwards.

'The energy in a dragon ley line is massive and as it is chiefly negative energy, it allows earthbound spirit and lower entities to travel along it like a supernatural superhighway and right through your house.'

These were exactly the words and the explanation that I needed to hear. Well, sort of. Does anybody really want to hear that they have a negative energy superhighway gushing through their home? Rebecca's psychic reading spoke of a wolf shaman with a 'dragon tattoo' and a 'jugular.' Rebecca's spirit guides had shown her the shaman's neck with a dragon tattoo upon it. Understandably, she had interpreted this to mean that the shaman would have a tattoo of a dragon on his neck. Whereas it was a coded message for me that when I saw the shaman point to his neck and speak of a 'dragon' energy line being like a 'jugular' I was to sit up and take notice. Sit up and take notice I did!

The dragon ley line and the massive amount of negative spirit energy that it brought explained everything as to why my house was always so spiritually active. The higher vibrational psychic sensitivity that I possess (suffer from?) was the explanation why it felt so energetically unbearable for me to live in the house, whereas many visitors barely noticed the low vibrational energy that powered its way through the building. Finally, it made sense as to why my neighbouring witch had moved next door to me and why she had launched a long campaign to take custodianship of the property. A witch practising dark arts and necromancy would be incredibly powerful if she could harness the abundant flow of negative energy and the spirits that came with it.

At home later that night, I realised that I had been given this information for a purpose. I ordered some copper divining rods online and they arrived in the post some three days later. I remembered that the curious scratching sound on the bedroom ceilings that heralded the night-time spirit manifestation occurred in one corner only of the principal bedroom and in one corner only of the second bedroom. If I were to draw a line between these two points, I would have a perfect line running diagonally through the house as to how it was originally built before the addition of the ground floor kitchen.

On a hunch, I stood in the sitting room with my new copper divining rods, holding them loosely in my hands as I had seen in an online tutorial video. I am not sure what I had expected to experience or find. I had not tried divining rods before and I had no idea whether they even worked, let alone would work for me trying to detect a dragon ley line. However, I received my answer instantaneously. Walking slowly and steadily across the sitting room carpet, the rods crossed quickly in my hands. Was this a coincidence?

I walked up and down the sitting room and began to get very excited when I realised that indeed yes, the copper rods crossed at the exact point where a diagonal energy line would be. I spent some half an hour walking through the house, both upstairs and downstairs achieving the same results each time. There was definitely an energy line passing diagonally through my home.

Other things began to make sense. I did some research using

historical maps. Plotting a line through my house following the envisaged diagonal energy line, I discovered that it passed directly through the creepy garden gazebo that stood in the churchyard gardens. This I have mentioned in an earlier part of the book was a very gloomy spot to spend any time and as such it was always deserted.

Moreover, the gazebo marked the site of the slum houses that had been cleared in the 1930s that had seen so much misery and deprivation in the town and where I suspected that my former resident troublesome ghost had originated. Following the dragon ley line further on the map, I realised with astonishment that it did not pass through any other property or house in this busy built-up little town. Mine was the first house for many miles around that this negative energy line would have encountered. Now looking at an old waterways map that I had photocopied previously at the town Historical Society, I studied the siting of the culverts, streams and rivers.

My earlier experience at the poltergeist house had told me that where there were strong negative spirit energies affecting a property, one could often find a waterway passing nearby or underneath. I wasn't disappointed as an old stream had originally flowed between my house and the witch's cottage next door, long before they were ever built. This had been covered over and long forgotten about until in the 1930s there was a roadway collapse nearby, when it was rediscovered. But the revelations didn't stop there.

The culvert passed directly under where my shower room was now situated. Suddenly the idea of a spirit portal opening above the contained and compressed energy of the water flowing beneath my shower room made more sense. And what of the two spirits who had stood in the rear yard? They had been directly over the culvert and creating a vortex of spirit energy. The culvert also explained why the rear of my house had an elevated floor. The surveyor said he had not seen anything like it and couldn't explain it, but the builders who constructed the house would have known that there may be a risk of flooding or damp from the contained water flowing close by. This culvert then skimmed under the corner of the witch's house and exited precisely under the place where her garden table was always sited and where we had regularly dined as I fell under her spell. 'Chop chop.'

The culvert then crossed the cottage gardens and exited somewhere northeast, presumably into the river. Giving considering to my house, I realised that the place on the stairs where the former coalman owner (and now spirit protector of my house) stood was dead centre in the property. The diagonal dragon ley line therefore passed directly through this spot where he regularly stood. This was like the picture suddenly becoming clear when nearing the completion of a jigsaw puzzle.

Out of the chaos clarity was now coming to my strange, haunted existence in this house. Further research of Historical Society records showed that yes, Pippins had been owned by a coal merchant in the early part of the twentieth century. Abigail was correct once more. It was he who was protecting my home and stood on the stairs and in the rear yard. My research revealed that in his retirement he had moved to a nearby cottage which backed directly onto the picturesque fast flowing river.

Tragically, during the war, his house had been washed away in a freak night-time flash flood, doubtless killing him in the process, the shock of which resulting in his spirit remaining earthbound. When on our dog walks together, Abigail and I often stood in a nearby public riverside viewing spot chatting about life while gazing at the river beneath. These were public gardens which unbeknownst to us had been created from the very ruins of his long-lost home. This was synchronicity following synchronicity and too many to ignore or dismiss.

Had the eighteenth-century builders of Pippins understood about the ley line? It was curious that no other buildings or houses fell along this line, except for the long since demolished slums. There surely must have been ancient local lore about the ley line? This was a powerful flow of energy which prior occupants of the town must have become aware of over the many passing centuries. If so, why had the builders constructed my house where they had? Certainly no other house in town had been constructed along this line.

The historical papers suggested that Pippins had been built in the eighteenth century for a doctor, a man of science. Had he ignored local advice and ancient lore when choosing the site for his home?

I wondered if the poor wretches who had resided in the nearby affected slums had also been negatively afflicted by this energy line? No-one would ever prosper under such negative energy. These were people described to me by townsfolk as 'the worst of the worst,' perhaps amongst them was my own recently rescued resident spirit. Was the ley line the connection between my home and where my former ghost once lived? I had sat in the public gardens late at night many months before when studying the house, I was to buy. Even back then those gloomy gardens felt 'wrong.' Had the spirit who came to haunt my house been watching me sit there from amongst the shadows of what had once been his home? Yes, quite probably.

Abigail and I discussed what to do. The ley line would possibly affect the house indefinitely unless something could be done about it. My property was on the market for sale and whilst those negative spirits who had lingered long past their time had now been sent to the Light, this energy line had to be dealt with. I did not however have to worry about my neighbouring witch and her husband. The town grapevine had it that their landlord had visited for the annual inspection and was not happy with what she had discovered! The house and garden were not in good order and June and Charles were threatened with eviction if they didn't improve matters.

In any case, soon after June and her husband discovered that I was selling my home, they had given notice to quit. It was exactly as my spirit circle had advised would happen. The witch had latched onto me as her project and aspiring to get my home from me she had used necromancy to cause chaos in my life in order to do so. Previously I had seen no motive other than I had a nice home that she wanted, whereas it was the energy from the dragon ley line she desired. She wanted to harness the energy of the ley line and use the spirits that travelled this supernatural superhighway for destructive means and financial gain. When that plan had failed and I was set to move on, she abandoned both the plan and the house that she lived in, perhaps having already discovered a new victim elsewhere.

Although I feared for her next target, in truth there was little that I could do. I was delighted for whoever was to buy my house that the witch and her husband were departing. The restless spirits had been dispatched to the Light and the house cleansed. It was an excellent result all 'round and I could be forgiven for believing that my spirit guides had set the whole thing up. Perhaps this was a part of my spiritual journey of awakening plotted out before I was even born. After all, the spirits formerly occupying my house had been around for a very long time and had doubtless caused much upset for decades to previous occupants.

The synchronicity of Terence coming from the same small town where I had grown up, that his ex-wife was descended from famous witches and that psychic medium Abigail lived only two doors down the road was all too much to accept as a coincidence. If you are still not a believer of synchronicity then I should perhaps mention that Abigail's next-door neighbour was also, by 'coincidence' a psychic medium.

But what to do about the dragon ley line? I began my research. Eventually, I discovered writings about diverting the path of a ley line. Whether one could also divert a major artery like a dragon ley line was not mentioned but I had to give it a go. I read that it was usual to rely upon hidden votive tokens to divert this energy field around any property but this seemed an unreliable method. Indeed, many psychics seemed to agree that even if this were to work, it would not continue to work indefinitely.

I needed a more permanent solution and this came in the suggestion that a ley line can be diverted up and over a house, high above the chimney tops and avoiding the property altogether. It was not long before one sunny afternoon I meditated and asked my spirit guides for their help, performing a lengthy, energy-filled ceremony to bring about the diversion of the dragon ley line that had troubled my house for centuries.

I was sceptical whether it would work but I was to be

pleasantly surprised. The energy in the house felt immediately different. I was used to this serene feeling in the house when I did my daily cleansing, but in the past the negative energy of the ley line had always returned within hours. This time the house fell still, it was as though someone had closed an upstairs window on a bad weather day. I found that the energy remained cleansed hour after hour, eventually stretching into the next day and then the day after, and the day after that, and so on. The diversion of the dragon ley line had been a success.

While my late mother continued to visit me from time to time, making her presence known to me by the switching on of my laptop and my bedside lamp in the small bedroom, all other spirit activity in the house ceased. There were no further night-time disturbances of any kind, no strange atmospheres or scent and the CCTV cameras, the wi-fi and all electrics no longer malfunctioned.

Within three days of my house going on the market a delightful couple came to view the property and they fell in love as soon as they walked in through the Regency front door. The day that the purchasers were due to view, I asked spirit for protection from the witch next door, placing an opaque shield of love and light around the house. I knew that the Satanists were packing up and leaving and would not be a problem for any new homeowners, but there was no desire on my part for any interaction between them and a likely purchaser.

As the allotted hour approached for the potential purchasers' viewing, passers-by and neighbours suddenly disappeared behind closed doors and a peace descended upon the town. This reminded me of my own viewing of the property several months earlier when I had immediately fallen in love with the peace of the house that was to become my home that I was to unwittingly share with so many unseen others. The potential buyers loved the house and its warm 'atmosphere' agreeing to its purchase at full asking price before they had even looked upstairs. If only they knew of the problems that I'd had in securing that warm and welcoming atmosphere!

The question was, where to move to next? I needed a new challenge. The answer to that, as always, came from my spirit guides.

Chapter Thirty-Six

A spiritual life

Karma, resistance and release

'I am sorry: please forgive me: I am grateful and I love you.'

In a never-ending emotional sea of unfulfilled wants and needs, each individual causes a reaction to their own personal circumstances. In a world of eight billion people, all these reactions create a very choppy emotional sea to swim in. Imagine those thoughts, words and actions as energy waves spreading outwards from each person on the planet. Colliding and interacting with others.

There is a lot of misunderstanding surrounding karma and what it is. The word 'karma' is Indian Sanskrit and means an 'act', so we may think of Karma as an 'action.' For every act or action, there is a consequence, 'good' or 'bad.' Karma is completely neutral, it is merely a reality of our existence in the physical 3D universe. It can perhaps be easier explained by using an allegorical representation of Newton's theory of gravity which is of course 'what goes up, must come down.'

It is that simple. There is no punishment behind karma. Karma is not 'out to get you' and bite you on the butt. Were you to toss a cricket ball into the air it eventually will come back down and hit you on the head, every action having an equal and opposite reaction. We can remember these basic truths about our physical universe from our school science lessons. Karma is no different. If you do something good, it will eventually come back around. The contrary is also true, and it is of course *this* that strikes fear into so many. It saddens me when I read some people's comments on social media that they 'wish someone would get their karma' or 'karma is going to get that ****' (fill in the blanks).

It is not for us to make judgment over anyone else, regardless of their actions and we spoke about that in an earlier section. Our own thoughts and deeds are creating our own karma. That karma may return to you in this life or in a future incarnation, it doesn't matter. Caution is therefore suggested as 'thoughts are things' and sending out the energy of vengeance, hatred, jealousy or anger will only come back to you just as surely as that cricket ball would. For those of you who feel wronged by someone, knowledge of how karma operates can allow you to release any negative thoughts and feel positive and free to live your own life without carrying the heavy burden of injustice.

Change is always with us, it is in the nature of the 3D universe that as with the seasons, everything must come to pass. Because all things in our 3D 'reality' are transient, the constant fear of loss makes us engage with a lifelong preoccupation with the material world and the accumulation of physical treasures that can only ever lead to disappointment and loss. Everything eventually breaks, decays, dissipates or dies. It is fruitless for us to base our happiness around the obtaining and retention of material things, whether that be property, beauty, money or indeed people.

All these things leave us eventually and so to only live in and for the material world is to guarantee a life of lack. The one thing that you have that will never leave you, is your consciousness. You are your consciousness, and your consciousness is the universe within you experiencing a human existence. The light within you is the Source and this is the energy of love. Everything else is material illusion. The one thing within you that will never fail you and never leave you, is you.

We all know this on a subconscious level, yet humanity resists this basic truth and rather than 'go with the flow' and move with life's currents, our fear-based ego tries to grab as much as it can while we are here, figuring that, 'If I don't have it, someone else will get it.' Yet to take more than we need for our basic wants may deprive another of their essential needs and in doing so we are exposing ourselves to karma.

The ego resists change that the universe offers, which is crazy when you think about it. What makes us think that we would win an argument with the entire universe?

The universe says, 'Stop polluting your planet.'

Humanity's collective ego resists and says, 'Yes, maybe tomorrow when we'll be clever enough to avoid the problem by finding a solution.'

The universe says, 'Slow down, here's a pandemic.'

Humanity's collective ego resists and says, 'Let's be clever and create a vaccine that has to be boosted every six months.'

So the universe says, 'Here's another pandemic, and another, and another ....' So, humanity's collective ego resists and says, 'We must be locked down until the pandemic is over.'

Big government then says, 'Actually, we quite liked the power that those lockdowns provided, so now we are considering keeping you forever locked down for your own safety and security.'

Resisting change in a physical universe of chaos can cause unintended consequences.

It is said that the Native Americans noted, when observing the European invaders, that when the invaders needed to cross the river, to get to where they desired, they would attempt to take the shortest route across, resisting the obvious. The movement and strong current of the water would wash their canoe further down the river and they would not land where they had intended.

When a Native American wished to cross the river, they found the best landing point, and then, observing the rocks and other obstructions in the waters, they walked upstream to their setting-off point. Once there, they gently pushed their canoe into the flowing water, and then navigated their way downstream, *using the obstacles* they had encountered to push against and gain momentum. They then alighted exactly where they had originally intended, having *'gone with the flow'* of the universe *rather than work against it*. It is such with life and spiritual development. There are no shortcuts to achieving spiritual nirvana and whether we know it or not, that is the multiple lifetime voyage of discovery that we are on.

You have been on a long journey down your own rapid flowing river of choice. Your life has led you into many highs and many lows. You have cried tears of joy and wept tears of sorrow. You have met some truly wonderful people and you have met with some truly awful people. Perhaps you have achieved everything in your life that you set out to achieve.

Perhaps your life has recently crumbled around you, and you feel as if you are on your knees with your hands fumbling about in the rubble of what remains. I experienced the latter before my spiritual awakening began. I am still on that spiritual awakening journey. Those who tell you that they have finished their spiritual journey and that they know all of the answers are far from the truth.

Before my awakening began, I had created a comfortable 3D life, it was the world that my fear-based ego had manifested for me to be safe in, to take comfort and refuge in and to return home to each night. Yet I watched as my material world dissolved around me. I was suddenly without everything that I had strived for, and I feared what was to come next. I was living in a state of lack.

I have since understood that it is not unusual for the physical life that you have carefully constructed for yourself in this 3D reality to rapidly fall away from you before your spiritual awakening blossoms. This then, is the ultimate test of your faith in a benevolent universe or God. Just when you believe that you have finally got it 'right' and understood the spiritual love-based construct of the universe, embracing the path that you should be travelling along, your personal world suddenly collapses around you. Why would this happen?

We incarnate on Earth many times over, perhaps hundreds of times, before we have experienced and learnt all that our soul set out to learn from a physical existence in this dense low vibrational plane. You have many incarnations of experience with emotional highs and lows, laughter, sorrow and trauma. All human experience is encountered and learnt over many lifetimes, creating and thereby collecting karma and karmic partners 'karmics' along the way.

Eventually, when we are almost done with the learning and when the karmic debts have been almost repaid over many lifetimes and when we are near to 'graduating', we may, eventually, have an 'awakening.' The awakening process has been likened to the film 'The Matrix' where you have a choice of two pills. One pill allows you continue to experience your 3D Earth plane existence, staying in the material-obsessed physical reality. The other pill wakes you up, awakening to the fact that the physical world is a low vibrational simulation, and that you actually belong elsewhere.

After thousands of years of human existence on Earth, humanity is now coming of age, so is it any wonder that so many people are experiencing an awakening right now. The human race has been pupating for centuries and many are about to emerge from the chrysalis.

Some of us, as indicated in my own personal astrological chart, are perhaps spiritual healers and teachers, born already awakened but just waiting to be 'switched on' when the appropriate moment comes. Others have their awakening at a time in their lives when their soul – or 'higher self' – knows that the spirit in the body incarnate is ready. Many are not yet ready to be awakened in this lifetime, and that's fine and exactly as it should be.

With an awakening you begin to realise that you are not the physical body itself but instead you are an infinite spiritual being of the universe, having a unique physical experience tailored to your needs. What happens to the awakened individual who wakes up one day and realises that everything is a stage play that we have put on for own elaborate journey of discovery? What happens to all that karma?

Our earthly existence cannot go unnoticed by others and our interactions are guaranteed to create a karmic pond that is rippled by a thousand actions. We are completely unaware of which actions are creating karma and which ones are solving them. Or to put it another way, we cannot know whether we are tossing the cricket ball into the air, or whether we are reaching out to catch it on its way back down.

When we awaken and become wise to the spiritual purpose and meaning of our existence on Earth, we are sending out a clear message to the universe that we can no longer play the game of life in quite the same way that we did before, in this lifetime at least. Where we have karmic 'debts', then those debts are 'called in.' This is in the same way that when the creditors of an insolvent person first hear of the future inability to pay their debts, they rush-in quickly to recover their losses, understanding and realising that this moment is their final opportunity to get back their investment. The insolvent individual is suddenly inundated with demands for payment.

So it is that when we find ourselves on the dawning of an awakening, the universe seemingly rushes up and bites us on the butt. Just when we think that we have a grasp on life, the universe recognises that we are awakening and all of those karmic debts which remain outstanding are suddenly to be repaid. I found myself, over a period of some four short months lose the only person I ever loved, I lost my home, I lost money, and I lost my career.

I was left with my one dearest possession of all, my beautiful cat and friend Monty. Only within months, he too was taken from me by illness. All of my physical comforts were stripped away and my integrity had been brought into question in the preceding months, with my dignity – or pride – dissipated. So, once we have awakened and maybe lost much that we hold dear, what happens next?

A spiritual awakening is not the end of the journey, it is the beginning of a new phase where you can see your life from the outside looking in, rather than from the inside looking out. You have a new awareness of the truth that you are inextricably linked to your higher self and to spirit and ultimately to the universe. You remain rooted in the 3D physical world but with much of your consciousness now forever in the 5D.

You soon discover that what you thought was a fully blossomed awakening was in fact just the budding of something new and you continue to encounter new challenges and tests placed along your path. In this way life continues as normal, only now you begin to recognise when you are being tested and when you are being supported by the universe and your spirit team. The physical world and all of its faux trappings of success and achievement loses its allure and it can even suddenly appear tawdry by comparison to the light that you now hold close in your heart and your connection to the whole.

While it remains the case that we are not permitted to know our destination for this lifetime you will become aware of your spirit guides leaving you messages and synchronicities if you care to look out for them. You will begin your life anew, and your co-dependency with the physical material world will begin to fade. You may begin to care less for physical belongings and instead seek experiences and joyfulness.

You may also discover that your friends suddenly begin to fall away. This is perfectly normal and should not alarm you. Since your awakening you will begin to vibrate on a higher frequency and those friends who are unable to vibrate on your wavelength will simply lose interest. Do not stress or be sad about those old friends who can no longer travel on your path, new friends and experiences more closely aligned with your new frequency will come into your life in the following months and years. Release. It is a universal truth that everything changes.

There have been many occasions when I thought that spirit, my guides and the universe had abandoned me in the physical world. Things have been pretty tough and I often wondered why I had seemingly been forsaken and why others, apparently not yet on this 'spiritual journey', seemed to be doing so much better in the 3D world than I felt I was. Yet everyone's journey and set of experiences are different and unique. Why should my journey be the same as the next person's? Just because my peers may perhaps be having a nicer time of things, doesn't mean that they actually are. Maybe I enjoyed an equally nice time in a previous or future incarnation, and maybe those others will have a difficult time in their next.

Crucially in my case the catalogue of negative experiences over a lifetime of people and events has taught me so much about the human condition and this, when teamed with spirituality, has brought me to where I am now, penning this book. There has been a divine purpose to all of the strange and questionable events and these had to happen to get me to where I am now.

I have written elsewhere in this book about the judgment of others and that it is folly to do so. The journey that others are on, their life, their expectations, their aspirations, interests or character, this is their journey and not yours. And guess what, *you don't have to like them or their journey*! We can just ignore someone who irritates the hell out of us, we don't need to judge or react or troll online, just ignore them. Like you, they are walking their own path and creating their own story and this should not affect us emotionally if we are working on our shadow.

If you have awakened you can now accept your existence and enjoy all the experiences that life offers you, both positive and negative, while fulfilling your destiny. You no longer have to worry about what others think or do. This is not your concern. You now recognise that life is a game, a very important and elaborate game, but a game, nonetheless. You have awakened to the reality that you can begin to do the job that you came here to do; to experience and enjoy life.

You have put in the hard effort, and you have worked on your shadow and you have come to an awakening. How do you know that you are truly awakened? How do you cleanse the karma that you have inherited in your family bloodline and from the accumulation of your own incarnations? We work through our karma in each lifetime. We often travel with a soul tribe and also with a karmic family.

You can easily spot the soul tribe as these are the people in your life who support, love and cherish who you are as a person and create little or no trauma for you. You may have your soul tribe with you from an early age, those wonderful people who have always been there for you. Or perhaps like me you had to learn tough lessons early on and deal with those on your own as part of your personal growth. I understand that my soul family are soon to be joining me and I welcome that day with much joy. If you have not yet met your soul tribe, then fear not for they will be arriving at the right time in your journey. Divine timing is in all things.

'Karmics' on the other hand teach us about ourselves and

we often learn valuable, if difficult, lessons from them. These lessons may be repeated from previous incarnations where we didn't learn that time around. Any outstanding karma may be worked through with our karmic team until it is cleared. Because we travel with the same people lifetime after lifetime, playing out differing roles until we 'get it right' we can often spot the karmic family. They may often be tight family groups, friends that turn out to be 'frenemies' and we all know of someone who attracts the same romantic mistake time and again. The universe will keep giving us the same lesson to learn until we have learnt it. So do yourself a favour, if the way you are trying to achieve success, whether that be romantic, friendship, family or financial keeps failing, then go about it a different way.

First, we must recognise that we have a problem with a person or situation in our life. Then we must make the ego shift to *release* the person or situation and choose that this will never happen again, releasing that old energy and then walking away from a failing relationship or situation will help to break the karmic cycle. In this way, the next new friendship or relationship will be markedly different to the old one and not repeating the same old issues to work through, though of course there may always be new issues!

There is a spiritual practice that I perform every morning in the shower. I find that the shower is a superb place to contact our spirit guides and angels and of course the universe, or God if you prefer. We are being cleansed physically by the water but also our auric field is being cleansed energetically by the purification that the water offers as we release what no longer serves us, including any toxic energy that we are holding onto.

Water is crystalline in structure and so your energetic body is being bombarded by a million crystals, carrying away your negative energy if you set that intention. While I am cleansing my body and my spirit, I repeat a mantra that originates from a Hawaiian tradition of repentance. This particular practice is called 'ho'oponopono' and this translates as 'correction.' While this has been adopted and altered in meaning by modern western spirituality, it is nonetheless important and relevant to our spiritual cleanliness. The westernised version of Ho'oponopono is a mantra spoken to open yourself up to the universe and ask for forgiveness. The wording that I use is:

I am sorry.
Please forgive me.
I am grateful.
I love you.

This sounds remarkably straightforward and inoffensive, but this simple statement carries a huge punch:

'I am sorry' – you are repentant to everyone that you have ever wronged in this life and in previous incarnations. This means everyone, including *all* of those people who did you wrong. You are also expressing your knowledge of your actions (karma) to the universe. You have to be truly repentant as you now recognise that we are all part of the collective and we are of the Source. Express it and feel it.

'Please forgive me' – you are asking for forgiveness from every person who you have wronged either wittingly or unwittingly in this life or in previous lives. Whether that person also did you wrong is irrelevant, this is time to release the ego. You have to be truly asking for forgiveness. Express it and feel it.

'I am grateful' – you are expressing your thanks to *all* of your ancestors, people you encountered, loved ones, enemies, karmics and to the universe for all that you have experienced and learned in *all* of your incarnations.

This is perhaps the most difficult to feel truthfully. We have doubtless gone through some horrendous and even terrifying experiences over many lifetimes. All of those people who did both good and bad deeds. To truly express thanks for all of those experiences both good and bad takes courage and true spiritual awakening.

For me, I recognised that I am grateful to be where I am today. When I understood that, I then realised that without *all* the good deeds and *all* the bad deeds done by people in my lifetimes, I wouldn't be where I am now. So, I have all of them to thank. Included in these pages are some of the bad deeds done to me by others but I was to discover an unexpected healing process began when I started writing this book and it has allowed a huge burden to be lifted from me. This is a self-help book of sorts and in writing it I am hoping to help the collective. The prospect of something good coming out of other people's bad deeds fills me with hope and leaves me grateful. Express your gratitude and feel it.

'I love you' – you are expressing unconditional love for everyone who you have ever encountered over many lifetimes, whether their influence on your life was direct or indirect. You are expressing unconditional love to the universe. Feel your love and feel the universe returning that love to you.

Many of you will be familiar with the Law of Manifestation (aka Law of Attraction) and that the key to getting this mantra right is not just repeating the words and hoping for the best. Instead, as with any prayer, you must put true *intention* into the words. To do this I begin by listening to appropriate high vibrational music in the shower. Then I think of something that makes me grateful.

Gratitude is a good starting point for any spiritual practice. Then I think of someone I love dearly, whether alive or deceased. The combination of gratitude and love is a powerful formula and beats hate every time. Now repeat the words slowly over and over, 'I am sorry. Please forgive me. I am grateful and I love you.' As you say each section apply the emotion behind the words. For example, when saying 'I am sorry' feel the sense of true remorse rise up within you. Continue with the sensation of repentance for those you wronged, gratitude to everyone alive or dead and finally the powerful emotion of love as you say the words.

You will discover that after only four or five incantations the energy within you and also the room will lift. Your spirit guides and angels are with you and the Source is listening. By truly asking for forgiveness and expressing gratitude to everyone who you have encountered, you are saying to the universe 'Ok, I get it now, I have learnt what I came here to learn, and I no longer need to keep repeating karmic cycles.'

Chapter Thirty-Seven

Bohemian Rhapsody

Czechmate

I nodded appreciatively while in the background the child repeatedly and impishly poked his head around the chimney stack.

I'd met John online some months prior. Over the years many people have kindly written to me on social media, but I am rarely one to make the first contact. John was to be the exception to that rule as something told me to write to him having seen his online social media presence in respect of his home interiors business. With the ghostly problems at Pippins still to reach their peak and I had yet to properly meet Abigail, my sudden new online friendship with Jonathan was like a lifeline.

I am not one to make new friends easily, but we hit it off straightaway, with shared interests and ideas about many or most things from design, interiors, gardening and cats. Always cats. He had enjoyed what was to me an exciting and colourful life in London and abroad and, for me at least, I felt we'd bonded.

We first met up for a day out while he was visiting his family in the UK. I had travelled up country to meet him and instantly we got along well, we must have done as he took me home and introduced me to his mother and I got to sample some of her fabulous homemade patisserie. It was therefore only a few weeks later that I was on a plane to Prague and about to spend a week's holiday at John's farmhouse in the rural mountains of what was once Bohemia and is now the Czech Republic.

Whilst it was immediately apparent that he and I would be good friends and no more, our relationship was nonetheless to be a close one. That sunny spring holiday we sat together for many hours each day, chatting over every imaginable topic whilst soaking up the sun on the terrace of his beautiful garden that he'd created entirely from scratch with his own hands and using very little money to achieve very big results.

We talked of politics, interiors, antiques, history, style, spirituality, psychology, religion and philosophy. We discovered that we, more or less, agreed on everything and yet approached each subject from a very different perspective. It was from the perspective that our own life experiences fashion the very lens through which we view the world. Days out together were spent at castles, on mountains, in the countryside and looking at old houses.

It was a lovely time, and it was like meeting with an old friend after decades apart. I began to wonder if the 'Adam' that the elderly psychic medium had referred to at a seance on the night of the UK 'Great Storm' of 1987 was the same person as Jonathan. She had said, 'The man that I would meet would be called 'Adam,"' and here, some thirty years later, after much water had passed under the bridge, perhaps this was him.

Casually, I asked John if he had used his middle name of 'Adam' at any time and he confirmed that yes, he had been known by the name of Adam many years prior when it proved expedient at work where there was another Jonathan in a small team. He had later swapped back to using 'Jonathan' (or 'John' for short) but some people would still remember him as Adam. Perhaps this was just a coincidence, but I had not known any other Adam in all of my previous years.

It was on this holiday with John that I experienced one of my most profound of 'psychic dreams.' Over many years I had encountered so much in the way of the supernatural and yet I remained an 'innocent abroad.' I had so much to learn, and I still do. I was certainly unaware of and thereby not expecting psychic dreams. I now know that these are premonitory dreams that in my case I only remembered years later when that premonition crystallised. It is not unlike the more well-known 'de ja vu' most of us experience, a feeling as though it has occurred before, however, unlike de ja vu, *you know in advance* what is *about* to happen because you have seen it before in your dreams.

It was on the penultimate day of my holiday with John, and we were travelling in my hire car to a nearby tourist destination. The feeling of strangeness or otherworldliness had stayed with me from my home to this new place, but I had dismissed this and put it down to (for me) the newness of the country. I had already experienced several sensations of psychic awareness that week and so perhaps through a degree of 'psychic fatigue', I ignored my claircognizance as we sped along countryside roads to our destination.

The destination in question was a lake and an abandoned nineteenth century hotel in a remote wooded area. This had once been a major tourist hotspot during the Belle Epoque of the early twentieth century and into the 1930s when thousands of Czechs and Germans would come to take their holidays here. I parked-up the car in the gravelled tourist car parking area but before I had even got out the car to buy a parking ticket, the sensation of familiarity began to creep over me.

As John chatted happily and got out of the car, I sat and stared through the windscreen at the derelict hotel opposite. It faced onto the main road in a picturesque valley surrounded by woodland and with the huge lake to the left of the large building. The hotel wore its decay well, with missing doors and windows sadly detracting from its once magnificent architectural splendour of past years.

Once I had returned to the car with the parking ticket, John began to recount to me the story about how he had once entered this abandoned and derelict building to have a look at the sadly decrepit architectural gems within, especially the old interior doors which he was only sorry that he'd been unable to salvage. However, I already knew the story as I remembered him exploring the hotel interior in the dark and I told him so. John was surprised. He said that he had not told me this tale before and yet I knew that it had taken place at night-time and that he was mostly interested in the historic doors that were abandoned inside.

He must have been mistaken and I told him so. John was a little confused and was convinced that he had not mentioned this to me before. Curious and thinking of an alternative explanation I said that perhaps I saw this place on his social media account within the last year. I had only been following John for a few months but again, John rebutted this idea and said that he had not posted pictures of this place at any time, and certainly not since I had started following him on social media. He finished by clarifying that he had not visited this place in some years. Yet to me, these events were fresh in my mind as *I had seen them* in my recent memory or my dreams, even down to watching John climb over abandoned piles of wood and fittings to get to the doors with the hope of salvaging them. But no-one had filmed John inside the hotel, so how could I have seen footage?

We turned and walked the short distance to the lake, only a few metres from the hotel. I discovered an overpowering residual energy of the 1920s and 1930s in this location, with a strong Germanic feel. This is perhaps unsurprising as this entire area had been a stronghold of German speaking influence and ownership in the early twentieth century and before. Powerful energies of that time still exist here, the landscape does not seem to have forgotten and yet to others, the area is as Czech as landscapes can come.

The lake was wide, beautiful and mysterious with only pine forest as far as the eye could see. John was a few metres ahead of me, soaking in the strange atmosphere of the lake. Still waters always seem to hold onto energy. John commented out loud two words 'Twin Peaks.' He didn't need to explain his comment. Those of you who have watched this 1980s television series will now immediately know what this woodland area looked like and it even comprised some of that strange televisual atmosphere in the surroundings. It was hauntingly beautiful.

On the same side of the road as the gravelled tourist car park was a brand-new construction. This was a modern timber and glass building, yet to be fully finished and as yet unopened. John told me that it was going to be a restaurant for the tourists. It was the only other building here aside from the hotel and although incongruous in this natural landscape, there was very little otherworldly about it, yet I had a strange sense of dread. I had been here before. *I had seen this modern building before.*

John told me that we were going to have a look at the local caves and he began to walk the lake pathway which took us past the new wooden restaurant. How could I have seen this new restaurant before if John hadn't been here for years? There was absolutely no prospect of me having seen photographs or having any prior knowledge.

I said out loud to John, 'Be careful, there are some people behind the restaurant,' more out of the need to silence this curious de ja vu than because I perceived any threat ahead. I couldn't have known anyone was behind the large building, there hadn't been anyone about when we arrived and yet, as we walked along the dusty footpath, there indeed was a gaggle of around ten or more young men and women gathered behind the construction site fencing, sitting about and enjoying the sunshine. *I had seen this before.*

While there was no apparent threat to us or anyone else, this unfolding of events or 'premonition' had begun for me to feel like a bad trip. How was it possible to have seen this gathering of people before? The unexpected psychic ability of knowing ahead of time what was about to occur freaked me out. Was this some kind of warning? Yet John and I were fine and unharmed, so we should have been enjoying a sunny afternoon together in this picturesque spot, but instead I was struggling with the precognition.

We reached the caves, only a short distance away, and they were of course beautiful but creepy in their own way. So remote that whoever lived here must have been desperate or very poor, perhaps both. Here there was a stone shrine to the Virgin Mary and judging by the votive candles and offerings that had been left it was obvious people still visited this site regularly and paid their homage.

Yes, it was a lovely place and very peaceful but the overwhelming energy of the area and my precognition was psychically stifling, the atmosphere heavy with a strange magical vibration of different times coexisting all at once. I was glad when we had returned to the car and put some distance behind us and it.

It had been a profound and life changing week for me. I had met someone with whom I shared so much in common – and simultaneously so little. The two of us had over many years encountered and endured a heady mix of different and sometimes extreme life experiences, many of them the same life lessons but approached in a completely different manner. The end result was that we had both become stronger and wiser.

Who was this man and why did I feel such an affiliation with him? Was it just through the similar lessons that life had thrown our way, or was it something deeper and spiritual? And did he feel the same strange spiritual connection? In my most recent psychic consultation with Rebecca my spirit guide described me and John as 'Blood Brothers' referring to the Willy Russell play. Those familiar with the play's plot will understand how our Twin Flame journey began, as though separated at birth and then finding each other many years later.

I hadn't had much experience of seeing anyone's aura before I had joined the spirit circle. While there, although I didn't tell anyone, I clearly saw the aura surrounding one of the psychic mediums present. This happened at most meetings and always with the same woman. There was a curious unspoken connection that I felt with this particular medium, and she often brought forward my late mother and many other deceased relatives. Perhaps we were on a similar vibration. It wasn't until I was staying with Jonathan on holiday that I once again experienced seeing an auric field.

It was always during good light and as we sat outside on the sun terrace. John would be chatting away and I would be listening when suddenly I would see his aura, shining some two or three inches out from his body. I'm sure that as I sat there in silence, studying his face, he must have thought that I was just deeply interested in what he had to say. I was of course but I was also transfixed by the bright auric field around him. Since that holiday this phenomenon has rarely re-occurred.

I was unknowingly still on high psychic alert from all that I had been encountering at my cottage in the UK and this made me powerfully aware of spirit energies within this large old German farmhouse. The two-hundred-year-old building has a double attic space running the full width and length of the property, a stretch of some thirty metres or more. It is an amazing area, completely in old timber and with its original beams.

The roof itself was replaced in 1905, as indicated by the handwritten and dated inscription on the attic timbers of the initials of the lover owners sealed within a heart shape. I do not find the attic overly creepy these days on account of being more in control of my own psychic energies and having strong protection. But back on that first visit I did find it very unsettling. John loves the attic, but I am less keen and with good reason. Standing by the attic chimney as John and I chatted that long ago summer holiday, I could clearly see out of the corner of my eye a small child playing games and peeping curiously around the large chimney stack which soared through the attic space.

Trying hard to concentrate on John as he spoke, I didn't lose eye contact and I nodded appreciatively while in the background the child repeatedly and impishly poked his head around the stack. It was a boy, I knew that much, even though I only saw his form as full-scale flashes of light. John must have seen my eyes veering off to the right as he asked, 'What is the matter?' I didn't know John that well then and so it was a difficult but quick decision I had to make whether to let him into my confidence.

In a matter-of-fact way I explained what I had seen, not wishing to tell a white lie. He seemed unsurprised. Nodding, he just said, 'Oh yes, perhaps,' somewhat less than shocked. Later I discovered that it was one of his jokes to tell guests about a mystery 'boy spook' that haunted the corridor outside the guest bedroom which is now the corridor to my own room. A coincidence perhaps or maybe John knew more than he was telling. Either way it seemed that John was far more psychic than perhaps he understood.

It was during this week that I noticed what seemed to be a movement of air but was in fact a vortex of energy on the ground floor in a part of the house that John had improved and altered. This was very similar to the vortex outside of my own rear door at home and believing it to be a spirit portal I later closed it with a small ceremony without John's knowledge.

It is not unusual, when rebuilding and alteration work is done in an old property, for a portal to be unintentionally opened. Why this would be I leave to conjecture, but open portals are rarely good news as they are like leaving the back door to your house open twenty-four hours a day and you never know who – or what - is going to come in.

My sleeping quarters for the holiday was a bedroom which came to be known as 'The Room of a Thousand Sleeps' on account that any guest who stayed in this room fell into a deep, peaceful and uninterrupted sleep. In my case it was a joy to not be disturbed by any nightly ghostly visitor, only ever woken by DeeDee the black and white cat early each morning. DeeDee, who has rather beautiful glamourous eyes, is one of thirteen rescue cats that occupy this house. The result of rescuing so many cats is that the house was jokingly renamed 'Grey Gardens' by Jonathan.

It was beautiful summer weather, and I would wake early, being nibbled and head-butted by a hungry restless DeeDee. The sunshine poured in through the window and warmly illuminating the yellow painted 'Room of a Thousand Sleeps.' The light was different here, it was clear, fresh and sparkling and not at all like the milk-of-magnesia skies that the UK suffers from. There were no background noises of busy traffic or airplanes. Here was peace, solitude and rest.

And boy, after what was going-on at home, did I need rest! I padded downstairs, descending down the two-hundred-year-old stone steps and moved through the vaulted ceilinged hallway, passing the open front door that led to the sunny garden and onwards into the vast vaulted kitchen for morning coffee. A surfeit of cats greeted me strongly protesting at their hunger and I passed them by as I headed for the open kitchen door and out to the sun terrace. The doors to the house were always kept open day and night in summer. Luca the German Shepherd Dog could then come and go and guard the house and grounds as he pleased.

It was early summer and yet the sunlight was startlingly bright here, reminding me of the blue crystal clarity of the light on the coast of far western Cornwall. The garden was a tribute to Jonathan, having begun it from scratch and with little money and much imagination and creative effort. Now filled with 'Old English Roses', hollyhocks, aquilegia, and other cottage garden flowers and organised by neatly clipped topiary hedges shaping formal zones, the garden was someway between the English Arts & Crafts cottage style and an Italian garden on Lake Como.

Visitors here call it 'The English Garden' and yet any Englishman arriving would be hard-pressed to establish in which European country they'd found themselves in. 'Mediterranean surely?' they would ask. 'Somewhere in Italy, or perhaps the South of France,' they would decide. Only the vernacular German and Czech architecture of the area giving away that they were further north.

Far from the high anxieties of home I began to relax, and I saw that life could be very different for me should I choose. I had achieved in my life everything that I had been reared to aim for by my parents and peers. I had a nice home, a nice car, nice antiques and I'd had a nice career, and yet something was missing.

I was yet to realise it, as I wondered amongst the head high roses and scented flowers, that in fact I had worked all my life for someone else's dream. I had been living my parent's dream, not mine. We all do this, only realising in middle age that what we wanted got left behind somewhere in our youth. I started each day here like this, strolling slowly around the glorious large garden, my feet feeling out the hand-laid cobbled paths that traversed John's creation.

Many of the rooms in this rambling huge old house had – unusual – energies. The room that I liked the least, even today, was John's own double bedroom at the front of the house which overlooks the village square and pond. John had painted it a shade of grey and it was adorned with manifold animal skulls and horns. For me, this gave it a depressing atmosphere. Was this due to the colour scheme and the bones, or was it something more than that? The décor has since been changed to more soothing greens, and the bones are gone but to me the energy remains the same.

John however loves this room and I often think that it is good that most folk do not sense some of the energies that enter into their personal space. Indeed, the house welcomes John, perhaps seeing him as its saviour. John does however recount the story of an event that occurred in this very bedroom and not long after he first moved into this house. He was to wake early one morning to laughter and male voices. Sunlight streamed through the front window which told that there was no-one in the room. 'Go on, give it to him,' said the voice, laughing. Then more laughter and that was it.

Those who visit and stay as guests in this house, whether they be those who believe in the supernatural or those others who are pleased to only believe in the reliability of science and cold logic, all say one thing in common, 'The house has to get to know you.' This is so true. Anyone just pitching up here, expecting the house to welcome them or expecting the cold indifference that modern day humdrum houses give, are to be sorely disappointed. This house greets the unwary visitor with a strange suspicious hostility. Is this the earthbound spirits that occupy it, or is it the soul of the old house itself? Perhaps both.

The main spirit entity made himself known to me on that first visit here. By 'main' entity I of course refer to the impact that a negative spirit in a house causes. Positive and benign spirits often go by unnoticed and doubtless there are many of those here too. A silent and sinister shade, in the past he would have scared me witless but after the experiences at home, he seemed of little trouble. Whenever I walked on the stairs, or the landing, I quickly became aware that I was not alone with that oh-so-familiar sensation of being watched. The same strange feeling of being alone in a room yet you know you are being watched. Observing and coldly assessing, rather like a cat might watch its prey before pouncing. Pounce he did, but not until much later.

From the landing of the first-floor stairs there was a curtained dark alcove which secreted a door to a corridor that led to further bedrooms. It was here, most times, whenever I passed, that the unmistakable scent of cigarette smoke pervaded. That week I chose to ignore my psychic abilities, dismissing them I had put my intuition down to flights of fancy brought about by the heightened imagination that an old house stirs.

Although I reasoned that I was merely wary after my experiences of the haunting at Pippins, each and every time I walked into the curtained alcove to access the corridor door, I smelt the familiar odour of cigarettes. Logically I presumed that the curtains had picked up the aroma of cigarettes from when a visitor to the house perhaps smoked there. This didn't however explain why the same scent was to be experienced in the toilet at the other end of the corridor, and why John had frightened guests with tales of the spirit of a small boy lingering in the same long windowless corridor, 'Pressing his face up against the darkened glass of the door.' Funny scary spook stories to terrify guests aside, what it failed to explain was why I sensed a man stood and observing me at both ends of the corridor.

At that time, whenever I 'saw' an earthbound spirit in my psychic third eye, I presumed that it was just my creative visualisation at work. However, I soon discovered that these 'visualisations' or 'sightings' could be later independently corroborated by the psychics that I spoke with. So the man's outline appearance was fairly clear to me, his energy providing me with sufficient information to sketch out a mental picture. Involuntarily I always moved over to the right each time I went through the corridor doorway. This reminded me of my cat Monty back at home on the staircase.

There was no-one physically stood in the alcove of course but instinctively I moved over to one side each time. It was like squeezing past someone stood there and not wishing to enter his personal space. I 'knew' for example that he was around 1.83 metres tall, a slender man in his thirties or forties and wearing a long dark overcoat, a dark hat, glasses and dark shoes. I also perceived that he was relying upon a walking cane. Most mysteriously of all was that I 'knew' he was German, and from an earlier part in the history of this old house, the clothing suggesting the early twentieth century. But what to do? What *can* we do when we are a guest in someone else's house? Ignore it of course and hope it goes away.

Chapter Thirty-Eight

Twin flames

A new life

'The Light Is Very Different There'

On the final day of my holiday with John, I drove us to a nearby town for some sightseeing. A historic and highly picturesque town, there was a rich heritage and a copious supply of historic buildings lining its high street and side streets. To the rear of the high street was a deep wooded valley and cliff faces cut from centuries old quarrying. Smoke wisped its way through the treetops from the houses below me and looking upwards was the rear of the buildings that faced onto the high street.

Here was also to be found the old former Jewish Quarter, containing a historically important and restored synagogue. It was another warm and sunny day, it seemed that all the days were warm and sunny here, and while John went off on foot shopping for groceries, I decided to have a leisurely stroll around town, paying special attention to this romantic and scenic area immediately behind the high street.

While the shops and houses fronting the high street were of a standard vernacular appearance being some two or three storeys in height, at the rear the land dropped away dramatically and these buildings had in fact been constructed into the cliff side many centuries before and several storeys high, towering well above the footpath from where I now looked up. It made for an impressive sight. I began to puff as the effort of the steep rise and the now very hot sunshine began to take their toll. Reaching two-thirds of my way along the footpath I paused to stare up at the rear elevation of the shops and houses once more.

Suddenly time slowed and my physical senses paused while I had a strange awareness of being a separate observer, half in my own timeline and half in another. I could still feel my physical body, my aching feet and my perspiring skin, yet my mind or perhaps my spirit was elsewhere. My attention had been taken by the rear elevation of one building in particular. Unlike most of the other stone buildings its façade was chiefly made of dark stained wood and comprised an external wooden staircase which rose up several floors to a door at the top. A sudden recall of a psychic dream that I'd had many months – or perhaps many years before – now flashed into my conscious mind.

In the dream I had stood exactly on this same spot and I had endured a feeling of being pursued and terrified as I watched some hideous historical event unfold before me. I had seen a man being chased by an angry mob and to escape his tormentors he had fled up the flights of wooden stairs. When he had nearly reached the top of the steps with his attackers in hot pursuit, my position had suddenly shifted and I had become this wretched man, feeling the full force of his terror. Now at the top and terrified for my life the gang of angry local men had closed-in on me and with horror I realised that I had nowhere to escape to. It was at this point that I had woken up from the dream, but my last memory was that the mob had carried out an execution of the man on the top floor by his hanging.

Finding myself back in the current moment and on the footpath, I was still staring up at the old building when I realised that John had finished his shopping and had come to find me, the heat of the day suddenly feeling overwhelming and stultifying. Asking what I had been looking at, I told John part of my 'premonition.' It was as we walked the hot and sticky stroll back to the car that John advised me that this part of town had been the Jewish quarter. On the terrifying Kristallnacht this area had been ransacked by Nazi thugs and the synagogue vandalised.

Could I, in my psychic dream, have seen a repeat play of a murder of some helpless local man? It may have been any poor desperate soul, but what did it mean for me that I had dreamt of this very same place long before I had ever stepped foot in the country? Puzzled and deeply troubled by what I had seen, thoughtfully I packed my bags that night and wondered what Abigail would think of my stories back at home.

When I did arrive back in the UK at the airport carpark very late the following night it was to find that my car headlight beam refused to work. It seemed to be a computer malfunction rather than an electrical problem as everything else was operating correctly. The car was less than a year old and I'd had no trouble with it before, so after a long day travelling and desperate to get home to sleep, I had to creep my car using dipped beam along dark unlit roads for the entire fifty kilometres.

Curiously I had been stopped and quizzed by the witch June the day before I had set off on holiday. I had told no-one except for Abigail and Monty's pet carer that I was going away, and it was clear that June had been 'tipped off' by the dark spirits who worked with her as she knew that I was flying somewhere. With visions of her dark magic making aircraft fall out of the skies, I chose to lie and tell her that I was heading for Germany to see friends who had an apartment there. This was only a white lie as I did have friends with a German apartment and after all, the Czech Republic is a neighbour. June smiled one of her large smirks and I knew that she knew that I was lying. She had known which day I was returning home and so when the headlights on my brand-new car failed without explanation that night, my mind immediately sought to blame her.

Fearing another large bill for repairs, the next morning I went to my parked car on the driveway only to discover that the headlights were now fully functional. Later that month the main dealership garage rang to inform me that they had made a thorough check of the car electrics and on-board computer and that there was no fault. A further expense had therefore been unnecessarily incurred and my suspicions about June's involvement in the curious incident were heightened. Had she touched the front of my new car in the same way that she had done with my classic car just before its engine failure and the later replacement engine failure? My new car sat on my unprotected driveway every day and every night, so yes, quite probably.

I was pleased to see Abigail and we went for tea and cake at the local garden shop café to discuss my holiday. I explained about my psychic dream of the old hotel by the lake, and I told her all about John's house and its strange spirits and energies. I had printed for her a handful of photos of the house and garden that I had taken on holiday. Showing her a picture of the house shot from the large garden she immediately was able to tell me that there was a, 'Small boy in lederhosen,' in one of the upper bedrooms that overlooked the garden and, 'A tall man in dark clothes on the upper floor.' Pausing, she added, 'He was a military officer and has been watching you two closely. He doesn't like either of you being there.' I was getting used to general weirdness in my life by now and this came as an unpleasant surprise but perhaps not a shock, especially as this man's energy was exactly what I had picked up myself in the alcove on the upper floor.

Confirming that the man smoked cigarettes, Abigail listened as I began to tell her about the rear wooden elevation of the townhouses, my psychic dream and the wooden staircase. Before I even had the opportunity to fully begin my story about the dream Abigail said, 'A man was hanged there by a mob, he was chased and then killed at the top of a wooden staircase. They chased him and they hanged him.' This was the corroborative clarification I sought. Whether the child spirit or the military officer came with the house or had drifted in on a 'psychic wind' rather like some of the spirits had at my own house, I did not know. What seemed certain was that they needed rescuing and transitioning to the Light. As for the psychic dream of the hanging, what was its purpose? Was this an energy imprint on the area, an indelible psychic stain? Or could it perhaps be a past life memory and I had travelled that way once before?

The next few weeks passed slowly for me. My house sale should have moved swiftly but instead it started to drag on for weeks, then months and then the whole year and into winter. The problems with both my cars and now the house made me suspect that I was cursed and given who my immediate neighbour was and her intentions towards me, that wouldn't have been much of a surprise.

On the positive side of things was that after Abigail's timely intervention and my daily house cleansing rituals I was troubled little by further spirit activity at Pippins. While the laptop and the bedside lamp continued to activate of their own accord, usually in the night when mum was close, this became comforting rather than alarming.

John and I began a regular Skype regimen, speaking every night and chatting away for hours at a time, often late. After a few months of this it was agreed that I would sell up in the UK and move to house-share his home the Czech Republic. A bold move people told me, yet I didn't have anything to lose. I had achieved all that I had wanted to achieve in the UK and the rat race had not brought me any happiness whatsoever, in fact quite the opposite. It was time for a change of life and that strange atmospheric house and pretty garden in Czech, a small piece of Englishness in a far-off country seemed exactly right.

Both John and I had read and learned all about Czechoslovakia as children. I'd had a set of second hand wartime encyclopaedias as a child, and I had lovingly pored over the colour plates of traditional European costume and traditions. John and I were especially excited about the architecture and Czechoslovakia's amazing burst of creativity and wealth during the Jugendstil or Secessionist artistic period of the early twentieth century. With a newfound friend living there too it suddenly seemed a natural place for me to move to, although I was very sad at having to say goodbye to Abigail.

The curious bad luck with the sale of the house continued and my money begun to get tight. I had spent far too much in recent months, with thousands spent on car repairs, a new roof and renovations and by now my capital was running out. A three week 'quick sale' turned into a ten month one. I began to question why things were always going wrong. With money short I discovered that the central heating system was about to pack-up after a routine service detected a major dangerous electrical problem and I was advised that it needed replacing. It was winter now and so I put my hand in my pocket once again and had the central heating boiler repaired by the replacement of the entire electrical circuit.

A rare trip out with Abigail brought yet more problems. We were travelling back on treacherous country roads from a psychic mediumship meeting in a far-off town when the car headlights failed for the second time. It was inky dark, and the weather was appalling, with snow settling on the roads, mud spraying on the windscreen and the threat of slippery black ice under the wheels. Only Abigail and I knew that we were out together that night.

It seemed too much of a coincidence that the headlights failed when we were together in the car on the worst night of weather for some time. Had June seen us depart together? Probably, as her bedroom window was in line of sight of my driveway. However, the car got us safely home after a slow cautious journey, the headlights miraculously returning to normal functionality the next day. They did not fail again.

Sometime before this I had decided to see my psychic medium Rebecca who had been so helpful with her shaman advice. The night prior to the reading I had been sat in my little bedroom study and feeling exhausted by all of the strange happenings and setbacks I said out loud that, 'I think that my flame is dimming.' I had begun to loathe my house and this small town which suddenly seemed so hostile. I thought of John's sunny garden and old farmhouse with all his rescue cats, and I imagined them playing in the beautiful crystal clear sunlight that always seemed to shine there. I then imagined myself working in the large garden, surrounded by Old English Roses and Aquilegia. Was it just a pipedream to be able to emigrate and move to this small haven at the foot of the Bohemian mountains?

The next day at a meeting in her calming consultation room Rebecca announced, 'Your father is here.' I shuffled excitedly in my seat and wondered what he had to say to me. 'He says that the light is different there and he is showing me cobbled paths.' This was very clearly John's garden that she was describing! I hadn't told Rebecca anything about John or the Czech Republic. John had hand laid all of the cobbled paths around the garden and indeed *the light was very different there* and sparkled when compared to the grey sunlight of the UK. My father had been a keen gardener and had always laid his own garden paths too, so it seemed entirely apt that he was talking about the paths.

'I can see a man, he has a jungle hat on,' she smiled at the vision being presented to her. John, a professional designer, always wore on his head a jungle hat that he had made himself. Nobody wears jungle hats these days and this was true evidential mediumship and I was delighted. 'I see two rings coming together.' Rebecca moved her hands to demonstrate.

'He is your Twin Flame.' Then, I had no idea what a 'twin flame' was but I did know that John always wore two silver rings on his little finger, gifts from many years before. Was the rings' reference in relation to this, or did it mean that John and I were to become partners? Then there was the reference to 'flames' when the night before I had said to spirit that I felt my flame was dimming.

I briefly explained to Rebecca that I had been to John's house for a holiday and that I was considering moving there. 'Your father says that many times in your life with people and events you have stepped on a garden fork, and it has come up and hit you in the face. He says that won't happen this time. If you stay with John, all the crap is behind you.' This is what I needed to hear. I mentally noted that the word 'fork' instead of the more commonly used 'rake' was given. I had my late keen-gardener father's 1950s garden fork and spade carefully preserved at home, powerful mementos of my childhood.

Rebecca continued, 'Your spirit guide says that you and John have been living parallel lives but now your paths are soon to cross and then merge.'

The reading went on to discuss other matters but the clarification that I needed had been given to me by my father. The light was indeed different in rural Czech. There were cobbled paths. John *did* wear a jungle hat and he *did* wear *two* rings on one finger. Two rings coming together. Twin flames. Could it really be that John was to be my partner? It seemed unlikely. We had indeed been living parallel lives, oddly similar since birth yet utterly different. Parallel lives, always destined to join together. But to what end? Romantic? Karmic? Something else?

There was only one way to find out, I needed to move to the Czech Republic. Life is to be lived and it is for the living. The arrangements were to be made. The psychic reading with Rebecca was over but not before my maternal grandmother gave me a message that, 'Money was tight and it was going to get wafer thin but things would work out ok,' and then Rebecca added, 'Your guide says that the reason your house sale is taking so long is because you are holding back making the arrangements to move. Set a date to move house and then this will send a message to the universe that you wish to move forward.' Rebecca couldn't have known about my plans for moving house and once again her evidential mediumship skills were astonishing.

It was December now and there was still no word about the moving date. I had been tearing my hair out trying to chase matters with a tardy solicitor at the other end of the property chain who had been messing about with minor legal technicalities for months. The months of anguish over my formerly active haunted house had now turned into mental anguish over my finances. I decided to take spirit's advice and take the plunge.

Without any completion to the house sale on the horizon, or even any certainty that it would proceed at all, I telephoned the house removal company and made the necessary arrangements to pack up and emigrate. Was I mad? I still hadn't sold my house. I also had Monty to get vaccinated and documented before I could take him on the long journey with me. Nevertheless the dates for moving out of my UK home were set. I made the arrangements with the estate agent to take control of the house keys and I instructed my solicitor to continue in the sale without me. I said goodbye to friends, and I sat back and waited for the universe to do its part of the bargain.

Within three days of making the telephone call to the removals company I received a call from my solicitor which confirmed that after nine months of delay, out of the blue we were to exchange contracts. I was elated. The universe had lived up to Rebecca's advice from my spirit guide. However, my elation wasn't to last long.

Abigail and I were due to make one of our very rare trips out together the very next day. Not unusually for the UK it was lashing down with rain the following morning and as we left the town outskirts behind and headed into the countryside the car made a strange exploding noise and lost power. Something had just blown inside the engine. It was the turbo. This was a brand-new car and we had only been travelling at 50kph when the turbo had failed. This was no coincidence. I was due to move to the Czech Republic in only two weeks and drive across Europe!

My heart sank, would I never get to the Czech Republic? I knew that the turbo repair costs would at least be covered by the warranty. Later that same day I called the garage.

'No,' they said, 'This had never happened before,' and as such, 'There wasn't a spare turbo part in the *whole of Europe*,' and the part would have to be special ordered in from the factory in Germany.

'How long would that take?' I demanded.

'Between a month and three months,' came the unbelievable reply.

I was leaving the UK in two weeks! I would just have to drive my car as it was, slowly across Europe and then get it fixed in the Czech Republic after I had arrived. A problem being that the nearest main dealership garage to where I was moving was some one-and-a-half hour's drive away. No matter, it had to be done. At least I had sold my house I reassured myself. My life savings had by now dwindled until I had huge debts and only

£900 remaining in the bank to last me until I moved. Surely nothing else could go wrong? The head of the removal company telephoned me the same day, 'We need another £1,600 from you for snow tyres.' I was speechless.

I had specifically chosen this firm because they did 'regular intercontinental trips' which clearly listed mountainous snowy countries. This request for more money was an obvious scam, but what could I do? They had already been to my house over the course of a couple of days and had packed up and removed all of my items into storage. I was sitting on a single wooden chair and Monty looked most disgruntled to have to relax on the floor. This was extortion and we both knew it. If I said 'no' then I would end up with all my belongings remaining in the UK in costly storage. If I said 'yes' then I had no money to pay and I had already maxed-out my credit card, owing thousands.

In desperation, I telephoned a friend who agreed to lend me a short-term loan of £10,000 to pay all off my bills, including the new up-front removals costs. If my house sale faltered at the last hurdle, then I was done for. And after the year that I had endured, anything was possible.

But the house sale didn't falter, the universe had decided that a new karmic cycle was beginning for me and it wasn't long before I said a tearful goodbye to Abigail and I was driving my broken car along the approach road to my new home in the Czech Republic. I pulled over just outside the village and paused at the roadside after an epic journey with the broken engine.

My spirit guides and angels had got me here safely and without incident. I stared at the village which was soon to be my new home. I wondered what was ahead. I couldn't possibly have guessed. Would I run a new business with John? Perhaps we would become partners in time, after all what was a 'Twin Flame' anyway? I had not actually done any research on the topic. Perhaps if I had, I wouldn't now be sitting in my car at the roadside in a strange new world. Instead, I had jumped headfirst into this new life.

This new life was to be the most intense period of spiritual growth that I have ever encountered. Meeting your Twin Flame is a spiritual awakening of seismic proportions. Mirroring each other you learn so much about yourself and it's either a fast-track to self-improvement or a downward slide into toxicity. I chose the former and with each lesson learned about the self or the ego, I received an increase in my spiritual vibration.

I understand from my spirit guides that at the time of writing, I have received at least three of these spiritual upgrades. In the process I discovered my life purpose. I have opened the box containing my shadow side in order to stare straight into my past and at my childhood traumas, many of them deliberately forgotten. It has allowed me to deconstruct and then reconstruct my ego and heal from the pain and sorrow inflicted by a thousand metaphorical cuts.

I now hope that my journey will help others. In my case my destiny was to transmute a lifetime of sorrow and suffering into the healing knowledge of the unseen spiritual world and provide comfort and reassurance to others that life is eternal, that death is a myth and that we are from and of the Light which is pure love.

Chapter Thirty-Nine

Physical, mental and spiritual wellbeing

The shadow

It is so psychologically damaging to us to even be prepared to consider that everything we know and think of as 'us' is not us at all, but instead the often-misplaced teachings of others that went before us.

We should always seek the professional assistance of a clinical psychologist or health professional in order to heal our burdensome mental health issues. I am a healer of the spiritual body, not the physical, and I believe that in order to live a healthy life it is essential that each of us brings into balance the physical body with our mental faculties and spirit energy. The stresses of the physical existence in the 3D are guaranteed to put these under strain during our day. If one of these three is out of kilter with the rest, then we can become out of balance.

This may perhaps manifest as a physical illness causing mental anguish, or maybe mental upset causing physical and spiritual problems. This is why it is important to not only maintain good physical health but also good mental health and spiritual wellbeing. If our spiritual health is neglected, then we can become anxious or too ego centred. In turn this anxiety puts pressure on our physical body as the negative energy has to be released or it can become stored in our physical body at a cellular level.

Regular daily exercise and good quality food provides the physical body with what it needs for healthy cell reproduction and wellbeing. Our mental faculties also require good exercise such as reading, music, good conversation, positive thinking and creative pursuits. In this way as we exercise our physical body and mental faculties we are also helping with good spiritual health. We have discussed meditation being good spiritual practice as it can help us to stay in contact with our higher-self and to restore our body's spiritual energy balance. Used in the correct way it can even help with our personal healing. Each day all of us balance our physical, mental and spiritual health like a stage conjurer with three spinning plates. Not an easy ask and not one where you can take your eye off the task at hand.

We have a light side and a dark 'shadow' or 'shadowside' as you'll hear me describe it in this book. In recent years the previously unspoken issues surrounding good mental health are thankfully now more freely and openly discussed without fear of derision or rejection. Anyone who says that they have not experienced mental health issues at some time in their life may be self-deluding. This is because the shadowside is relevant to every person on Earth. The shadowside is within all of us and it is a lifelong process to bring this into balance with our light side.

In my lifetime I have engaged and tackled my shadow without even understanding what it was or that it had a name. An abused and misunderstood child and adult, like many I have been through the ringer of mental health difficulties. I am here to tell you that the battle to bring your shadow into balance can be won but first you must accept that you have one and then actively heal the wounded inner child within you.

It is my belief that healing the inner child and balancing your shadowside will help with many mental health difficulties. Working with the shadow and healing from childhood trauma and learnt behavioural issues and expectations is one of the best things that you can do for your mental wellbeing and thereby your physical and spiritual health. Our physical, mental and spiritual health is interconnected energetically. By healing your inner child, your mental health will improve, your shadowside rebalance and your physical body will respond positively to this reprogramming.

Working with your shadow side is transformational and will ultimately be empowering and life affirming. A truly moral person is not free of shadow, he or she identifies their shadow and controls it. But to face your shadow is to face the one thing we all fear the most; the bits of ourselves that we don't like. The shadow is where the dark side of ourselves exists and this darkness we all have within us, it is part of the human existence.

Most will be familiar with the tale of 'Dr Jekyll and Mr Hyde.' Dr Henry Jekyll is the epitome of the outer mild mannered professional gentleman, intelligent, articulate and perfectly integrated with the requirements of society. His alter-ego of Mr Edward Hyde however is angry, fearsome and brutal, the very antithesis of polite late-Victorian society when the book was originally published. The transformation from Dr Jekyll to Mr Hyde comes about when this dark side of his ego is 'triggered' by the consumption of a serum in his laboratory. He becomes the raging beast that has always existed within but through a triggering event has now been unleashed.

While these stories are fictional, they are closely based on the truth of the psychological beast that lies within all of us in our subconscious; the shadow. Only the brave amongst us would want to tackle that raging angry beast within and yet that is what we must do on an individual and collective basis. The old expression to 'Face Your Demons' is never truer than in this regard.

Consider your shadow like one of those out-of-town storage containers. Many of us keep so many material possessions that we run out of space in the home for them. These belongings may serve no further use to us or may even represent something we no longer need in our life, or even like to have around us. These are the physical memories of past relationships, poor life judgments and toxic situations that we may farm-off to a storage container on an industrial estate somewhere.

Instead of getting rid of these unwanted things, we instead remove them from our home (our conscious mind) and hire a storage facility and keep all this junk there instead (our subconscious mind), literally 'out of sight, out of mind.' Only it isn't out of mind because as each month passes, when you check your bank balance you discover that you are paying good money to retain all this clutter. Money is energy.

Think of all the things that have occurred to you in your life that you no longer wish to carry with you in your present-day thinking. Past relationships, past hurts, upsetting memories and lost opportunities. These are things that made you unhappy, upset, jealous or angry. Where do you store these memories? They are kept in your mental storage container where secretly you know that you can access them at any time that your ego wishes to go on a 'downer.'

Just as a physical storage container filled with disused household junk is a waste of your money and thereby your energy, so too is a mental storage container filled with negative emotions and thoughts wasting your valuable mental, physical and spiritual energy. It's time for a mental clear-out!

Once you begin to face-up and challenge your shadow side you will start the lifelong process of accepting and healing yourself. You will no longer need the approval and acceptance of others through social conformity, instead this will come to you via you being a healed and genuine person. You will provide yourself with your own approval as that is all that you will require to feel good. With the shadowside healing and less of a dominant mental structure, your emotional triggers begin to heal, and you will discover that you accept others for whom and what they are and that they can no longer hurt you emotionally.

Partly as a result of western religion-based philosophy, we consider that we must identify and completely expunge and reject our shadowside elements, leaving only the love and the light side. Historically, the Church identified many aspects of shadow as 'sinful' and thereby avoidable. Yet as part of our life journey as spiritual beings enjoying a physical existence on Earth, we carry with us the darker side of our ego as well as the light side. These two live together.

You cannot remove the darker elements of our psyche altogether. Rather than the dichotomy of western religions where people are told that they can be 'light' or 'dark', 'good' or 'bad,' eastern philosophy talks of Yin and Yang. Yin and Yang co-exist. This is as obvious as day and night, the paint needing a canvas, or obviously, the shadow needing the sun before it can cast itself across the ground. So we must co-exist with our dark side and not reject it.

If we try to reject and expunge the shadow as many religions may tell us to do, we merely end up boxing up those shadows and then carrying that box with us throughout life, the box getting heavier and heavier as we place more and more inside. We pretend that the shadow elements do not exist and yet every moment of every day they are gabbling away in your subconscious like a bunch of angry monkeys shoved inside a leaky bucket with an ill-fitting lid. Perhaps it is time to gently ease open that lid and see what's inside for healing with self-love and compassion.

Our sense of identity is completely based upon what you perceive others will find acceptable. In this way we seek approval from others for our conscious being and not from ourselves. These are the sandy foundations where our conscience, or ego is built upon as we disregard the essence of our own being and fail in self-love merely in order to not stand out and so to fit in. As children, we have to be taught by our parental and guardian figures how to behave in order to survive. All babies are born without ego and largely unaware of the inherent dangers of the 3D world.

As small children we discover that our parental figures give us approval and perhaps rewards for what they deem 'good' behaviour, whether that be *not* licking the toilet seat, *not* sticking our hand in the fire or *not* trying to kill grandma when she visits. When the infant does something that gets a reaction of disgust, or worse anger, we respond accordingly and learn our parental version of what is acceptable and what is not.

The problem for society as a whole is that our parental

guardian's parameters of what is acceptable and what is not may differ when compared to other sections of society or society at large. Social behaviours have to be learnt in order for the human to be accepted by the group. This is nature's pack or herd mentality. The lone wolf is often punished and sent into the wilderness alone. Humans are social creatures, and we therefore seek to avoid this public isolation by changing ourselves to fit-in.

Acceptance becomes the main parameter within the child's mind in order to cope and most importantly to be loved by others. While safety obviously matters and parameters surrounding the basic lawful and socio-survival needs of the future adult are clearly essential, this is nonetheless codependent behaviour being deliberately taught to our children and thereby to the adults of the future. The codependency occurs where the young adult now steps forth into life either having been trained to accept another's commands for a quiet life or trained that making demands of others gets physical results.

This can be considered as the grounding for the child to be exposed to mental abuse later in life being unwittingly taught by parents. Rather than provide their children with the appropriate survival techniques as they had intended, they may instead have exposed their offspring to the likelihood of future abuse or be creating the future abuser. In all cases what it also induces is an inner rage brought about by the need to not be yourself. This hidden rage becomes the fuel supply of the shadow.

Imagine yourself as the small child, a perfect energetic ball of light and shadow. Each time that you got a negative response to an action that was deemed unacceptable by your parental guardians you chipped off a little piece of that energetic ball of your life source. You then packed that little chip of your source away into an unseen and discarded box in the subconscious marked 'do not open.'

Once you began school the process began afresh where not only your teachers told you what is unacceptable thinking and behaviour but also your peers from their own learnt set of rules of approval from *their* parental guardians. Since then, you have chipped away tiny fragments of your life source for the remainder of your school career, your teen years and into your adult years and beyond.

By the time we become adults that ball of energetic light has had so much chipped off it and stuffed into the box of shadows in our subconscious that it's heavy and laden with all of the clutter that we consider 'unacceptable', 'undesirable' or 'disgusting.' Our once beautiful energetic ball of light has been carefully and unwittingly manipulated and carved into a cube. In short, we have become a square. This square we then hope slots neatly into societal norms of behaviours and thinking. But what of that box filled to the brim with shadowside stuff?

By our own actions we have recreated ourselves and our identity not in the image of 'God' as we were born but in the image of society. Societal norms that are more often than not are based on ignorance, prejudice and restriction. Many bemoan that society these days is sick, so why on Earth would you want to shape your image to conform to a sick society? We have created a false narrative about who and what we are, based solely on the learnt behaviour of other people's fears, perceptions and prejudices. Yet it is so *psychologically damaging to us to even be prepared to consider that everything we know and think of as 'us' is not us at all, but instead the often misplaced teachings of others that went before us.*

Rather than become uncomfortable and face the contents of that box and actively engage with our shadowside, we would rather go through our entire lifetime in denial of the truth of who we truly are. Rather than confront our addiction to our own ego, many of us with huge shadow boxes filled with negative perceptions may instead end up in therapy.

We have learnt that the rejected part of us is now opposite to all that that our ego is prepared to accept. Because it is in opposition to all that we now hold acceptable we intentionally ignore the existence of those rejected elements within us that make up our shadowside. They remain buried deep within our subconscious. However, they do not lay dormant but instead affect us every waking moment of every day. We just don't realise it. This is our shadow, and this is why it is so hard for us to face it.

A result of the over-vigilance of the ego against any social faux pas is the risk of anxiety disorders, of which I am a sufferer. As a result of my dysfunctional childhood, I suffer from Complex (Childhood) Post Traumatic Stress Disorder (CPTSD) and Obsessive Compulsive Disorder (OCD) and my hyper anxiety leaves me hyper vigilant at all times and thereby exhausted when in any social situation. It is probable that the more the 'dos' and 'don'ts' that we have learnt, the greater the risk of anxiety disorders.

My own personal list was a mile long and I became easily triggered by other people's behaviour towards me, their actions rejected by my ego as 'unacceptable' and any criticism cutting deep as it rejected my carefully crafted 'square' of life source energy which I had been so lovingly shaping over decades using other people's parameters of what was acceptable as my template.

The victim of the unhealed inner child with a rampant raging shadow discovers all of life's interactions to be nothing more than a series of unfortunate events and unpleasant encounters. Where the shadow has been healed, we instead experience life, with all of its joys and pitfalls as a panoply of chaotic events on a stage where learning and even pleasure is to be gained and enjoyed. We accept others for who they are, without any direction to attempt to change them for our own ego's comfort.

The healed and balanced shadow has to coexist with everyone else's shadows. Where we are unhealed, the problem is obvious that everyone's shadow differs and therefore everyone's standard of what is or what is not acceptable or repugnant also differs. This then is where the collective shadow comes into play on a global scale. By learning our own shadow from our parents and those in our karmic circle, we have inherited their karmic shadow. So we not only have our own learnt shadow to attend to, we also have the karmic shadow of our family and peers to heal. That is quite a big ask and healing for the self and for humanity is one of the reasons that I have a need to write this book.

It is exhausting to repress our shadowside indefinitely. I believe that to do so will make you physically ill. The rise in psychological disorders I believe directly comes from our unattended shadow and our reluctance to engage with its healing. The modern world is filled with physical and mental distractions that take us away from our spiritual and heart-based centre and these distractions block the inner peace required that enables healing.

The fast-moving images of television and the internet teamed with the abstract reality of social media platforms and computer gaming serve only to ever-distance us from our inner connection to the Source and the Light. Our 3D 'reality' is a virtual physical creation to enable the Light to experience itself as individual personalities. Because the dark and the light co-exist, we have created laws to help prevent deeds and actions considered undesirable or inhuman.

So what does humanity do to expunge its shadow if it cannot openly commit undesirable acts? Instead of healing the shadow, we have instead created violent computer games and toxic virtual reality worlds where any acts of anger, terror and violence is 'acceptable.' This is merely the shadow in the subconscious making an appearance in the virtual world. It must surely follow that we should also police and have criminal penalties in the virtual world. There is also great irony that we have created an electric virtual world within a virtual energy physical world.

Our shadow exists in our subconscious thoughts, and this feeds through to our conscious ego throughout our waking day. Our brain monitors every moment to establish whether it is under attack from any outside intellectual or emotional influence that it deems unacceptable or liable to shatter the fragile ego construct that is the repressed shadow. Many of us are empathic, and while this is a hugely positive attribute, this does keep us on the look out for any attack to the unhealed shadow and we often become over sensitive to the criticism of others.

Others of us instead become desensitised and thereby insensitive. Over-opinionated we give others the benefit of our ego's opinion, thereby setting out our stall before anyone else can get there first. We have all encountered someone who refuses to give way to anyone else's opinions or reconsider their lifelong held self-beliefs. This is because their ego has an overwhelming need to be right about everything as anything less leaves them feeling less than.

The undealt with shadow doesn't only influence the ego into a range of anxiety disorders. It can create coercive or manipulative behaviours and at its extreme clinical narcissism. These psychological disorders are often the result of the unhealed wounded inner child. Depending on what we have been taught to reject as unwholesome or unacceptable there is the danger of the individual becoming racist, homophobic or bigoted in some other way, which they perceive as being their societal norm as this is what they were taught as being approved thoughts and acceptable behaviour.

Humanity has been about for a few hundred thousand years, and that's a lot of inherited karmic shadow for us to deal with. Wars, invasions, genocide, imperialist colonisation; is it any wonder that those of us alive today have a huge shadow to tackle.

In order to avoid dealing with the shadow and to protect the fragile ego, we push back against everything we perceive as unacceptable. In this way when we perceive ourselves as a victim of another's shadowside, we may as a result become an unwitting aggressor. But humanity is not an individual, it is a collective of individuals acting energetically as one. With the collective karmic shadow becoming disproportionately large and unhealed, and an unwillingness to tackle it and look into our own box of shadows, we end up with sections of society turning against other sections, all with differing shadows and ego-based accepted norms.

Politicians and rulers with their own unhealed shadows, rub up against other geopolitical shadowsides. Collectively the unhealed global human shadow can cause entire nations to turn against other nations and whole peoples turning against other peoples on the grounds of ethnicity, creed, sexual orientation or beliefs.

Our shadow is intentionally manipulated and triggered by the unscrupulous and power-hungry politician. They have their own geopolitical shadow agenda and their shadow element of choice extracted from the collective shadow box is usually 'disgust.' Human history has so many examples to choose from but at this point in the twenty-first century we often use Nazi Germany as the ultimate in the shadow of the masses being mobilised against anyone who didn't fit with the shadow-based political agenda.

With a manipulative propaganda campaign of hatred and fear, the Nazis were able to weaponize the shadowside of the majority of the people in Nazi Germany. Indeed, elsewhere in the world at the time, many saw no issue with the rounding up of Roma, Jews, gays, disabled and anyone seen as 'disgusting' or 'unworthy' by those in charge and these innocents were sent to the Nazi death camps for their ultimate destruction into dust.

The 'Final Solution' was the shadowside gone rampant, where it was fuelled by disgust whipped up into fear and hatred by a repressed and shadow corrupted society. But do not think that this won't happen again. After the fall of Nazi Germany humanity recognised that we have a collective shadow that had become culturally acceptable and the long hard struggle for liberty and freedom of choice, expression and diversity began. But as long as we refuse to deal with our personal and our collective shadow element, these terrors from history will continue to occur and history *will* repeat itself. Many may argue that this process has already begun.

In recent years we have seen the revival and the mobilisation of the collective shadow by shadow-ambitious politicians and global leaders as a weapon either against their enemies, or to divide and rule. By our failure to attend to our own personal shadowside we are silently contributing and permitting the slide into the depravity of the collective shadow taking ground once again and history repeating. Unless what you are being told by global leaders, politicians or even self-proclaimed spiritual advisers comes from a place of all-accepting unconditional love for all of humanity *without* exception, you *must* question the authority of the person speaking to you.

When we consider that the shadowside is a wounded child that has never been accepted for who he or she is and who wants everyone else to adhere to their own learnt restrictive values, we begin to understand why globally politicians rarely agree and let humanity down. We are in fact being served, or indeed ruled, by angry children. And importantly, *we continue to allow this to happen.*

There is a terrifying fear for the ego in having to face its own shadow. For what the ego has intentionally avoided and boxed up as shadow, becomes so dominant in the individual's daily existence that it becomes the bogeyman, a terrifying shadowside that only the brave will tackle, because to do so may mean the ultimate deconstruction of the ego itself.

There is much fiction written about the dangers of the ego,

the computer Hal in the film '2001: A Space Odyssey', the aforementioned book by Robert Louis Stephenson 'Doctor Jekyll & Mr Hyde' and the 1956 film 'Forbidden Planet,' where Doctor Morbius's own shadow side is made physical. Sadly, as the horrors of genocide and war continue to demonstrate, there is a powerful need to tackle the shadow from childhood development onwards, as the dangers of the shadow are all too real. Humanity has become the greatest threat to humanity.

Clinical psychology remains a rare medical art, where only the most troubled receive help. Similarly, few ever seek assistance from spiritual healers such a Reiki practitioner. While it has become normal to see a doctor for a chemical pill to 'fix' a physical ailment, by the time that the physical body is displaying symptoms, the delicate balance of mind, body and spirit has been out of kilter for some time.

In the same way that good physical health is brought about through good food and regular exercise, it would be better to bring about good mental health by supporting children and young adults at the developmental stage of the ego, rather than try to repair the problem later on in adulthood. The overarching need is one of good spiritual health which comes from physical and mental wellbeing together with good spiritual practices such as meditation, yoga or even walks in nature. Once we bring the physical, mental and spiritual into alignment, we lose the restrictions that create the mental turmoil that keeps us from enjoying life.

Chapter Forty

Epilogue

Love, gratitude and spirit guidance

What we have as spiritual beings experiencing a human existence is love and gratitude. Love and gratitude survive death, and they are the greatest possession and power of all.

Perhaps readers will be keen to know what happened to the spirit of the German male on the stairway landing and to the child peeking around the chimney stack in the attic. I shall save these curiosities for a future book when I shall give an up-to-date report of events at my new home in the Czech Republic and of my life in general where it pertains to my spiritual and personal growth as aided by my spirit guides.

Everyone has spirit guides, and they are incredibly willing to help you along your journey in life here on Earth, only they are not permitted to intercede on our behalf unless specifically invited to do so. As spiritual beings enjoying a human experience, we have complete freewill to think, create and do as we please. We are therefore at liberty to create and do wondrous things or free to squander our time on petty earthly squabbles and material possessions, the choice is ours.

Sadly, out of our unhealed emotional wounds, many choose the latter option and then we wonder why the Earth can be such an inhospitable place to live. Better to create and do wondrous things with your life for others and for yourself. And should you want assistance with this (and why wouldn't you?) then there can be no better start than ensuring that you are following your divine destiny as set out by you before birth. To do this and follow the right path for you, then all you have to do is ask your spirit guides for help.

It is wise to be diligent when you call in your spirit guides. Your guides are of the Source, or the Divine, and they will always act for your highest good, but as you will have read in the pages of this book, there are many earthbound spirits and negative entities just waiting for an invitation to cause mischief or worse. So how to differentiate between the two?

When you choose to contact your spirit guides, always do it in the correct positive vibration of love and light. I would always recommend that you are in a positive , preferably sober and hopefully feeling gratitude and love. This will ensure that you have a clear connection with their energy and also ensure that you are protected from any passing negative influence. A simple 'Hello, I wish to invite in my highest vibration spirit guides to assist me in my life at all times for the highest good' will do nicely.

You can do this just the once, or at any time that you need guidance. The purpose of stating 'highest vibration' is to ensure that no other type of lower vibrational energy comes in to deceive and 'help' you. The purpose of requesting 'for the highest good' is to ensure that you receive the best guidance and help that your soul *needs*, which is not necessarily always the same as what your ego might *want*. Asking for 'the highest good' will also ensure that no karmic issues are created for you or for anyone else when the help is received. When requesting guidance from your spirit team, always *feel* the intention of the request. You must really want their help in love and in gratitude.

Your spirit guide(s) or 'spirit team' are only too ready and willing to come in and help you. You most probably won't notice the difference at first. You may however see clues left for you by your guides. The classic ones are white feathers or seeing specific animals, but I consider these to be a little passe these days! They can do so much better and more. Keep an eye open for something that means something to you personally or sentimentally that only you know about. Maybe a song will play on the radio or over a shop loudspeaker at just the right moment. Perhaps you'll be in a second-hand store and something familiar to you from childhood will just pop-up in front of you which may answer a question that you were thinking earlier that day.

Your spirit guides will have a very keen sense of humour and I often find myself laughing at some of the strange things that they place on my path that have been sent to make me jolly but also to recognise that they are saying 'hello, just letting you know that we are with you.'

Always have respect for your guides as they love you and want the best for you. I would also take this opportunity to ask that we have respect for all living things and also for spirit, including earthbound, even the most troublesome kind. It is very saddening to see 'ghost hunter' television programmes made for entertainment, where the 'ghost hunters' swear at, chide and verbally abuse the trapped spirit, sometimes claiming that they are 'demonic' or 'evil.'

I implore those involved in this to please remember that in

life these people were perhaps in mental turmoil, in anguish, or are now in anger at their premature demise. There can be manifold reasons why a spirit may be an unhappy tortured soul, the spirit rescued from my own house had, for example, been murdered. Whatever or however they were in life, it is not ours to judge. There is no such thing as death, there is only consciousness which transmutes from one plane to another. These are not 'ghosts' or 'spirits' or 'ghouls', these are trapped people and they deserve the same respect as the living – because they are living. Please remember that all humankind deserves to be treated with love and the sanctity of life.

I still receive an annual consultation with Rebecca, and these have been truly invaluable with my spiritual development and destiny. Without Rebecca's psychic help I would not now be on my true path. When I moved to the Czech Republic, I had no idea what I was going to do for a career, expecting an online business or something very normal and dull. I wasn't anticipating my spiritual journey to continue with four years of hard lessons about the shadow self and regular spiritual tests, not all of which I'm sure that I passed.

I have been guided to practice my latent psychic abilities and also encouraged to develop my healing abilities. When I was spiritually guided to write this book, the decades of strange supernatural incidences and a life replete with trauma and sorrow suddenly made perfect sense and all of it worthwhile. If I can help just one person through the writings contained in this book, then I have accomplished my task. I just hope that I have done it well as I do not wish to let any of you, or my spirit guide 'team' down, or indeed myself.

And there this book would have ended. However, only a

few days prior to writing these end words, at my most recent psychic consultation with Rebecca, I was given a conclusion to my story at Pippins by my spirit guide, timed presumably so that it could end up in the final pages of this book. I have undergone a huge amount of spiritual and inner-healing work over the last few months. A part of this was forgiving everyone's role played in my life where that caused friction or trauma. Often these life events are karma playing out. Even if they aren't, there is no need to continue or carry forward with that newly created karma in this life, or your next.

I detailed in a previous chapter about the Ho'oponopono mantra which I use daily, whereby I declare to the universe that I am grateful to everyone I knew in this life and in past lives, and I truly mean it. Accordingly, everything that occurred at Pippins I am truly grateful for, because without it, I wouldn't be as healed as I am today, heading in a positive new direction and writing and sharing my story with you in this book.

In the final stages of my most recent consultation with Rebecca she asked me, 'Do you know of your previous incarnations?' I confirmed that yes, I knew of some of them.

Rebecca then asked of me, 'Did you know that you were cursed in an earlier life?' While I was surprised at the question arising, I was perhaps not surprised by the notion of being cursed. Listening to my spirit guide, Rebecca went on to explain that I was, 'Cursed in a previous life,' and 'Also in this one.' 'It has something to do with a chimney' Rebecca said. I then knew exactly to what this alluded.

Five years prior, Abigail and I had stood in the sitting room of Pippins a few days before I set off for my new life in the Czech Republic. I can still remember Abigail deep in thought and staring at the curious cobweb design on the front of the cast iron woodburner. 'There's something about that woodburner,' was all she said. I knew that Abigail was referring to my centre-of-a-web witch neighbour. In line with advice from my spirit team I had protected the house by charged crystals placed at all access points to the house, both doors and windows. Aware that a chimney is technically an access point of sorts, I had sought to protect this by placing a large Selenite crystal on the woodburner, but it seems that this wasn't enough.

Rebecca continued, 'They're telling me that you were cursed in a previous life and the same woman, reincarnated, cursed you again in this life because she thought that you had wronged her.' This was truly revelatory information!

'She cursed you via the chimney somehow.' So, Abigail had been right. The fireplace had always bothered me and I knew not why. I also suspected that the difficulties had begun long before June and her husband had moved in next door. June's own claim that she had 'been watching me' for some time after I moved in to Pippins but before she had become my neighbour was evidence of that. The fireplace was in full view of the main sitting room window which faced onto the street and my neighbour often made a point of oddly commenting on the furniture and belongings inside my home that she had spied through the various downstairs windows.

After June had begun her curious campaign of enticing Monty into her house, my dear old cat and best friend went a little strange. Monty was always friendly and rarely aloof, and he knew better than to sit atop the frequently lit woodburner. Yet at around this time he stopped sleeping on my bed, preferring to be out on the stairs landing, and in the daytime he would jump onto the woodburner and stare at me unblinkingly, unmoving and unsettlingly quiet. This was very unusual behaviour for my cat and quite hostile. What had June done to him?

Monty fell ill the very week we arrived in the Czech Republic and went into a long terminal decline over twelve months before passing away of an incurable disease of the head. Had this been part of June's curse? I can still recall the curious day where the three of us were in the alleyway outside my house and her pointedly touching him softly on the head with three pointed fingers in a similar manner to how she had touched the hood of my classic car just before it too became 'faulty.'

Rebecca continued that my spirit guide was explaining that I had carried the curse through from the previous incarnation where June and I had met, and then been cursed once more in this lifetime. I wondered how many incarnations there had been in between which had also been negatively affected? I have since learnt that we can carry the dark negative energy of curses in our energy field each time that we incarnate.

However, my guide then revealed that I had 'worked through' the curse and that it was 'no longer in my energy' but that it had still to be cleared from around my physical body and further *physical* healing was required. Finally my guide advised that because I had resolved the issue I need not worry further and I would 'not have to meet her in another incarnation.' Well, at least that was a relief!

Suddenly all of the curious dogged bad luck that had occurred, not only since I had met June but throughout this incarnation, and also in what little I knew of my previous incarnations flooded my consciousness. When I was much younger, there was a comedy television programme called 'Chance In A Million' where impossible bad fortune would happen to the leading hapless character on a daily basis. No matter what choices the poor man would make, hilarious bad luck would dog him. People I knew would innocently laugh at the similarities between me and this comedy character. Was this just a fanciful victimhood mentality leading to its own self-fulfilling prophecy?

But then what of Pippins and all of its ghostly problems? I had just lost my career, my home and my mother in three short months. I had walked straight into Pippins with its numerous troublesome ghosts. With June openly stating that she had been 'watching me' after I had moved in, and still with unopened packing cases about me, I had been obliged to buy a new car after my old one developed random electrical faults, rendering it unusable. This new car was then damaged by a hit-and-run driver in a car park within three days of buying it.

Then there was the fault that wasn't with the headlights on the new car. There was the failed turbo only two weeks before I was due to drive across Europe. Then there was the removal company successfully extorting money from me at a time when my personal finances were in freefall due to seemingly endless financial demands and pressures. Then there was my classic car with the engine that seized without warning after June had strangely touched the hood of the car in a very pointed manner. Then there was the brand-new replacement engine also being faulty and a subsequent fruitless battle taking place over several weeks with the supplier over the warranty.

I haven't mentioned in these pages the instances of the local authority trash lorry which hit my house not once but twice, damaging the brand-new Georgian lead portico that I'd just had beautifully restored at great expense. This caused minor structural damage to the house but with the laughing driver denying liability on both occasions. The first occasion may have been an accident. The second time it occurred it seemed as if it were intentional. Then there was the central heating failure and the plague of flies followed by a plague of fleas, and all these things June spitefully and impossibly told me about.

There was the simple cash-buyer 'three weeks' house sale that turned into ten months and financial Armageddon. Since moving to the Czech Republic, I have been obliged to purchase another new car, and this too was reversed into by a hit and run in a car park within three days of ownership. This car too has been beset by faults and issues which the main dealer has been unable to resolve or adequately explain. Finally I invested my life savings into a new business venture which was up and running *the very same week* that the pandemic lockdown began, causing it to fail with a massive financial loss that I struggled to repay and I lost my pension as a result.

Each time that I tried to manifest something in the physical material world, it ended in the same financial quagmire. It wasn't so much that there were many failures, this can happen to anyone and sadly it frequently does, it was that *nothing came to fruition*. Snatching defeat from the jaws of victory had become an unhappy pastime and anyone would think that I was cursed, with this often being suggested to me over the years, including by my own family. A suggestion that I always rebutted with a nervous laugh.

To hear at my last psychic consultation that there indeed was a curse, in fact not just *one* but *two*, and the fog began to clear. To then hear that I have worked through the dark energy of both curses and that they no longer exist is like being let out of jail! In that moment I felt a huge burden lift from my shoulders, in the knowledge that things may now begin to start moving forward positively and that failure in new material ventures won't now always be the inevitable outcome. If you are reading this book it means that it has been published and the reversal of fortunes has at last begun.

So, what does 'worked through it' actually mean? Well, I believe that when writing this book and putting so much of my heart, emotion and soul into it, I became truly grateful to June and her husband. Without them none of this would have been possible. To feel genuine gratitude and love towards someone who wishes you ill, or who has gone to the extreme of cursing you is a wonderful thing and extremely liberating. Liberating mentally and emotionally yes, but also liberating on a spiritual level. We must forgive and be thankful, for in that moment we have released ourselves from the prison that another has placed us in.

To also feel regret, upset and sadness that their actions have created a karmic debt that they must repay will also have aided the dissipation of the curse energy. It now made sense why June got so incredibly angry with me when I had said to her that she was very 'kind.' I had always found it curious that she became so very angry at being called 'kind.' Had she already cursed me by this point in time? By my thanking her for her kindness, it would have weakened any curse energy and perhaps inadvertently returned it to sender. Anger and hatred only work if they are met with the same response. This is in our personal lives and on the world stage.

Within only weeks of hearing that I have 'worked through' the curses from both incarnations, my material and emotional fortunes have turned 180 degrees, blockages have been removed, and I have experienced sudden amazingly good financial fortune. I enjoy healthy emotional wellbeing and at fifty-three years, I have met the love of my life. I am advised that a powerful and protracted karmic cycle has ended and the future looks bright.

In the physical world, when people's actions cause loss and injury to others in order to seek short term gain, whether that be theft, deceit, mental torture or even a curse, they cause themselves the same level of harm each time. That's how the universal law of karma functions, what goes up must come down – the universe operates on the principle of balance and harmony. Whether the karmic 'debt' is repaid in this life or in a future incarnation, one thing is always certain, where bad intention or actions occur at the hands of an individual, the universe will create balance. We often hear that 'karma is a bitch', well I would suggest that karma is a bitch only if you are too.

The reverse is also true, where good thoughts and deeds will always be returned eventually. We cannot break the inevitable laws of the universe and however clever or sly we may think that we are, *there is nothing to be gained by deception because the universe is always keeping score*. This is why I practice the mantra of Ho'oponopono, because by forgiving the other person and also asking for their forgiveness and expressing love and gratitude for everything that has happened, we stop the karmic cycle.

Unwittingly I 'worked through' June's curse energy with my love and my gratitude towards her and to others.

As humans we allow ourselves to be beguiled and bewitched by the materiality of the physical world. Yet possessions and power are transitory and delusionary and separate us from the truth.

What we have as eternal spiritual beings experiencing a human existence is love, gratitude and our connectedness through the Source to all things. Love and gratitude survive physical death, and they are the greatest possession and power of all.

I wish you peace, I wish you contentment, I wish you joy and I wish you love.